Ka

Singa
& Bangkok

2nd Edition

Fred S. Armentrout

Prentice Hall Travel

New York • London • Toronto • Sydney • Tokyo • Singapore

THE AMERICAN EXPRESS ® TRAVEL GUIDES

Published in the United States by
Prentice Hall General Reference
15 Columbus Circle
New York, NY 10023

PRENTICE HALL is a registered
trademark and colophon is a
trademark of Prentice-Hall, Inc.

First published 1992 in the United
Kingdom by Mitchell Beazley
International Ltd, Michelin House
81 Fulham Road, London SW3 6RB and
Auckland, Melbourne, Singapore and
Toronto as *The American Express
Pocket Guide to Singapore & Bangkok*.
This edition, revised, updated and
expanded, published 1994.

Edited, designed and produced by
Castle House Press, Llantrisant
Mid Glamorgan CF7 8EU
Wales

© American Express Publishing
Corporation Inc. 1994

Contact Library of Congress for full
CIP data.

ISBN 0-671-86830-6

The editors thank Neil Hanson, Alex
Taylor and Steve Ramsay of Lovell
Johns, David Haslam, Anna Holmes
and Sylvia Hughes-Williams for their
help and co-operation during the
preparation of this edition. Special
thanks are due to the Singapore
Tourist Promotion Board and the
Tourism Authority of Thailand, for
their invaluable contribution to the
preparation of this book. Advice and
information were also provided by
the Royal Thai Embassy, London, the
Sentosa Development Corporation,
Singapore, and the Office of the
Narcotics Control Board, Bangkok.

FOR THE SERIES:
Series Editor:
 David Townsend Jones
Map Editor: David Haslam
Indexer: Hilary Bird
Gazetteer: Anna Holmes
Cover design: Roger Walton Studio

FOR THIS EDITION:
Edited on desktop by:
 Sharon Charity
Art editor:
 Eileen Townsend Jones
Illustrators: Karen Cochrane,
 Sylvia Hughes-Williams,
 David Evans
Cover photo: James Davis Travel
 Photography, Singapore

FOR MITCHELL BEAZLEY:
Art Director: Andrew Sutterby
Production: Katy Sawyer
Publisher: Sarah Bennison

PRODUCTION CREDITS:
Maps by Lovell Johns, Oxford,
 England
Typeset in Garamond and
 News Gothic
Desktop layout in Corel
 Ventura Publisher
Reproduction by M & E
 Reproductions, Great Baddow,
 Chelmsford, Essex, England
Linotronic output by
 Tradespools Limited, Frome,
 England

Contents

Singapore

Bangkok

Maps

How to use this book

Few guidelines are needed to understand how this book works:

- For the general organization of the book, see CONTENTS on the pages preceding this one.
- Wherever appropriate, chapters and sections are arranged alphabetically, with headings appearing in **CAPITALS.**
- Often these headings are followed by location and practical information printed in *italics*.
- Subject headers, similar to those used in telephone directories, are printed in CAPITALS in the top corner of each page.
- If you still cannot find what you need, check in the comprehensive and exhaustively cross-referenced INDEX at the back of the book.
- Following the index, LISTS OF STREET NAMES for both Singapore and Bangkok provide map references for all streets, squares etc. mentioned in the book that fall within the area covered by the main city maps (color maps 3–4 and 5–7 at the back of the book).
- Cross-references are printed in SMALL CAPITALS, referring you to other sections or alphabetical entries in the book. Care has been taken to ensure that they are self-explanatory. Often, page references are also given, although their excessive use would be intrusive and ugly.
- We use the European convention for the naming of floors in this book: "ground floor" means the floor at ground level (called by Americans the "first floor").

AUTHOR'S ACKNOWLEDGMENTS

Fred Armentrout would like to thank the following for their help and advice in the preparation of this book. In Singapore: for hospitality at the Shangri-La hotel and its Sentosa Beach resort, Joanne Watkins in Hong Kong, Adelina Ko, Judy Choo and Benson S. Puah, general manager of the Sentosa Beach resort. • Josephine Lau of Doris Lau Ltd., Lee Geok Suan of Baldwin Boyle Shand and Wong Seng Kit of the Singapore Tourist Promotion Board (STPB).

Help on the ground in Singapore was provided by: • Julie Ong (Sentosa Development Corporation). • Audrey Mok (Port of Singapore Authority). • Rita Goh (Beaufort Hotel). • Jennifer Wee-Almodiel (Raffles Hotel). • Candice Su Lin and Kirby Kwek (Inn of the Sixth Happiness). • Margaret Wong and Dave Goh (Duxton Hotel). • Kerensa Ang (Club Excel at Royal Holiday Inn Crowne Plaza). • Clark Corey (Peter Burwash International) at the Beaufort.

In Bangkok: Henrietta Ho, Savas Rattakunjara and Israporn Posayanond for arranging hospitality at the Grand Hyatt Erawan hotel. • Pusdi Angsuvat, director of the Hong Kong office, and Meenawat Satraphay, Bangkok director of the Tourism Authority of Thailand (TAT), for arranging transport and a guide in Bangkok. • Pornnun (Jane) Sunhachan, for being that very able and hardworking guide. • Eumport Jiragalwisul, director of TAT in Phuket.

Key to symbols

☎	Telephone	AE	American Express
Tx	Telex	◉	Diners Club
Fx	Facsimile (fax)	◯	MasterCard
★	Recommended sight	VISA	Visa
❀	Good value (in its class)	◠	Quiet hotel
i	Tourist information	♨	Garden
▥	Building of architectural interest	♣	Good beach nearby
◙	Free entrance	≈	Swimming pool
▨	Entrance fee payable	⚲	Tennis
⚔	Guided tour	✓	Golf
◄	Good view	♔	Gym/fitness facilities
✿	Special interest for children	⚓	Sauna
⬧	Hotel	⚱	Spa
═	Restaurant	♟	Conference facilities
▣	Cafeteria	⌨	Business center
♿	Facilities for disabled people	❢	Bar
		◉	Disco dancing
		♫	Live music

PRICE CATEGORIES

▢	Cheap	▥	Expensive
▨	Inexpensive	▦	Very expensive
▧	Moderately priced		

Our price categories for hotels and restaurants are explained in the WHERE TO STAY and EATING AND DRINKING chapters for each city.

About the author

Fred S. Armentrout has lived in Hong Kong for 16 years and has traveled widely in Asia as the editor of numerous arts, business and travel magazines. Books he has written include *Images of Hong Kong; Taipan Traders* (to which he was contributing author); *Spirit of Yenan, A Wartime Memoir;* and, in this series, *Hong Kong and Taiwan* (which he co-wrote with Ann Williams) and *Hong Kong, Singapore and Bangkok* (with Keith Addison and Brian Eads), a predecessor of this edition. Forthcoming is *Outlier's Island: The Secret Life of Cheung Chau.*

He has also edited some 20 books on Asian arts, business and politics, including *China: The Long March; Bayan Ko: The Aquino Revolution; Living in Hong Kong; Doing Business in Guangdong Province* and *Who's Who in Hong Kong Communications.* His newspaper and magazine assignments have included work for the *International Herald Tribune, Asian Wall Street Journal,* and *Fortune* and *Departures* magazines.

The **research associate** for this edition was Rodelia Delizo, Sheen Co. Ltd., Hong Kong.

A message from the editors

Months of concentrated work were dedicated to making this edition accurate and up to date when it went to press. But time and change are forever the enemies, and between editions we are very much assisted when you, the readers, write to tell us about any changes you discover.

Please keep on writing — but please also be aware that we have no control over restaurants, or whatever, that take it into their heads, after we publish, to move, or change their telephone number, or, even worse, close down. Some restaurants are prone to menu notices like the following genuine authenticated example: "These items may or may not be available at all times, and sometimes not at all and other times all the time." As to telephone numbers, everywhere on earth, telephone authorities seem to share a passion for changing their numbers like you and I change shirts.

My serious point is that we are striving to change the series to the very distinctive tastes and requirements of our discerning international readership, which is why your feedback is so valuable. I particularly want to thank all of you who wrote while we were preparing this edition. Time prevents our responding to most such letters, but they are all welcomed and frequently contribute to the process of preparing the next edition.

Please write to me at **Mitchell Beazley**, an imprint of Reed Illustrated Books, Michelin House, 81 Fulham Road, London SW3 6RB; or, in the US, c/o American Express Travel Guides, **Prentice Hall Travel**, 15 Columbus Circle, New York, NY 10023.

David Townsend Jones, Series Editor, American Express Travel Guides

Singapore
& Bangkok

Ancient wisdom, modern strength

The two exhilarating cities that form the subject of this book are windows opening onto four great cultures in Southeast Asia. They are, respectively, the cultures of the immigrants from the two great neighboring civilizations — the Chinese and Indian — that have shaped the region's history and traditions, and the two dominant indigenous cultures of the region, those of the Thais and Malays.

The first, Singapore, is a city–state entrepôt, developed mostly on the backs of overseas Chinese laborers as a 19th century British colony, which only in 1965 became a new pioneering "Singaporean" polyglot nation built and led into independence by its People's Action Party (PAP), in some ways more akin to Australia or North America than the ancient seats of Malay civilization that surround it.

Singapore is a new culture as well as a new country. The progeny of Western industrialization and trade with Asia, it is probably the easiest place in Asia in which to live or do business. Set prettily between two of the most fascinating countries in the region, Indonesia and Malaysia, it provides an appealing introduction to Asia. It is also the less hectic of the two cities and by far the more compact and efficient. Singapore is the second-best city in Southeast Asia for shopping, after Hong Kong, and a good place to dispel any idea that Asians are unsophisticated when it comes to 20th century ways.

Bangkok, the second city featured in this book, is the capital of one of the most complicated social systems on earth, potentially one of the news world's flash points, and determinedly impassive to the presence of curious foreigners. Thais can tell a northerner from a southerner at 50 paces, to say nothing of Burmese or Khmers — and that seems about the limit of their geographic concerns.

The Thai creed of *sanuk* (roughly translated as "have fun") is infectious and subtly undermines efficiency. In Bangkok the most sober intentions seem to dissolve in the sweet scent of jasmine flowers — like the ones that children sold in garlands to drivers stuck in the interminable traffic jams, until the government banned the trade in an effort to persuade them into the classroom. Bangkok is a place for the strong-willed and the weak-willed. Those in between often feel uneasy there.

To appreciate these cities to the full, they must be put in their general geographical and cultural context. The Eastern Hemisphere encompasses huge stretches of ocean, several continents and subcontinents and more than 30 countries. Socially and culturally it is a vastly diverse and complicated part of the world. Economically it is becoming increasingly significant as commercial ties strengthen between the countries of the "Pacific Basin," to use a term much heard nowadays whenever world economic affairs are discussed.

At the same time, the region suffers from the familiar problems of poverty, racial and sectarian violence, corruption, organized crime and systematic exploitation of women and children. Harsh and primitive features are often found in close juxtaposition with things seen as enlightened — by Western standards — and ultramodern.

Bear in mind that the economic zone known as the "Pacific Basin" extends as far as the west coast of America and includes such highly developed societies as California, Japan and Australia. Mexico and the South American countries facing the Pacific have also made moves to become included in what is expected to be the world's fastest growing economic region in the closing years of the 20th century.

Too often Westerners think of the Eastern Hemisphere as socially and economically backward. It is salutary to recall that many of the innovations that we think of as Western were known to the major cultures of the East while we, by our own historical reckoning, were still barbarians.

Remember too that these mostly agricultural nations have, for thousands of years, supported a far larger population than that of the Western hemisphere, on a far smaller amount of arable land. China alone supports 20 percent of the global population on about seven percent of the earth's surface — and less than 15 percent of the land on that surface is arable.

The East it was that developed the delicately balanced economies of the rice paddy and the bamboo grove with their attendant way of life and of looking at life. *We* tell our sons to "stand firm," with the strength and solidity of the oak tree; *they* tell theirs to "bend strong" — like the sinuous bamboo, which bends, but never breaks, in the fiercest monsoon winds. Both civilizations still have much to learn from each other, especially at a time when Asia is in the curious position of having some of the world's oldest developed cultures and youngest population bases.

No one would seriously lump together all the inhabitants of this sprawling region as "Asians." The typical Asian, if one is to imagine such a being, defies our Western stereotypes: there are black aboriginals in Malaysia and the Philippines, and in Melanesia. There are Armenians, Parsees, Jordanian Jews and White Russians who have traded and lived in Asia for centuries. There is a Portuguese-speaking enclave in Malacca, which has not been a Portuguese colony since the late 17th century. In fact, there are probably more languages spoken in the Indonesian and Philippine archipelagoes combined than there are in the rest of the world altogether.

The common image of the inscrutable Chinese, venerable and secure in the accumulated wisdom of his ancient culture, hardly survives an encounter with the noisy, superstitious, materialistic reality of modern Chinese societies — which is not to say the ancient wisdom isn't there.

THE OVERSEAS CHINESE

The "Overseas Chinese" are such an important part of the ethnic equation in Asia that it is important to take a glance at their history and examine how they came to be so widely dispersed.

The Chinese were roaming the high seas long before the Western age of discovery. The exports they carried with them included mass-produced but high-quality pottery, large quantities of which have been unearthed in the Philippines, Indonesia and Malaysia. China was desperately short of iron and had set up iron-smelting industries in the Southern Seas, and there were flourishing Chinese ports in Luzon, North Borneo and elsewhere in the region.

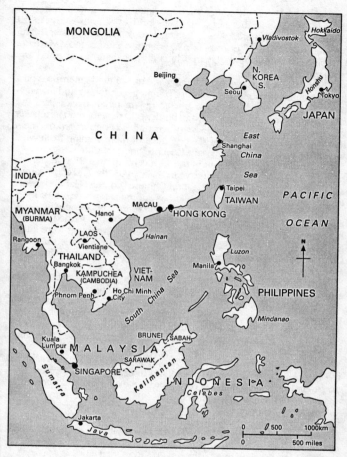

The junks would sail from ports along the South China coast, laden with ceramics and other cargoes, and return the following spring with iron. Unlike other nations they seem not to have carried much in the way of cultural or religious cargo; the Chinese did not, and still do not, proselytize. They were content to trade, and they were highly successful — it was, after all, the Chinese who invented money.

In the 15th century the Europeans arrived from the west via the new Cape of Good Hope route, taking over the trade routes with advanced armed ships that could go anywhere. First came the Portuguese, seizing ports such as Malacca, building up new ones such as Macau and taking control of huge areas of trade. Then the Spaniards followed from their base in Mexico, to the east, bringing Christianity and 300 years of colonization to the Philippines. The Dutch took over Indonesia; Britain took Malaya, parts of Borneo and Burma; the French took Vietnam, Cambodia and Laos. Only Japan, China and Thailand maintained any independence.

The new empires developed mining and agricultural enterprises on a hitherto unknown scale, the big ships bringing technology and management from home and carrying extracted raw materials back again. But labor was in short supply locally, and bottlenecks developed. The answer was to employ imported Chinese workers under a contract arrangement that was in fact little short of slavery, most of them coming from what were then the famine-stricken southern provinces of China.

This trade reached its peak in the 19th century. In a 25-year period, between 1850 and 1875 (the same years that marked the end of the formal slave trade out of Africa), 1.28 million Chinese "contract" laborers were used to supply manpower to plantations and mines in a dozen or more countries around the world. Virtually all were men. Generally, some three-fifths of those who made the crossing on the overloaded arks did not survive the journey; of those who did, 50 to 60 percent were killed by disease and/or suicide. It was through this horrific trade that most Chinese came to Singapore and many to Bangkok. Their way station was Hong Kong.

The legacy of the Chinese traffic in men, which was not finally abolished until 1916, is seen in the Chinese communities that now thrive all over Southeast Asia. Astute, enterprising and hard-working, they have prospered and thus often earned the resentment of other ethnic groups. Their social, economic and political impact on the region has been considerable. They are often referred to as Nanyang Chinese, "Nanyang" meaning Southern Seas.

The Chinese were not the only people imported into Southeast Asia to provide manpower. Some two million Indians were also brought in, and their descendants likewise contribute to the ethnic kaleidoscope that characterizes the region's cities today.

Southeast Asia is an endlessly absorbing part of the world. Western visitors will find a great deal that is baffling, impenetrable and disturbing, but with perseverance and an open mind they will also encounter much beauty, adventure and real excitement. This book aims to enrich the reader's experience of two of the region's most vital cities.

Singapore

Singapore — the Garden City

"Instant Asia," the tag line once used by the Singapore Tourist Promotion Board, remains a succinct description of this city–state. Singapore is not just tiny: by the standards of most Asian nations it is a micro-dot, with a population of $2\frac{1}{2}$ million that would barely fill a suburb in one of Asia's larger cities, let alone one of its nations.

Singapore is also known as "Garden City" — a reference to another of its distinctive features: whereas much of Asia is more jungle than garden, Singapore is planned and controlled. From its founding by Sir Stamford Raffles as a British colonial entrepôt to its modern incarnation as a virtual one-party state run as a self-conscious meritocracy by a Cambridge-educated Chinese lawyer, Singapore has always been a product of human intellect. The conveniently small scale plus a firm belief in the optimistic canons of the Western creed of Progress make it a planner's paradise.

INSTANT ASIA (1)

There are two "Instant Asias" on view in Singapore. The first offers remnants of Raffles' Singapore and serves as an introduction to Asia's major civilizations; in an attempt to avoid racial clashes, ethnically homogeneous districts were set up around the port's central wharf.

The city's development dates from the great era of "coolie" labor migrations in the second half of the 19th century, which sent thousands of Chinese men (sojourners) around the globe in search of work and wealth. The forebears of Singapore's many Chinese dialect groups arrived that way. Indians were brought in as contract or prison laborers and later as rubber plantation workers. The third main group are the Malays, who were the original settlers of the island, although many farmers, fisherfolk and laborers migrated to the island from Malaysia much later.

Today, in a population of 2.65 million, 76 percent are Chinese, 15.1 percent Malay and 6.5 percent Indian. The remaining 2.4 percent includes about 25,000 Westerners (mostly expatriates working abroad) and 30,000 Eurasians, Japanese and Arabs.

Singapore, largely Chinese, has a love–hate relationship with its two neighbors: Muslim Malaysia to the north and east, and ethnically similar Indonesia, the world's largest Muslim nation and fifth-largest in population, on all other sides. Both countries espouse specific policies against Chinese business interests, which had come to dominate their economies in the colonial era, and both experienced violent anti-Chinese riots during the 1960s.

Yet simultaneously both neighbors acknowledge their need of Singapore as a financial and logistical service center. Prime Minister Lee Kuan Yew, Singapore's only leader for 30 years from 1959, was sensitive to the tensions and cultivated close ties with his political neighbors. On the domestic front, he aimed to transcend ethnic differences by encouraging the fusion of the island's disparate races into a single "Singaporean" national identity.

Modern Singapore's efforts to establish its own identity are demonstrated by its hot-and-cold relationship with the colonial tongue. In the immediate post-independence period, English was downgraded, then made the first language again in 1987. At the same time, Mandarin Chinese was encouraged as a second language for the country's Nanyang Chinese, Malays and Indians, most of whom continued quietly to ignore all exhortations and inducements to learn more than English and the two or three dialects or languages that they already spoke at home, none of which was ever likely to be Mandarin.

INSTANT ASIA (2)

The second "Instant Asia" in Singapore has proved a perfect complement to the first in promoting tourism to the island. The stability of a single, progressive leadership community of planners has allowed for the rapid development of infrastructure. The government has housed more than 80 percent of the population in public housing estates. It has created distinct industrial districts, hotel and shopping districts, a business district in Shenton Way, as well as a leisure district on Sentosa Island, and on others of its 57 tiny islands to the south.

This development has tended to be at the expense of local color, and much of the original "Instant Asia" has been planned out of existence — to the extent that, since 1987, government planners have also taken to establishing preservation districts, which comprise about 4 percent of the central land area and teeter somewhere between actual living neighborhoods and American-style theme parks.

A S$1-billion Tourism Development Plan is intended to support Singapore's new convention center at Raffles City, with upgrades at existing sites as well as neighborhood conservation (see JURONG BIRD PARK, SENTOSA, HAW PAR VILLA, RAFFLES HOTEL and CHINESE GARDEN). Raffles City itself looks set to be overshadowed by the opening (in 1994) of the ambitious Suntec City complex, a massive development in the Marina Centre that will incorporate the gigantic Singapore International Convention and Exhibition Centre. The plan has also led to a virtual tripling of annual events staged in Singapore, particularly in the form of sports competitions such as international road and speedboat races, tennis and golf championships.

One result of this self-conscious flurry of development is that Singapore tends to lack the authentic air of Asian traditional life. Another, however, is that, much as "old Asia hands" may grumble, the transplanting of such local traditions as informal evening food-stall centers, from empty parking lots to permanent concrete homes such as Newton Circus, guarantees improved inspection and better hygiene. For visitors this means a "safe" introduction to Asian cuisines.

While for some visitors Singapore is just too squeaky-clean for travel to feel like adventure, the truth is that for most newcomers "Instant Asia" is a good place in which to build up courage for more serious excursions to the region. Singapore's farsighted planners correctly understood that efficiency, service and cleanliness would attract the average traveler as much as the authentic exoticism of neighboring countries.

Income from tourism in the 1990s has been rising steadily, the number of visitors climbing to reach an annual figure approaching six million. Echoing this trend, the number of meetings and conventions staged in Singapore has doubled since 1985, and will certainly receive a further boost with the grand launch of Suntec City.

Manufacturing, finance and commerce have thrived, so that Singapore often feels more like suburban London or Bethesda, Maryland, than an enclave of Asia's great agricultural civilizations. Even the superb shipping facilities, which long ago left Rotterdam behind and allowed Singapore to compete annually with Hong Kong to rank as the world's busiest container port, have been carefully shunted out of sight.

Singapore cares more about its reputation as a clean "garden city" than it does about appearing exotic to Western tastes — the planner's paradise was built primarily for residents, not tourists, and it enjoys Asia's second highest per capita income, after Japan. It is a model of the condition to which most Asian capitals aspire: modern and middle-class. There is a telephone for every three people, a television for every five, and a doctor for every thousand. Just as in comfortable suburbs in America, Canada and Australia, "boredom" is its citizens' most common complaint.

This status has helped make Singapore attractive also to those Asian tourists who perceive the West as exotic. Small wonder that more than a quarter of its visitors are recorded as coming from six ASEAN member states (the Association of Southeast Asian Nations: Indonesia, Thailand, the Philippines, Malaysia, Singapore and Brunei); and the overwhelming majority of those come from Indonesia. Some 70 percent of all visitors come from Asian nations.

Singaporeans tend to consider their nation an outpost of progress in an untidy world — a 19th century English colonial outlook transposed into a "modern" Asia grounded on hard work and intelligence. That's understandable, for Singapore is an object lesson in how to set national priorities — and follow them through, year upon year.

Culture, history and background

A brief history of Singapore

For 2,000 years traders from points as distant as the Red Sea and the Sea of Japan have sailed before monsoon winds to the Straits of Malacca — the great causeway, between the Malay Peninsula and the island of Sumatra, that links the Indian Ocean with the South China Sea and the Pacific. The island of Singapore, strategically guarding the Pacific entrance to the Straits, has a long and rich mercantile and military history.

From the **7th–13thC**, Temasek (Sea Town), the first recorded name for Singapore, was an important port of the powerful, seafaring Srivijayan Empire of Sumatra, and it prospered from tolls levied on ships passing through the Straits. A Sumatran prince later gave Temasek the bolder name of Singa-Pura, "Lion City." In the **14thC**, Javanese, Siamese and Chinese merchants established a trading state on the island. But, conquered by Muslim Malacca, which rose to power as Srivijaya declined, Singa-Pura fell into obscurity.

During the Christian Crusades, ships carrying spices from the Spice Islands (now Indonesia), sailing via the Straits, helped pay for the Arab armies fighting for Allah; in medieval Europe, spice profits helped finance the Italian Renaissance. The desire to seize control of the spice trade from the Muslims explains the zeal with which the Christian nations took their crusading legacy to sea — first the Portuguese, later the Spanish, Dutch, French and English. In **1511** Malacca fell to the Portuguese, who used it as a base for the spice trade.

By the late **18thC** the Portuguese had been overtaken by the Dutch as the dominant European influence, and the Dutch in turn were losing ground to the British. In **1789**, Francis Light leased from a local sultan an island at the top of the Straits. He founded Penang, the easternmost port in the Indian Ocean. Then, in **1819**, Sir Stamford Raffles, acting on behalf of the British East India Company, paid 33,200 Spanish dollars to lease Singa-Pura from the Sultan of Johore, ruler of Malacca.

Raffles was a sailor with a sense of history and, recognizing the potential of Singa-Pura's protected port and remembering its former stature, he re-established the place as a trading station and called it the "Emporium of the Southern Seas." When Raffles landed at the mouth of the tiny Singapore River, the population was about 150 — Malays and a few Chinese. In the 15thC, following seven extraordinary expeditions to the South Seas and the Indian Ocean by Admiral Zhenghe (Cheng Ho),

China's greatest navigator, and for reasons still not entirely clear, the Ming Dynasty rulers had closed China's borders and forbidden unofficial travel overseas on pain of death. However, such rules were easier to declare than to enforce, and the Chinese trading communities, even in the early 19thC, had managed to maintain their footholds in the region.

Raffles' interest in Singapore stemmed from his frustration at having to return Batavia (Java in Indonesia) to the Dutch as part of the treaty terms ending the Napoleonic Wars. Raffles convinced his superiors in London that Britain needed an entrepôt in the area. His business acumen proved accurate: within four years of its founding, Singapore's population had increased to 10,000; people were brought in from South China on the Chinese "credit ticket" system to work the tin mines of Malaya and the pepper and gambier farms on Singapore island itself.

By 1823, Raffles was already attempting to curb what would later become the "coolie" traffic, or "pig trade." He passed an ordinance that imposed a ceiling on passage fares and limited the indentured period to two years. To discourage kidnapping and deceptive recruiting, he required that every engagement for labor be entered with free consent of the parties before a magistrate.

By that time, however, the Chinese secret societies had gained control of the coolie trade and set up a network of brokers in South China and in the port towns of Southeast Asia. Raffles' far-sighted ordinances were never enforced. The traffic in men, not abolished until 1916, left legacies that would haunt the region's leaders.

The opening of Treaty Ports for foreign trade in China and Japan strengthened Singapore's commercial and maritime position. With the opening of the Suez Canal in 1869 and the emerging Western technologies of cable and steam, the island was naturally positioned to benefit from the trade in raw materials moving west and manufactured products moving east.

From growing prosperity through various boom-and-bust cycles from the 1880s to the 1920s emerged the Singapore of shaded verandas and slow ceiling fans depicted in the short stories of Somerset Maugham.

In 1942 the invading Japanese army surprised everyone by riding down the Malayan Peninsula on bicycles and destroying "fortress Singapore," and with it what had appeared to be the impregnable dominance of the White Man in Asia. The island was bombed, occupied, and its defenders remained imprisoned until the Japanese surrender in 1945.

After the war the British returned with the promise of eventual independence for their colonies east of Suez, including the Malay Straits Settlements. Japan's defeat notwithstanding, her wartime victories had severely punctured the illusion of White supremacy, and the prewar colonial idyll was never to return. The only question was the shape of independence.

The first challenge came from ethnic Chinese Communists, inspired largely by events in their mother country, where Mao Zedong's Red Army was close to nationwide victory over Chiang Kaishek's Nationalists (Guomintang) and had been seasoned in battle by their successful guerilla war against the Japanese occupation forces.

For 12 years (**1948–60**), Chin Peng, a Straits Chinese and former anti-Japanese guerrilla fighter, waged war on the British in Malaya. Thousands were killed, 50 battalions of British and Commonwealth troops were tied down, 90,000 Chinese were deported back to China and another 20,000 were imprisoned.

When Singapore's Prime Minister Lee Kuan Yew and his colleagues of the People's Action Party took control in **1959** of a self-governing Singapore under British protection, they had counted on joining an independent Malaysia as one of its Federated Malay States. The **1963** union lasted only two years, dissolved by a Malaysian government who succumbed to anti-Chinese pressure from its Malay Muslim majority.

Well aware of his small island state's vulnerability to the appeal of Chinese Communism and Chinese secret society gangsterism on the one hand, and Malay–Indonesian anti-Chinese hostility on the other, Lee has governed the country with an iron hand. Even today, with friendly Malay and Indonesian neighbors and regional Communist insurgencies on the wane, few non-Communist societies are so tightly regimented.

Speaking from the podium of practical economic success, Lee has become a regional advocate for hardliners in the People's Republic of China and Hong Kong, arguing that national affluence *leads*, in some unspecified future, to democratic values, rather than growing out of them.

From **1959** until **1989**, Lee had been the country's only Prime Minister, and his People's Action Party, despite winning the 1992 election with a reduced majority, still has a firm hold on the reins of power. Many believe Lee's soldier-turned-politician son Lee Hsien-Loong is being groomed for succession. A former Brigadier-General in the army, popularly known as "BG," he was named as one of two Deputy Prime Ministers when Lee Snr. stepped down to become "Senior Minister" rather than "PM" — as he had been known for 30 years. However, recent ill-health may have cast a shadow over "BG"'s prospects.

The Prime Minister is Goh Chok Tong, who has recently hinted at moves toward liberalizing Singapore's social environment. Meanwhile, however, Lee Snr. has been attempting to make himself a spokesman for "Confucian" versus "Western" values — supplying a neat rationale for strong-arm politics. Nobody expects him to relinquish his grip on power just yet.

From an inhospitable swampland has emerged a modern affluent city–state — part financial services center, part hi-tech manufacturer, part oil industry base, part entrepôt to its less developed neighbors. Few doubt that, by the end of the century, living standards in Singapore will be on a par with those of the developed world.

Singapore's architecture

Singapore is a modern, planned city, much of whose architectural heritage has been replaced by formal estates of public housing apartment blocks, sleek hotels, multistory indoor shopping centers, and the linear towers of commerce and finance.

As plans go, it is a good one, although not without its disasters. The ergonomics are good, services and communications excellent, building standards high. There is a good ratio of breathing space, for the "Garden City" image reflects the reality: extensive landscaping is a required part of major building contracts, and there is greenery and open space in abundance, to the city's great benefit. Most important, people are adequately housed, healthy and well fed; as a social and economic machine, the city is clean and efficient — it works well. In Asia, all these features are rarities.

Whether you perceive the brave new city or the remnants of the old depends on where you go, and perhaps on whether you're of the West or the East. The new style is international, with local cultural content mostly confined to decorative detail.

Westerners will find more interest in the remaining colonial buildings, in the streets of old shophouses (simple but functional structures combining living and working quarters, one of which is illustrated on page 27), terrace (row) houses, bazaars and temples, where styles express the traditions of each of the ethnic groups that together built old Singapore, occasionally mingling to produce some odd hybrids.

THE COLONIAL PERIOD
St Andrew's Cathedral, illustrated on page 74, was built in 1836 and is a fusion of Western design and Eastern technique. Architect **George Drumgoole Coleman** gave it an early-Gothic style and an imposing scale, with a 22.5m-high (74-foot) nave.

The graceful interior is plastered in *Madras chunam*, a strange blend of shell lime, egg white and raw sugar, mixed with water from soaked coconut husks. The resulting rocklike surface was rubbed smooth as marble with immense labor by gangs of Indian convicts using lumps of rock crystal.

The **Sultan Mosque** (1928), a British colonial architect's interpretation of traditional Moorish design.

The **Hajjah Fatimah Mosque**, designed by another English architect, **John Turnbull Thomson**, in 1846, also has a touch of Gothic: the minaret is said to have been modeled on the spire of St Andrew's Cathedral. An earlier mosque, the **Nagore Durgha Shrine**, has a facade of intricate Muslim calligraphic designs, along with Doric columns and Palladian doors. The **Sultan Mosque** (1928, illustrated opposite), the largest place of Islamic worship in Singapore, has a traditionally Moorish design: an imposing white building with gold-painted domes.

Singapore's early colonial public buildings were constructed in the Palladian style, adapted from the formal designs fashionable in 18thC England. The term refers to the work of the Venetian High Renaissance architect Palladio (1518–90), who revived and interpreted Greek and Roman Classical forms. Wealthy Englishmen traveling in Italy took the style home and patterned their country houses after it. From England, it traveled to the East.

Coleman, a consultant to Raffles on the 1822–23 Town Planning Board of Singapore, had previously worked in Bombay and Calcutta, where merchants' houses were built in the Palladian tradition. He adapted the style to local conditions, combining Doric and Corinthian elements, using elegant plasterwork, deep, wide verandas, high ceilings, roof overhangs for shade, louvered windows and open floorplans. Other surviving Coleman buildings are the **Armenian Church** (1835) and the former Maxwell House (1826), later enlarged and modified to become the present **Parliament House**.

Coleman's Neoclassical
Armenian Church (1835).

Thomson arrived in 1841 and designed many solid buildings, including the **Cathedral of the Good Shepherd** (1846) and the **Thian Hock Keng Temple** (c.1842) as well as the **Dalhousie obelisk** (1850).

A third leading architectural light was **Regent Alfred John Bidwell**, who joined the architectural firm Swan and Maclaren in 1895 and introduced a style that has been described as neo-Renaissance. Examples of his work include the 1899 main wing of **Raffles Hotel**, the **Teutonia Club** (1900), now part of the Goodwood Park Hotel, and **St Joseph's Church** (1913).

Colonial Englishmen built similar homes wherever they went in the tropics, and the Singapore version is a variation on a theme to be found in Malaysia, Kenya and wherever the equatorial map was colored pink for Britain. Some of these houses are magnificent, and fine examples can be found in **Goodwood Hill**, **Alexandra Park**, **Rochester Park** and **Nassim Rd.** They are mostly big, airy and comfortable, with large gardens.

Typically there are two reception rooms and a kitchen downstairs and two or three large high-ceilinged bedrooms upstairs, all with balconies. At the top of an imposing staircase is found a big "day-room," open on all sides, supported by columns, and set under a deep-eaved pitched roof like a large upstairs porch. The "day-room" is fitted with shutters or bamboo blinds, and is delightfully airy even with the blinds down. Behind the house are the servants' quarters with two or three rooms, bathroom and laundry, connected to the house by a covered walkway against monsoon storms.

Many of these houses still have European occupants, although these days some of them choose to live in the comfortable servants' quarters while renting out the house. Many of the open day-rooms have now been enclosed and air conditioned, perhaps because they offered no security against burglars.

CHINESE AND HINDU ARCHITECTURE

The most striking of Singapore's traditional buildings are the Chinese and Indian temples, and here the city's colonial past has left little mark: thus the **Thian Hock Keng** Chinese temple may be ascribed to Thomson, but it is typically Chinese with its gate of carved wood and stone, its curving tiled roofs alive with dragons, its halls with brightly lacquered columns and pillars, surrounding a tiled courtyard. The sheer proliferation of Chinese motifs leaves no room for other influences. Like all Chinese temples, it is ornate, colorful and jumbled.

Chettiyar Temple

Hindu temples have spectacular gate towers *(Gopuram)* topped with tiered pyramids of intricately sculpted processions of deities in bright and elaborate array, often wrought by craftsmen brought from India. The **Arulmuga Thandayuthapani Temple,** known as the Chettiyar Temple after the subcaste of money lenders who built it in the 1850s, is a showpiece of Hindu craftsmanship. The original was demolished in 1981, but rebuilt in 1984.

A row of typical
shophouses

The other major traditional features are the **shophouses** and **terrace (row) houses**. Shophouses were introduced to Singapore from South China via Malacca (where fine examples of the form can be seen) by immigrant "Straits Chinese." Originally unadorned timber buildings with thatched roofs, they serve as both living and working quarters. The first floor extends over the sidewalk onto pillars at the roadside, forming the "five-foot way," where storekeepers display their wares along the sidewalk and lower bamboo blinds between the pillars, creating a virtually enclosed shopping bazaar, shady and cool.

The terrace houses are much the same, without the shops, and with a small courtyard under the extended first story, walled off from the sidewalk.

The **Tanjong Pagar Conservation Area** offers a glimpse of the genre, with some 200 restored shophouses. Other examples are **Boat Quay**, on the bank of the Singapore River opposite **Empress Place**, and **Clarke Quay Festival Village**. The **Little India** and **Arab Street** areas also exemplify the style.

Up to the 1880s, shophouses were built by locals with local materials to standard patterns, but then the wealthier Straits Chinese started to retain English architects to design their houses, and to introduce Western motifs. The style that emerged from this collaboration is variously called "Chinese Baroque," "Palladian Chinese" or "Straits Chinese": shophouses and terrace houses with ornate facades incorporating classical Chinese, Malay and European elements.

Fine examples of Chinese Baroque can be seen among the terrace houses on **Emerald Hill**, **Koon Seng Ed** *(off Joo Chiat Rd.)* and **Petain Rd.** The houses are narrow but long and spacious, with two stories and pitched Chinese-style roofs. Front doorways and windows are ornate and brightly colored, the walls below the windows finished with floral tiles from Europe.

Palladian columns replace the standard pillars supporting the extended first story; intricate upstairs window louvers are flanked by more (false) columns. Colors are cream, green, pink, blue — the same bright colors as Straits Chinese porcelain and embroidery.

Shophouses and terrace houses are functional and comfortable, an attractive approach to urban living in the Singapore of old, and in today's Penang and Malacca. Parts of Singapore's preservation areas manage to continue life much as before, but many historic streets have only a few old buildings left, anachronistic tokens of traditional Asia in clean, functional streets with no pedigree.

China also reached out to influence Singapore architecture, although only remnants and rather gaudy reproductions in hotels remain as reminders of the Middle Kingdom's tradition of buildings erected around a courtyard.

Thong Chai Medical Institution (now rechristened the **Seiwan Arts Centre**) was a free hospital using traditional Chinese medical techniques and medicines. Its former location, built in the 1890s in Wayang St., is said to have been designed by a Beijing architect. Seiwan Arts Centre, now relocated to a modern structure nearby, displays and sells Chinese arts and crafts.

North of Fort Canning is the **House of Tan Yeok Nee**, which has housed the headquarters of the Salvation Army since 1940. Mr. Tan was a wealthy 19thC Teochew trader who built his house in a style then flourishing in southern China. Only four such homes were built in Singapore and only this one survives.

MODERN SINGAPORE

Singapore's planners are not unaware of the fact that their model city lacks the basic artifact of a modern urban identity: a unique skyline, instantly identifiable from a distance.

They plan to rectify that with a "showcase Downtown of the 21stC," to be built on reclaimed land around Marina Bay. This area already houses a number of massive hotels and shopping complexes, as well as the towers of the new **Suntec City** convention and commercial center.

The centerpieces of the new downtown will be twin 50-story office towers, intended to link the old downtown area to the new developments on Marina Bay. The MRT system will be expanded, with four new stations serving the district. Up to five rows of trees will line all boulevards, in an effort to suggest what city planners refer to as a "sprung from nature" ambience. Part of something called the "Concept Plan," a master scheme that envisions an eventual population of four million people, construction of the new downtown is expected to be completed by the year 2010.

Singapore's new hi-tech, high-rise skyline has been the cause of some odd juxtapositions. The Gothic spire of St Andrew's Cathedral, once the tallest point near the Padang, now dwarfed by the soaring cylinder of the **Westin Stamford Hotel** (see illustration on page 74), is a good example of how the city of Raffles coexists with a thrusting commercial city focused on a new millennium.

The arts in Singapore

Like the people, religions and languages, the arts in Singapore comprise a vivid multicultural cocktail. In some respects they are a straightforward continuation of artistic traditions evolved in ancestral homelands, feeding both local tastes and the tourist industry.

Thus, there are stylized Mandarin operas, Bersilat performances (a Malay version of kung-fu), Tamil- and Bengali-language movies, Chinese woodcarvers fashioning sandalwood into temple gods, and Malay craftsmen working tin and silver into pewter artifacts. But, just as English has emerged as the *lingua franca* of this diverse community, so "the performing arts" frequently means Western music, theater and dance.

Its diversity notwithstanding, no one would describe Singapore as a cultural dynamo; the traditional arts are rendered much better in China, Malaysia, Indonesia and India, the Western arts much better in the West. As is frequently the case when tourism is a major moneyspinner, the easiest option is the canned cultural show, with digestible cameos of traditional song, dance and acrobatics. Several major hotels offer these shows. But education and economic success have fed local demand for the arts. Theaters inherited from the colonial era have been renovated and supplemented with new auditoriums. Never before have so many artists, local and visiting, been creating and performing there.

The watershed year was probably 1963 when, a century after the **Victoria Theatre** became Singapore's first permanent theater, a new **National Theatre** opened and the country hosted the First Southeast Asian Cultural Festival. They offer an eclectic mix — from Malay drama to Western ballet; Chinese classical music played on traditional instruments to Gilbert and Sullivan. That evolved into the biennial **Singapore Festival of Arts** — the next one takes place in 1994. More than 60 international and local groups from almost a dozen countries take part.

Musical life got a boost in 1979 with the setting up of a full-time **Singapore Symphony Orchestra**, and the **Singapore Broadcasting Corporation** now maintains a full-scale Chinese orchestra.

The half-dozen museums and art galleries still most often exhibit imported works, but there are notable exceptions such as **Alpha Gallery**, a proponent of contemporary regional art for more than 20 years. The **National Museum** houses the **National Art Gallery**, which emphasizes Southeast Asian artists and has a gallery devoted to Straits Chinese culture, including antique furniture touched by Portuguese, Dutch and Chinese influences. It also contains the **Haw Par jade collection**, 385 pieces that form what is thought to be the world's largest private collection, and a good array of trade porcelain from China.

The **University of Singapore Art Museum** has watercolors and lithographs from the earliest days of the British settlement. Efforts to stimulate distinctive Singaporean schools of art have been rather less successful than accumulating the past and importing from the West. Perhaps the most significant progress has been in painting, thanks mostly to the **Nanyang Academy of Fine Arts (NAFA)**. NAFA sought above all to blend established multicultural traditions into a Singaporean style, christened Nanyang, or "Seas South of China." Initially, it drew heavily on an idealized vision of life in the Malay *kampong* (village). More recently artists have begun addressing the late 20thC, with some of the finest work done in batik painting — a 2,000-year-old technique of coloring cloth using wax-resist methods, which lends itself as much to abstract and contemporary themes as to traditional designs. Their work is often exhibited at the National Art Gallery.

Contemporary artists are on show and in action at the **Sentosa Arts Centre** *(Block 4, Carlton Hill, Sentosa Island)*. Exhibitions take in the best in local painting, calligraphy, batik, woodcarving and ceramic work, all areas where traditional techniques can be channeled into modern expression. The **Substation**, a renovated power station site on Armenian St., has been developed by a local dramatist into a thriving center of artistic experimentation.

Practical information

This chapter is organized into seven sections:
- **BEFORE YOU GO**, below
- **GETTING THERE**, page 34
- **GETTING AROUND**, page 36
- **ON-THE-SPOT INFORMATION**, page 39
- **BUSINESS IN SINGAPORE**, page 44
- **USEFUL ADDRESSES**, page 45
- **EMERGENCY INFORMATION**, page 48

Each section is organized thematically rather than alphabetically. Summaries of subject headings are printed in CAPITALS at the top of most pages.

Before you go

SINGAPORE TOURIST INFORMATION OFFICES OVERSEAS
The **Singapore Tourist Promotion Board** has much useful information for prospective visitors. It has offices in the following cities:
- **London**   Carrington House, 126-130 Regent St., London W1R 5FE, UK ☎(071) 437-0033 ☒(071) 734-2191.
- **New York**   590 5th Ave., 12th floor, New York, NY 10036, USA ☎(212) 302-4861 ☒(212) 302-4801.
- **Los Angeles**   Suite 510, 8484 Wilshire Blvd., Beverly Hills, CA 90211, USA ☎(213) 852-1901 ☒(213) 852-0129.
- **Chicago**   333 N Michigan Ave., Suite 818, Chicago, IL 60601, USA ☎(312) 220-0099 ☒(312) 220-0020.

DOCUMENTS REQUIRED
British and Commonwealth visitors may stay for up to three months without a **visa**, US citizens for 14 days with extensions up to three months; visas are needed for residence and employment. Confirmed **onward or return tickets** are required. For further information contact Singapore overseas missions or the Immigration Office (see USEFUL ADDRESSES on page 46).

Health documents are not needed unless you are arriving from South America or Africa, in which case a yellow-fever certificate is required. Check current regulations when making travel reservations.

National **drivers' licenses** or international **drivers' permits** issued in most Western countries are valid in Singapore. Visitors from other countries can apply to the Traffic Police for a Singapore driver's license on production of a valid national driver's license.

TRAVEL AND MEDICAL INSURANCE

It is important to take out insurance cover before you depart on your trip to Singapore. American Express provides comprehensive travel and medical insurance including on-the-spot 24-hour emergency coverage. Contact **American Express Travel Service** offices for details of this. It may also be worth checking whether other insurance companies have a reciprocal agreement with companies in Singapore for refund of medical expenses.

For US citizens, the **IAMAT** (International Association for Medical Assistance to Travelers) is worth joining, and membership is free. It has member hospitals and clinics throughout the world, including several in Singapore, and has a list of English-speaking doctors who will call, for a fee. It also provides information on health risks overseas.

For further information, and a directory of doctors and hospitals, write to IAMAT headquarters in the US or Europe (*at 417 Center St., Lewiston, NY 14092, USA or 57 Voirets, 1212 Grand-Lancy, Genève, Switzerland*).

MONEY

The unit of currency is the Singapore dollar (S$), which is divided into 100 cents. Daily currency exchange rates are provided in banks and in the "Timesdollar" section of *The Straits Times*. Brunei dollars circulate freely in Singapore; Malaysian dollars exchange less favorably and are not accepted as payment. **Travelers checks** issued by American Express, Barclays, Thomas Cook and Citibank and major **charge and credit cards** (American Express, Diners Club, MasterCard and Visa) are widely accepted.

Always read the instructions included with your travelers checks. It is important to note separately the serial numbers of your checks and the telephone number to call in case of loss. Specialist travelers-check companies such as **American Express** provide extensive local refund facilities for lost checks through their own offices or agents.

CUSTOMS ALLOWANCES

The international allowance of one liter for alcohol applies. Duty-free concessions on tobacco were removed from January 1991 to encourage Singaporeans to stop smoking. All travelers arriving by any means of transport must pay around S$17 duty per carton of cigarettes. Cameras, radios and other such items are free of duty, but goods in excess of "reasonable personal effects" must be declared on entry and exit.

There are no restrictions on currency or other negotiable instruments, nor on imports and exports of gold, gems and jewelry. Firearms and other weapons, including swords and *kris* (Malay daggers), must be declared and handed over; flora and fauna are restricted. Airport tax is levied on departure. **Airport Passenger Service Coupons** reduce check-in time at the airport and can be purchased in advance from airlines, hotels and travel agents.

Magazines such as *Playboy* and *Penthouse* are considered pornographic and are subject to confiscation.

NARCOTIC DRUGS

Before you depart, you should be warned that Singapore strictly enforces harsh **anti-drug laws**; there have been many executions, including those of foreigners.

The **death sentence** is mandatory for anyone convicted of trafficking more than 15 grams ($\frac{1}{2}$ ounce) of dimorphine; more than 30 grams (one ounce) of morphine or cocaine; more than 200 grams of cannabis resin, 500 grams of cannabis or 1.2 kilograms of opium. Lesser offenses are punishable by long prison sentences or corporal punishment.

When arriving in Singapore, you are strongly advised:

- **NEVER** to agree to carry any amount of drugs;
- **NEVER** to check in baggage on behalf of someone who claims to have excess baggage;
- **NEVER** to carry packages or baggage for anyone unless you are absolutely sure they don't contain drugs.

TIME ZONES

Singapore is 12 hours ahead of US Eastern Standard Time, 13–15 hours ahead of other US time zones and eight hours ahead of Greenwich Mean Time. It is one hour ahead of Bangkok and Tokyo and two hours behind Sydney.

CLIMATE

Singapore lies one degree N of the equator and has a tropical climate and hot weather all year. The temperature ranges from 24°–31°C (75–88°F), and humidity is generally high. There are two very wet monsoon seasons, March to May and November to January.

WHAT TO WEAR

Light, casual clothes are the most comfortable and are accepted almost everywhere. You will need a pullover to cope with the air conditioning in some restaurants. A jacket and tie are required in only the most exclusive restaurants.

You may feel more at ease if you dress to match your surroundings: most hotels and restaurants are luxurious, and Singaporeans dress very well. Avoid flipflops in hotels or private homes; some discos forbid jeans or running shoes. Singaporean male office workers do not wear suit jackets, just shirts and ties.

PREPARATORY READING
Culture

The two best books to document the disappearing life-style of the Nanyang Chinese are *Singapore's River: A Living Legacy*, a sensitive book-length photo-essay by Linda Berry (1982) and *"Can Survive, La"*: *Cottage Industries in High-rise Singapore*, by Margaret Sullivan with photographs by Henry Wong and Michael Neo (1985).

Indians are the third largest ethnic group in the former Straits Settlements of the British. The most comprehensive explanation of their presence is *Indians in Malaysia and Singapore,* by Sinnappah Arasaratnam in the Oxford in Asia series of monographs (1979).

History

C.M. Turnbull is the most noted Singapore historian, with his *History of Singapore* and *A Short History of Malaysia, Singapore and Brunei.* Maurice Collins has written a popular biography of the city's founding father, *Raffles.*

Wartime Singapore

Out in the Midday Sun, by Kate Caffrey, relates the hardships and suffering of the captured. The novel *King Rat,* by James Clavell, tells the POW story from the inside. The fall of "Fortress Singapore" and its consequences is looked at in *Sinister Twilight: The Fall of Singapore* by Noel Barber, who was a journalist in Singapore before World War II, and in *The Singapore Grip,* by J.G. Farrell. Barber also wrote *Tanamera: A Novel of Singapore.*

Getting there

BY RAIL

There are several trains a day from various Malaysian towns and cities, arriving at Singapore's Tanjong Pagar Station, not far from Orchard Rd. and the city center.

Butterworth, near Penang (about 14 hours), and **Kuala Lumpur**, Malaysia's capital (about seven hours), are the two most frequented Malaysian stops. Air-conditioned sleeper cars are the most comfortable means of train travel. The customs and immigration checkpoint for visitors arriving by road or by rail is at Woodlands, on the Singapore side of the causeway that joins Singapore to Malaysia.

The Eastern and Oriental Express

Well-heeled railway buffs can relive the opulence of the "golden age of travel" on **The Eastern and Oriental Express**, a luxury train developed by the company that created the Venice–Simplon Orient Express in Europe.

The train runs from Singapore to Bangkok, by way of stops in Malaysia and southern Thailand. It departs from Singapore on Sunday at 3.30pm, arriving in Bangkok the following Tuesday at 9.30am, with five stops en route. The round trip starts in Bangkok on Wednesday at 8.30pm and ends in Singapore on Friday at 8.45am.

If a shorter sample of interwar elegance will do, there are also weekend excursions to Malacca that leave Singapore on Friday at 6.30pm, returning on Saturday at 5.30pm.

For **reservations**, contact: Eastern and Oriental Express Co Pte Ltd, 90 Cecil St. #14-03, Carlton Bldg., Singapore 0106 (☎ *227-2068* Ⓕˣ *224-9265*). In Europe, contact: Venice–Simplon Orient Express Ltd, 20 Upper Ground, London SE1 9PF, UK (☎ *(071) 928-6000* Ⓕˣ *(071) 620-1210*).

The People's Express

Another way of exploring the Malay–Thai peninsula at leisure, and of traveling between the two cities covered in this book, is to take the **Rakyat** — or **People's** — **Express**, a clean and modern train that, belying its name, ambles along the 1,250 miles from Singapore to Bangkok at a top speed of 80kph (50 miles per hour).

The journey can be completed in 39 hours, but this is not the way to travel if you are in a hurry. The People's Express offers a chance to sit back in air-conditioned comfort as it chugs along through the Malaysian jungle, past the palm-fringed beaches and Buddhist temples of southern Thailand. A first-class, one-way ticket from Singapore to Bangkok costs about S$140, and allows you to stop off whenever and wherever you want. Second-class is also perfectly adequate.

For **reservations**, contact Malaysian Railways at this address: Passenger Services Department, KTM Berhad, Jalan Sultan Hishamuddin, 50261 Kuala Lumpur, Malaysia (☎ *(603) 2749-422* ⟨Fx⟩ *(603)2757-331)*.

BY AIR

Singapore's **Changi International Airport** is the largest in Asia and was twice voted the finest in the world by readers of *Business International* magazine. With its second passenger terminal recently completed, Changi is served by 47 scheduled airlines with direct links to 91 cities in 51 countries. Intra-Asian flights are usually direct and nonstop.

Approximate flying times from Singapore are as follows: Hong Kong, $3\frac{1}{2}$ hours; Bangkok, 3 hours; Perth, $4\frac{1}{2}$ hours; Sydney, $7\frac{1}{2}$ hours; Tokyo, $6\frac{1}{2}$ hours; European capitals, about 15 hours; San Francisco, 17 hours; Chicago or New York, 23 hours.

BY SEA

Singapore has succeeded in becoming the major port of call in Asia for cruise liners. They dock at the **International Passenger Terminal**, near the new **Singapore Cruise Centre** at the World Trade Centre Ferry Terminal. Week-long fly-cruise vacation packages, using Singapore as a base, are available from a number of tour operators including Club Med, Renaissance Cruises, Delfin Cruises and Seven Seas Cruises.

Most Southeast Asian cities are only one or two days away by ship. The *QE2* stops over as part of her 20-day Asian cruise out of Tokyo, as do the *Royal Viking Sun* and the British liner *Canberra*. Two round-the-world voyagers, *Sagafjord* and her sister ship *Vistafjord,* also call. Regional ships include Thailand's *Andaman Princess, Sea Goddess II* and *Ocean Pearl*.

BY ROAD

A 1.2km/$\frac{3}{4}$-mile road-and-rail causeway connects Singapore to Malaysia and the Asian Highway. **Fly-drive** packages are popular in either direction. Good places to stop over on the 14-hour drive between Singapore and Penang are **Kuala Lumpur** or **Kuantan** in Malaysia *(both a 7-8hr drive from Singapore)*, and the former Portuguese and Dutch colony of **Malacca** *(5hrs)*.

Getting around

Singapore is a small city, easy to get around in, and the public transport system is predictably efficient.

The Central Business District (CBD) has peak-hour restrictions on taxis and private cars to reduce traffic congestion. Cars and taxis carrying fewer than four people (including the driver) must display special daily license stickers Monday to Saturday 7.30–10.15am.

FROM THE AIRPORT TO THE CITY

Moving walkways and elevators provide an effortless glide to Immigration at Changi Airport. The luggage area has eight conveyor-belt systems, each clearly marked with the relevant flight number.

The public **Arrival Meeting Hall** is beyond the clearance counters, with baggage storage facilities, a duty-free emporium, restaurants and snack bars, a 24-hour money exchange, a bank, a 24-hour post office, public phones (local calls are free within the hall), international telephone booths, car rental and hotel reservation counters, private reception and VIP rooms. The **Tourist Promotion Board desk** provides a wealth of information, including maps and the official guide book.

The city is about 20km (12½ miles) from the airport. The **taxi stand** is at the concourse outside the arrival hall. There is a small airport surcharge; trunk (boot) luggage is extra, but wheelchairs and baby carriages are carried free of charge. The journey takes about 30 minutes.

Buses leave for the city from a terminal on the lower ground floor of the arrival hall. Bus #390 goes to the Orchard Rd. hotel area, and takes around 45 minutes.

MASS RAPID TRANSPORT (MRT)

Singapore's **Mass Rapid Transit (MRT)** trains run at intervals of three to eight minutes from 6am–midnight, on separate N–S and E–W lines. Stations serving the city and Orchard Rd. areas are Orchard, Somerset, Dhoby Ghaut, City Hall and Raffles City.

Three-stop travel costs 60 cents. Routes are color-coded, and there are clear maps at the ticket-dispensing machines and change machines. Keep your ticket: you will have to show it to get out at the other end of your journey. A good *MRT Guide* is sold at newsstands and in bookstores.

BUS SERVICES

This popular mode of public transport is inexpensive and efficient. **Singapore Bus Service (SBS)** (☎ 287-2727), with its red-and-white buses, is the leading company, followed by **Trans Island Bus Services (TIBS)** (orange-and-yellow buses) as well as a host of independent operators who use school buses outside the school rush hours. Buses run from 6am–11.30pm.

Fares on SBS and TIBS buses are by zones ("stages"), which you must calculate yourself. Pay as you enter; change is not given. There are inspectors, so keep your ticket. Independent buses are slightly cheaper than the "official" buses. Smoking is prohibited on buses and can incur a hefty fine. *The Bus Guide,* available from bookstores and newsstands, is an indispensable and comprehensive source of information, with routes and a map (70 cents). The STPB publishes a free brochure, *See Singapore By Bus.*

The **"Singapore Explorer"** ticket, issued for one or three days, can be bought at most major hotels and entitles the holder to unlimited travel on any SBS or TIBS bus. The ticket includes a map showing six color-coded sightseeing routes such as "Historic Singapore" and "The Temple Route," and signs posted at bus stops along these Explorer routes indicate nearby attractions.

Trolley buses

Singapore Trolley *(62 Cecil St., #01-00 TPI Bldg., Singapore 0104* ☎ *227-8218* [Fx] *227-0802)* operates distinctively decorated, air-conditioned and motorized trolley buses, which stop at 22 places convenient for the city's hotels and tourist sights *(daily 9am–9pm)*. Discounted admission (usually half-price) to museums and other attractions is offered with the tickets.

TAXIS

Taxis are plentiful (there are more than 13,500), and relatively inexpensive compared with other cities (meters start at about S$2.20). All taxis are metered and are licensed to carry four passengers, with a surcharge for more than two adults.

Surcharges are also levied on the following: trunk (boot) luggage (excluding wheelchairs and baby carriages); radio or telephone reservations (advance reservations cost more); trips from (but not to) Changi Airport; waiting time; trips out of the Central Business District Monday to Friday 4–7pm, Saturday noon–3pm; trips into the CBD Monday to Saturday 7.30–10.15am (waived if a taxi already has a daily license sticker); and on trips from midnight to 6am, when 50 percent is added to the fare.

Most taxi drivers speak fair English (but make sure the driver understands exactly where you want to go before you set off), and are known for their honesty; newspaper stories abound about their returning valuables or large sums of money found in their taxis. Taxi drivers are not supposed to take tips but won't refuse some change — it's up to you. Smoking in taxis is an offense that incurs a fine.

A **24-hour radio taxi service** is available (☎ *452-5555/250-0700).*

London cabs

There are ten of the familiar, spacious "London taxis" in Singapore. They are air conditioned and can seat five passengers. They apply the same metered rates as regular cabs, with a S$1 surcharge. Reserve ahead with **TIBS Radiophone** (☎ *481-1211).*

DRIVING IN SINGAPORE

The roads can be packed, especially at peak hours, but driving in Singapore is more manageable than in other Asian cities. Traffic density is controlled by restricting the growth of the car population with heavy import duties and road taxes. Gasoline prices are moderate. Clearly indicated routes make driving easy.

As **parking laws** are strict, it is advisable to use officially designated parking lots. Rates are double in the Central Business District (CBD). Housing-estate parking areas managed by the Housing Development Board (HDB) and Urban Redevelopment Authority (URA) require coupons, which are sold at shops, gas stations and at booths on the estates.

If you need to drive in the Central Business District at any time from Monday to Saturday between 7.30 and 10.15am (see page 36), you are required to buy a **daily license** from a booth just outside the CBD.

Seat belts are compulsory. The speed limit, which is enforced, is 55kph (34mph) within the city and 80kph (50mph) on the expressways.

If your car breaks down en route, move it to the side of the road, use a warning triangle or leave the hood (bonnet) open, and phone for a breakdown crew immediately. The **Automobile Association (AA)** provides a 24-hour service (☎ 748-9911); if you're not a member you can join when the breakdown crew arrives and transfer the membership to the equivalent organization in your home country. The *Yellow Pages* lists car repair and maintenance workshops under "Garages."

Visitors bringing their own cars do not need an import license. The AA issues a free **International Circulation Permit** lasting 90 days. To receive the permit, a current certificate of insurance with minimum third-party cover, issued by a Singapore company, is required.

RENTING A CAR
The A–Z section of the telephone directory lists **car firms** under "Motor car renting and leasing." Both chauffeur-driven and self-drive cars are available, and it is advisable to shop around. Drivers must have held a valid **driver's license** for at least one year; the minimum age is 23.

Mileage is usually unlimited and cars are supplied with a full tank, which you must refill on return. There is no extra charge for one-way rentals of three or more days between Singapore and major Malaysian cities.

Car rental companies
- **Avis**   Changi Airport ☎542-8855; Boulevard Hotel at Cuscaden Rd. ☎737-1668
- **Hertz**   c/o Sime Darby Services Pte Ltd ☎447-3388 ☏345-7247

For **limousine and chauffeur services**: contact **Elpin Tours and Limousine Services Pte Ltd** (☎ 235-3111) or **Presidential Pacific Limousine Pte Ltd** (☎ 223-3668).

GETTING AROUND ON FOOT
The causeway between Singapore and Malaysia has a footpath, making it possible to walk across both ways. Most pedestrians are residents of the border "town" of Woodlands going over to Johor Bahru. Most visitors to Malaysia enter by bus, train or car. If you walk, don't forget your passport, which will be checked at the Immigration checkpoint.

Jaywalking — crossing a street within 50m (160 feet) of a pedestrian crossing, bridge or underpass — can incur a fine. Cross at traffic lights if no alternative crossing is available. Singapore has a low crime rate and the streets are relatively safe.

FERRIES

Regular ferries and water taxis (bumboats) connect Singapore to the offshore islands.

- **Kusu Island and St John's Island:**   Regular ferries leave at 10am and 1.30pm from the World Trade Centre ferry terminal, leaving St John's at 11.15am and 2.45pm and Kusu at 11.45am and 3.15pm. On Sunday and holidays the ferries run hourly from 9am, the last ferry leaving Kusu at 8pm and St John's at 8.20pm. It takes 15 minutes to St John's and 30 minutes to Kusu.
- **Sentosa Island:**   Ferries leave every 15 minutes from the World Trade Centre ferry terminal, from Monday to Thursday 7.30am–10.15pm. The last boat departs from Sentosa at 11pm. On weekend (Friday to Sunday) and holiday evenings, the last ferry leaves the World Trade Centre at 11pm and Sentosa at midnight. The journey takes six minutes.
- **Other islands:**   Bumboats leave for any of the islands from Jardine Steps and Clifford Pier. There are no scheduled services; just ask the boatman. You can also charter a boat for a round trip; negotiate the price before embarking.

CRUISES

STPB's *Singapore Official Guide* lists three pages of local cruises from more than a dozen vendors. These include a **Singapore river cruise**, for which another free brochure, *Discover the exciting contrasts of the Singapore River,* is available from one of the operators, **Singapore River Cruises and Leisure Pte Ltd** (☎ *227-9678* ﹝Fx﹞ *227-7287).*

You can also cruise round the harbor on a *Tongkang* (Chinese junk), a catamaran, even a "pre-war luxury cruise boat." Another popular option are the chartered cruises for beach parties on surrounding islands or day trips with water sports.

On-the-spot information

TOURIST GUIDES

There are almost 900 mainly English-speaking tourist guides licensed by the STPB, many of whom speak an additional European or Asian language. Inquire at any STPB office (see page 45 for addresses).

LANGUAGE

Singapore has four official languages: English, Mandarin, Tamil and Malay. The national language is Malay, but English is the *lingua franca* and the administrative language. In fact, English is the passport to a good job and future and is widely used, particularly in the tourist trade. For example, most taxi drivers, especially the young ones, and guides speak and understand English.

The standard of Singaporean English is generally high (higher than it is in Hong Kong, for instance), with one peculiarity: the ends of spoken sentences are punctuated with a "lah." This "lah" has no special meaning, but adds a lilt to the English, making it closer to the tonal qualities of Chinese languages.

The government actively encourages the Chinese communities to speak Mandarin instead of their dialects, and bilingualism is encouraged in schools; most students study English and their mother tongue, and some take a third language, such as French, German or Japanese. When older members of the different ethnic groups meet, however, they favor their native language and dialect.

ADDRESSES IN SINGAPORE

Singapore has a proliferation of high-rise developments, which accounts for what, on first acquaintance, appears to be a peculiar numbering system for local addresses.

Two **sample addresses**: the STPB tourist information centers are at #01-19 Raffles City Shopping Centre, 250 North Bridge Rd., Singapore 0617 ☎330-0432 and at #02-02/03 Scotts Shopping Centre, 6 Scotts Rd., Singapore 0922 ☎738-3778-9. The #01 or #02 indicates the floor or story in apartment or commercial blocks. The -19 and -02/03 shows the unit number on that floor.

PUBLIC HOLIDAYS

There are 11 official public holidays when all offices and government departments are closed. However, most department stores, supermarkets, shopping complexes, restaurants and places of entertainment remain open on all holidays except **Christmas** and **Chinese New Year**, when many are closed. On Christmas Eve, New Year's Eve and the eve of Chinese New Year, most establishments close early. Restaurants in hotels stay open on all public holidays and offer special celebration dinners.

SHOPPING HOURS

Most shops, including department stores and boutiques in shopping centers, are open from 10am–9.30pm and closed at Christmas and at Chinese New Year. Smaller shops close at around 6pm.

RUSH HOURS

Peak traveling hours are from 12.30–3pm and 5–6.30pm; the Orchard Rd. area is crowded on weekday evenings between 4.30 and 6pm. Government and most offices still work on Saturday mornings, which means a midday rush.

BANKS AND CURRENCY EXCHANGE

Banks, money changers and most hotels will change foreign currency. Banks are open Monday to Friday from 10am–3pm and on Saturday from 9.30–11.30am. The **DBS** (Development Bank of Singapore) is open Saturday until 3pm at its Orchard, Katong, Toa Payoh, Thomson and Bukit Timah branches. There are no currency exchange dealings in most banks on Saturday.

Passports must be shown when cashing travelers checks; some banks charge a commission for cashing travelers checks in the currency of the checks, so inquire first. Visa cardholders can draw cash from automatic teller machines. American Express Cardholders can cash personal checks at **American Express Travel Service** offices (see USEFUL ADDRESSES on page 45).

American Express also has a **MoneyGram®** money transfer service that makes it possible to wire money worldwide in just minutes, from any American Express Travel Service Office. This service is available to all customers and is not limited to American Express Card members.

Hotels often charge a service fee for changing foreign currency. Money changers in shopping centers sometimes give higher rates and may be prepared to bargain. They usually operate Monday to Saturday 10am–5pm; some are open on Sunday. Travelers checks often command higher rates than cash.

All post offices supply money orders (primarily for neighboring countries) and postal orders in Singapore dollars and pounds sterling. Banks issue bank drafts to most countries for a small commission, but only accept cash for the transaction. Cable and telex transfers can also be made, at a higher fee than bank drafts.

DISABLED TRAVELERS

Facilities such as ramps are provided in ever more public places and hotels. Changi Airport and most hotels have lavatories (bathrooms) for disabled people. Taxi drivers are generally helpful.

The **Singapore Council of Social Services** (*11 Penang Lane, Singapore City, map 4 C4*) publishes a guide to easily accessible attractions, *Access Singapore,* which charts facilities for the disabled at public places and buildings.

MAIL SERVICES

Mail services are available at most hotel desks and there are post offices all over the island, open Monday to Friday 8.30am–5pm, on Wednesday until 8pm and on Saturday 8.30am–1pm. The post office in **Tang's Department Store** in Orchard Rd. is open Monday to Saturday noon–8pm; the **Orchard Point Post Office**, also in Orchard Rd., is open 8am–8pm; the **General Post Office** and the post offices at **Changi Airport** and **Comcentre** are open 24 hours (see USEFUL ADDRESSES on page 46).

TELEPHONE SERVICES

Singapore is the telecommunications hub of Southeast Asia, with 24-hour telephone, telex and telegram services worldwide. It costs 10 cents for a three-minute call from a public pay telephone; extra coins buy an extra six minutes. There are pay phones in sidewalk booths, in shopping complexes and in coffee shops on public housing estates. Visitors can call most major cities direct from their hotel rooms.

The **Telecom offices** (*General Post Office; Comcentre; and Telecommunication Building*) provide a useful 24-hour international call service;

Telephone House is open 8am–9pm (see USEFUL ADDRESSES.) Telexes and telegrams can be sent from the above offices and from most hotels.

- To **call the US from Singapore**, dial 001 1, then the area code and the number. To **call the UK**, dial 001 44, then the number, omitting the initial 0 of the area code.

PUBLIC LAVATORIES/BATHROOMS

Most shopping centers have public lavatories, with a 10-cent charge. Department stores, restaurants and hotels have them too. Failing to flush a public toilet is a finable offense.

ELECTRIC CURRENT

The current is 220–240V 50-cycles AC, and most hotels have 110–120V 60-cycles transformers.

LAWS AND REGULATIONS

Singapore is clean: any form of littering can incur a S$1,000 fine. Other offenses include jaywalking; smoking in public areas such as cinemas, theaters, elevators, public buses, taxis and government offices; topless swimming and nudity; and gambling, with the exception of official lotteries, charities, horse racing and social mahjong games.

Drug abuse carries heavy penalties: sentences range from ten years and/or a S$20,000 fine for possession or consumption, to the death sentence for trafficking in morphine (1 ounce) or heroin ($\frac{1}{2}$ ounce). See also NARCOTIC DRUGS on page 33.

Singapore has so many ordinances that attempt to control public behavior — including fines for failing to flush a public toilet and a law against chewing gum — that local wags have produced a tee-shirt (sold in Tanjong Pagar tourist shops) that reads "Singapore is a very fine city" on the front and lists all the local infractions and amount of fines on the back. The government has not yet found a way to outlaw the Singaporean sense of humor.

CUSTOMS AND ETIQUETTE

Singapore's government believes in the use of law to modify social behavior. There is now a fully adult generation that has grown up under ordinances that in other countries are seldom enforced, if indeed they exist.

Legalism here is akin to religious conviction. In the 1960s Singapore gained notoriety for "Operation Snip-Snip," as arriving male visitors whose hair was considered too long were forced to have a haircut or leave. Policemen will piously serve summonses on jaywalkers or spitters. Street life is strictly controlled. There was a major police crackdown on the wave of teenage "break dancing" that swept through the streets of Singapore, along with those of the rest of the world, a few years back.

Foreign publications are carefully monitored for pornography, and for "inappropriate" slurs on Singapore (which in one case was defined as suggesting Singapore was dirty because a photo was used depicting an Indian hawker food chef in an undershirt, cooking *murtabak* over an open flame). The ruling People's Action Party has long used libel suits to intimidate opposition candidates — of which, after more than 30 years, there are only two in Parliament.

Singapore has even experimented with ways to encourage its educated women to have more babies, in an effort to counter what the government believes is a threat to the community's gene pool: the fact that poor, uneducated women outproduce affluent, educated ones.

At its worst, this pervasive government influence on virtually every aspect of social life has produced a tendency toward contentious, narrow thinking by lower-level government servants. At its best, it has made Singapore a city whose streets are safe and pleasant to roam — comparable, perhaps, to a reasonably affluent middle-class suburb of an American city.

The family unit itself was the one area the government had virtually avoided until the gene pool controversy. Arguably, the common denominator among Singapore's ethnic groups has less to do with government policies *per se* than with the fact that all the major ethnic and religious groups of the population have traditions of strong, extended families. The Chinese with their polyglot religion, Malay Muslims, Eurasian Catholics and Indian Hindus and Muslims are all family people, and beneath the tourist tinsel, Singapore is a family-man's town.

To an outsider it can seem a society of forms without much social content, but this is not so: officially, Singaporeans have shed their ethnic ties, but unofficially they remain close to the systems of kinship inherited from their forebears.

The main ingredients in the blend that is "Singaporean" are materialism, ambition, education and the family unit; the government has supplied the means of fulfilling the first three, and, usually, the deference required for the autonomy of family and religion. Singaporeans have in turn accepted what is often privately viewed as the government's obsession with social engineering; the rule by law, rather than of it.

The official government publicity defines Singapore as a nation of shared Confucian values. These are: nation before community and society above self; respect and community support for the individual; conflict resolution by consensus rather than conflict; racial and religious harmony.

This coda reflects Lee Kuan Yew's championship of the concept of benign dictatorship of a ruling party, over pursuit of Western democratic ideals and liberties, as the right road to economic prosperity for "Confucian" societies. "Confucian" is a code word meant to encompass China, Hong Kong, Taiwan, Macau and, of course, Singapore.

Singaporeans, at first seemingly aloof, will almost always ask new acquaintances if they have eaten. Eating out is a national pastime and an easy way to move beyond the shy civilities of initial encounters. As with most Asians, the meal is a social event for families and friends; visitors should accept *every* invitation if they hope to meet Singaporeans at their ease. Friends and family bring out the best in the Singaporeans: to enjoy this small country to the full it is essential to get to know as many of them as possible.

Short-term travelers need know only two things: Singaporeans follow the rules, and they expect the same of you. Most of them are proud of themselves and their country and like to compare it favorably with virtually anywhere else. This kind of provincialism is perhaps the more noticeable because their first language is usually English, and because it's surprising in what is otherwise so cosmopolitan a community. But it pays to remember that Singapore has good reason for self-satisfaction.

Ask permission before entering **temples and mosques**. Dress respectably: shorts are inappropriate, and women must have covered arms; leave your shoes at the entrance. Visitors are not allowed on Friday, when the prayer hall is packed. Islamic law forbids menstruating women from entering mosques.

Tipping is not customary. It is forbidden at the airport and is discouraged in hotels and restaurants, which levy a 10-percent service charge.

MAPS AND LOCAL PUBLICATIONS

The Singapore Visitor, This Week Singapore and *Lion City* are published weekly and distributed free at all hotels, with visitors' guides to shopping, restaurants, entertainment and sightseeing, and a "What's on" list. *The Map of Singapore* is published monthly and also freely distributed. The English-language daily newspaper *The Straits Times* also publishes a "What's on" list.

The American Express/STPB *Map of Singapore* is free, and available at airport arrival halls and in most hotels. *The Singapore Visitor Map* is also free, but leaves more to be desired as a source of direction. The *Nelles Singapore Map* is expensive but thorough. Less expensive is the *Singapore Street Directory,* available at bookstores.

Business in Singapore

No more than 150 years ago, Singapore was a fishing village on an island of mangrove swamps. Today, thanks to its location at the crossroads of Asia, and to the dynamism of its people, Singapore is one of the world's big financial and business centers, with an enviable international airport and a highly developed infrastructure.

Every facility for the traveling executive, from the business and secretarial centers in the major hotels, through a state-of-the-art range of conference venues, to superb restaurants and golf courses, is on tap in Singapore. A great deal of effort is being put into the promotion of the island as a top destination for incentive travel, using the lure of luxury playgrounds such as Sentosa Island, the country's flagship attraction.

CONFERENCE FACILITIES

Following the leads of Hong Kong and Bangkok, both of which have recently opened massive convention and exhibition centers, Singapore is moving beyond its existing facility at **Raffles City**, which anchors the two Westin hotels and associated office buildings, to create **Suntec**

City, a massive development that will contain the **Singapore International Convention and Exhibition Centre**.

Due for a grand opening in 1994, the 98,582sq.m. (1,061,116 square-foot) Convention Centre is a giant business complex that will sit astride the existing Marina Centre. Its main convention hall will have seating for 13,000 delegates. An associated complex, of four 45-story office towers and an 18-story office building with retail podium, will follow in 1996.

The 11.69ha (29-acre) site is one of the largest privately-owned commercial projects in Singapore, capable of supporting a workforce of 22,000 people. There will be 200 shops, a 4-story department store and a supermarket in the retail podium.

To complement the launch of the new facility, the Singapore Convention Bureau will host its first mega-convention: **Meet in Singapore (MIS) '95**, to promote the country's entry into world-rank conventioneering and celebrate 30 years of independence.

For further information, contact the **Suntec City Development Pte Ltd** *(100 Beach Rd., #21-06 Shaw Towers, Singapore 0718* ☎ *295-2888* ℡*RS 20131* ℻*294-0880)*.

BUSINESS CONTACTS
- **American Chamber of Commerce**   1 Scotts Rd., #16–07 Shaw Centre ☎235-0077.
- **British Business Association**   450/452 Alexandra Rd. ☎475-4192.
- **Indonesian Business Association**   #07–03, 158 Cecil St. ☎221-5063.
- **Singapore International Chamber of Commerce**   Denmark House #05-00, 6 Raffles Quay ☎224-1255.
- **Singapore Manufacturers' Association**   20 Orchard Rd. Map 4C5 ☎338-8787.

Useful addresses

TOURIST INFORMATION
Singapore Tourist Promotion Board
- #01-19 Raffles City Tower, Stamford Rd., Singapore 0617, map 4C5 ☎330-0431, open Monday to Friday 8.30am–6pm; Saturday 8.30am–1pm.
- #02 Scotts Shopping Centre, map 3B2 ☎738-3778, open Monday to Friday 9.30am–9.30pm.

American Express Travel Service
The American Express Travel Service is a valuable source of information for any traveler in need of help, advice or emergency services. Offices in Singapore are at the following addresses:
- #13-01/08 UOL Building, 96 Somerset Rd. ☎299-8133.
- #01-06 Lucky Plaza, Orchard Rd., map 3B2 ☎235-5789; 24-hour emergency service ☎235-5288.

Others
- **Changi International Airport Flight Information** ☎542-5680.
- **Singapore Immigration Office** Empress Pl. Map **4D4** ☎337-4031.

TOUR OPERATORS
There are almost 550 registered travel agencies, but four inbound operators handle the bulk of tours in Singapore:
- **RMG Tours** 5001 Beach Rd., #08–12 Golden Mile Complex. Off map **4B6** ☎298-3944.
- **Siakson Coach Tours** 3 Miller St. Map **4C5** ☎336-0288.
- **Singapore Sightseeing** 401 Havelock Rd., #02–16 Hotel Miramar. Map **3D3** ☎737-8778.
- **Tour East** 114 Anson Rd., #14-00 Tunas Building. Map **4E4** ☎220-2200.

MAIL AND TELECOMMUNICATIONS SERVICES
- **General Post Office** Fullerton Building. Map **4D5** ☎533-0234; after hours ☎449-3377.
- **Comcentre** 31 Exeter Rd. Map **3C3** ☎734-3344.
- **Telecommunication** 35 Robinson Rd. Map **4E4** ☎534-3111.
- **Telephone House** 15 Hill St. Map **4C4** ☎734-9466.

AUTOMOBILE CLUB
- **Automobile Association of Singapore (AA)** ☎737-2444.
- **AA breakdown service** ☎748-9911 (24 hours).

PLACES OF WORSHIP (ENGLISH-LANGUAGE)
Anglican
- **Chapel of Christ the Redeemer** 2 Tampines Ave. 3. Map **2C6** ☎72-6653. Services 10.15am.
- **Christ Church** 1 Dorset Rd., just N of Farrer Park ☎2502544. Services 8am.
- **Church of Our Saviour** 130 Margaret Dr., off Tanglin Rd. ☎474-7222. Services 8am, 10.30am, 5pm.
- **St Andrew's Cathedral** Coleman St. Map **4C4** ☎337-6104. Services 7am, 8am, 11am.

Jewish
- **Synagogue Maghain Aboth** 24 Waterloo St. Map **4C4** ☎336-0692 or 337-2189. Services weekdays 7.30am, 6.45pm; Saturday 9am; Sunday 8am.

Roman Catholic
- **Church of the Risen Christ**, 91 Toa Payoh Central. Map **2D4** ☎253-2166. Services Saturday 6pm, Sunday 9am, 11am, 6pm.
- **Christ The King Church**, 2221 Ang Mo Kio Ave. 8. Map **2C4** ☎459-9957. Services Sunday 9.30am, 11am, 6pm.

AIRLINES

- **Air Canada**   100 Orchard Rd., #02-43/46 Meridien Shopping Centre. Map **3**B3 ☎732-8555.
- **British Airways**   101 Thomson Rd., #09-03 Goldhill Sq. Map **2**D4 ☎253-8344.
- **Cathay Pacific**   10 Collyer Quay, Ocean Building, 16th story. Map **4**D4 ☎533-1333.
- **Garuda Indonesia** 101 Thomson Rd., #01-68 United Sq. Map **2**D4 ☎250-2888.
- **Japan Air Lines (JAL)** 16 Raffles Quay, #01–01 Hong Leong Building. Map **4**E4 ☎221-0522.
- **Malaysian Airline System (MAS)** 190 Clemenceau Ave., #02–09 Singapore Shopping Centre. Map **4**C4 ☎336-6777.
- **Northwest Airlines** 435 Orchard Rd., #20–01 Wisma Atria. Map **3**B2 ☎235-7166.
- **Qantas** 300 Orchard Rd., #04–02 The Promenade. Map **3**B2 ☎737-3744.
- **Singapore Airlines**   77 Robinson Rd., SIA Building, map **4**E4 ☎223-8888; Mandarin Singapore Hotel, 333 Orchard Rd., map **3**E3 ☎229-7293/4; Raffles City Shopping Centre, North Bridge Rd., map **4**C5.
- **Thai Airways International**   133 Cecil St., #08-01 Keck Seng Towers. Map **4**E4 ☎224-9977.
- **United Airlines**   16 Raffles Quay, #01–03 Hong Leong Building. Map **4**E4 ☎220-0711.

EMBASSIES

- **Australia**   25 Napier Rd. Off map **3**B2 ☎737-9311.
- **Canada**   80 Anson Rd., #14-00 IBM Towers. Map **4**F4 ☎225-6363.
- **Indonesia**   7 Chatsworth Rd. Off map **3**C1 ☎737-7422.
- **Ireland**   541 Orchard Rd., #08-02 Liat Towers. Map **3**B2 ☎732-3430.
- **Japan**   16 Nassim Rd. Map **3**B1 ☎235-8855.
- **Malaysia**   301 Jervois Rd. Map **3**C1 ☎235-0111.
- **New Zealand**   13 Nassim Rd. Map **3**B1 ☎235-9966.
- **Thailand**   370 Orchard Rd. Map **3**B2 ☎737-2644.
- **United Kingdom**   Tanglin Rd. Off map **3**B1 ☎473-9333.
- **United States**   30 Hill St. Map **4**C4 ☎338-0251.

Emergency information

EMERGENCY SERVICES
Police ☎999
Fire/Ambulance ☎995

MEDICAL SERVICES
In an emergency ☎995 or call the hotel doctor. Most doctors and dentists have emergency 24-hour telephone services.

HOSPITALS WITH EMERGENCY ROOMS
Government hospitals:
- **Alexandra Hospital** Alexandra Rd., Singapore 0511 ☎473-5222
- **National University Hospital** 5 Lower Kent Ridge, Singapore 0511, map 1E3 ☎779-5555
- **Singapore General** Outram Rd., Singapore 1316, map **3E3** ☎222-3322
- **Tan Tock Seng Hospital** Moulmein Rd., Singapore 1130, map 2D4 ☎256-6011

Some private hospitals:
- **East Shore Hospital** 321 Joo Chiat Place, Singapore 1542, map 2D6 ☎344-7588; emergencies ☎345-1516
- **Gleneagles Hospital** 5–6 Napier Rd., Singapore 1025, off map 3B1 ☎473-722
- **Mount Elizabeth Hospital** 3 Mount Elizabeth, Singapore 0922, map 3B3 ☎737-2666

PHARMACIES
The following branches of **Guardian Chemist** are open from 10am to 9.30pm:
- **Jelita Cold Storage Supermarket** 293 Holland Rd., map **2D4** ☎469-0700; open until 9pm
- **Centrepoint** Orchard Rd., map **3B3** ☎737-4835
- **Changi Airport**

LOST PASSPORT
Contact the local police (☎999) and your embassy immediately.

LOST TRAVELERS CHECKS
Notify the local police immediately. Follow the instructions provided with your travelers checks or contact the issuing company. **American Express** provides a 24-hour emergency service (☎ *737-8188*).

Planning
your visit

When to go

The climate in Singapore is generally constant, with high humidity averaging 85 percent and temperatures hovering pleasantly around 28–30°C (80–85°F). Because of prevailing monsoons, March, November and December are wetter than other months; rain pelts down in heavy torrents, then stops as suddenly as it began. February has the most sunshine and December the least.

Events in Singapore's calendar

To confirm venues and celebration dates for feasts that follow the Buddhist or Muslim calendars, contact the **Singapore Tourist Promotion Board (STPB) Information Centre** (☎ 330-0431 or 738-3778). The Centre can provide brochures describing each festival. Days and months of such festivals may change slightly from year to year.

JANUARY
Mid-January, **Ponggal**. Celebrations for the four-day Tamil Harvest Festival are best experienced at the Srinivasa Perumal Temple on Serangoon Rd. Mid-January, the **Singapore River Raft Race** is the only occasion in the year when boats return to the once-busy river waters, but this time it is just for fun. Bands, cheerleaders, arts and crafts stalls and elaborate raft designs to amuse the crowds are hallmarks of the event.

Late January to early February, **Thaipusam**. This extraordinary two-day Hindu festival begins with a procession following the image of Lord Subramaniam through the streets. On the second day of the festival the devout, in self-induced trances, turn themselves into human pincushions by piercing their bodies, foreheads, cheeks and tongues with hooks and steel skewers.

Then, donning a metal arch bedecked with feathers and fitted with steel spikes that jab into their torsos, they proceed along the 3 kilometers ($1\frac{1}{2}$ miles) from the Srinivasa Perumal Temple in Serangoon Rd. to the Thandayuthapani (Chettiyar) Temple in Tank Rd., accompanied by large crowds of chanting well-wishers. Eerily, although the wounds are genuine, they do not bleed.

Late January to early February: **Chinese New Year**. Preceding the main event of the Chinese calendar, and weeks before the date, Chinatown becomes vivid with bright red and gold bunting and lanterns. A time for family visits, gifts of fruit and flowers and "lucky money" *(laisee)* in red packets for children.

The festival lasts for two weeks, with what is called locally a "light up" in Chinatown, wherein festive lights are strung about the building exteriors and arched over roads.

FEBRUARY

The week following Chinese New Year: **Chingay Parade**, a Singapore celebration of its multi-ethnic heritage. Lion and dragon dances, stilt-walkers, acrobats, pugilists, traditional Malay tableaux, Indian dancers and floats. The length of Orchard Rd., from Scotts Rd. to Doby Ghaut, is closed off for the day of the spectacle.

Epson Singapore Golf Open is held during Chinese New Year holidays at Tanah Merah Country Club. International-rank golfers.

February to March: **Rawan, South East Asian Rally Raid**, the first major international car rally event in Southeast Asia, was launched in 1991. The race begins in Singapore, traverses Malaysia and southern Thailand and ends about two weeks later in Bangkok. The event is modeled on the Paris–Dakar Rally.

MARCH

Birthday of the Monkey God, celebrated twice a year at the Monkey God Temple in Seng Poh Rd., opposite Tiong Bahru Market. This features shamanist devotees trance-dancing with skewers through their cheeks and performing other feats of apparent indifference to pain.

The Monkey God is a celebrated character in Chinese mythology, made famous in a book entitled *Journey to the West*. This tells the tale of a Buddhist pilgrim monk sent to India to collect sacred *sutras* by his emperor during the Tang dynasty (9th–11thC). He is accompanied and protected by the mischievous Monkey God, who gained immortality by stealing sacred peaches from the garden of one of the Taoist Eight Immortals.

March or April: **Easter** services are held in Christian churches; on Good Friday in the grounds of St Joseph's Cathedral, a candlelit procession follows a figure of Christ.

Ramadan, the ninth month of the Islamic calendar (a moveable feast therefore). The strict daytime fasting makes for special ways to offset hunger at night, and food stalls for the faithful are set up along Bussorah St., in front of Sultan Mosque. Ironically, fasting makes this a good time to sample Malay foods — but only after sundown.

March or April: **Singapore International Film Festival**. Includes visits by well-known actors and movie directors.

APRIL

Early April: **Ching Ming**. During this festival, which is roughly equivalent to the Christian All Soul's Day, Chinese families visit cemeteries to honor their ancestors: graves are tidied and decorated with flowers, and incense-burning and prayers are followed by a cheery family picnic at the graveside.

Epson Singapore Super Tennis features top-rank players on the Association of Tennis Professionals World Tour men's circuit. 32 players compete for a US$250,000 purse at the Kallang Tennis Centre.

Hari Raya Pusa indicates the end of the Ramadan fast, and the Malay district in Geylang is transformed into a fairyland of lights and decorations on the streets and in Malay homes. The bazaar along Jalan Pasar Baru bustles with people dressed in traditional finery, en route to visit family and friends. Outsiders are welcome.

Mid-April: **Songkran**. Thai Buddhist water festival to celebrate the traditional New Year: an entertaining affair with ceremonies, folk dancing and uninhibited flinging of water — especially at monks and elders. Most lively at the Sapthapuchaniyaram and Ananada Metyrama Thai temples.

MAY

Birthday of the Third Prince, a child god bearing a magic bracelet and spear, who rides wheels of wind and fire. Arcane rites are conducted, and Chinese trance-dancers go into action, cutting their tongues with swords or spikes and then licking inscriptions on yellow paper charms, which are sought by devotees. Rituals are held at various Chinese temples. At outdoor processions such as that held on Queen St., street operas *(wayang)* are performed.

Late May: **Vesak Day**. This sacred day in the Buddhist calendar commemorates the birth, enlightenment and death of Buddha. Celebrations start at dawn with monks chanting *sutras*. Free meals are given to the poor, and worshipers accrue merit by releasing caged birds. In the evening, temples hold candlelit processions; the best ones are at the Temple of a Thousand Lights and the Meng San Phor Kark See Temple.

JUNE

All month: **Singapore Festival of Arts** (every two years, next scheduled for 1994). This extravaganza includes performing artists from all over the world and is the biggest single performing and visual arts event held in Singapore.

The festival has brought to Singapore international names such as the Ellis Marsalis Jazz Quartet from New Orleans, the Swingle Singers from Britain, the Zimbabwe Theatre, the National Ballet du Senegal and the Houston Ballet. Painting and sculpture exhibitions are also held. A fringe festival is a recent addition. Be warned that tickets purchased by mail (with remainders sold through the central box office at Victoria Hall) can be sold out weeks in advance.

Mid-June: **Dragon Boat Festival**. Teams from many countries compete in this exciting race, which originated as a fishermen's homage to a legendary Chinese hero. It is a thrilling spectacle to watch the 12m (38-foot) dragon-prowed boats slice through the water, the paddlers straining to keep up with the pace set by the captain, who pounds a large drum in the bow.

AUGUST

Early August to early September: **Festival of the Hungry Ghosts**. In the seventh lunar month, spirits are freed from the underworld to roam the earth. To appease them, the Chinese offer prayers and paper money ("Hell banknotes") and lay food at the roadside; market stalls and tents offering tables of food burn huge, ornate incense sticks. This is the best time of the year to see Chinese opera, when it takes to the streets to entertain the spirits (or perhaps frighten them away).

August 9: **National Day**. Displays by the armed forces, school bands, trade unions and so on.

SEPTEMBER

Mid-September: **Mooncake Festival**. Also known as the Mid-Autumn Festival, this traditional Chinese celebration commemorates the overthrow of the Mongols (Yuan dynasty, 1280–1368AD), which was expedited by Chinese rebels who passed hidden messages in cakes and signaled to each other by lantern. Today the Chinese light colorful lanterns, sweet mooncakes are eaten (with a salted egg yolk in the middle), and children form lantern processions in the street.

September to October: **Navarathri Festival**. During this 9-day Hindu festival, held in honor of three goddesses, lavish offerings are made in temples. Nine evenings of classical Indian music, dance and singing are held from 7–10pm at the Chettiyar Temple. On the tenth evening a grand procession sets out from this temple.

OCTOBER

Early October: **Volkswagen Super Challenge** draws top international tennis players to the Singapore Indoor Stadium with an exhibition match between two top seeds. These have in the past included players such as André Agassi, Stefan Edberg and John McEnroe.

October to November: **Kusu Island pilgrimage**. Boatloads of Chinese Taoists flock to the Da Bo Gong Temple at the sacred island of Kusu to pray for prosperity, fertility and good luck, offering fruit, flowers and food. The crowds are daunting — and, in many cases, they have assembled merely for the amazing purpose of hanging stones in little plastic bags from the island's trees. This, and an offering at the temple, is meant to express gratitude for the granting of favors asked the year before.

Mid-October: **Double Ninth**. On the ninth day of the ninth lunar month Chinese families bring offerings to ancestors' graves and then picnic beside them. Kiu Ong Yiah and other temples celebrate the spectacular Festival of the Nine Emperor Gods. Priests write charms with the blood of entranced mediums who flagellate themselves, and the images of nine particular Chinese gods, set in sedan chairs, are taken out on parade. The gods' spirits are said to possess their images, causing the sedan chairs to career wildly.

Late October to early November: **Thimithi**. The Hindu goddess Duropadai is honored in this spectacular firewalking ceremony, which is not for the faint-hearted. After being whipped by a priest, supplicants walk barefoot and uninjured over a 4m (13-foot) pit of burning coals at the Sri Mariamman Temple in South Bridge Rd. The spectacle begins at 3pm. Arrive early.

NOVEMBER

Early November: **Deepavali**. During this Festival of Lights, Hindus honor the spirits of ancestors who return to earth. Families make offerings, burn rows of oil lamps and decorate their homes with colored lights and candles; temples are lit, shrines are draped with lights and garlands, and images of deities are taken out on procession. Festivities are best viewed at the Perumal Temple. Serangoon Rd. and the rest of Little India are alight with decorations.

Early to mid-November: **Singapore Formula One Powerboat Grand Prix** is a world championship event held in Marina Bay, completing Grand Prix rounds held in Europe.

DECEMBER

December 25: **Christmas on the Equator**. All the traditional trimmings, Singapore-style: Giant Christmas sales, spectacular light-displays on Orchard Rd., carol-singing and artificial snow.

Where to go

Singapore is a small island that lies 135 kilometers (85 miles) north of the Equator at the heart of Southeast Asia and on the main channel (the Straits of Malacca) between the Indian and Pacific Oceans. To the north lies Peninsular Malaysia, whose Johore State is linked to the island nation by a one-kilometer ($\frac{1}{2}$-mile) rail-and-road causeway. To the south lies the Indonesian archipelago.

The city's British founders recognized its strategic location and superb natural harbor and thus its potential as a trading center linking Asia, Africa and Europe. Today, Singapore ranks as the world's busiest port.

The island's terrain consists of predominantly swampy lowlands; its highest points are **Bukit Timah** (Tin Hill) at 177 meters (581 feet) and **Mt. Faber**, which at only 105 meters (345 feet) hardly deserves the appellation. The land area, even including coastal reclamation, is only 640 square kilometers (247 square miles).

The island state governs 57 smaller islands within its territorial waters, some of which have been developed as resorts and others as oil-refining centers. Some islands, still dotted with traditional fishing villages, are idyllic tropical paradises, and Singapore's northern coastline at **Sembawang**, sufficiently removed from the bustling city, has retained a similar timeless quality.

Singapore's neighborhoods

Singapore is a small island and is easy to explore, with most places of interest concentrated within a few areas:

JURONG DISTRICT *(map 1 D1-2)*. Sightseeing here is best done with a rented car or on a bus tour, especially if you have children. The CHINESE GARDEN, modeled on the one at Beijing's Summer Palace, the JAPANESE GARDEN, with Zen Buddhist-inspired stone gardens, and the CN West Leisure Park are next to each other.

Nearby is the fascinating SINGAPORE SCIENCE CENTRE, with around 500 exhibits and a "Crazy Room" where children are able to learn the effects of scientific principles through the medium of play. A short distance away, TANG DYNASTY CITY is a gigantic theme park devoted to one of China's greatest historical epochs. It is surrounded by a massive city wall that is typical of the period.

A short drive away are the brilliantly designed JURONG BIRD PARK and Jurong Crocodile Paradise (see CROCODILES), across the road.

LITTLE INDIA *(map 4 B4-A5)*. Concentrated around SERANGOON ROAD, the exotic and colorful ethnic Indian neighborhood is rich with temples, spice shops, garland makers and *sari* sellers.

CHINATOWN *(map 4 E4)*. The lively Chinese ethnic quarter, its old two-story shophouses festooned with bamboo poles of drying laundry, is laced with narrow alleys crowded with shops selling preserved fruits, Chinese crockery, pots and pans. See also pages 63–65.

NORTH BRIDGE ROAD *(map 4 B5)*. This is an area full of mosques, synagogues and churches. ARAB STREET is the main artery of the Muslim quarter, and batik, spice and traditional crafts stalls, as well as sidewalk fortune tellers, are found along Waterloo and Rochore Rds.

ORCHARD ROAD/SCOTTS ROAD *(map 3 B2-3)*. Most of the deluxe hotels and upmarket shops are concentrated in this very chic tourist, shopping and entertainment belt.

HISTORIC SINGAPORE *(map 4 C4-D5)*. Along the waterfront, the Esplanade, MERLION PARK, the Padang with its old colonial buildings, the Boat Quay and Raffles' Landing Site are all thriving reminders of the island's colonial past.

SENTOSA ISLAND *(map 2 F4)*. With parks, specialty museums, arts, sports, an old fort, a new aquarium where you can walk under the water, a theme park that takes you around Asia in an afternoon . . . this is quite literally Singapore's national playground. Unless you thrive on crowds and want to see half of Singapore at play, allow a full weekday if possible. On weekends the island is full and there are no tours from the hotels. (See pages 74–77.)

THE EAST COAST PARKWAY *(map 2 E4-5)*. Many of Singapore's best sports and recreation facilities are located on this strip of reclaimed land, including the Big Splash swimming park, golf, tennis, sailing and seafood centers.

Organizing your time

On a short visit to Singapore, the way to avoid frustration is to be selective. You may already have decided what you want to see, but if not, here is a suggested program for a four-day visit.
Day 1
- In the morning explore CHINATOWN, visit the SRI MARIAMMAN TEMPLE (Hindu) and the THIAN HOCK KENG TEMPLE (Chinese), then lunch at either the People's Park Complex food center or any of the Chinese restaurants on Mosque St. Visit Change Alley, then board a Chinese junk at Clifford Pier for a dinner cruise.
Day 2
- Explore Little India and the TEMPLE OF A THOUSAND LIGHTS, then lunch on a curry served on a banana leaf at the Banana Leaf Apolo (see RESTAURANTS, page 105).
- In the afternoon, visit the SULTAN MOSQUE and wander along ARAB STREET. Then explore the colonial area: visit Queen Elizabeth Walk, ST ANDREW'S CATHEDRAL, City Hall, the Supreme Court, the Padang (a grassy field around which the colonial center of Singapore was situated), Singapore Cricket Club, Parliament House, Victoria Theatre and Concert Hall, finishing at Raffles' Landing Site and Boat Quay. Return to Queen Elizabeth Walk in the evening and take a night tour of the city, or go on a "pub crawl" through Tanjong Pagar's many distinctive bars.

Day 3

- Breakfast with an orangutan at the SINGAPORE ZOOLOGICAL GARDENS, take a side trip to the Mandai Orchid Gardens and lunch at the Zoo's Swan Lake cafeteria. Alternatively, spend the morning chatting up parrots over breakfast at JURONG BIRD PARK, then move on to the CHINESE and JAPANESE GARDENS, where you can have a panoramic *teppanyaki* lunch at the Japanese restaurant on Jurong Hilltop.
- A visit to the Nonya showpiece, PERANAKAN PLACE, could be followed by shopping in Orchard Rd. and capped with drinks at one of the many bars with live jazz or rock music (see NIGHTLIFE, pages 115–117).
- Dine at one of the city's grand hotels, such as the Mandarin, Shangri-La, Hyatt Regency or Raffles — or catch an "Instant Asia" show at the Pasir Panjang restaurant. (See NIGHTLIFE, page 118.)

Day 4

- Spend the day on SENTOSA ISLAND. Visit the museums and other sights in the morning; in the afternoon, swim and bask at one of its three beautiful beaches, or take in some golf at one of its two 18-hole courses. For dinner and a fine night-view of the city, take the cable car to Mt. Faber.
- Alternatively, spend the day at the East Coast Parkway, which is a popular place to swim, windsurf, sail or play squash and tennis; after lunch at the Lagoon Food Centre near the Sailing Centre, visit the nearby Crocodile Farms, and end the day with a seafood dinner at any one of the East Coast restaurants.

Sights and places of interest

Introduction

In this "garden city–state," it is hardly surprising that parks, preserves and playgrounds on a theme dominate any sightseeing program. This A to Z listing of the major sights of Singapore is no exception, but also introduces Singapore's most intriguing neighborhoods, the finest buildings from each of its many cultures, and the best museum collections.

PARKS AND PLAYGROUNDS
The ten entries in this category span the gulf between the dignified serenity of the Botanic, Chinese and Japanese gardens, through the crocodile wrestlers and oriental white-knuckle rides of Haw Par Villa, to instant immersion in Chinese culture at Tang Dynasty City. There is also a compact guide to the many attractions of Sentosa Island, Singapore's playground and a major resort in itself.

NEIGHBORHOODS
The four neighborhoods described recall the "like to like" planning principle of the city's 19thC founder, Sir Stamford Raffles: the Arab Street district of Middle Eastern traders; Chinatown; the Serangoon Road district of ethnic Indians; and the Colonial Area, in Raffles' time mostly for Europeans. All are in the immediate environs of the mouth of the Singapore River, where Raffles first landed.

MOSQUES, SHRINES, TEMPLES AND CHURCHES
Singapore's ethnic areas surround the river like a mixed bag of sweets, each wrapped in its own language, customs, clothing and cuisine, and guided by its own religious leaders. The result is that there is probably nowhere on earth with such a variety of religious establishments within so small an area. Our sampler includes 12 of the most interesting: three Hindu shrines, three mosques, five Chinese Buddhist or Buddhist/Taoist temples, and the Neo-Gothic St Andrew's cathedral.

ARCHITECTURE AND AMBIENCE
Five locations are included for their unique exterior and/or interior architecture and ambience: Alkaff Mansion, Raffles Hotel, Peranakan Place, the Chinese Scholar's Gallery and the unique House of Tan Yeok Nee. A pleasant aspect of this group is that, save for the last, they all serve refreshments.

HOW TO USE THIS A TO Z SECTION

- **Bold type** generally indicates major points of interest.
- **Cross-references** to other entries or to other sections of the book are printed in SMALL CAPITALS.
- Some lesser sights do not have their own entries but are included within other entries: look these up in the INDEX.
- The ★ symbol identifies the most important sights.
- The 𝔪 symbol indicates buildings of considerable architectural interest.
- The ◁€ symbol is used to indicate places from which the view is especially panoramic or picturesque.
- Places that are likely to be of special interest to children (❀) are also indicated.
- For guided tours, look for the ✗ symbol: details follow this symbol where appropriate.
- **For a full explanation of all the symbols used in this book, see page 7.**

Singapore's sights A to Z

ALKAFF MANSION 𝔪
10 Telok Blangah Green. Map 2E4 ☎ *278-6979 (restaurant)* ▣ *(to grounds)* ⇐ *MRT: Tiong Bahru.*

The Alkaff Mansion is a grand villa that was once owned by the illustrious Alkaff family of Arab traders, whose considerable fortune was made in the lucrative trade in spices, coffee and sugar from Indonesia. They arrived in Singapore in 1852, when Shaik bin Abdul Rahman Alkaff sailed his ship into port.

The family owned four such sumptuous mansions; this one was built in 1888 and was later enlarged in the 1920s to be used only for entertaining on a grand scale. The massive building could seat 100 people on each floor and could service 1,200 if the grounds were in use. Those must have been some parties!

The mansion is set in sprawling, 19thC hillside gardens overlooking the sea, on the ridge of Mt. Faber, which was known as Mt. Washington in the Alkaffs' times.

In recent years, the house has been the subject of a costly restoration exercise by local hotelier, Mr. Ong Beng Seng, who leased the building from the government, imported reproductions of Dutch colonial furniture from Indonesia, and has turned it into one of only two restaurants in Asia serving traditional *rijstaffel*, the Indonesian multiple-course banquet. The whole experience recalls the opulence of plantation days in Jakarta, when each of ten dishes was served by a different young maiden. It is the only restaurant of its kind outside Indonesia. See also EATING AND DRINKING, page 105.

The mansion itself is open only for meals and drinks; the estate is now a 19ha (47-acre) public park.

ARAB STREET DISTRICT ★
Map 4B5.

In the early 1830s, Stamford Raffles' town planners determined that the area around this street should be set apart as an Arab village, or "Kampong Glam," that would house people united by language and Islam. Always a small community, which in the years between 1834 and 1947 increased only from an original 66 souls to just over 2,000, its leaders became wealthy; their belief in education gave them influence among their Malay co-religionists.

No social register of prominent names in Singapore's history could exclude the Alsagoffs, Aljunieds or Alkaffs (see ALKAFF MANSION). Still today, the progeny of the Arab traders and artisans who settled here walk streets lined with shops selling the wares of the Middle East's *souks,* bearing names that resound in the collective memory of Araby, such as Baghdad, Muscat, Bussorah and Kandahar.

The area is ripe for exploration. Start on **Arab St.** itself, where it joins Beach Rd. The 195 bus goes there from Orchard Rd. via Bras Basah Rd., Victoria St. and Jalan Sultan, or you can take a short walk from Bugis MRT station. Here, shops spill out onto some of Singapore's only "five-foot ways" (covered sidewalks, see illustration of shophouses on page 27) that remain *in situ,* with delicately designed Malay and South Indian batiks, rich Madras silks in emblematic weaves of royal houses long forgotten, and cleverly constructed basketware.

Turn right onto **Baghdad St.** to find shops selling jewelry, nonalcoholic perfumes (in adherence to the Islamic prohibition of alcohol) and the accouterments of Muslims at prayer. Take the first turn left, **Bussorah St.**, and you will find the golden domes of the SULTAN MOSQUE (illustrated on page 24) right in front of you. **Muscat St.**, in front of the mosque, is alive with evening foodstalls in the fasting month of Ramadan, when Muslims are forbidden to eat before sundown — and then make up for lost time (see CALENDAR OF EVENTS on page 50).

Turn right onto Muscat St., then right again onto Kandahar St., to arrive back on Baghdad St. Turn left and walk on to the next junction (Sultan Gate). The Sultan's palace, the **Istana Kampong Glam**, stands behind the two old gateposts.

Retrace your steps back to the Sultan Mosque and follow the street round the building to **North Bridge Rd.** There are many Muslim restaurants here (see VICTORY and ZAM ZAM on page 111) and places where you can buy an unusual souvenir: slivers of what is said to be the most expensive wood in the world. This rare Burmese wood became so extremely highly prized because it burns with a fragrance of incense.

There are two old **Muslim burial grounds** (one of which contains the graves of Malay princes) in the area bounded by Jalan Sultan, Rochor Canal and Jalan Kubor.

BIRD-SINGING CONTESTS ★
Various locations. Sundays 8–10am. Arrive early.

There is no known explanation for the attraction, to Chinese middle-aged men, of having a songbird in a beautiful bamboo cage, which they take for morning walks, as Westerners would a dog. The birds are taken to the park, where they commiserate with their free-flying brethren. Then, over early morning tea each day, bets are laid on their relative powers of song. The old men are giving away no secrets, but they will let a stranger sit in on the action.

Bird-singing contests in Singapore are not typical tourist brochure fare. They are very much a local entertainment, and that is precisely their charm. Singapore bird owners congregate in various districts early on Sunday mornings, with their best singing birds in their most beautiful cages. You can see them on **Petain Rd.** *(off Serangoon Rd.)* — a street notable for lovely old terrace (row) houses painted in gay pastels with panels of decorative tiles — and at the corner of **Tiong Bahru Rd.** and **Seng Poh Rd.**

Sharmas and merboks are the preferred birds. Training a prize songster is a popular hobby and is sometimes profitable for the owner, but the ancient roots of this Chinese pastime are obscure.

BOTANIC GARDENS
Napier/Cluny Rds. Map 2D4 ☎474-1165 ▣ ▆ ✿ Open Mon–Fri 5.30am– 11pm; Sat, Sun and hols 5.30am–midnight. Bus 7, 14, 95, 106, 174 (40C) from Orchard Blvd.

Within the 47ha (116 acres) of "the Botanics," as locals call them, there is a 4ha (10-acre) section of virgin tropical jungle, one of two such indigenous environments left in the city–state (the other is at BUKIT TIMAH NATURE RESERVE). For the less adventurous, there are large lawns, and lakes with gliding swans. The **Orchid Enclosure** contains 250 hybrids, including Singapore's national flower, Vanda Miss Joaquim.

There is a **Palm Valley**, one "resident" of which has the world's largest seed, which can measure up to a half-meter, a sundial garden, a marsh garden, a topiary garden, rockeries and an aviary. On Sundays, school and military bands play classical and popular music at the octagonal, gazebo-style, Victorian bandstand at the top of **Bandstand Hill** *(between 5.30 and 6.30pm)*, and recently there have even been jazz concerts. In the early morning, this is a popular place for Singaporeans to jog or practice *tai chi*.

Had mankind a better understanding of the 19thC legacy to the 20thC, there would surely be a grand monument in this garden's Palm Valley to *Hevea brasiliensis*. In 1877 the botanist **Sir Henry N. Ridley**, otherwise known as "Mad Ridley," successfully transplanted Brazilian rubber trees by way of cuttings brought from Kew Gardens. He drove Malaya's colonialist planters to distraction with his missionary zeal for the virtues of growing rubber trees, which won him the "mad" moniker.

Ridley's trees eventually made of the Malay peninsula a plantation economy largely based on rubber exports, and that economy put the Western world on mechanized rubber wheels.

Sir Henry had the last laugh, and within the gardens are perhaps the best monuments to his memory, the **School of Ornamental Horticulture** and the research branch of the **Parks and Recreation Department**. The building where Ridley worked is near the main office. Research today has mainly to do with orchids, soils and plant breeding.

Ridley ran the Botanics from 1888–1912, and fancied orchids as well as rubber trees. So to him came running **Agnes Joachim**, an Armenian resident, with an orchid she'd stumbled upon amid a stand of bamboo in her garden. He verified it as a natural hybrid, and **Vanda Miss Joaquim** became Singapore's own true flower.

BUGIS STREET
Bounded by Victoria St., Queen St., Rochor Rd. and Cheng Yan Pl. Map 4B5. MRT: Bugis.

A legend in its colonial lifetime, when it catered to all the entertainment needs of servicemen far from home, Singapore's red light district has been restored, polished and pressed into service as a food and nightlife center suitable for family viewing.

For those who want a hygienic and risk-free visit to a theme-park built around Singapore's raunchier past, Bugis St. is a must. For a full description of its past and present, see NIGHTLIFE, page 114.

BUKIT TIMAH NATURE RESERVE
Upper Bukit Timah Rd. Map 1D3 🔲 ✻ *Bus 171 or 173 (80C) from Orchard Blvd. or Scotts Rd. Alight at Bukit Timah Shopping Centre.*

Bukit Timah, which means "Tin Hill," rises to 175m (570 feet) and is Singapore's highest hill. Bukit Timah Nature Reserve is a 60ha (148-acre) stretch of primary jungle through which you can follow well-marked trails that lead you to the top. Most people will experience little difficulty following these paths, but the first section is steep, so wear good walking shoes. Jungle Fall Path to Rock Path and up is a popular route to the top, which takes about one hour to reach.

A word of caution: unlike most outdoor sights in Singapore, this is a "reserve," not a man-made theme park. There are dangerous snakes, spiders, scorpions, red weaving ants *(kerengga)* and the like — most of which have learned to avoid nature's most dangerous predators, some 60,000 of whom trek these carefully widened and fenced paths each year. Still, it's best to remember that this is indeed primeval forest: watch your step and travel in pairs or groups.

CHANGI PRISON CHAPEL AND MUSEUM

Main entrance, Changi Prison, Upper Changi Rd., near Changi International Airport. Open Mon–Fri 8.30am–12.30pm, 2–4.45pm; Sat 8.30am–4.45pm; Sun 3.30–5.30pm. MRT: Simei.

This simple chapel, with thatched roof and outdoor pews, is a replica of one built by Allied prisoners of war. Its setting is charming: a small garden filled with bougainvilleas, which visitors are welcome to pick in remembrance of the people who died in the region in World War II.

The museum's modest display records the living conditions of these prisoners, held during the Japanese occupation of Singapore in World War II. The prison itself dates from the 1930s and was used shortly after its completion to house European prisoners of war. Many of them died in the construction of the Thai-Burma railroad and are buried beneath the Bridge over the river Kwai in Thailand's Kanchanaburi province (see pages 255–6).

CHETTIYAR TEMPLE (Hindu) ▥

15 Tank Rd. Map 3C3 ☎737-9393 (trustees) ☒ Open 8am–noon, 5.30–8.30pm. Bus 123, 143 (40C) to River Valley Rd., then walk back to Tank Rd.

The original Chettiyar Temple (or Arulmuga Thandayuthapani Temple, see illustration on page 26) was built by Chettiyars (Indian money lenders) in the 1850s. In 1981 the original temple was demolished, and a new one was completed in 1984. The temple is dedicated to one of Shiva's sons — Lord Muruga, the provider — and contains six representations of him. There are also nine figures of his father in different dance poses.

The entrance-tower (or *gopuram*) is 23m (75 feet) high and is covered in six tiers of pastel-colored carvings. The temple ceiling has 48 glass panels, positioned to catch the morning and evening light; chandeliers and depictions of lotus flowers add to the beauty.

The Chettiyar Temple is particularly popular at the spectacular festival of **Thaipusam** *(Jan or Feb)* and at **Navarathri** or "Nine Nights" *(Oct)*. At Thaipusam, an image of Lord Subramaniam is carried from here to the **Vinayagar Temple** in Keong Saik Rd. At dawn the next day, crowds accompanying the petitioners walk from the **Sri Perumal Temple** in Serangoon Rd. to this temple.

Petitioning for specific favors or in thanksgiving for favors given, participants in Thaipusam parade through the streets in various expressions of self-mortification, some having long skewers run through their lips, others wearing large harnesses supported by hooks pierced into their back and torso.

Navarathri is a joyous festival. This temple is the stage for classical Indian music, song and dance, for nine nights from 7–10pm. On the tenth day, at 6.30pm, a silver horse is carried in a procession through the neighboring streets, which then returns to the temple.

CHINAMAN SCHOLARS GALLERY

14B Trengganu St., Chinatown. Map 4D4 ☎222-9554. Open Mon–Fri 9am–4pm ▨

Go up a narrow, wooden staircase to the third floor of a restored shophouse, and you will find yourself in a re-creation of the life-style of the Chinese merchants and scholars of the 1920s and 1930s. The house could be a million miles from the noise and bustle of 1990s Chinatown in the streets below.

There are sleeping, dining and living areas, and a fascinating collection of Chinese musical instruments, photographs and other memorabilia, gathered lovingly together by antique collector Vincent Tan. If they arrange it in advance, some tour groups are invited to share a tea ceremony, listen to music and gain an insight into the period.

CHINATOWN ★
Map 4E4.

There are many Chinatowns tucked away here and there in Singapore, but *the* Chinatown is in the area around New Bridge Rd. and South Bridge Rd., to the south of the Singapore River *(near MRT Outram Park station).* Here the sleek geometrical planes and angles of the planned city give way to highly exotic Oriental vistas of compressed, bustling detail, making a blaze of color and variety. The streets are narrow and intimate.

Open-fronted shops spill unfamiliar wares onto the sidewalk, so that you walk as often through them as past them. The surroundings seem almost too perfectly "Chinese," like a skillfully-made movie set: a jade store; a medicine hall with wooden drawers of herbs from floor to ceiling; an embroiderer's, whose fine silks and brocade are made to order;

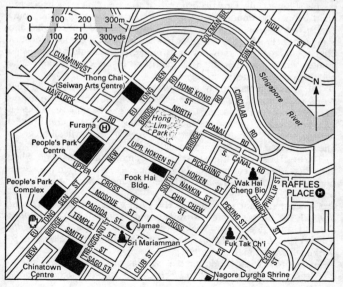

Chinese screens, furniture, porcelain; Chinese lanterns, Chinese gods, elaborate altars; wooden clogs; bottles of crushed pearls, sold as a tonic; dried snakes and lizards; Chinese cakes; a goldsmith; traditional clothing; teas and teapots; rattanware; highly decorative paper clothing for the gods; *bonsai* trees; a *mahjong* tile-maker; a seal carver; a fortune-teller; a Chinese clan association; bamboo and paper effigies to be burned at funerals (the modern deceased invariably has a Mercedes sent to him in the Underworld this way); Chinese opera mask makers; a sidewalk calligrapher; a carpet made of shark's fins, laid out in the road to dry; an ancient barbershop with an old man having a crewcut; Chinese books; a martial arts shop; a man who sells newborn mice, to be taken live as a cure for ulcers.

Virtually everything about Chinatown is old, except perhaps the ubiquitous bristle of TV aerials. The streets are an old-fashioned maze of asymmetry, the shophouses (illustrated on page 27) old in style and scale as well as in fact. There is a timeless sense to the place, a vision of the ancient continuity of Chinese life, as of the centuries stacked behind the way people live here, the strange foods they eat, their odd customs, their clothes.

Shops cluster together, with nine Teochew restaurants in a row, a street of goldsmiths, another of medicine halls, another of craftsmen carving household gods. Your bill will be totted up on an abacus, not a calculator, but the speed and accuracy are the same.

China has a real presence in this part of Singapore: it is the homeland that people look back to — or at least part of it is, for most of the old people still speak the local dialects of their ancestral Chinese villages and often cannot communicate with each other unless they share some English or Mandarin. All young people, however, speak both English and Mandarin well, and they look not to China but to Singapore. Most of Chinatown's sons have moved away to modern apartments in the housing estates, where they and their children live in the comfort and style befitting prosperous Singaporeans.

The grandparents remain. Many of them still work a full day in their shops, stalls, workshops and factories, just as their forebears have always done (but not their children). Others spend the day sitting on the spiral stairs outside their houses, or standing at the deep, half-shuttered upstairs windows, staring out at the street. In a few years they will all be gone. The planners and developers are waiting.

The best time to visit Chinatown is at early morning market-time, when the streets are at their liveliest. Evenings are also good, with the streets brightly lit, the families home for dinner, and most shops open till 9pm or later.

Chinese temples to note are **Wak Hai Cheng Bio** (circa 1850s) *(Phillip St.)*, **Fuk Tak Ch'i** (Temple of Prosperity and Virtue, c. 1820) *(#76 Peking St.)* and THIAN HOCK KENG (Temple of Heavenly Happiness) *(near the corner of Telok Ayer and Boon Tat Sts.)*. Before the 1880s, Telok Ayer St. marked the shoreline.

Singapore's oldest Hindu temple, SRI MARIAMMAN (c. 1827), is also in this district *(South Bridge Rd., a block square between Pagoda, Temple and Trengganu Sts.).* If you are near Trengganu, visit the CHINAMAN SCHOLARS GALLERY (#14B).

Chinatown is a fascinating place to explore, great for local eating and for shopping too, both on the streets and in such shopping centers as **People's Park Centre**, **People's Park Complex** with its adjacent food stall center, and **Chinatown Centre**, where the hawker stalls of China-town were relocated by the planners. You will find good-value clothing, textiles and Chinese food.

A walk through Chinatown

Begin at the river and travel sw down South Bridge Rd., one of the main arteries of Chinatown. This road and its tributaries contain many fascinating open-fronted shops and three shopping centers. A short way past the junction with Cross St. is JAMAE MOSQUE, near the corner of Mosque St., with a variety of restaurants.

Parallel to Mosque St. are a number of side streets, lined with more shops. Follow one of these through to New Bridge Rd. and continue into Eu Tong Sen St. Then turn right and go past the People's Park Complex, the People's Park Centre and the **Thong Chai** (see SHOPPING on page 123), an attractive 1890s former hospital building, now a curio market and rechristened "Seiwan Arts Centre," a name by which it may someday actually become known. For now, it is wisest to stick with Thong Chai when asking directions.

By continuing along New Bridge Rd., you will eventually find yourself back at the river.

CHINESE GARDEN (Yu Hua Yuan)

Jurong Park, Yuan Ching Rd., Jurong. Map 1D2 ☎ *265-5889* ▨ *dual entrance fee with Japanese Garden* ✗ ▣ ⇚ *Open Mon–Sat 9am–7pm; Sun and hols 8.30am–7pm. MRT: Chinese Garden.*

The Chinese Garden is a reproduction of classical Sung dynasty (AD960–1280) gardens in the style of the gardens of the Peking Summer Palace. Like the adjacent JAPANESE GARDEN, it is actually an island in the Jurong Lake, and each is about 13ha (32 acres) in size. A nine-tiered pagoda has a panoramic, 360° view from the top. Dotted around the gardens are miniature bridges, fountains, lakes, serene courtyards, bamboo groves and many beautiful flowers. You can rent a paddleboat, for a leisurely chug around the lake, and the teahouse shops sell fine souvenirs and batik fabrics.

If you have time and can take the heat, combine the Chinese Garden with a visit to the Japanese Garden.

CLARKE QUAY

Across River Valley Rd. from Fort Canning Park on one side, across the Read St. Bridge from Ellenborough Market. Map 4D4 ☎ *339-8377* ⓕ*339-1713. River taxis operate between Empress Place, South Boat Quay and Clarke Quay. Taxi stop and parking lot on River Valley Rd.*

Clarke Quay is an ambitious combination of actual architectural resto-ration, Disney-style theme park and pedestrian tourists' town. Sixty godowns (warehouses) and shophouses, some dating back to the late

1880s, most to the 1920s, are being renovated to provide space for about 180 shops and 20 restaurants and pubs.

A 12-minute ride in a "bumboat train," modeled on Disneyland's "Pirates of the Caribbean" in California, will use Disney-style "animatronics" special effects techniques to tell the tall tales of Singapore's history: the legend of Sang Nila Utama, who found and named the island; those of Orang Galang pirates from the 1830s; and those of the Hoey Chinese secret societies that flourished among the "coolie" laborers who dominated these former working docks until the 1950s.

Daytime at Clarke Quay offers jugglers and stilt-walkers; at night there are walks along the gaslit quay, a beer garden in the central square and shaking and singing in the **Suzie Wong** disco and *karaoke* bar.

The rough-and-tumble history of this district has, like Singapore's hawker foodstalls and so much of the raunchier side of Singapore, been made safe and sanitized for popular consumption. Clarke Quay is the most ambitious project to date of the same government-sponsored company that is responsible for the restoration of Raffles Hotel and Tanjong Pagar district.

THE COLONIAL AREA ▥ ★
Map 4C4.

Sir Stamford Raffles, when he stepped ashore in 1819, chose the area N of the river for the heart of his city. To explore it, start from Dhoby Gaut MRT station. The NATIONAL MUSEUM on Stamford Road is a superb example of Victorian architecture. On the same road you will also find the **National Library**, whose reference section contains guidebooks in many languages.

Continue along Stamford Rd., then turn right at Armenian St. At the far end of this street, the **Armenian Church** on the left (see illustration on page 25) has an extremely peaceful setting. This lovely little white-spired church is said to be the only Armenian–Christian place of worship in Southeast Asia. In 1835, a dozen Armenian families commissioned the well-known architect George Drumgoole Coleman to build the church, known to the faithful as the Church of St Gregory the Illuminator.

To avoid traffic noise a little longer, turn right at the Armenian church and walk up Canning Rise. About 400m (440 yards) from the church, there is a white stone entrance gate on the left. This is the entrance to FORT CANNING PARK and leads on through to an old Christian cemetery. Also here is a Malay grave, thought to be the burial place of the last prince of Singa-Pura, and the ruins of the old **Fort Canning**. This was the seat of power of an ancient empire before the founding of Singapore by Raffles. An old fortress on the hill became the British Command Headquarters during the Japanese invasion of Singapore in World War II.

From here go back down the hill, noting several environmental sculptures en route, walk past the Armenian Church, then turn right into Hill St. Continue until you get to the river, then turn left and walk along the **North Boat Quay**. Follow the quay until you come to the statue of **Sir Thomas Stamford Raffles**, which marks the point at which he is supposed to have landed in Singapore.

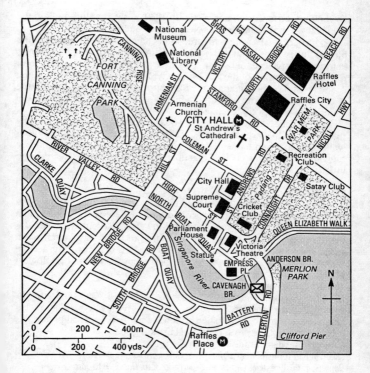

The food centers here are a good place to stop for a drink, a snack and a look at the old shophouses and warehouses that line the Boat Quay on the other side of the river. Until recently, you could see gigantic lighter boats anchored here and men in shorts and singlets busily loading and unloading goods, just as their forefathers did in the early days after the founding of Singapore. Today, the boats are gone, anchored in the "Outer Roads" (sea lanes), and the Singapore River dozes in ghostly serenity.

Behind the food center is the **Cavenagh Bridge**, dwarfed by the nearby **Anderson Bridge**, which was built to replace it. It is worth crossing one of the bridges to see the fishing boats and sampans moored near **Clifford Pier**. Then walk away from the river to visit the collection of artifacts from mainland China in EMPRESS PLACE. As you cross the bus-stop area, you will see **Victoria Theatre** in front of you. Across the street that runs alongside the theater is the imposing **Parliament House**, the oldest government building in Singapore.

Walk between these two buildings to the **Padang**, the city's green lawn and site of grand parades. Field hockey and cricket matches are played here. This area is bordered on the right by the sea and on the left

67

by the **Supreme Court**, completed in 1939, and **City Hall**, built in the late 1920s. Both are impressive Neoclassical buildings.

To the E of the Padang is the treelined Queen Elizabeth Walk and the **Satay Club**, where Malay stallholders sell grilled meat on skewers (satay) eaten with a spicy peanut sauce. This area, and RAFFLES HOTEL, are the best remaining examples of the late 19th-early 20thC style of the colonial era. At the far end of the Padang is the **Singapore Recreation Club**. To the w of the Padang is the beautiful, white ST ANDREW'S CATHEDRAL, a superb example of Neo-Gothic architecture.

To reach RAFFLES HOTEL, cross the busy Stamford Rd. and walk to the right or left of the large modern Raffles City complex of hotels. End your walk by relaxing in Raffles Hotel's **Long Bar**, and sipping a legendary "Singapore Sling," the cocktail that made Singapore famous, created here in 1915.

CROCODILES

Singapore has a whole lot of crocodiles. Fortunately, most of them are kept under good control, at crocodile farms where you can visit them in their natural habitat. Bred for their skins, they also provide entertainment while awaiting their long-term fate, and you can watch them being wrestled, and, of course, being fed. You can also buy a wide variety of goods made from reptile skins, but get written zoological identification in case it is demanded by customs officers.

The Crocodile Farm

*790 Upper Serangoon Rd. Map **2**D5. Open daily 8.30am–5.30pm* 🖭 *Feeding at 11am and 3pm except Mon.*

Singapore's longest established crocodile farm breeds other reptiles too, and stocks jade products as well as skin goods.

Jurong Crocodile Paradise

*Jalan Ahmad Ibrahim. Map **1**D2 (5mins' walk from JURONG BIRD PARK). Open daily 9am–6pm* 🖾 *Wrestling shows 11.30am and 3pm. Bus 198 to Jurong interchange 250, 251 and 253.*

More than 2,500 crocodiles are to be seen here, and the underwater viewing areas put a new perspective on croc-watching.

The Singapore Crocodilarium

*730 East Coast Parkway. Map **2**E5* ☎447-3722. *Open 9am–5.30pm daily. Feeding 11am Tues, Thurs, Sat. Wrestling daily (except Mon and if raining) at 1.15pm and 4.15pm* 🖾 *Take a taxi from MRT Paya Lebar Station.*

Close encounters can be had with more than 1,000 specimens here, perhaps combined with a trip to the East Coast.

EMPRESS PLACE

*1 Empress Place. Map **4**D4. Open 9.30am–9.30pm daily* 🖾 ➾ *Walk from MRT Raffles Place Station.*

Before 1988, this impressive Neoclassical building was best known to travelers for housing the Immigration Dept. Built in 1865, it has always until now been a government facility, first as a courthouse, then housing the Legislative Assembly, then a succession of government offices. Empress Place was chosen to be Singapore's first major conservation project and, presto! US$13 million later it had metamorphosed into a massive exhibition hall with a taste for things from mainland China.

Empress Place has exhibited a number of important collections of Chinese artifacts since it opened. The opening exhibition showed the famous **Han dynasty** (206BC–AD221) **collection**, which traveled the world from the People's Republic of China. This was followed by the **Silk Road collection**, focusing on cultural and archeological treasures of the Tang dynasty. Another exhibition, **Gems of Chinese Art**, gave a rare glimpse of Chinese bronze and ceramics spanning 5,000 years.

There is also a terrace restaurant, **House of Four Seasons**, and souvenir stores on the ground floor, behind a bank of walk-in vaults, now used for storage. Almost as incongruous as the vaults is the presence of the **Philippines Handicraft Centre**, which is not entirely a misnomer, in that much of its stock and some of its staff are from the Philippines.

But perhaps one should not be too particular about authenticity in a British colonial building set in Singapore, featuring exhibitions from the People's Republic of China.

FORT CANNING PARK
Fort Canning Rise. Map 4C4 🔲 ⇶ ➧ ◈ *Entrance near MRT Dhoby Ghaut Station.*

Fort Canning Park spreads over a hillside once known as Forbidden Hill (in Malay, *Bukit Larangan*). No one is completely certain of its history before 1819, but excavations carried out in recent years suggest that a 4m/13-foot-square brick platform, found and described by a Dr John Crawford in the 1820s, could have been the site of an important temple.

Sir Stamford Raffles soon discovered that the local people believed the hill to be a sacred place, not to be visited. Nevertheless, within a week of arriving he had ordered that guns and signaling equipment be taken up there, its height (45m/150 feet) being ideal for observing unannounced visitors.

Here eventually was built **Fort Canning**, from where guns were fired at dawn, noon and dusk. It was on this hill that Raffles, on his third, longest and final visit to Singapore, chose to build his home. He felt that it was a relatively healthy area, being high and cool. It was rechristened **Government Hill**. Today all that remains of the 3ha (7-acre) fortified compound are the metal gates, the guardhouse and the earthworks.

Another interesting feature of the park is the old **Christian cemetery** (1822–65). Here rest the bones of many early settlers, and those believed to belong to the last monarch of old Singa-Pura, Sultan Iskandar Shah. Ascend the steps from Canning Rise *(behind the National Museum)* to pass through the old Gothic-style cemetery gate.

At the sw foot of the hill there is a 25-court squash complex and a swimming pool. Also in the park is a restaurant, which specializes in Chinese seafood and Vietnamese dishes.

HAJJAH FATIMAH MOSQUE 🏛
Java Rd., off Beach Rd. Map 4B6 🔲 *Nearer MRT Lavender Station than Bugis.*

The Hajjah Fatimah Mosque, built in 1845–46, is a favorite of the local Muslims. It was built by an exceedingly rich and pious Malay Muslim lady, Hajjah Fatimah, who commissioned a British architect, J.T. Thompson, to design its minaret and central building.

The result is a small but attractive mosque, a successful melange of Classical, Chinese and Islamic architectural styles, with hints of Gothic. The leaning minaret is alleged to have been modeled on the spire of the original ST ANDREW'S CATHEDRAL.

HAW PAR VILLA DRAGON WORLD (formerly Tiger Balm Gardens)

423 Pasir Panjang Rd. Map 1E3 ☎ 774-0300. Open daily 9am–6pm 🎫 ✳
Buses 10, 30, 51 and 143 direct to Pasir Panjang Rd., or SBS 200 bus from MRT Buona Vista Station. Taxi from Orchard Rd. about 20mins.

Mythology meets hi-tech in the enlarged and completely renovated environs of a rich philanthropist's 1937 creation.

Mr. Aw Boon Haw, who made the famous Tiger Balm salve, was a man of means who owned a dozen or so newspapers in Asia. He built a pair of virtually identical villas and gardens depicting the various special hells to which the bad folks of Chinese mythology go, in both Singapore and Hong Kong. These constructions were meant to inspire moral uprightness among his Overseas Chinese brethren, who could wander through artificial caves and ogle at the tableaux of punishments meted out to sinners. To Western eyes, they were notable only as tasteless, grotesque caricatures.

The new theme park opened in October 1990, after a US$43 million facelift. Mr. Aw's strange statues of dismembered bodies and gruesome punishments were carefully restored, but they are now merely a pretext for thrills'n'spills-type water rides such as *Wrath of the Water Gods* and the *Ten Courts of Hell* (the gruesome entrance, illustrated above, is through a dragon's gaping mouth). There is also a number of sound, movie and light-effects theaters whose extravagant themes are self-evident in their names: *Spirits of the Orient, Legends and Heroes, Creation of the World*.

Live entertainments are provided at three more theaters, including Singapore's answer to Punch and Judy: a children's puppet show conveying cautionary moral tales on the perils of being naughty. A modern generation of Overseas Chinese has made of Mr. Aw's bizarre morality play a money-spinner, in the form of a playground billed as "The Seat of

Chinese Mythology" and attracting some two million visitors a year. Which suggests, perhaps, a cautionary tale for didactic philanthropists.

HOUSE OF TAN YEOK NEE (Chen Xu Nian) 🏛

207 Clemenceau Ave. (corner of Penang Rd.). Map 3C3 ☎737-9122. Near Cockpit and Meridien hotels, close to MRT Dhoby Ghaut Station. Bus 143 from Orchard Blvd. or Orchard Rd. Mon–Fri 8.30am–4.30pm, Sun 9.30am–6pm.

The House of Tan Yeok Nee is one of the finest examples of Straits Chinese-style architecture. Roofed in terracotta tiles, the house has huge granite pillars that were probably brought from China, and, like Singapore's Chinese temples, it has upswept eaves.

It was built in 1885 for a Chinese merchant, **Tan Yeok Nee**, who, like many of his generation who could afford it, returned to South China and died in 1902. Tan began as a cloth peddler but later became a very rich man dealing in pepper and gambier. His house was acquired for use by a railroad company, whose main terminus was on nearby Tank Rd. The house has been the headquarters of the Salvation Army since 1940. Like many other important buildings in Singapore, it was occupied briefly by the Japanese during World War II as part of their army command center.

JAMAE MOSQUE (Masjid Chulia)

218 South Bridge Rd. (corner of Mosque St.). Map 4D4.

The Jamae Mosque, like the NAGORE DURGHA SHRINE, owes its existence to the Chulias, Indian moslem merchants from the southeast Indian Coromandel coast. It was built between 1830–35, shortly after the Shrine. Recognizable by its twin towers and simple, uncluttered style of architecture, it is only a few steps from the SRI MARIAMMAN TEMPLE. Both are within a few yards of CHINATOWN.

JAPANESE GARDEN (Seiwan)

Jurong Park. Map 1D2 ☎265-3474 🎫 dual entrance fee with Chinese Garden ✗ 🍴 MRT: Chinese Garden Station.

This 13ha (32-acre) garden (in fact an island in the Jurong Lake), opened in 1973, is one of the largest of its kind ever built outside Japan. One significant feature is the tranquil "dry landscape garden," a style developed in the Muromachi period in Japan (1392–1568) and based on Zen ideas. Some 500 tonnes of stones were imported from Japan, to help create a truly Japanese atmosphere. The bridges and buildings are all in the Japanese style, sustaining the impression of authenticity.

You can buy a special entrance ticket covering both this and the nearby CHINESE GARDEN. Visitors, especially those with children, might find it too hot and tiring to visit both. One solution is to go from here to the **CN West Leisure Park**. The park, only minutes away, includes a swimming pool with a 50m (160-foot) slide and a wave-making machine.

JURONG BIRD PARK ★

Jurong Hill. Map 1D1 ☎265-0022 🎫 includes entrance to all shows; tram/monorail fares extra ✗ 🍴 ♿ Open daily 9am–6pm. MRT: Boon Lay Station, then bus 251, 253 or 255.

Breakfast with the birds at this 20ha (49-acre) bird park, beautifully landscaped, and containing 4,500 birds from 420 species from all over the world. It has the world's largest enclosed, **walk-in aviary** and a man-made waterfall 30m (98 feet) high. Parrots will be your hosts over toast and coffee, while songbirds serenade nearby *(breakfast daily from 9-11am)*.

The park also boasts the world's largest collection of Southeast Asian hornbills and South American toucans. Its **Penguin Parade** re-creates arctic conditions and houses about 100 penguins *(feeding times 10.30am and 3.30pm daily)*. It is second in size only to the similar facility at San Diego's Sea World exhibit, upon which it is modeled.

If you don't want to walk, there's now a **monorail** to take you around the park. This is a great place for children. Shows such as *Birds of Prey* are screened in a Nature Theatrette throughout the day.

KONG MENG SAN PHOR KARK SEE TEMPLE (Buddhist)
88 Bright Hill Drive. Map 2C4 ☎ *453-7384* ☎ *Open 10am–10pm.*
Built at the beginning of this century, this is one of the largest Buddhist temples in Singapore and is in fact a huge complex of separate temples and pavilions joined by covered walkways. It also has funeral chambers and a columbarium (a building with tiers of niches for urns containing the ashes from cremations). There are many intricate gold-leaf decorations, most of them hand-worked. As at the SIONG LIM TEMPLE, monks are happy to show visitors around.

MERLION PARK
Fullerton Rd., near Anderson Bridge. Map 4D5.
Merlion Park is simply a narrow stretch of green next to the Singapore River. From here you can sit and watch the fishing boats entering and leaving the area around Collyer Quay. Flowering shrubs line the paths and at the end, next to the Anderson Bridge, is the **Merlion Fountain** (see illustration on page 18), which guards the river mouth and is brilliantly lit at night. The Merlion, half lion and half fish, is the national symbol of Singapore.

At the end of this green stretch is a **cenotaph**, which commemorates the dead of Europe's 1914–18 war. Just beyond this, there is an open-air food center.

NAGORE DURGHA SHRINE ▥
140 Telok Ayer St./Cross St. Map 4E4 ☎ *Bus CBD1 to Robinson Rd., then walk; or walk from the MRT Tanjong Pagar Station.*
The Nagore Durgha Shrine, also known as Masjid Chulia, was built in about 1827 for the Indian Muslims from the SE Indian Coromandel Coast, who were known as Chulias. Its Doric columns and Palladian doors are architectural curiosities. The facade comprises intricate calligraphic designs and is typical of Islamic art, which forbids the use of human or animal figures.

As with other mosques, you may find that shrine attendants discourage non-Muslim visitors.

NATIONAL MUSEUM AND ART GALLERY 🏛

Stamford Rd. Map 4C4 ☎ *330-9645* 📧 *Open Tues–Sun 9am–4.30pm. Closed Mon* ✗ *departs from the information counter 11am every Tues, Wed, Thurs, Fri. Short walk from MRT City Hall Station.*

Opened in 1849 as the Raffles Museum, this collection was moved to its present site in 1887; the impressive Neoclassical structure was designated the National Museum in 1960. In 1975 the National Art Gallery (emphasizing the work of contemporary local artists, with some changing exhibitions) was moved to the same building.

In the **History of Singapore Galleries**, there are 20 miniature dioramas depicting aspects of Singapore's history. The **Straits Chinese** (or **Peranakan**) **Gallery** contains many interesting features of the history of this unique culture, including a traditional bridal chamber, embroidered ceremonial garments and colored enameled porcelain (see also PERANAKAN PLACE). At the back of the museum is the **Southeast Asian Gallery**, containing ethnographic collections from the region.

Other sections of the museum contain a great variety of Oriental riches ranging from textiles to silverware and from ceramics to jade. There is also a lively "hands-on" **Young People's Gallery** *(unfortunately open Sat only 10am-noon).*

PERANAKAN PLACE 🏛 ★

Corner of Orchard Rd. and Emerald Hill Rd. Map 3B3 ☎ *732-6966* 📧 *except for Peranakan Museum* 🍽

The Malay word *peranakan* describes the culture evolved by those Chinese tin miners, traders and plantation workers who took Malay wives and first settled in the Malay Peninsula. Elements of this culture are preserved in Peranakan Place, a large, pastel blue and white property development at the foot of Emerald Hill preservation district. Within the distinctive complex, which is jointly sponsored by the government and a group of private investors, are shops and restaurants meant to recall the *peranakan* style.

Peranakan Place is frequented by locals and tourists, and at night its large outdoor courtyard area is a lively gathering point for cocktails. *Peranakan* "taste" is an eclectic blend of ornate Western furnishing and architectural styles, embellished with the rich design patterns of China.

Done today it would be tacky. With the patina of a century or so, the culture clash has the same charm as a cardboard-stiff portrait of one of the Straits Chinese families of the late 19th to early 20thC, where, typically, the man would assert his modernity by topping his traditional Chinese, pajama-like silk suit with a bowler hat — the incomprehensible tastes of China's mandarinates made more so by the addition of the incomprehensible taste in headdress worn by City of London bankers.

RAFFLES HOTEL 🏛 ★

Corner of Bras Basah Rd., Beach Rd. and North Bridge Rd. Map 4C5 ☎ *337-8041. Bus CSS 1 or 2, CBD 1 or 14.*

No visit to Singapore would be complete without paying homage to Singapore's most famous hotel. See HOTELS on page 87.

ST ANDREW'S CATHEDRAL 🏛
Coleman St. Map 4C4 ☎ *337-6104 (recorded message giving times)* 📷 *Outside MRT City Hall Station.*

The Anglican Cathedral of St Andrew is one of Singapore's most famous buildings. Raffles chose the site in 1823 but never lived to see it built. The present early Neo-Gothic building was completed in 1861, the work being carried out by Indian convicts. (For a full explanation of their labors, see page 24.)

The main door is to be found under the spire at the w end of the church. Above it is a fine **stained-glass window** depicting the Four Evangelists. In the chancel, there are four more stained-glass windows with floral designs.

The simple white spire of the cathedral was at one time a dominant feature of the skyline of colonial Singapore, when it was the tallest structure around the Padang. In the 1990s, its setting could be taken as a symbol of the changes that have taken place in this dynamic city–state since the time of Raffles: it is dwarfed by the soaring tower of the Westin Stamford hotel.

SENTOSA ISLAND ★
500m (550yds) s of Singapore and reached in 5mins by ferry (from the World Trade Centre Ferry Terminal), cable car (from either the Jardine Steps or the Mount Faber Cable Car Station; operates 10am–7pm), bus (from WTC bus terminal and MRTTiong Bahru Station) or taxi. Map 2F4. For more information, contact Sentosa Development Corporation (SDC) (☎ 270-7888). Open Mon–Thurs 7.30am–11pm; Fri–Sun and hols, to midnight 📷 ✗ ⇌ 💺 ✦ ✓ 🌿 🍴
⇐ *Hotel guests are allowed to enter by taxi at any time, but still must pay an admission fee.*

• A **bus service** (📷) *circles the island with 4 routes (A, B, 7.30am–11.30pm; 1, 2, 9am-7pm; departures every 10mins). The* **monorail** (📷) *traverses a loop with 7 stops: 1) Ferry Terminal, 2) Gateway Station (at the vehicular causeway), 3) golf courses and Beaufort Hotel, 4) Central Beach and Campsite, 5) Cable Car Plaza/Butterfly Park and Insect Kingdom, 6) Fort Siloso, 7) Underwater World, Shangri-La Sentosa Beach resort. Bicycles for rent.*
There are those who argue that tourism will destroy itself as an industry by despoiling the very locations it seeks to promote, unless it creates

equivalents of Walt Disney Worlds in strategic places around the world. In 1990, that former cow patch in Orlando, Florida reportedly hosted more than 28 million visitors — more than half the number of tourists who visit Spain each year. Theme parks and theme parties at hotels within them are the rage with incentive travel groups, and Singapore appears to have taken the pundits' advice about tourism's future and applied it in Asia.

Chinese maps of the 14thC called this island *Blakang Mati*. The British called it St George Island and built three forts and an artillery battery there in the 1880s. After World War Two it became a naval base, *HMS Sultan*. In the early- to mid-1960s, during the period of Indonesian Confrontation, Gurkha infantry units patrolled and defended the island against Indonesian saboteurs.

Following the withdrawal of all British forces in 1967, the island was handed back to the Singapore Government. In 1972, the Sentosa Development Corporation was formed to create a leisure resort island on the rechristened Sentosa.

Enter Sentosa Island, cleared of its inhabitants in 1972 and ever since a leisure park promoted as an escape from the bustle of the city, for visiting residents and some tourists. The Malay name, Pulau Sentosa, means "Island of Peace and Tranquility." No more. Singapore's planners mean to make that the misnomer of the century.

A causeway now links Sentosa to the mainland, opening access to much larger numbers of visitors. Two resort hotels have opened: the **Beaufort** and **Shangri-La Sentosa Beach** resort. Visitor arrivals have grown to over three million per year, about evenly divided between locals and foreigners.

Sporting attractions include swimming lagoons and two 18-hole golf courses, **Tanjong** and **Serapong**. There are plenty of opportunities to jog, canoe, cycle, roller-skate or camp, or to rent canoes, pedal boats, aquabikes and wind-surfing boards. That is the sedate side.

For a number of years, Sentosa has had attractions such as a **Maritime Museum**, **Fort Siloso**, the **Coralarium**, **Insect Kingdom** and the **Rare Stone Museum**, linked by monorail, with a food center, **Rasa Sentosa**. It made a pleasant day out for people of all ages and interests.

Now, with a view to enticing incentive travelers to spend a week there, a frenzy of new attractions has been added to what was already there, with more still to come.

Already flourishing is **Fountain Gardens**, which features classical European landscaping and ornamental fountains, with a light show at night. Nearby are a **Flower Terrace**, ablaze with tropical blooms, and a **Butterfly Park** with 2,500 specimens flitting about a "free flight" enclosure. This last is partnered by **Insect Kingdom**, with, for those who can face them, such treasures as rhino beetles, jungle grasshoppers and scorpions.

Giving new meaning to the the phrase "Instant Asia," one of the most recent attractions, the **Asian Village**, lets visitors tour the whole continent in a single day. Next to the ferry terminal, in 8ha (20 acres) of landscaped tropical lushness, the S$60 million theme park has three villages, representing Southeast Asia, North Asia and South Asia, all set around a lake.

The experience is a sort of cultural picnic: visitors can travel round the mini-region on foot or by boat, dipping into a whole different ethnicity at every port of call. Each village comes equipped with its own "street life," with entertainers, food stalls, demonstrations and handicraft displays.

An **Orchid Fantasy** park, billed as one of the world's most comprehensive displays of tropical orchids, opened in April 1993. A giant clock made of orchids of every hue is a permanent feature, and occasional exhibits of rare varieties and hybrids are planned.

1991 saw the opening of **Underwater World**, Southeast Asia's largest oceanarium, which features a 100m/110-foot circular acrylic tunnel over a moving walkway. When they stand inside this, visitors can gaze at sea life from the bottom looking up; 400 species of marine life glide all around them.

The **Rare Stone Museum** has a collection of 4,000 rare stones, most of them from China, of which around 1,000 are displayed at any one time.

A curiosity is the Inca-inspired **Lost Civilization and Ruined City**, less reminiscent of South America than of those wacky 19thC German princes who rebuilt ruins in their gardens for effect.

History closer to home is immortalized in an attraction dubbed **Pioneers of Singapore**, where a waxwork of Sir Stamford Raffles signs the lease on the island of Singa-pura, to start off a diorama of Singapore's colonial past. Close by are the **Surrender Chambers**, with more waxwork dioramas showing the surrenders of the British and the Japanese during World War II. A voice-over intones details of daily life under Japanese occupation.

Fort Siloso, with its maze of underground tunnels, was used to house Prisoners of War during World War II, a fact that is commemorated in a further use of wax: another diorama, this time of life behind bars. The museum traces the history of the fort from its construction in the 1880s until independence, and makes a fascinating detour despite, or perhaps partly because of, something called the Sounds of Siloso — a fusillade of gunfire, shouting and footsteps that is triggered off as you make your way around the site.

Another of the more long-standing attractions, the **Maritime Museum**, is devoted to the history of the Port of Singapore Authority. Housed mostly in three Malay-style corrugated wharves, it has various types of boat on display, including one used to carry Vietnamese refugees, and a dragon boat.

If all this frenetic activity is just too much, you can laze around on Sentosa's three beautifully-kept beaches, **Tanjong**, **Siloso** and **Central**.

Finally, for those who have still not succumbed to entertainment-lag, **Fantasy Island**, "an adventure-packed water theme park" is expected to open in the very near future. As well as a breath-catching menu of watery thrill-rides, visitors are promised a submarine that will transport visitors to the lost city of Atlantis — which may, after all, have been a grand tourist center of the ancients that sunk under its own weight.

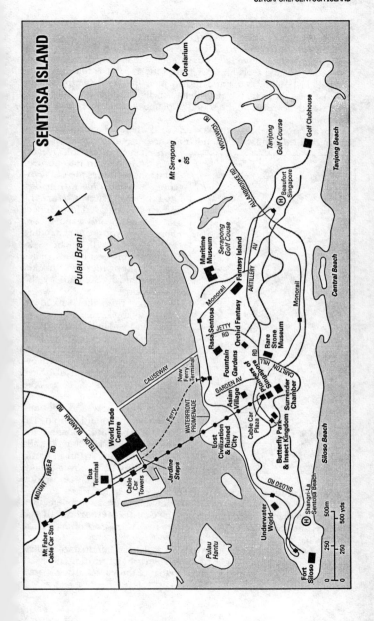

SENTOSA ISLAND

Coralarium

Golf Clubhouse

Mt Serapong
85

Tanjong
Golf Course

Tanjong Beach

WOODBRIDGE RD

ALLANBROOKE RD

Beaufort
Singapore (H)

Pulau Brani

Serapong
Golf Course

Maritime
Museum

Fantasy Island

ARTILLERY AV

Monorail

Monorail

Rasa Sentosa

Orchid Fantasy

JETTY RD

Rare Stone
Museum

Central Beach

Fountain
Gardens

CARLTON HILL

CAUSEWAY

New Ferry
Terminal

Asian
Village

Pioneers of
Singapore &
Surrender
Chamber

GARDEN AV

PIONEERS RD

Ferry

WATERFRONT
PROMENADE

Lost
Civilization
& Ruined
City

Cable Car Plaza

Butterfly Park
& Insect Kingdom

Siloso Beach

TELOK BLANGAH RD

World Trade
Centre

Jardine
Steps

SILOSO RD

Shangri-La
Sentosa Beach (H)

MOUNT FABER RD

Bus
Terminal

Cable
Car Towers

Underwater
World

Mt Faber
Cable Car Stn

Pulau Hantu

Fort
Siloso

500m
500 yds
250
250
0
0

77

SERANGOON ROAD DISTRICT (Little India) ★
Map 4B4–A5. About 6 blocks from MRT Bugis Station.

The first Indians to come to Singapore settled s of the Singapore River. In about 1880 they moved N, to the area in and around Serangoon Rd. A walk in this area feels like a step into India, for it is full of women wrapped in beautiful *saris* and Indian men in *dhotis* (wrapped loin cloths). Open shops fill the air with the smells of freshly ground spices, jasmine and incense, and the sound of plaintive romantic ballads set to *sitar* music.

Start at the bridge across the Rochor Canal where Selegie Rd. becomes **Serangoon Rd.** Walk on the left in the same direction as the traffic and

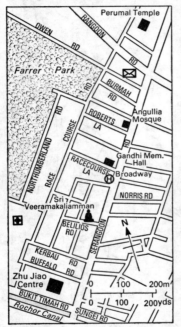

turn left into **Buffalo Rd.** Over on your left is the **Zhu Jiao Centre**, which now houses the old **Kandang Kerbau** (*Tek Ka*) market and the old **"Thieves' Market,"** which was removed from Sungei Rd. It is well worth wandering in here even if you are not intending to buy anything. If you are seeking directions, be advised that it is still best known as "KK" market (from Kandang Kerbau) by the local people.

Across from the market are shops selling *saris,* audio equipment and garlands of flowers. If you are not in a hurry, stand for a while and watch the garlands being made. Chettiyars (moneylenders) and goldsmiths also have stalls here: again, patience is the best policy.

Go back now and continue along Serangoon Rd., turning left onto **Kerbau Rd.** to see some interesting old buildings. At #85 Serangoon Rd. is an Indian **handloom store**. Cross over Belilios Rd. to see the **Sri Veeramakaliamman Temple**, dedicated to the Hindu goddess Kali.

Continue on down Serangoon Rd., drinking in the atmosphere, then turn left onto Race Course Lane to find the **Gandhi Memorial Hall and Library**, and some interesting old terrace (row) houses (**Robert's Lane** also has these).

Back on Serangoon Rd., go on to #253, which has hundreds of tropical birds. Walk four more blocks to the **Sri Perumal Temple**. This has a towering decorative gateway similar to that of the SRI MARIAMMAN TEMPLE in South Bridge Rd. (see CHINATOWN).

Return by retracing your steps, this time on the other side of the street and walking against the traffic. There are many local coffee shops in which to pause for a drink or a snack. In Norris Rd., just before the Sri Veeramakaliamman Temple, there is a good coffee shop that serves curry and *chapati*.

To take a taxi or a bus back to Orchard Rd., turn left onto any of the side streets (you may have to cross one or two intersections) and you will soon come to Jalan Besar, on which the traffic is one-way in the other direction.

SINGAPORE SCIENCE CENTRE

Science Centre Rd., Jurong. Map 1D2 ☎*235-3111* ▩ ✿ *Open Tues–Sun, hols, 10am–6pm. Closed Mon. MRT: Jurong East.*

More than 500 exhibits help visitors to understand the marvels of science. Children (and adults too) can find out how the body works and what creates magnetic attraction; or they can get to grips with the principles of flight, in the **Aviation Gallery**.

There is a changing program of **Omnimax movies** *(8 shows daily, 10am-10pm),* and a twice-daily **Planetarium show** that illustrates how the Earth is influenced by the sun and the moon. Be prepared to drag your children kicking and screaming from the "**Crazy Rooms**" — custom-built for child-sized experience of science. They simply refuse to leave so much fun behind.

SINGAPORE ZOOLOGICAL GARDENS

Mandai Lake Rd. Map 1C3 ☎*269-3411* ⌧*367-2974* ▩ ✦ ▣ ✿ *Open 8.30am–6pm. Take SBS bus 137 from MRT Toa Payoh Station, or bus 171 from MRT Yishun Station or TIBS bus 926 on Sun, hols. A Zoo Express leaves twice daily from major hotels* ☎*235-3111 or 732-2123 (fare includes zoo admission and stop at* **Mandai Orchid Gardens***). By car take Pan Island Expressway w toward Jurong to Bukit Timah Expressway N to zoo exit. Breakfast at 9am or High Tea with an Orang Utan at 4pm daily (except Sun, hols) must be reserved in advance.*

Acclaimed by zoologists and tourists as one of the best to be found anywhere, and averaging more than a million visitors a year, Singapore's zoo is set in 28ha (170 acres) of parkland next to a lake. There are more than 1,600 animals in residence, representing 170 different species, 50 percent of which are endangered species from Southeast Asia. You will see no animals degraded here. Most of them are restrained not by bars but by natural barriers such as water or rock walls.

A **Children's Zoo**, where children can feed and play with tame animals, and two 30-minute animal shows every day, are special attractions. Another is the world's first **Night Safari Park**, opening in 1994, on a 40-ha (99-acre) site adjoining the zoo. The concept is a marriage of zoo and national park, set in hilly secondary jungle. It is being developed, at a cost of S$60 million, under the guidance of specialists such as Lyn de Alwis, former director of national parks and the National Zoological Gardens in Sri Lanka, who are coordinating the collection of species from all over the world.

The park (as it name suggests, it will open at night) will provide a rare opportunity to see nocturnal animals in their active state, illuminated sufficiently to enable them to be seen, but not so much as to send them scuttling for cover.

The emphasis of this new attraction will be on protecting and nurturing endangered species — such as the *anoa* or dwarf buffalo, the Nepalese rhinoceros, the Indian *ghavial* or fish-eating crocodile, the Malayan tiger and the golden cat. There will also be Asian elephants, tapirs, cattle and deer.

The animals will be viewed from either a 1.3km (1-mile) footpath or a 3km (2-mile) tram route along two loops. First to open will be an East Loop, for Asian wildlife. An eventual West Loop will host animals from Latin America and Australia. Initially, about 1,200 animals of 100 species will find a new home in Singapore.

Why a "night safari"? The fact is that 90 percent of tropical animals are nocturnal. This limits what can be seen in a zoo, such as the existing one, in which only 25 percent of the animals exhibited are nocturnal. About 600,000 visitors a year are expected.

SIONG LIM TEMPLE (Shuang Lin Si — Buddhist) ▥

184E Jalan Toa Payoh. Map 2D5 ☎251-1836 ▧ Bus 64, 65, 92, 106.
MRT: Toa Payoh Station.

This is one of the largest and most impressive Chinese Buddhist temples, built between 1898 and 1908. Within the walls are many marble Siamese Buddhas, and at the entrance are the **Four Guardian Warriors**. The central point of the temple is the inner sanctuary, which contains a statue of **Gautama Buddha** perpetually surrounded by burning incense. The goddess **Kuan Yin** has a shrine here too, overlooking the gardens.

About 12 monks and two or three nuns live in rooms within this temple and willingly explain to visitors the significance of the different statues. Visitors need not remove their shoes unless they wish to enter the special shrine. The monks will indicate when this is required. You may want to leave a small donation.

SRI MARIAMMAN TEMPLE (Hindu) ▥ ★

244 South Bridge Rd. Map 4D4 ☎223-4064 ▧ Open 5am–11.30pm.
Recommended times to visit: 8–11.30am, 6–9pm. Bus 124, 167, 174, 143.

The oldest Hindu Temple in Singapore began its life in 1827 as a wood and thatched-roof shrine. By 1844 it had been rebuilt of stone and had almost reached its present size. Since then, it has frequently been re-faced and redecorated. As recently as 1984, sculptors from southern India undertook restoration work. The temple is in the Chinatown area and stands as a reminder of a time when Indians also lived s of the Singapore River.

The temple is easily recognizable from the road because its front wall is decorated with almost life-sized, enameled cows resting on top at 5–6m (16-foot) intervals. They are of a light blue/gray color and wear garlands around their necks.

The **entrance tower** (*gopuram*) is elaborately arrayed with figures of gods and goddesses surrounded by brightly dressed attendants in a processional tableau. By some accounts, there are thousands of Hindu deities, all of whom seem to be carved into entrance towers of temples. The Sri Mariamman Temple shows only 72 deities — but then it's small.

The fire-walking festival, **Thimithi**, takes place at this temple in October or early November, dedicated to the goddess Droba-Devi. It takes place in the courtyard, where entranced devotees walk over a 4m/13-foot-long pit of burning coals. Although the festival begins at 3pm, the temple crowds arrive several hours beforehand.

SRI PERUMAL TEMPLE (Hindu) ★
397 Serangoon Rd. Map 2D5 🚌 *Bus 23, 64, 65, 111.*

This began as a simple shrine until its expansion in 1855. Like most Hindu temples, it has a brightly colored entrance tower, and the figures are painted in pastel blues and pinks. During the festival of **Thaipusam**, this temple is the gathering center for petitioners with pierced bodies (see page 49). From here they walk in procession to the CHETTIYAR TEMPLE.

SULTAN MOSQUE 🏛
North Bridge Rd. Map 4B5 ☎ *293-4405. Open 5am–9.30pm.*

Part of Stamford Raffles' deal for purchasing Singapore from the Sultan of Johore was that the British East India Company should underwrite the cost of a mosque, which was built on this site in 1825. Completely reconstructed with its large golden dome in 1928, the Sultan Mosque (illustrated on page 24) is the largest in Singapore. Its high dome and minarets can be seen from several streets away.

The prayer hall is massive, with walls inscribed with passages from the Koran; non-Muslims can view it only from the upper gallery. Five times a day, the *muezzin* chants to call Muslims to prayer *(at dawn, 12.30pm, 4pm, sunset and 8.15pm)*. Noon on Friday is a special time of worship for Muslims, and the hall then becomes crowded with men at prayer. Visitors who would like to see inside should telephone beforehand and make arrangements with the attendants.

There is a strict **dress code**, especially for women (arms and legs must be covered at all times), and photographs should not be taken without permission.

TAN SI CHONG SU TEMPLE (Chen Shi Zong Ci) 🏛
15 Magazine Rd. Map 3D3 🚌

The small but ornate Tan Si Chong Su Temple was built in 1876. The roof at the front of the temple was restored in 1964, but the one at the rear is original. It was built by the Tan clan and is an ancestral temple and assembly hall. The original building materials were brought to Singapore from China as ballast for sailing junks.

An attendant will read your fortune for the day from a numbered bamboo joss stick — you shake a number of them in a bamboo pot until one falls out, and the number on the stick corresponds to a text in the temple keeper's book. A simpler way is to use the two crescent-shaped blocks (usually kept in front of the temple's main god). Devotees first make an offering, then say a prayer stating the question. The divining blocks are then thrown on the floor before the altar. If both blocks fall with the flat side down, the answer is no. If only one falls with the flat side down, it is yes. Both flat sides up means yes/no.

TANG DYNASTY CITY
Jalan Ahmad Ibrahim. Map 1D2 ☎271-6111. MRT: Jurong East.
This is Singapore's answer to Universal Studios in Burbank, California or Shaw Brothers' Studios in Hong Kong — a massive, 12ha (30-acre) walled city with architectural reproductions of what was the great city of Chang-An, capital of China's Tang dynasty and home of the first emperor in what is now Xian province in China — fully equipped with three separate studio blocks for local and overseas film producers to crank out ever more *kung fu* movies.

The theme park, which claims to be the largest cultural and historical theme park in Asia, can accommodate 3,000 guests at any one time, 2,000 of whom can eat together in its banqueting hall. It is designed to take visitors through re-created scenes of historical anecdotes. These include the seven-story **pagoda of the Monkey God**, with appropriate acrobatics, and the **replica of Emperor Tang Tai Zong's palace** and the **Hua Ching Pool**, beside which he whiled away his time with the concubine, Yang Kwei-Fei, while his empire was whittled away.

There is, of course, an **Underground Palace**, where 1,200 reproductions of the **terracotta armored warriors** who guard the Yellow Emperor's tomb in Xian stand ready to amuse.

TANJONG PAGAR CONSERVATION AREA
Tanjong Pagar, Craig and Neil Rds. Map 4E4.
The once-dowdy shophouses in this maze of winding lanes are as bright as new paint, having undergone the thorough treatment characteristic of the city's approach to preserving its past. In this flagship of Singapore's conservation policy, a host of traditional crafts, such as lacquer painting, wood carving and flower arranging, flourish in its crafts center (see SHOPPING, page 124). It is an excellent place to wander around in, with no shortage of restaurants and pubs (see NIGHTLIFE, pages 116–7).

TEMPLE OF A THOUSAND LIGHTS (Qian Fo Si)
371 Race Course Rd. Map 2D5 🔲 Open 7.30am–4pm. Bus 64, 65, 92, 106.
Sakya Muni Buddha Gaya Temple, or the Temple of a Thousand Lights, was built in the 1950s in the SERANGOON ROAD area by a Thai monk called Vutthisasara.

Inside the temple is the 15m/50-foot **Buddha** figure (illustrated opposite), encircled by lights, which gave the temple its name. These are illuminated when a donation is made.

Around the base of the massive Buddha, Vutthisasara carved the story of Gautama's search for Enlightenment. He also collected other relics from the Buddha's life, including bark from what Buddhists believe is the original Bodhi tree in India under whose shade Buddha Gautama passed from this world.

THIAN HOCK KENG TEMPLE (Tian Fu Gong) 𝕀𝕀𝕀
158 Telok Ayer St. Map 4E4 ☎222-2651 ⊡ Open 6.30am–5.30pm. Bus CBD1 to Robinson Rd., or MRT Tanjong Pagar Station, then walk.

The Thian Hock Keng Temple, or the Temple of Heavenly Happiness, was completed in 1841. It is the oldest Chinese temple in Singapore and is probably the most important to the Hokkien-dialect Chinese. Their temples represent a combination of beliefs, called Shenism, which melds elements of Buddhism, Taoism and Confucianism. Immigrants from Amoy (Hokkiens) built a *joss* house (or temple) on this site in 1821, and dedicated it to the Mother of the Heavenly Sages and Goddess of the Sea (Ma-Chu-Po). A carved figure of her was brought from China in 1840 to adorn the new temple, still to be seen in her shrine in the inner courtyard.

Also from the homeland are intricately carved roof-ornaments, including many dragons, and an inscribed memorial plaque from the Chinese Emperor of the time.

TIGER BALM GARDENS   See HAW PAR VILLA.

Buddha, Temple of a Thousand Lights

Singapore:
where to stay

Making your choice

The rise and rise of Singapore as one of the commercial capitals of the dynamic Pacific Basin has been in tandem with a boom in the hotel business. Glittering executive palaces dot the skyline, as expensive and as uniform as a string of pearls, with a full complement of atriums, imported Cantonese and French chefs, and gymnasiums to tone up the executive muscles.

Tourism in Singapore is a S$8.7 billion industry. About six million tourists, nearly three times the resident population, visited the country in 1992. To cater to these multitudes, there are now some 70 hotels with 26,000 hotel rooms, and most of these are of international or first-class standard. By 1996, the number of hotels is projected to rise to 89, with more than 31,500 rooms.

The mid-1980s saw occupancy rates plummet to 45 percent, due to over-building, but today accommodation is again at a premium, with rates at around 80 percent. This makes it essential to reserve in advance.

RESERVATIONS AND PRICES
Reservations can be made direct through the hotels' booking services, which usually quote the standard "rack rates." Ask if packages or corporate rates are available. Another option is to reserve through a travel agent, who will usually benefit from lower rates. First-class hotels add a 10-percent service charge to the bill, and there is a four-percent government tax.

Air conditioned rooms in middle-range hotels are available at budget travelers' rates. Prices in smaller hotels usually include the service charge and tax, but you should always check if that is so. There are some lower-priced hotels, particularly in Bencoolen St., where backpackers can find basic dormitory accommodation.

The Singapore Tourist Promotion Board (STPB) offers a free booklet, *Singapore Budget Hotels,* listing more than 60 hotels in six room-rate categories, starting from S$20 and below up to S$71–S$100.

WHAT TO EXPECT
Most of Singapore's hotels fall into the deluxe or first-class categories. The city has its fair share of grand old hotels in dignified colonial buildings, notably the legendary **Raffles** (renovated and reopened in 1991) and the **Goodwood Park**. More common, inevitably, are the

towering concrete slabs, with predictable comforts, but little to choose between them.

Rooms are uniformly plush, lobbies favor multistory atriums, IDD telephones are standard, televisions feature teletext messages with airline schedules, and furnishings include self-lock safes in the closets. Good 24-hour **room service** can be expected. **Swimming pools** (🏊) and **health clubs** (💪) — which may include anything from sauna (🛁) and massage facilities to a fully-fledged gym with instruction from professional body-builders — are also common fare in mid-range through deluxe-class hotels. All rooms are **air conditioned**, and have **color TV** and **private bathroom** unless otherwise indicated.

A recent phenomenon has been the appearance of the **resort hotel,** notably the two on **Sentosa Island**, where easy access to the business and commercial centers of the city is combined with palm-fringed tropical beaches and a welter of theme-park attractions.

Virtually all hotels now have **business centers** (💻) and most have created separately serviced, privileged and priced **executive floors** or "clubs." These go by prestigious names, such as Dynasty Club, and offer guests a blend of perquisites ranging from late check-in/out to free extras such as newspapers, laundry, breakfast, fruit basket and evening cocktail. Some also offer separate meeting rooms, concierge services and reading lounges.

Singapore Hotels, a free guide published by the STPB, profiles almost 80 hotels. A useful information source is the *Singapore Yellow Pages Buying Guide,* 26 pages of which are devoted to hotels and hostels.

FOOD AND DRINK
In most large hotels the following are now *de rigueur:* two or more Asian food outlets, typically Japanese and Chinese, a French, Italian or "Continental" restaurant (🍽) and a disco, *karaoke* bar or live music pub (🎵) in the basement.

Breakfast is charged separately (unless included in a package) but is reasonably priced in most hotels, often with a choice of Continental, American or local dishes, such as meat or fish *congee* and *nasi lemak* (rice cooked in coconut and served with fish and spices). For a local breakfast, try **The Good Earth** *(Shenton House, 3 Shenton Way, map 4 E4).*

TIPPING
This is officially discouraged in hotels. A service charge is added to all bills, but if you are really pleased with someone's assistance, why not show it and leave him/her a tip?

LOCATION
Singapore is small and compact and, for most purposes, it matters little where you choose to stay. Getting around is easy by taxi or MRT, and unless you are walking in the equatorial sun, distances are short. Singapore is a city of distinct districts, which are seldom contiguous for pedestrian purposes. Shopping and commercial complexes have replaced shaded walkways. Wide streets, with footbridges for crossing

them, are made for easy movement of cars, not people, and jaywalkers risk stiff fines.

The combination of the heat and the distance between districts conspires to make the city somewhat inhospitable to all but the most devoted walkers. In a place whose ultramodern identity owes so much to the power of the planners, vehicular transport seems to have been decreed as the politically correct way of getting from A to B.

If you are determined to buck the trend and take to the streets on foot, it is worth noting the district within which your hotel is located and others within close walking distance. Most of the international and first-class hotels are concentrated in three areas: most are on **Orchard Rd.** and **Scotts Rd.**, the recognized tourist and premier shopping belt developed in the 1970s. The **Raffles City** complex boasts what is claimed to be "the world's tallest hotel" at 73 stories, plus others in and near Singapore's largest convention complex; and **Marina Square**, billed as "the city within a city" and developed, with Raffles City, in the mid-to-late 1980s, includes three large hotels.

Havelock Rd., close to **Chinatown**, has a half-dozen hotels, and more are to be found in the older parts of town around **Coleman St.** and **Bras Basah Rd.**, an area containing such historic colonial landmarks as the City Hall, Supreme Court, St Andrew's Cathedral, the Esplanade and Boat Quay. Others are scattered around the fringes of these hotel areas, and some are tucked away in the residential areas, with peaceful, green surroundings.

Many hotels are high-rise with good panoramic views of the city and its surroundings, and those close to the waterfront have beautiful sea views. The **Mandarin Singapore** on Orchard Rd. has a revolving restaurant atop its 40 stories, as does the **Pan Pacific Singapore** (37 stories) in Marina Sq. The **Westin Stamford**, at Raffles City, has a stationary bar and restaurant tucked into its 70th and 71st floors. From this vantage point, you can look out beyond Singapore, toward Malaysia and Indonesia (N and S respectively).

HOW TO USE THIS CHAPTER

- **Symbols**: See the KEY TO SYMBOLS on page 7 for an explanation of the full list.
- **Prices**: The prices corresponding to our price symbols are based on average charges for two people staying in a double room with bathroom or shower. For this purpose, breakfast and tax are not included. Although actual prices will inevitably increase, our relative price categories are likely to stay the same. **Singapore dollars** are quoted here.

Symbol	Category	Current price
▨▨▨	very expensive	over S$300
▨▨	expensive	S$200–300
▨	moderate	S$100–300
▨	inexpensive	S$80–100
▢	cheap	under S$80

HOTELS CLASSIFIED BY PRICE

VERY EXPENSIVE ▥
Beaufort Singapore Sentosa
  Island
Duxton
Goodwood Park
Hyatt Regency Singapore
Mandarin Singapore
Marina Mandarin
Oriental
Pan Pacific
Raffles
Regent
Shangri-La
Westin Plaza

EXPENSIVE ▥
Allson
Amara
Crown Prince
Dynasty
Holiday Inn Park View
Imperial Singapore
King's
Meridien Changi
Meridien Singapore
New Otani
Novotel Orchid
Omni Marco Polo
Royal Holiday Inn Crowne Plaza
Shangri-La Sentosa Beach
Sheraton Towers
Singapore Hilton International

Westin Stamford
York

**MODERATELY PRICED TO
EXPENSIVE** ▥ to ▥
ANA Singapore
Inn of the Sixth Happiness

MODERATELY PRICED ▥
Bencoolen
Cockpit
Concorde
Furama
Garden
Lion City
Orchard
Singapore Paramount
Singapore Peninsula

INEXPENSIVE ▥
Broadway
Harbour View Dai-ichi
Ladyhill
Metropole
RELC International House
Royal
Sea View
Sloane Court
YMCA

CHEAP ▢
Cameron
Lloyd's Inn

RAFFLES — SINGAPORE'S LANDMARK HOTEL 🏛 ✿
Corner of 1–3 Beach Rd. Map 4C5 ☎337-1886 ◰RS 39028 ◳339-7650
▥ *104 suites* AE ◉ ◎ VISA ⇥ 🍴 ≋ ♨ ♬ 💺
Location: On the E side of the city, close to the harbor front, with Orchard Rd. shopping within easy walking distance to the E. It seems that every city in Asia has at least one hotel that has transcended the commercial concerns of hostelry and become part of the city's cultural life. In Singapore that hotel is the Raffles.

"Raffles stands for all the fables of the exotic East," wrote Somerset Maugham, who often stayed there: fables such as that of the tiger shot under the billiard table by a guest at the turn of the century (like all good fables, although not true, it ought to be). The hotel was once probably better known in the West than its host city (Singapore was famous for one thing only: the Singapore Sling sundowner, concocted at Raffles **Long Bar** in 1915). The Long Bar was rebuilt, in a new wing, in the 1980s.

Even if you can't afford a room here, no stay in Singapore would be complete without a visit to Raffles, and the obligatory Singapore Sling in the **Writers' Bar**. Raffles opened as a "tiffin room" in 1886, serving lunches to the expatriate elite. By the boom years of the 1920s it had become the "Savoy of Singapore," attracting a world elite of princes and potentates, writers and stars of stage and screen. However, by the time former general manager Roberto Pregarz was appointed in 1972, his predecessor was predicting that it would be pulled down within six months.

Instead, Raffles flourished into its second century — a bit seedy, and the floorboards creaked, but a *grande dame* all the same. It was designated a National Monument in 1987. Finally, in 1989, the old girl was shut down for a well-earned, S$100 million facelift, and the addition of a S$51 million extension, similar in concept to the refurbishment of Bangkok's legendary Oriental, but with far more sensitivity to maintaining its architectural elegance.

The original 127 rooms have been cut back to 104 suites, furnished in "colonial style." More than 400 pieces of original furniture and some 8,000 pieces of silver and chinaware from its early days have been used or are on display in the made-up lady's new quarters.

Reopened in September 1991, the new Raffles has already reclaimed its role as the jewel in the crown of Singapore tourism, winning an array of international plaudits: in 1993 it was judged "Top Individual Hotel" in Berlin's prestigious TTG Europa European Travel Awards series, edging out Bangkok's Oriental and Hong Kong's Regent hotels. It is also ranked among the top in the American Express (UK and Europe) list of "Best Hotels of the World." In 1992 it was voted "Urban Sanctuary of the Year" by the US-based *Hideaway Report,* which also cited it for having the "World's Best Hotel Breakfast."

The management has succeeded brilliantly in packaging the hotel's history, and the prestigious identity it has always sought to promote, into a kind of architectural theme park. Key public areas have been restored as food and beverage outlets; **The Bar and Billiard Room** is now a dining area, retaining its billiard tables only for decorative effect. (A display case of old photos abruptly shatters the myth of the tiger shot under one of the tables in 1902, by explaining that it was actually shot under the building, which was at the time elevated.)

Famous-name suites have retained their period furnishings, and have been decked out with photographs of the person in question (Charlie Chaplin, Noel Coward, Somerset Maugham are some of the names).

There is also the **Raffles Hotel Museum** and **Museum Shop** *(open daily 10am–9pm),* with all manner of memorabilia, genuine and reproduction, as well as several shops done out in period garb, which are in fact the usual hotel bookshop, pharmacy and sundries store.

The Raffles arcade carefully follows the look of the renovated buildings beside it and contains a number of dining outlets, including the famous **Long Bar,** in which the Singapore Sling was created in 1915, as well as 70 specialty shops and international designer-label boutiques. There is also the **Tiffin Room**, for traditional afternoon tiffin curry, and

Ah Teng's Bakery, for curry puffs, fragrant breads and a dash of durian ice cream (see also SEAH STREET DELI on page 110).

So much for colonial nostalgia. The cosmetic surgeons have somehow managed to tuck a swimming pool discreetly onto one of the building's roofs, and today's Raffles bows quietly to the perquisites attached to a *grand luxe* hotel of the 1990s, with the inclusion of a business center, conference rooms and a fitness gym.

Singapore's hotels A to Z

ALLSON
101 Victoria St., Singapore 0718
☎336-0811 ℞RS 21151 ℻339-7019.
Map 4C5 〓 *412 rms, 27 suites* AE ▣
▣ 〓 ☵ 〓 〓 〓 〓 〓 〓
Location: Near Raffles City Convention Centre, beside the Bras Basah Shopping Complex. This is a luxury hotel, formerly the Tai-Pan Ramada. Lavish use is made throughout of Italian marble, with delectable Chinese *objets d'art* and antiques, including Ching Dynasty screen paintings and sculptures. The facilities include a nonsmoking floor and long-stay serviced apartments. There is also a Chinese restaurant, Western grill room and *karaoke* lounge.

AMARA
165 Tanjong Pagar Rd., Singapore 0208
☎224-4488 ℞RS 55887 ℻224-3910.
Map 4E4 〓 *332 rms* AE ▣ ▣ 〓
〓 〓 〓 〓 〓
Location: Close to the Tanjong Pagar conservation district, Chinatown Plaza and People's Park Shopping Complex in Chinatown. Five minutes by car from the World Trade Centre or on foot from an MRT station, this hotel is well located for business, smack dab within the city's financial district, and near an area of preserved row houses of architectural interest surrounding Chinatown Plaza. Royal Club floors offer late check-in and check-out, among other perks. There is a choice of oriental eateries: the **Fragrant Hill** restaurant serves Sichuan cuisine, while the **Thanying**'s specialty is Thai food. If neither of these suits, the **Chicago Grill**, the **Tivoli** restaurant and the **Scanwicherie** snack shop

speak for themselves, unlike the **Wall Street Pub**, which is actually a *karaoke* bar. The fitness facilities include squash courts and a jogging track. The shopping annex has more than 200 outlets.

ANA SINGAPORE
16 Nassim Hill, Singapore 1025
☎732-1222 ℞RS 21817 ℻235-1516.
Off map 3B1 〓 *to* 〓 *456 rms* AE ▣
▣ 〓 〓 〓 〓 〓 〓 〓
Location: Exclusive position, in the embassy district and within walking distance of Orchard Rd. Lush greenery, a mock turn-of-the-century lobby with rich wood paneling, crystal chandeliers, antique tapestries, Carrara marble and an excellent grill room all distinguish this luxurious hotel. An Executive Floor offers special guest privileges. The hotel is only a short walk from the Singapore Handicraft Centre and the Botanic Gardens, from which the hotel disco draws its name, **Ridley's** (after Henry Ridley, who brought the rubber tree to Singapore). It is part of the hotel chain associated with All Nippon Airways (ANA) that is growing in tandem with the expansion of ANA's air routes throughout the region. Its Bangkok sister is the ANA Grand Pacific.

BEAUFORT SINGAPORE SENTOSA ISLAND
Bukit Manis Rd., Sentosa, Singapore 0409
☎275-0331 ℞RS 39133 ℻275-0228.
Map 1F4 〓 *214 rms, 4 garden villas* AE
▣ ▣ 〓 〓 〓 〓 〓 〓 〓 〓 〓
Location: At the extreme SE stop on the monorail system, off Allan Brooke Rd., set between two 18-hole golf courses.

This looks and feels like the Oriental mansion of a wealthy corporate recluse; a maze of columned pavilions facing reflecting pools dotted with tastefully placed water lilies, shaded by steeply pitched red teak roofs. The guest rooms feature "built-in" sofas and walls paneled in burlwood. The S$100 million property opened in 1991, designed by renowned Kerry Hill Architects, with interiors by the French firm, Design Realisation.

Unlike Sentosa Island's other hotel, the SHANGRI-LA SENTOSA BEACH resort, this is no family playground. Strictly business. Even the main swimming pool is tiled in a restrained midnight blue. The superb sports facilities, including a de-salinated exercise pool, squash courts and gym with state-of-the-art machines, are shunted some distance away. Tennis instruction is managed by an American firm that provides pro-fessionally-rated coaches to sports centers around the world. Golfers should be satisfied with a location be-tween Sentosa's two manicured 18-hole courses, Tanjong and Serapong (tee-off at Tanjong starts across the road from the hotel's entrance). As you would ex-pect on Sentosa, jogging and cycling routes are plentiful, and good public beaches are easily accessible.

For those who find any human com-pany too much to bear (and who can afford S$2,000 a night), there are four two-bedroom Garden Villas set in se-cluded corners of the grounds. Each villa has its own midnight-blue swim-ming pool, garden terrace and stereo sound system in a magnificent sitting and dining room, under a vaulted teak ceiling. Beyond the waiters and house-keepers, who come and go in golf carts, there's no need to see another human soul for the duration of your stay.

BENCOOLEN
47 Bencoolen St., Singapore 0718
☎336-0822 ⊠RS 42380 ⊠336-4384.
Map **4B4** ▥ 62 rms ▩ ▦ ▬ (no cards in ▬) ❄ ◁€ ▦ ▱
Location: In a busy, crowded street of Chinese shophouses and budget hotels.
This one, at the upper end of the scale,

is a ten-story building topped by a roof-top restaurant, **The Roof Garden**. It is within walking distance from the Na-tional Museum and Art Gallery, several churches and Singapore's main syna-gogue, Magnain Aboth.

BROADWAY
195 Serangoon Rd., Singapore 0821
☎292-4661 ⊠RS 36714 ⊠291-6414.
Map **4A5** ▥ 63 rms ▬ ▣ ▩ ▦ ▱
Location: On a busy street in an old district. In a modern, seven-story build-ing, set in the center of Little India's old shophouse district, the Broadway may be unpretentious, but it is perfectly ad-equate.

CAMERON
547 Upper Changi Rd., Singapore 1648
☎545-1816 ⊠545-6602 ▥ 24 rms.
No cards.
Location: 16km (10 miles) from the city center, close to the Airport and Changi Beach, in a quiet, middle-class resi-dential area. Near Simei MRT Station.
This is a small, simple and inexpensive choice — there's no restaurant, but a caterer provides good, simple meals.

COCKPIT
Penang Rd., 6/7 Oxley Rise, Singapore 0923 ☎737-9111 ⊠RS 21366 ⊠737-3105. Map **3C3** ▥ 176 rms
▣ ▣ ▩ ▦ ▬ ❄ ◁€ ▼ ▱
Location: Near Orchard Rd. In its orig-inal, colonial incarnation, this hotel was a favorite with aircrews: hence the name. It was rebuilt in 1972, in a style pur-ported to be Georgian, with pseudo-colonial decor. Queen Elizabeth II stayed here that year, but her suite has since been turned into a boardroom. A com-fortable place to stay, the Cockpit has Sichuan and Cantonese restaurants as well as a 24-hour coffee shop, and a daily "Instant Asia" cultural show.

CONCORDE
317 Outram Rd., Singapore 0316
☎733-0188 ⊠RS 50141 ⊠733-0989.
Map **3D2** ▥ 497 rms, 26 suites
▣ ▣ ▩ ▦ ▬ ▭ ◁€ ▨ ▰ ▼ ▱
Location: In the Havelock Rd. area, on

the edge of Chinatown. This 27-story tower of brown glass is imposing, although the decor — a hybrid of contemporary and Oriental — is not without its clashes. Originally destined to be the Hotel Nikko, it was taken over by an Italian hotel group, leading to an engaging mix of styles. Four of the 26 suites are in Japanese style, down to *tatami* mats (for sleeping on) and Japanese hot baths (for use *after* you have washed). The Concorde Floors provide all the pampering a busy executive could ever need, including its own pool. The hotel complex houses 30 shops, Chinese and Japanese restaurants, and a poolside terrace serving local specialties. A useful plus is the free shuttle service to Chinatown and the CBD.

CROWN PRINCE
270 Orchard Rd., Singapore 0923
☎732-1111 ⌷RS 22819 Ⓕ732-7018.
Map **3**B3 ⫸ 303 rms AE Ⓞ Ⓒ VISA
≈ ◁€ ≋ 🏊 ⚐

Location: At the heart of downtown Orchard Rd. A bright, cheery hotel, whose two exterior glass-bubble elevators and cauldron-shaped coffeehouse make a distinctive, if confused, architectural statement. Inside, some of the rooms are supplied with steam or whirlpool baths. Authentic Chinese and Japanese cuisine is on offer. Managed by Prince Hotels of Tokyo, the Crown Prince can also boast a feature common in Japanese hotels, a department store.

DUXTON
83 Duxton Rd., Singapore 0208
☎227-7678 Ⓕ227-1232. Map **3**E3
⫸ 49 rms AE Ⓞ Ⓒ VISA ≈ ⚐ 🏊

Location: In the center of the Tanjong Pagar Conservation Area, beside the business district and bordering Chinatown, opposite Selangor's Pewter Museum. This, Singapore's first stab at a "boutique hotel," is a tasteful adaptation of a number of former Chinese shophouses into an inn with a distinctly European flavor. The choice of guest rooms includes nine duplex suites. Some of the best French food in the city is served at its **L'Aigle d'Or** restaurant (see EATING

AND DRINKING, page 105). A free shuttle service (8.15-11am Mon-Sat), laid on by the hotel, ferries hotel guests to and from the busy Shenton Way/Orchard Rd. area.

DYNASTY
320 Orchard Rd., Singapore 0923
☎734-9900 ⌷RS 36633 Ⓕ733-5251.
Map **3**B2 ⫸ 400 rms AE Ⓞ Ⓒ VISA
≈ ◁€ ≋ 🏊 ⚐

Location: At the corner of Orchard Rd. and Scotts Rd. It takes more than a 33-story, octagonal tower block with a steeply pitched, deep-eaved, green-tiled Chinese roof to make a pagoda, although this is a valiant attempt. The decor is Chinese-opulent, in rich Coromandel reds: the three-story atrium lobby is bedecked with carved teak murals of legendary Chinese warriors, and has a staircase styled after drawings by a leading local artist and created by craftsmen brought from Shanghai. Singapore is an international crossroads, and the Dynasty is right at the main intersection, where Scotts meets Orchard Rd. You can take a seat at the sidewalk café and watch the world go by; or you can travel about as far from China as one hotel can take you, to **Fabrice's World Music Bar** (see NIGHTLIFE, page 118).

FURAMA
60 Eu Tong Sen St., Singapore 0105
☎533-3888 ⌷RS 28592 Ⓕ534-1489.
Map **4**D4 ⫸ 352 rms AE Ⓞ Ⓒ VISA
≈ ⚐ ≋ ⚐ 🏊 ⚐

Location: In the middle of Chinatown a good base for exploring the bustling alleyways; five minutes' walk from Orchard Rd. The elegant curvilinear architecture, with two descending rows of arched domes falling back from the center to form a sloping triangle, stands out like an Egyptian pyramid among the Furama's neighbors — some old Chinese shophouses and low-cost government apartment blocks bristling with bamboo poles of washing hung out to dry. Facilities include executive floors, with privileges such as advance check-in and late check-out, a choice of Japanese and Chinese restaurants, and an arcade of shops on the third floor linked to two separate shopping centers by an overhead bridge.

GARDEN

14 Balmoral Rd., Singapore 1025
☎235-3344 ☎RS 50999 ⊠235-9730.
Off map 3A2 ▥ *209 rms* AE ◉ ◙ ▦
≡ & ≈ ♈ ☷ ⌂

Location: In a quiet residential area, surrounded by greenery. From outside, it looks more like a block of apartments. Within the precincts of the Garden, however, the vegetation starts to appear. Rooms have balconies overhung with lush foliage, set around a central atrium lobby. All in all, the Garden bears a resemblance to an American courtyard-style motel, *sans* cars, of course, with a roof for cover and a coffeeshop in the parking lot.

GOODWOOD PARK

22 Scotts Rd., Singapore 0922
☎737-7411 ☎RS 24377 ⊠732-8558.
Map 3A2 ▥ *231 rms* AE ◉ ◙ ▦
≡ ♨ ≮ ≈ ☷ ⌂

Location: A short walk from the Orchard Rd. shopping belt. Perched on a promontory over 6ha (15 acres) of very expensive real estate, and oozing elegant, old-world charm, the Goodwood Park is one of the grand hotels of Asia. In 1899, the original building was the Teutonia Club, designed by Bidwell, the architect of Raffles Hotel. Later it became an entertainment palace for the gentry, and in 1929 a hotel, which has since been much added to. In 1978 the 19thC wing was restored as an historic landmark. An extravagantly plush hotel, the Goodwood has an excellent choice of dining, including some of the city's choicest Chinese cuisine, at the **Min Jiang Sichuan** (see EATING AND DRINKING) and **Chang Jing Shanghai**. The **Gordon Grill** has a continental menu, Japanese specialties are offered at the **Shima**. Informal seafood grills *(dian xin)* are available at the poolside **Garden Seafood Restaurant**.

HARBOUR VIEW DAI-ICHI

81 Anson Rd., Singapore 0207

☎224-1133 ☎RS 40163 ⊠222-0749.
Map 4E4 ▥ *420 rms* ≡ AE ◉ ◙ ▦
≈ ♈ ☷ ⌂

Location: A block either way from Shenton Way business district and Chinatown. This Japanese-managed property features two special *tatami* suites for homesick Tokyo businessmen and anyone else who likes to sleep Japanese-style. Executive Floors provide the usual amenities. *Sashimi* and other raw fish delights are served downstairs in the **Kurumaya Japanese Restaurant**, but there is also a steak house for stray Westerners, and a Cantonese eatery that caters mainly to tour parties from Hong Kong and South China. Tanjong Pagar MRT station is nearby.

HILTON INTERNATIONAL

581 Orchard Rd., Singapore 0923
☎737-2233 ☎RS 21491 ⊠732-2917.
Map 3B2 ▥ *406 rms and 12 suites*
AE ◉ ◙ ▦ ≡ & ♨ ≮ ≈ ♈ ☷ ⌂

Location: In the main shopping belt, snugly set between Forum Galleria and Far East Shopping Centre. Until the early 1980s, the Hilton chain was the benchmark of excellence for other Asian hoteliers. Things are different now, however, with new Asian-based hotel chains striding ahead of the field, more leading US and European management groups in competition, and the London-based management company under new ownership. The comfortable Singapore Hilton, however, with its reliably high standards, happily hasn't changed. Its rooftop swimming pool offers a breathtaking view of the island. Twelve exclusive suites were styled by Givenchy and are served by a volley of butlers and maids. The **Tradewinds** restaurant (see EATING AND DRINKING, page 111) screens current movies, and its foodstalls serve delicious local specialties. Other options are the **Inn of Happiness** (Cantonese) or the **Harbour Grill** (Continental).

HOLIDAY INN PARK VIEW

11 Cavenagh Rd., Singapore 0922
☎733-8333 ☎RS 55420 ⊠734-4593.
Map 3B3 ▥ *320 rms* AE ◉ ◙ ▦
≡ ≈ ♈ ☷ ⌂

Location: Just off Orchard Rd., facing Singapore's Presidential Palace, the Istana. East Asia's Holiday Inns are more upmarket than Americans familiar with their humbler roadside motel origins might expect. The two in Singapore are both deluxe properties. This one has an elegant atrium lobby with lavishly landscaped gardens inside and out: the garden lounge has a four-story waterfall, and the rooms surrounding the atrium have foliage cascading from their inner balconies. The Executive Club has its own floor and access by private elevator key, leading to 12 suites and a lounge where free afternoon tea and cocktails are served. Cantonese, at **Loong Yuen**, and North Indian *tandoori* cuisines are featured, as well as American "cajun" food in the **New Orleans Restaurant**.

HYATT REGENCY SINGAPORE

10–12 Scotts Rd., Singapore 0922
☎733-1188 ☒RS 24415 ☒732-1696.
Map 3B2 ▥ 421 suites 🆎 💳 💳 💳
≡ ✿ ⍾ ∞ ⚲ ♨ ♉ ⌂

Location: Off the Orchard Rd. tourist belt, between two major shopping complexes — Far East Plaza and Scotts. This massive, L-shaped hotel complex was built in the early 1970s and recently renovated to a very high standard. At a cost of S$70 million, 700 rooms were reworked into just over 400 suites. Its cool, restrained lounge area, divided with black lacquer window panels and beveled glass, is a study in mood lighting and coy placements of Asian sculptural artifacts. It also has what must be the classiest hotel bookstore in town — chandelier and all. **Scotts** lounge bar looks out on a vista of 16 man-made waterfalls up to four stories high, hidden above and behind which are two pools (one for laps, another free-form, with one end reserved for children), a jogging track, a state-of-the-art health center, as well as tennis and badminton courts. **Pete's Place**, an Italian eatery, and **Brannigan's** pub, both of which are in the basement, are such Singapore institutions that they were left untouched by the renovators. Also unscathed were

the oddly angled glass entrance doors and fountains out front, in deference to the belief of the Chinese owner in *fung shui* — a Chinese system for obeying the immutable laws of nature, as expressed in geographic configurations that must properly align their direction with the interplay of wind, land and water. Executive floors offer round-the-clock butler and valet services, in addition to other perks such as a private lounge, complimentary coffee, newspaper and cocktails.

IMPERIAL SINGAPORE

1 Jalan Rumbia, Singapore 0923
☎737-1666 ☒RS 21654 ☒737-4761.
Map 3C3 ▥ 600 rms 🆎 💳 💳 💳
≋ ⍽ ⚲ ≡ ♉ ⌂

Location: Near the Chettiyar Temple, just across the street from Fort Canning Park and within walking distance of Orchard Rd. The Imperial is large, comfortable and fully equipped to deluxe standard, but otherwise fairly nondescript. Restaurants feature Continental, Sichuan and North Indian *tandoori* cuisines. The Imperial Club features executive floors with private butlers. Another feature is what may be the only discotheque in the city that offers chess or backgammon boards for non-dancers (who must, presumably, be deaf as well). A free shuttle is laid on to Orchard Rd.

INN OF THE SIXTH HAPPINESS ▥

9–37 Erskine Rd., Singapore 0106
☎223-3266 ☒223-7951. Map 4E4 ▥ to
▥ 48 rms and suites 🆎 💳 💳 💳 ⚲ ≡
Location: Takes up most of a small lane between South Bridge Rd. and Kaday Awallur St., a block NE of Maxwell Rd. on the edge of Chinatown and very near the Tanjong Pagar Conservation Area. The magic of this unique hotel is in its peculiarly Singaporean mood of eclectic Straits Chinese *Chinoiserie*. A row of nine traditional 19thC Chinese shophouses has been converted into a lively dragon's lair (the hotel's Chinese name translates as "Dragon's Gate"). The guest rooms have tubs built for two and rosewood "opium" beds, while the

Heritage Suites contain the famous Chinese covered wedding beds (of impractical proportions for most Westerners). Another delightful touch is the *Kopi-Tiam* (café), featuring Chinese restorative teas and local candies. Manifestly *not* intended to be part of the international upmarket circuit of "boutique hotels," which includes such places as the DUXTON, the Inn of the Sixth Happiness aims at a broader audience of those interested in recalling the experience of Straits Chinese life-style. Part of a Singaporean family business, it has been painstakingly created by the owner, architect Lin Chung Ming and his daughter, Candice Lin.

KING'S

403 Havelock Rd., Singapore 0316
☎733-0011 ▦RS 21931 ▣732-5764.
Map **3D3** ▦ *319 rms* 🅰🅔🅓🆅
🖭 ◖ ⊗ 🍴
Location: Close to Chinatown, with a good view of the river. An older hotel, with a modern extension in the form of a cylindrical 20-story tower. Dorchester Club floors cater to traveling executives. It has contemporary Chinese décor and a largely Asian clientele. The **Tien Court** Chinese restaurant does a good "steamboat" (a sort of northern Chinese fondue). A Japanese department store is nearby.

LADYHILL

1 Ladyhill Rd., Singapore 1025
☎737-2111 ▦RS 23157 ▣737-4606.
Off map **3A1** ▦ *171 rms* 🅰🅔🅓🆅
🍴 🖭 ◖ ⊗
Location: Away from the Orchard Rd. bustle, although not far from it. Request a poolside cabana rather than a standard room in the main building. They cost a bit more, but they are worth it. There is a children's playground, babysitting services and, an interestingly untropical touch, good Swiss *fondue* at **Le Chalet** restaurant. Free shuttle to Orchard Rd.

LION CITY

15 Tanjong Katong Rd., Singapore 1543
☎744-8111 ▦RS 21789 ▣742-5505.

Map **2D5** ▦ *163 rms* 🅰🅔🅓🆅
👥 MRT: Paya Lebar.
Location: In the Malay quarter of Geylang Serai, halfway between the city and Changi Airport. Not quite in the sticks: the hotel has a built-in shopping mall (complete with bank and supermarket), there's a high-rise shopping complex across the road, another one two minutes away *(open to 2am),* and a movie theater next door. There is no food worth mentioning in the hotel, but there are plenty of food centers in the vicinity. The East Coast Sailing Centre (see SPORTS, page 130), is nearby.

LLOYD'S INN

2 Lloyd Rd., Singapore 0923 ☎737-7309
▦RS 21157 ▣737-7847. Map **3C3** ▢
20 rms ◖ 🆅 ⊗ ◖
Location: Off Killiney Rd. in a quiet residential area, five minutes from Orchard Rd. Strictly functional, low-budget accommodation is the attraction of this hotel, near Somerset MRT Station and the Specialists' Shopping Centre. Guest rooms have private bathrooms, but no TV or telephone.

MANDARIN SINGAPORE

333 Orchard Rd., Singapore 0923
☎737-4411 ▦RS 21528 ▣732-2361.
Map **3B3** ▦ *1,200 rms, 52 suites* 🅰🅔
◖ 🆅 ◖ ⊗ ♨ ⚲ 🍴 🖭 🛓
Location: In the main tourist belt. No relation to the famous Hong Kong hotel of the same name, this Asian-owned and managed property is one of the city's great banquet centers. There is probably no Singaporean who has not attended a relative's wedding or special party here. Although both the decor and style of doing things show its age, the Mandarin has been a great anchor of hotel life on Orchard Rd. since the area became a tourist belt 20 years ago. The lobby is all chandeliers and giant, gold-etched murals of Chinese fairies flitting up a white marble wall. The Mandarin Club offers executive floors with the usual extras. In 1992, the hotel ranked 10th, 17th and 37th among leading hotels in the world in reader surveys by *Business Traveller, Conde Nast Travel-*

ler, and *Institutional Investor* magazines. There are squash and tennis courts and a putting green. Chinese, Japanese, English and French cuisines are featured in the restaurants in its two 40-story towers. **The Top of the M** is a rooftop revolving restaurant with panoramic views of the city, stretching out toward Malaysia and Indonesia. **The Library** disco is one of the city's trendiest (see NIGHTLIFE, page 113).

MARINA MANDARIN

6 Raffles Blvd., Marina Sq., Singapore 0103 ☎338-3388 ⊠RS 22299 ⊠339-4977. *Map* **4***C5* ▥ 575 rms ▣ ▣ ▣ ▥ ⟨€ ♨ ⇌ ≋ ♪ ✓ ♈ ♠ ♬

Location: In the Marina Sq. complex near Raffles City. Sister hotel to Singapore's original **Mandarin** and one of the three new hotel complexes that encircle Marina Sq., this luxury property rises like an Egyptian pyramid stage-prop for *Aida* astride Singapore's largest shopping center, **Marina Square**. Every room has a balcony view over the city, Marina Bay, where the Singapore River meets the ocean, or the open sea. The facilities are fit for a pharaoh, with four tennis and two squash courts and three Marina Club executive floors with private butlers and a lounge. Specialty restaurants serve Italian cuisine, at **Ristorante Bologna**, and Cantonese, at **House of Blossoms**.

MERIDIEN CHANGI

1 Netheravon Rd., Singapore 1750 ☎542-7700 ⊠RS 36042 ⊠542-5295 ▥ 280 rms, 4 suites ▣ ▣ ▣ ▥ ⇌ ⟨€ ≋ ♈ ♪ ✓ ♈ ♨ ♬

Location: Off Upper Changi Rd., ten minutes from the airport, 30 minutes from the city and a five-minute walk from Changi Beach. The only accommodation near the airport, this is a luxury resort hotel, with golf, tennis and water-sports available nearby. Free shuttle service to airport and city.

MERIDIEN SINGAPORE

100 Orchard Rd., Singapore 0923 ☎733-8855 ⊠RS 50163 ⊠732-7886. *Map* **3***B3* ▥ 407 rms, 16 suites ▣ ▣

▣ ▥ ⇌ ⟨€ ♨ ≋ ♣ ♨ ♬

Location: In the main shopping belt. An atrium is *de rigueur* in today's deluxe hotel: the Meridien's is a cheery affair with fountains and seven tiers of cascading greenery. The hotel is part of the French-owned Meridien group, linked to Air France, and its **Le Restaurant de France** is said to have the best French cuisine in town (SEE EATING AND DRINKING). Apart from its two French eateries, there is the **Nusa Dua Lagon** Indonesian restaurant. The hotel is part of an exclusive shopping complex with 18 designer-label boutiques and 70 other outlets including **Printemps**, the Parisian department store. Le Club President has its own private floor, with all the usual complimentary services for executive travelers.

METROPOLE

41 Seah St., Singapore 0718 ☎336-3611 ⊠RS 21852 ⊠339-3610. *Map* **4***C5* ▥ 54 rms ▣ ▣ ▣ ▥ ⇌ ♨ ⟨€ ♬

Location: Near the business district. A cozy nine-story hotel favored by Asian visitors. It has a coffeehouse and a Chinese restaurant, and there are several food centers in the vicinity, with good hawker stall fare. Some rooms have harbor views.

NEW OTANI

177A River Valley Rd., Singapore 0617 ☎338-3333 ⊠RS 20299 ⊠339-2854. *Map* **4***C4* ▥ 386 rms ▣ ▣ ▣ ▥ ⇌ ⟨€ ≋ ♈ ♨ ♠ ♬

Location: On the riverbank, close to Chinatown and Orchard Rd. Standard 1st-class luxury is what you get inside this hotel, whose tan color is said to have been chosen for good fortune as, to the Chinese, it suggests gold. Inexplicably, the lobby is on the seventh floor. Although it is Japanese-owned, the New Otani finds favor with Germans and Americans. Most rooms have a good view of the river and old Singapore. There are Chinese and Japanese eateries, and **Trader Vic's** of San Francisco serves exotic eats and drinks from Asia and the South Seas. Nonsmoking floors are available.

NOVOTEL ORCHID INN

214 Dunearn Rd., Singapore 1129
☎250-3322 ᴛᴇᴌRS 21756 ꜰᴀх250-9292
▦ 412 rms ᴀᴇ ⊙ ▣ ▦ & ❤ ≈ ✓ ♈ 🏊 ♨

Location: In a residential area within five minutes' ride of Scotts Rd./Orchard Rd. tourist belt. Set prettily in 2ha (5 acres) of garden, the inn offers extensive outdoor facilities, including cycling, a jogging track and a putting green. Rooms have recently been renovated, and some are adapted for use by disabled guests. The Orchid Club has special rooms and complimentary services for executive travelers. Free nonstop shuttle to Orchard Rd.

OMNI MARCO POLO

247 Tanglin Rd., Singapore 1024
☎474-7141 ᴛᴇᴌRS 21476 ꜰᴀх471-0521.
Off map **3B1** ▦ 603 rms ᴀᴇ ⊙ ▣ ▦
≈ & ❤ ≪ ≈ ♈ 🏊 ♨

Location: In the chic embassy district, quiet, near the Botanic Gardens, and not far from Orchard Rd. Another deluxe hotel: this one is built like a spaceship, to a prizewinning design. Lovely gardens, good service and an excellent French bistro-type restaurant, **La Brasserie**, with provincial food, are some of its attractions. **Le Duc** restaurant offers Continental *haute cuisine* with an extensive wine list. **The Club** disco is in the basement. The Tudor Court Shopping Gallery is next door.

ORCHARD

422 Orchard Rd., Singapore 0923
☎734-7766 ᴛᴇᴌRS 35228 ꜰᴀх733-5482.
Map **3B2** ▦ 350 rms ᴀᴇ ⊙ ▣ ▦
≈ & ≪ ≈ ♨ 🏊 ♨

Location: In the main shopping belt, next to Delfi Orchard shopping complex. The Orchard is quiet and cozy for a big hotel. The Harvesters' Club offers three executive floors with the usual personal and complimentary services. The **Orchard Terrace** sidewalk café is a pleasant vantage point for people-watching on the bustling Orchard Rd. **Blooms** continental restaurant serves more sophisticated fare. Squash, tennis courts and a rooftop pool are available.

ORIENTAL

5 Raffles Ave., Marina Sq., Singapore 0103
☎338-0066 ᴛᴇᴌRS 29117 ꜰᴀх339-9537.
Map **4C5** ▦ 515 rms, 61 suites
ᴀᴇ ⊙ ▣ ▦ ≈ & ≪ ≪ ℀ ✓ ≈ ♈ 🏊 ♨ ⚓ ♨

Location: Marina Sq. This 21-story triangle of luxury accommodation was designed by the world-renowned architect, John Portman. It features an 18-story-high atrium and six observation elevators from which to view it as you rise to the fourth-story lobby. This is the sister to two hotels that consistently vie for honors as "the world's best": the **Mandarin Oriental** in Hong Kong and Bangkok's **Oriental**. Marina Square, the two-story complex over which it towers, along with the MARINA MANDARIN and PAN PACIFIC hotels, contains international department stores, two movie theaters, a supermarket and 240 specialty shops, boutiques and restaurants. In-house gastronimic opportunities include **Fourchettes** for continental and the **Cherry Garden** for both Sichuan and Hunan cuisines. In the unending grand-luxe hotel struggle of luxurious one-upmanship, the Oriental has scored yet another point: an underwater sound system piped into its swimming pool. Other sporting facilities are two squash courts, two tennis courts, and steam baths.

PAN PACIFIC

7 Raffles Blvd., Marina Sq., Singapore 0103
☎336-8111 ᴛᴇᴌRS 38821 ꜰᴀх339-1861.
Map **4C5** ▦ 800 rms ᴀᴇ ⊙ ▣ ▦
≈ ≪ ℀ ✓ ♈ 🏊 ⚓ ♨

Location: Marina Sq. At 37 stories, this is the largest of the Marina Sq. hotels, managed by the Tokyu Hotels International group, a name familiar to Japanese department store *aficionados*. **Hai Tien Lo**, the rooftop Chinese restaurant, offers grand views of harbor, city and neighboring countries. It is built into what appears, from the ground, to be a precarious overhanging platform jutting out like a space station, into which two external bubble elevators vanish. Other restaurants offer Japanese and Polynesian cuisines. The Pacific Floor caters to traveling executives with private access, personal butlers and other privileges. As in the nearby **Oriental**, the swimming pool has an underwater sound system. *Karaoke* must be a challenge.

RAFFLES
See entry on page 87.

REGENT OF SINGAPORE
1 Cuscaden Rd., Singapore 1024
☎733-8888 ᴛᴀRS 37248 ꜰᴀx732-8838.
Map *3B1* ▥▥ 440 rms ᴀᴇ ⊕ ⊙ ᴠ⁄ˢᴬ ⇌ ⴞ ⟨⟨ ⩰ ♈ ⸙ ⵔ

Location: Tanglin area, near the Tudor Court Shopping Gallery. This was the first luxury hotel in Singapore to benefit from those modern standards, an atrium lobby and skylight, and foliage cascading from the balconies. Its outstanding **Summer Palace** Chinese restaurant (see EATING AND DRINKING) benefits from the skills of Cantonese chefs, imported from Hong Kong. By contrast, **Maxim's de Paris** offers French cuisine from the famous Parisian *Belle Époque* eatery of the same name. The seventh floor is reserved for nonsmokers.

RELC INTERNATIONAL HOUSE
30 Orchard Grove Rd., Singapore 1025
☎737-9044 ᴛᴀRS 55598 ꜰᴀx733-9976.
Off map *3A1* ▥ 128 rms ᴀᴇ ⊕ ⊙ ᴠ⁄ˢᴬ ⇌ ⴞ ⟨⟨ ⸙ ⵔ

Location: In a quiet area, next to the Shangri-La hotel. This has all the facilities of a hotel, but with a hostel atmosphere, and it is actually within the premises of the Regional English Language Centre. Many of the guests are visiting scholars, often teachers on training fellowships. There is a designated nonsmoking floor and executive floors, with all the usual amenities for traveling businesspersons.

ROYAL
36 Newton Rd., Singapore 1130
☎253-4411 ᴛᴀRS 21644 ꜰᴀx253-8668
▥ 331 rms ᴀᴇ ⊕ ⊙ ᴠ⁄ˢᴬ ⇌ ⩰ ♈ ⸙
Location: The only hotel in this quiet, middle-class area, convenient for Newton Circus Hawker Centre and 10 minutes' walk from Orchard Rd. The Royal has a shopping arcade, Chinese,

Japanese and Western restaurants, and a facade adorned with large Indonesian murals. American Express Cardholders are entitled to a free breakfast.

ROYAL HOLIDAY INN CROWNE PLAZA
25 Scotts Rd., Singapore 0922
☎737-7966 ᴛᴀRS 21818 ꜰᴀx737-6646.
Map *3B2* ▥▥ 493 rms including 30 suites
ᴀᴇ ⊕ ⊙ ᴠ⁄ˢᴬ ⇌ ⴞ ⟨⟨ ⩰ ⸙ ♈ ⸜ ⵔ
Location: In the main shopping belt, near Far East Plaza and Scotts Shopping Centre. This 15-story hotel is about 20 years old, but was renovated in 1990. As well as an executive floor catering to traveling business executives, the hotel has a wide choice of eating places on offer. The **Cafe Vienna**, in the lobby, is a popular local meeting place. There are other good choices — particularly the special international oyster menu at the **Baron's Table** (which has ceased to serve German cuisine in favor of Continental). The **Sukmaindra** restaurant's highest accolade is its popularity with resident and visiting Malays from Indonesia, Malaysia and Brunei (it has a live cultural show nightly except Thursday). The decor features beautiful textiles from Brunei. **The Bar** is all wooden paneling, brass trim, etched glass mirrors and Georgian furniture in a streetside club style. There is also the **Meisan Sichuan** Chinese restaurant.

Since it has no health center of its own, the hotel offers guest memberships of the **Club Excel** fitness center, with state-of-the-art equipment and a computerized fitness evaluation program. Guests are also allowed to join **Le Spa**, billed as "Singapore's first and only sybarium," which offers the full range of body works and is linked to Termi Di Saturnia in Italy and Doral Saturnia in the United States. Both health clubs are on the hotel premises.

SEA VIEW
Amber Close, Singapore 1543
☎345-2222 ᴛᴀRS 21555 ꜰᴀx348-4335
▥ 435 rms ᴀᴇ ⊕ ⊙ ᴠ⁄ˢᴬ ⇌ ⸜ ⟨⟨ ⩰ ♈ ⸝⁄ ♈ ⸙ ⵔ
Location: Close to the sea, at the East Coast, and Parkway Parade Shopping

Complex. Originally planned as an apartment block, this older hotel offers fine sea and city views, as well as easy access to the sports facilities of East Coast Park. Popular with Australians.

SHANGRI-LA

22 Orange Grove Rd., Singapore 1025
☎737-6888 ⌷RS 21505 ⌷733-7220/
1029. Map 3A1 ▥ *810 rms* ⌷ ⌷ ⌷
⌷ ⌷ ⌷ ⌷ ⌷ ⌷ ⌷ ⌷ ⌷ ⌷

Location: five minutes' walk from the Orchard Rd. shopping belt. One of Singapore's best hotels, and the flagship property of the Kuok group, the Shangri-La is famed for its excellent service, and has been voted one of the world's top hotels by business magazines in Europe, Japan and the United States. "The Shang," as local journalists call it, is attractively set in 6ha ($12\frac{1}{2}$ acres) of landscaped tropical garden with lawns, said to have reduced George and Barbara Bush to speechless admiration on their 1992 state visit to the island republic.

The newer **Valley Wing**, built in 1985 with 24 suites and 112 rooms (each 52sq.m in size), where the ex-presidential couple stayed, is the most exclusive, with its own lobby entrance off Anderson Rd. and furnishings designed for CEO's and heads of state. This is, predictably, reflected in its higher room- and mini-bar rates (about US$10 for a small bottle of nuts). The business center is open 24 hours daily. Even the older **Tower Wing** (1971) and **Garden Wing** (1978) will do any world traveler proud.

This is one of the few hotels in Singapore that boasts of the fact that it has *no* special floors or clubs for business travelers, because every floor and room offers their equivalent in services. Five restaurants include the Japanese **Nadaman**, specialized in the ancient *kaiseki* style of cooking, the excellent **Shang Palace** Chinese restaurant, the **Latour** French restaurant (named for the Chateau Latour vineyard in France, with a wine cellar to match) and a "waterfall café." **Xanadu** is its razzle-dazzle disco (see NIGHTLIFE on page 120).

Extensive recreation facilities in the grounds include a golf putting green, four floodlit tennis courts, two squash courts and both adult and children's pools and an outdoor Jacuzzi. It has one of the city's best-equipped health clubs with yet another "dipping pool" and offers professional fitness and sports instruction. Free shuttle to business and shopping districts. Joggers are shuttled the five minutes' drive to the Botanic Gardens free of charge at 6.30am, returning at 7.30am (maps for joggers, shoppers and businesspersons are provided in guest kits).

SHANGRI-LA SENTOSA BEACH

101 Siloso Rd., Sentosa Island,
Singapore 0409 ☎275-0100 ⌷RS
20817 ⌷275-0355. *Map 2E4* ▥ *459 rms and suites* ⌷ ⌷ ⌷ ⌷ ⌷ ⌷ ⌷
⌷ ⌷ ⌷ ⌷

Location: At the NW end of Sentosa Island, across the road from Underwater World, with its monorail and bus stops. Billed as an escape to "the lighter side of Singapore," this is a daring effort to tap into the market for exclusive resorts close to home. It aims to attract both local conference organizers and business travelers with families in tow, who may want to enjoy offduty watersports and the theme-park world of SENTOSA ISLAND (see pages 74–77) with their families after serious sessions with colleagues in the nearby business district (about a half-hour taxi ride).

The resort opened in March 1993, not long after the opening of a vehicular causeway to the island. It is determinedly informal, with staff decked out in Club Med-style beachwear. For younger visitors, there is the **Playhouse** nursery/playroom, a play-pool with waterslides and directed sports activities from kite-flying to roller skating (not to mention the **Soda Fountain** ice cream bar next door). Playful adults can opt for professional watersports instruction, cycling, beach ball competitions, wall-climbing (for the hardy set) and shared access to the BEAUFORT's tennis courts and instructors. Golf is available at the island's two public courses. The resort's general manager, Benson Puah, runs this happy "Gilligan's Island" with a light touch, cheerfully greeting guests at **The Sandbar** outdoor barbecue pavilion or **Breakers** fun pub and disco, like the captain of television's *Love Boat*.

SHERATON TOWERS
39 Scotts Rd., Singapore 0922
☎737-6888 ⎰RS 37750 ⎙737-1072.
Off map **3A3** ⎏ 407 rms ≒ 🛏
⚅⚄⚃⚂⚁⚀
Location: Near Newton MRT Station and a short walk from the Newton Circus Hawker Centre. **The Terrazza** coffee shop is probably the most distinctive feature of this 21-story tower — diners look out through massive picture windows at the spectacular man-made waterfalls and rock pool. Like its upmarket chain-hotel rivals, Sheraton maintains a high standard of service in all of its many Asian properties. This one has been ranked among the world's top ten hotels by the UK's *Business Traveller* magazine. Specialty restaurants feature Italian cooking at **DOMVS** and Cantonese cuisine at **Li Bai**.

SINGAPORE PARAMOUNT
25 Marine Parade Rd., Singapore 1544
☎344-5577 ⎰RS 22234 ⎙447-4131
⎏ 250 rms ≒ 🛏
Location: In a respectable middle-class district, a short walk from East Coast beach. A mid-range, 12-story hotel with fine views of sea and city. Adjacent to the Paramount Shopping Centre, with three floors of shops and a roller-skating rink. Sister hotel to the PENINSULA and **Excelsior** hotels, with free shuttle to Orchard Rd.

SINGAPORE PENINSULA
3 Coleman St., Singapore 0617
☎337-2200 ⎰RS 21169 ⎙339-3580.
Map **4C4** ⎏ 315 rms ≒ 🛏
Location: In the city's old shopping hub, opposite the Raffles City Shopping Complex; a good base for exploring historic Singapore. Just across the road from ST ANDREW'S CATHEDRAL, and close to the

Armenian Church. There are 20 shops in the arcade, mostly selling electronics and fashion clothes, and several shopping malls nearby. The well-appointed rooms have great views of the harbor and river. The **Golden Million Club** offers cabaret performances much favored by Indonesians.

SLOANE COURT
17 Balmoral Rd., Singapore 1025
☎235-3311 ⎰RS 55058 ⎙733-9041
⎏ 32 rms ≒ 🛏
Location: In an upmarket residential area, across from the Garden Hotel, 10-15 minutes' walk from Orchard Rd. This congenial hotel occupies a Tudor-style building with an old-world English atmosphere, particularly noticeable in the **Balmoral Berkeley** restaurant (a seriously English pub for serious draft beer drinkers), which serves home-cooked meals.

WESTIN PLAZA and WESTIN STAMFORD
2 Stamford Rd., Singapore 0617
☎338-8585 ⎰RS 22206. **Plaza**
⎙338-2862. Map **4C5** ⎏ 796 rms, 40 suites; **Stamford** ☎337-8585
⎙337-1554 ⎏ 1253 rms, 80 suites.
Both ≒ 🛏
Location: One of two hotels within the Raffles City complex, a city-within-a-city with all kinds of recreational, entertainment, shopping and convention facilities, based on New York's Rockefeller Center. The 42-story Westin Plaza has spectacular views of the harbor and city, and is the home of the excellent **Inagiku** Japanese restaurant (see EATING AND DRINKING, page 107). Its other restaurants include Italian, Cantonese and Sichuan cuisines. Rooms are larger than usual, with two "super suites" on the top floor, each of which is equivalent to 14 standard rooms. Its sister hotel, **Westin Stamford** (illustrated, soaring up behind ST ANDREW'S CATHEDRAL, on page 74), is 73 stories high and is billed as the tallest hotel in the world. The two hotels share sports facilities, which are extensive: two swimming pools, four squash courts and six tennis courts. The Executive Club floors offer business

travelers private access, the usual array of personalized services and complimentary privileges.

The hotel also manages the Raffles City Convention Centre in the complex, and there is a 39-story office tower. The **Compass Rose Restaurant and Bar** offers panoramic views from the 70th and 71st floors. **Somerset's Bar** offers live jazz music and **Scandals** is a popular discotheque. There are 16 restaurants altogether in the two hotels.

YMCA OF SINGAPORE/ METROPOLITAN YMCA
1 Orchard Rd., Singapore 0923
☎336-6000 ☎RS 55325 ☎337-3140.
Map 3B2. 111 rms. **Tanglin Centre,** 60 Stevens Rd., Singapore 1025 ☎737-7755
☎RS 56100 ☎235-5528. Map 3B2.
87 rms ⇌ **Both** ▥ ≈ ☂ ⚓ ◇ ⚑
Location: On the main tourist belt and nearby at Tanglin. The first is across from the MRT station and in the middle of the Orchard Rd. tourist action, at much lower prices than its tourist neighbors are paying in deluxe hotels. The

Orchard Rd. hostel houses a **McDonald's** and the **El-Shaddhai Cafeteria**, which serves local fare. The YMCA at Tanglin Centre is nearby, with a full-service restaurant. Both hostels have pools, squash courts, gyms and conference rooms; Orchard Rd. has a business center.

YORK
21 Mount Elizabeth, Singapore 0922
☎737-0511 ☎RS 21683 ☎732-1217.
324 rms. Map 3B3 ▥ ⇌ ▦ ◇ ◎ ▦
⌂ ≈ ⚓ ⚑
Location: Behind the Goodwood Park Hotel, off Scotts Rd. The York's attractions include a suites-only tower and a poolside wing with cabana rooms on two levels. Guests are also entitled to use the facilities of the **Goodwood Park** hotel. The **Balalaika Room,** which was renowned for its Russian borscht and shashlik, closed recently, in favor of the new **Zen** restaurant, which is named for the Japanese Buddhist sect. It serves Thai–Chaozhou Chinese cuisine — a kind of Asian culinary Glasnost.

Singapore:
eating and drinking

Dining out in Singapore

Asians of whatever ilk are rather French about food. It is their passion, and when it comes to eating, most Asian cities are special. But Singapore has the edge on them all, especially from the visitor's point of view. First, the food is consistently good, and few cities can make that claim. Wherever you may choose to eat, there is virtually no risk of being served poor-quality food. The ingredients are fresh, always well cooked, with tasty results. Don't, therefore, be fooled by local opinion: locals are spoiled by all this, and tend to judge anything less than a superb meal as bad. But it never is bad.

It is also safe. Hygiene standards are high: higher than elsewhere in Asia, as good as or better than European countries, and strictly maintained — Asia's fearful stomach bugs are held at bay in Singapore. The water, too, is clean and safe to drink. It would be, of course: that's what Singapore's like, and it's a blessing — in contrast to Jakarta or Bangkok, where Western digestive tracts fall like flies.

WHAT TO EAT

The variety of food in the city is kaleidoscopic, thanks to Singapore's multiracial makeup: all the major and many minor regional cuisines of China and the Indian subcontinent are here, plus Malay/Indonesian food and a liberal sprinkling of the other Asian styles (Japanese, Thai, Korean, Vietnamese), as well as a colonial heritage of British and Continental cooking.

In cuisine, very much as in architecture, this cultural mélange has produced some unique blends, such as the Portuguese- and Malay-influenced Nonya food of the Straits Chinese, and the excellent seafood, where cultures have mixed to produce some spectacularly Singaporean results, like the chili crabs and prawns for which Upper East Coast Rd. became justly famous before its waterfront was reclaimed and its denizens relocated to the seafood centers on East Coast Parkway.

WHERE TO EAT

Hotels dominate the international food scene, as they do throughout Southeast Asia. They will typically feature one or more Continental or European ethnic eateries, such as **Restaurant de France, Pete's Place** and **Prego** and two or more Asian outlets — usually Chinese and Japanese (**Min Jiang Sichuan, Inagiku**) of very high caliber.

It is worth remembering that (unlike in the US and Europe) Asia's very best restaurants, by international standards, are commonly found in hotels, which formed the first air-conditioned family entertainment centers. Outhier, Bocuse and Ken Hom are but the best known names of a very long list of Michelin-starred and star-quality aspirants who regularly parade through the Asian hotels circuit on one- or two-week guest spots, or as consultants with more permanent relationships. Likewise, hotels bring in big-name chefs from Hong Kong and Tokyo. Thumb your nose at your hotel's restaurants and you may miss one of the best meals to be had anywhere, by anyone's standards.

There is a nascent movement toward more upmarket decor and imaginative menus in **freestanding restaurants**, which moves apace with the growing affluence of Asian urbanites. These usually take the form of stylish revivals, the best examples of which in Singapore are **Alkaff Mansion** (with Indonesian *rijstaffel,* a Dutch colonialist hybrid), **Bibi's** (Nonya cuisine from the marriage of Chinese men, Malay women and Portuguese colonialist legacies), and **Aziza's** or **Bintang Timur** (with refined Malay foods).

There is an element of theater in all this, with attention to details of period or ethnic costume and, in most cases, furnishings, as ambience helps justify the "added" part to their value-added pricing. In these early days, when only people truly devoted to their revivals will take the trouble, such restaurants are almost always worth the extra price. That will change one day, when success and the gleam of future franchises makes portion control more important than authenticity. For the present, however, these places should not be missed.

Singapore also now has some 50 Japanese restaurants, many clustered about the **New Otani hotel/Liang Court** shopping mall complex.

Note that restaurants classified as "tourist class" (a category that includes all hotel restaurants and most upmarket freestanding establishments) add a 10-percent service charge and a four-percent government tax.

HAWKER CENTERS

For local fare, there is no better place to eat than at the food stalls of Singapore's legendary **hawker centers**, where for S$2–3 a dish you can discover a world of "fast foods," before which Western hot dogs, hamburgers and chicken legs pale in comparison. Yes, Big Macs are churned out in some 34 locations, as is the colonel's Southern Fried Chicken, Dunkin' Donuts doughnut holes and Denny's pancakes, but in the hawkers' centers converge the culinary traditions of three of Asia's great cultures: Chinese, Indian and Malay.

In other Asian cities you're never far from a street food stall or a congregation of them. Likewise in Singapore, with the difference that they are no longer found in the streets. Like everything else, they have been "cleaned up," which in this case has meant moving them to big, modern, clean, mostly open-air "food centers." Although the scrubbed-down centers to which they've been removed lack local color, there has been no known negative effect on the food, which remains delicious.

The hawker centers best known to tourists are **Rasa Singapura**, formerly beside the Handicraft Centre in Tanglin Rd., but now removed to Dunearn Rd., beside the Bukit Turf Club; **Newton Circus**, at the junction of Scotts, Bukit Timah, and Newton Rds., a round-the-clock food paradise; **Satay Club**, a white-collar lunch location and night haunt for satay lovers on Elizabeth Walk, near Connaught Drive; **Cuppage Centre**, adjacent to Centrepoint in Orchard Rd.; **People's Park** in Eu Tong Sen Rd., on the edge of Chinatown; **Lagoon Food Centre** on East Coast Parkway, next to the lagoon, on the beach; the **Botanic Gardens**, just across the road from the main gate in Cluny Rd.; and **Funan Centre**, an open-air affair on the top level of this shopping center.

Variety is the major attraction of these centers, and stallholders welcome your curious questions. Diners are proprietary about their favorite outlets and don't at all mind if you ask them what they are eating, and which stall supplied it. Order several dishes from different stalls, especially if you are in a group.

Stallholders at work are an entertainment in themselves. This is traditional Asian fast food, Chinese, Indian and Malay, and the cooks' style and sheer blinding skill can be as good as any theater. The man who sells hot fresh milk drinks (with egg, or chocolate) doesn't mix his drinks so much as stretch them: he pirouettes with a full mug in one hand and an empty one in the other, the milk passing in a miraculously curved torrent around his body, every drop going into the empty mug; then once again, and it's done.

Prata (Indian pancakes with or without curry fillings) start off as a lump of dough tossed, or rather flapped, over and over on a hot plate, the cook's fingers flying, tugging and shaping it into a super pancake, wonderful to watch. The chicken-rice lady's meat-cleaver misses her fingers by a hair's breadth as she deftly chops the chicken — perhaps a million cuts in 30 years, and she's never missed once.

Service is also entertaining. The idea is to make your rounds of the stalls, order up your choice and tell the stallholder where you're sitting (sometimes there are table numbers to assist). Return to your stool, relax and enjoy the show: stallholders-cum-waiters waltzing through the chaos of customers seeking theirs.

Remarkably, using a mysterious radar known only to stallholders, your food will soon arrive, which is when the bill is settled. Seafood is often priced by the 100-gram unit, based on current market rates, so settle on a price when you make your order, to avoid paying more than you bargained for later.

Normal hawker center hours are 11am–2.30pm for lunch, 6–11pm for dinner on weekdays, 7pm–midnight on weekends. Save for desserts and drinks, most hawker foods are built around noodles, rice or soup bases. Their profusion of flavors is outdone only by the confusing collision of languages from whence individual dishes get their names, and these include several transliterations of Chinese dialects that are mutually incomprehensible to foreigners. For instance *Bee Hoon* and *Mi Fun* are the same thing — rice vermicelli; *Kwey Teow* and *Hor Fun* mean flat rice noodles; *E Mee* or *E Mian* mean fried wheat flour noodles.

COFFEE SHOPS

Singapore's coffee shops are a variation on the food stall theme: open-fronted, with bentwood bamboo chairs and marble-topped tables, and old men in T-shirts serving coffee, tea, soft drinks or beer. Remember that "coffee-o" means black, just "coffee" means white. This is true local eating.

Similar coffee shops tend to cluster in groups. There are, for example, South Indian **banana-leaf restaurants**, serving superb curries on a banana leaf with fresh yogurt to quench the fire (see BANANA LEAF APOLO on page 105), and the **fish-head curry restaurants**, which serve what has to be Singapore's national dish.

USEFUL TO KNOW

Malay words

Helpful Malay terms to know are *ayam* (chicken), *ikan* (fish), *kambing* (mutton), *kerang* (cockles), *sotong* (squid or cuttlefish), *udang* (prawn), *nasi* (rice), *sayor* (vegetable), *lemak* (coconut, especially sauces), *soto* (soup), *goreng* (fried), *sambal* (a hot and spicy condiment of fried ingredients: chilies), *langkuas* (ginger, turmeric) and *blachan* (prawn paste). *Roti Pratha* and *Murtabak* are Indian crepes and omelets, and *Biryani* is saffron rice.

Gourmet reading

Serious gourmets may want to purchase a monthly guide, *The Food Paper,* published by leading local food critic, Violet Oon. There is also an annual entitled *Where to Eat and Drink in Singapore. The Guide To Singapore Hawker Food* by James Hooi is a must, and the STPB's booklet, *Feasts and Fun — A Guide to Food and Entertainment,* offers a sampler introduction to the myriad cuisines of this melting-pot city. These include: 11 Chinese cuisines, four Indian, seven from elsewhere in Asia, 15 Western cuisines, as well as seafood and cuisines of mixed ethnic origin, such as *rijstaffel.*

The booklet also gives details of eight outdoor **hawker centers** and six air-conditioned **food centers** (in shopping complexes), with their hybrid cuisines.

Smoking

Smokers should be advised that Singapore forbids any smoking in air-conditioned restaurants. There are no sections for smokers. It is, however, allowed at outdoor eateries.

HOW TO USE THIS CHAPTER

- **Symbols:**   See the KEY TO SYMBOLS on page 7 for an explanation of the full list.
- **Prices:**   The prices corresponding to our price symbols are based on the average price of a meal (dinner, not lunch) for one person, inclusive of house wine, tax and gratuity. Although actual prices will inevitably increase after publication, our relative price categories are likely to stay the same. **Singapore dollars** are quoted here.

Symbol	Category	Current price
▨	very expensive	over S$85
▨	expensive	S$35–85
▨	moderate	S$17–35
▨	inexpensive	S$10–17
▨	cheap	under S$10

Singapore's restaurants A to Z

L'AIGLE D'OR (The Golden Eagle)
French
The Duxton Hotel, 83 Duxton Rd. Map 3E3 ☎227-7678 ▨ 🆎 💳 💳 🆚
MRT: Tanjong Pagar.
Affiliated with the Paris restaurant of the same name. The French chef has 14 years' experience, including a stint with La Tour d'Argent at the Eiffel Tower. The menu changes seasonally, but is always light and mildly adventurous, with dishes such as fillet of roasted lamb with a coffee sauce, or crabmeat ravioli scented with anise. The combination of the Duxton's cozy ambience and reliably excellent cuisine has already caused this new eatery to reach the heights implied in its lofty name: bookings are a must and can be hard to get.

ALKAFF MANSION *Indonesian*
10 Telok Blangah Green. Map 2E4
☎278-6979 ▨ 🆎 💳 💳 🆚 *MRT: Tiong Bahru.*
This exquisite 19thC mansion, set in sprawling hillside gardens on the ridge of Mt. Faber, and former home of the Alkaff family of spice and sugar traders, has enjoyed a multi-million dollar facelift. Local hotelier, Mr. Ong Beng Seng, leased the building from the government, imported reproductions of Dutch colonial furniture from Indonesia, and has turned it into one of only two restaurants in Asia that serve traditional *rijstaffel*, in a manner recalling the opulent plantation days in Jakarta, when each of ten dishes was served by a different young maiden. Only Jakarta has another such restaurant.

The three *rijstaffel* (rice table) menus change weekly, and there is also a set lunch, a breakfast menu and curry tiffin in the afternoon. And there is no better place in Singapore, apart from the **Raffles**, of course, in which to ease back into an overstuffed sofa and sip a sundowner. Dinners must be reserved about two weeks in advance, but for other meals a day's notice will do. Start with the sundowner, which needs no reservations. See also entry in SIGHTS on page 58.

AZIZA'S ♣ *Malay*
36 Emerald Hill Rd. Map 3B3 ☎235-1130
▨ 🆎 💳 💳 🆚 *Lunch 11.30am–3pm, dinner 6.30–11pm. Closed Sun lunch.*
MRT: Somerset.
Malay food is traditionally served in eating-houses and at open-air food stalls. This was Singapore's first real Malay restaurant, and air-conditioned to boot: a cozy place with the personal touch of Aziza Mohammed, a charming man who befriends his guests. Try the *ayam percek, nasi minyok, radih mas* and *nasi ambang.* If you are unsure as to what to order, ask one of the waitresses; they are friendly and helpful.

BANANA LEAF APOLO ♣ *South Indian*
56–58 Race Course Rd. (a block off Serangoon Rd. and on Little India's "Curry Row"). Map 4A4 ☎293-8682
▨ 🆎 💳 💳 🆚 *Open daily 10.30am–10pm. MRT: Dhoby Ghaut, then taxi.*
This is South Indian food, and hot stuff, too — eat it off a banana leaf with your fingers as all the best curry *aficionados* do (forks and spoons are available for the fastidious). Try the fish-head curry — literally the head of a fish (usually red snapper) cooked till tender in spicy hot

gravy with eggplant and okra; also *masala* and *biryani* rice. This is simply among the two or three hottest cuisines on earth, not for those with weak stomachs or taste buds over-sensitive to spices. Some like it hot. For them this is the ultimate chili-induced high: every body pore opens, sinuses drain and a very warm sense of well-being envelops the body. Curries are normally served with yogurt to temper the heat of the chilies. A lime drink also helps. There is an art to eating with your hand (for hygienic reasons in s Asia, only the right hand is used, as the left is used for personal cleansing). Watch the clever fingers of locals singlehandedly roll the curry ingredients into tidy little rice balls and prepare to feel the fool at your own inability to do the same.

BIBI'S RESTORAN *Nonya*
Peranakan Place, 2nd floor, 180 Orchard Rd. Map **3**B3 ☎732-6966 ⅢⅢ AE ⒸⒹ ⅦⅥ Open 11am–3pm and from 6pm. MRT: Somerset.

From the rickshaw at its entrance to the ornate side cupboards, this Nonya restaurant is as much theater as eatery — and, appropriately, it becomes just that in the evening. For people-watching over lunch, ask for a table facing Orchard Rd. To watch plays by local writers or hear the music of local bands, come back for dinner with a *Peranakan* cultural show (see NIGHTLIFE, page 117).

BINTANG TIMUR *Malay*
14 Scotts Rd., #02–08/13, Far East Plaza. Map **3**B2 ☎235-4539. MRT: Orchard. Golden Landmark Hotel, 390 Victoria St., Level 5. Map **4**E4 ☎299-2996. Both ⅢⅢ ⒸⒹ ⅦⅥ Open daily 11am–10pm.

This "Star of the East" (*bintang timur*) is run by Malay Muslims and therefore *halal*, meaning it adheres to Islamic dietary laws. Aloyah, the chef, offers what she claims to be both traditional and contemporary Malay cuisines, the latter being spicier than the former. Her *Satay Goreng Bintang Timur*, *Satay Udang* and *Ukop Belanga* are the contemporary prides and have been highly praised by the local restaurant reviewers. Fur-

nished to create a restrained, family-style ambience, with uniformed waiters and waitresses, these places are mostly about food and quiet comfort rather than high-styled historical re-creations. The dishes noted are beef satay dipped in flour, prawn satay and hot and sour seafood soup, in that order. There is a take-out counter in the Far East Plaza location for Malay bakery desserts.

CUPPAGE THAI FOOD RESTAURANT *Thai*
49 Cuppage Terrace (opposite Cuppage Plaza, behind the Holiday Inn Park View hotel). Map **3**B3 ☎734-1116 or 734-5767 ⅢⅢ AE ⒸⒹ ⅦⅥ MRT: Somerset.

Cuppage Terrace is lined, on one side, with hawkers' stalls in front of Cuppage Plaza (from about 8pm) and, on the other, with a row of bars and eateries that spill onto the pedestrian promenade. These include **Saxophone**, which has some great music but forgettable Continental cuisine (see NIGHTLIFE, page 119), a North Indian eatery and this family-run Thai restaurant, owned by Alan Yeo. The food is good and, with the exception of the *tom yam kung* (prawn soup), the spicing does not seem sanitized for tourists — meaning it's hot. A good place to build up a thirst for drinks and music at Saxophone.

FRISCO RESTAURANT ✿ *American*
B1–02 Hong Kong Bank Building, 21 Collyer Quay. Map **4**D5 ☎220-3777 ⅢⅢ AE ⒸⒹ ⅦⅥ Closed Chinese New Year. MRT: Raffles Place.

Superb US beefsteaks, lobsters, Dover sole, salmon soup and snails in pastry, with attentive service and elegant surroundings. It is pricey, but the four-course set dinner and Saturday lunch offer good value and the same quality.

HAADYAI BEEFBALL RESTAURANT *Thai*
467-C Joo Chiat Rd. (ε of city in Geylang and Katong districts between East Coast and Geylang Rds.). Off map **4**B6 ☎344-5070 ⅢⅢ ⒸⒹ ⅦⅥ Closed Chinese New Year. MRT: Paya Lebar.

Popular with locals, especially with Thais — great food, garish decor. Try *pandan* leaf chicken, fish cake, the spicy salads, *pla merg pahd kra* (stir-fried cuttlefish) and *tom yam* seafood soup. Desserts give new meaning to the term "sweet tooth."

INAGIKU RESTAURANT ♣ *Japanese*
Westin Plaza, 2 Stamford Rd., Level 3. Map 4C5 ☎338-8585 *Ⅷ ⒜ ⒪ ⒞ ⒱* *Closed Sun. MRT: City Hall.*

A branch of a celebrated restaurant in Japan, the Inagiku is noted for its *tempura*. It is spacious, with separate areas for *teppanyaki, tempura* and *sushi,* an *à la carte* dining area and three *tatami*-matted rooms, all under personable and efficient management. A typical set lunch might be *tempura Inagiku* (prawns in batter) with rice, *miso* soup, pickles and fruit. *Sushi* or *sashimi* (raw fish) cost extra.

JACK'S PLACE ♣ *Western*
117-A Killiney Rd. Map 3C3 ☎734-2921 *Ⅷ ⒜ ⒪ ⒞ ⒱ MRT: Somerset.*

In the good old days this was the haunt of hard-drinking newsmen, who would drop in after deadline to top up with beer and shoptalk. Some of the old clique still survive, but the new newsfolk talk shop at the **Front Page** and **Next Page** (see NIGHTLIFE, pages 115–16). Jack's Place is a bit tacky and frayed at the edges, with ancient furniture to match, but it reeks with atmosphere. The place and its owners are the stuff of legend. Now there's a string of Jack's Place **steakhouses**, 13 in all, but this is the mother of all the houses Jack has built. All of them, perhaps not surprisingly, serve excellent steaks — try the steak *sambal* (laced with chili sauce) — and marvelous pizzas: tell them what you want, they'll throw it in.

KEDAY KOPI *Nonya*
Peranakan Place, 180 Orchard Rd. Map 3B3 ☎732-6966 *▢ Open 24hrs. MRT: Somerset.*

Nonya food in a setting based on the traditional Chinese coffee shop, with marble-top tables and old bentwood coffee-shop chairs. This is BIBI'S downstairs little brother.

KHENG LUCK SEAFOOD *Seafood*
Block 1204, East Coast Parkway #01–06, UDMC Seafood Centre. Off map 2D6 ☎241-0291 or 442-2690 *ⅧⅦ ⒜ ⒪ ⒞ ⒱ Open Mon–Fri, Sun, hols 5pm–midnight; Sat 5pm–1am. MRT: Paya Lebar and taxi.*

The old "Seafood Strip" along Upper East Coast Rd. is no more. Once, the strip ran right along the shoreline, but the sea has become ever more distant, due to government land reclamation, and the popularity of the many restaurants there led to complaints of traffic jams and parking problems. So most of the old places moved to East Coast Parkway, eight to the UDMC Seafood Centre, including this classic restaurant, once set in its own grand house in the old style. No matter. In its new surroundings, Kheng Luck is still a real paradise for piscivores, particularly on weekends. They serve superb crunchy squid balls, deep-fried squid, black pepper or chili crab, *satay* and *rojak* (salad with prawn paste sauce).

KINTA MANI INDONESIAN RESTAURANT ♣ *Indonesian*
Level 3, Apollo Hotel, 405 Havelock Rd. Map 3D3 ☎733-2081 ext. 1025 *ⅧⅦ ⒜ ⒪ ⒞ ⒱ MRT: Outram Park.*

The place is pleasant, the food good, and a meal won't blow your budget. Excellent chili prawn, *gado gado* and *ikan siakap apik* for dessert. Be sure to have the *chendol* drink, an exotic concoction of coconut milk, brown *gula melaka* (sugar from the *melaka* tree), green jelly strips and large kidney beans — a sheer delight.

LUNA COFFEE HOUSE *Nonya*
Apollo Hotel, 405 Havelock Rd. Map 3D3 ☎733-2081 *ⅧⅦ ⒜ ⒪ ⒞ ⒱ Closed dinner. MRT: Outram Park.*

This was one of the first restaurants to offer Nonya food and air conditioning, which were once a novel combination. They used to offer a set Nonya lunch, which was changed daily, but it's now a buffet with a wide range of dishes to choose from: *otak, ikan assam pedas, sambal udang* and beef *rendang* are all worth a try.

MARINA VILLAGE INTERNATIONAL
Continental/Chinese
78 Shenton Way #23-01. Map 4E4
☎ *221-6500. MRT: Tanjong Pagar.*
Under its revolving globe, this global village turns the West's ethnicity into a gastronome's playground. Nearly 20 restaurants and bars, mostly of European stock, bring the West to the 70 percent of Singapore's tourists who are Asian, as well as to its residents. It all seems rather precious, but no more banal than much of DisneyWorld's pretensions to internationalism in Florida. For those who like to collect theme park experiences, here is the "been there, done that" checklist: **Tic Toc** (Swiss), **Bierstube** (German), **Ocean Spray** (seafood), **H C Andersen** (Danish) ughhh!, **Café Bonjour** (French), **Greece My Love** (Greek) ughhh!, **Bouzouki Bar** (Greek), **Via Veneto** (Italian), **Marrakesh** (Moroccan), **Que? Manuel** (Spanish), **American Fifties Parlour**, **Makan** (local dishes), **Paisley Park** (English pub), **I-Scream** (ice cream), **Cosa Nostra** (pizza of undetermined nationality), **Diamond Head Grill** (American steakhouse), **Lexington Avenue** (American bar), **Kun Ming** (Cantonese). There is also an amphitheater, **Rhythm and Blues**, which can hold 180 people.

MILANO PIZZA HOUSE *Italian*
04-26 Orchard Plaza, 150 Orchard Rd. Map 3B3 ☎ *734-6050* ▯ *Closed Good Fri, Christmas. MRT: Somerset.*
Despite being one of several in a chain (there is another in Holland Village), this serves good and inexpensive Italian food in a simple, homely atmosphere with no frills: choose from three types of pizza with a choice of 13 toppings, also spaghetti and garlic bread.

MIN JIANG SICHUAN RESTAURANT
Chinese
Goodwood Park Hotel, 22 Scotts Rd. Map 3A2 ☎ *737-7411* ▯ ▣ ▣ ▣ ▥
MRT: Orchard.
Here you dine in the "Chinese imperial splendor" that is *de rigueur* for such banquet restaurants, with, at the Min

Jiang, food and service to match. Given what you get, prices are surprisingly low. The menu has all the piquant specialties that make this provincial cuisine so very popular — camphor-and-tea-smoked duck, diced chicken with dried red pepper, and so on.

MITZI'S CANTONESE RESTAURANT
Chinese
10 Murray Terrace (Food Alley). Map 4E4 ☎ *221-5236* ▯ ▣ ▥ *MRT: Tanjong Pagar.*
A family-run restaurant. Not much to look at, but the food is excellent, especially the deep-fried intestines, deep-fried chicken in prawn paste, and almond soup dessert (which must be ordered in advance).

MOMO YAMA JAPANESE RESTAURANT
♣ Japanese
Picnic Food Court, B1-15 Scotts Shopping Centre, 6-8 Scotts Rd. Map 3B2 ☎ *734-1035* ▯ *MRT: Orchard.*
Good Japanese food with no frills — it's serve-yourself in this tiny restaurant, and if you can't find a seat there are plenty in the air conditioned courtyard outside, shared with a number of other low-priced restaurants, from Italian to Chinese vegetarian. Good value. Food courts are an air conditioned version of the hawkers' centers set up in several shopping plazas. Other such gentrified centers include **Marina Square** (Rasa Marina), the 6th floor of **Lucky Plaza** and the basement of **Wisma Atria**.

MOTI MAHAL *North Indian*
18 Murray St. (at Food Alley beside Maxwell Rd.). Map 4E4 ☎ *221-4338* ▯ ▣ ▣ ▣ ▥ *MRT: Tanjong Pagar.*
Kashmiri, Punjabi and Mughlai cuisine with well over 100 recipes and a wall papered with accolades from visiting journalists of the *Financial Times, The Asian Wall Street Journal* and *Business Traveller Asia Pacific*. It no doubt helps that journalists and other customers are offered a free bottle of wine for every S$100 in cash or $150 by credit card spent on the food . . . which just gets better and better!

OMAR KHAYYAM ✿ *North Indian*
55 Hill St. Map 4C4 ☎*336-1505* ▥
🄰🄴 🄲 🄲🄳 📼 *MRT: City Hall.*

A favorite with locals, serving N Indian, Mughlai and Kashmiri cuisine, in an intimate setting with Moorish decor and antique oil lamps in wall alcoves. Attentive service and good food, especially the Harem's Joy (a rich chicken curry) and *Shah Nauz* (roast lamb in a sticky sauce), also, from the *tandoori* brick oven, the gently spiced *shish kebab* and the aromatic chicken *tikka*. The Mughal recipes are genuine, down to the gold and silver leaf sprinkled into some dishes, which have no notable value in terms of flavor, but do make the meal seem "fit for a king."

PANDAN GARDENS RESTAURANT ✿ *Seafood*
200A Pandan Gardens Estate (near Jurong Town). Map 1D2 ☎*560-2907* ▥ 🄰🄴 🄲🄳 📼 *MRT: Chinese Garden or Jurong East.*

This seafood restaurant lacks charm: it's loud and garish, it could be cheaper, it gets crowded at lunch, and it's rather out of the way. Trouble is, the food's so good. Frankly, it's like this, Scarlett, they can afford "not to give a damn." Specialties are freshly steamed prawns, fried chili crabs, salt-and-pepper prawn and crabs. Also beancurd stuffed with salted egg and *pandan* leaf chicken.

PAREGU VIETNAMESE SEAFOOD RESTAURANT *Vietnamese*
01-24/34 Orchard Plaza, 150 Orchard Rd. Map 3B3 ☎*733-4211* ▥ 🄰🄴 🄲 🄲🄳 📼 *MRT: Somerset.*

The fare is widely acclaimed, although it could be cheaper. Try the prawns barbecued on sugarcane, or spring rolls wrapped with mint leaves in a large lettuce leaf and dipped in chili sauce.

PARKWAY THAI RESTAURANT *Thai*
02-08 Parkway Parade, 80 Marine Parade Rd. Map 2E5 ☎*348-0783* ▥ 🄲🄳 📼 *with two branches at Centrepoint and Bideford Rd. (near Orchard Rd.). MRT: Paya Lebar, then taxi.*

Classy, which is a rare quality in local Thai eateries, and not cheap, but local Thais rate the food here highly, and with good reason. Specialties include the Thai classic, hot-and-sour *tom yam* soup, crispy *garoupa* fish, *pandan* leaf chicken, and a wonderful dessert — water chestnut in coconut milk.

PASTA FRESCA DA SALVATORE *Italian*
#30 Boat Quay ☎*462-0073, map 4D4 and Blk. 833, #01-03 Royalville, Bukit Timah Rd. (opposite Singapore Turf Club)* ☎*469-4920* ▣*779-5384, map 1D3* 🄰🄴 🄲 🄲🄳 📼 *Daily 10am–10.30pm. MRT: Newton, then taxi.*

The management has turned its position — as a wholesaler of Italian foods to hotels and other restaurants — to advantage in its own eateries, with the promise of fresh pasta and other delights manufactured on the premises. A good place to eat before or after drinks at **Harry's**, next door (see NIGHTLIFE, page 116).

PETE'S PLACE *Italian*
Hyatt Regency Hotel, 10–12 Scotts Rd., Basement. Map 3B2 ☎*733-1188* ▥ 🄰🄴 🄲 🄲🄳 📼 *MRT: Orchard.*

Excellent fare, using recipes from the land of *gnocchi* and *fettuccine alfredo*. The studied informality of its "Cheers" local bar decor and coy Americanisms of various menu items are deceptive, as the food follows original Italian recipes, even to bringing visiting chefs out from restaurants in Rome. The characteristic Italo–American flourishes are best expressed by "The Godfather" — an ice cream concoction dreamed up by its manager, William Cheng, which won the "Magnolia Dessert of the Year" competition. (Magnolia ice cream, made in the Philippines, is Southeast Asia's best-known brand; it sponsors regional awards to encourage imaginative uses of its products.)

PREGO *Italian*
Westin Stamford Hotel, 2 Stamford Rd., Level 3. Map 4C5 ☎*338-8585* ▥ 🄰🄴 🄲 🄲🄳 📼 *MRT: City Hall.*

Home to antipasto, pizza and chianti wines and, like **Pete's Place**, a casual *ristorante Italiano*.

LE RESTAURANT DE FRANCE ✿ *French*

Hotel Meridien Singapore, 100 Orchard Rd.
Map **3B3** ☎733-8855 ▭ AE ◉ ◯ VISA
Closed lunch, weekends and hols.
MRT: Somerset.

Rated as the best practitioner of *haute cuisine* in Singapore, this restaurant offers fine French cuisine in a setting modeled on a château. Master chef Louis Outhier, top-rated by Michelin and Gault-Millau, was its founding consultant. This is food-as-art and, like all original creations, it does not come cheap, but the three- and four-course luncheons are more modestly priced.

SAMY'S CURRY RESTAURANT *South Indian*

Singapore Civil Service Club House, Block 25, Dempsey Rd. (near Tanglin Rd.)
☎472-2080. Off map **3B1** ▭ ◯ VISA
Open daily 11am–10pm. Closed Thurs, hols.
One of the most popular South Indian restaurants, and still moderately priced. Traditional favorites here are fish-head curry, fried mutton and *masala* chicken curry. There is a separate air conditioned dining room, with a nominal extra charge of under S$2 per person.

SATE SATE RESTAURANT ✿ *Malay*

Gold Hill Sq., B1-12/14 Newton Rd.
☎254-4357 ▭ ◯ VISA MRT: Novena.
Traditional Malay fare, especially *satay* — skewers of grilled minced meat in large, crunchy chunks, and good value with it. Try *mee siam*, *laksa* and *soto ayam*, the local favorites.

THE SEAFOOD INTERNATIONAL MARKET AND RESTAURANT *Seafood*

902 East Coast Parkway. Map **4F4**
☎345-1211 ▭ ◄€ AE ◉ ◯ *Closed Wed lunch.* MRT: Kembangan or Bedok.
If you're a fresh seafood fanatic, this is for you. Choose your meal in the market, it's weighed and priced, then you pay at the register and select the cooking style: grilled, steamed, or fried. Then dine, preferably on the open-air terrace overlooking the sea, or under thatch beside the pool. Excellent lobsters, crabs, steamed fish, all quite fresh and made to appear more so with special lighting.

SEAH STREET DELI *Jewish-American*

Raffles Hotel Arcade, 328 North Bridge Rd
☎337-1886. Map **4C5** ▭ AE ◉ ◯ VISA
MRT: City Hall.

This delightful "New York Deli" is for those who find themselves a bit stifled by all the historical artifacts around them at the RAFFLES HOTEL (see page 87). Cut loose for a potato "Knish Upon A Star," a "Lox, Stock and Bagel" or "Ike and Tina Tuna," or a host of other impiously tagged dishes in large helpings. You make your choice from a New York smart-aleck menu that threatens a dollar charge for "Too Much Grief and Aggravation to the Waiter" and challenges the undecided to "Be creative, invent your own sandwich." As the management says, who knows? Maybe you'll become famous. Good food served in a spirit of good fun.

SEOUL GARDEN KOREAN RESTAURANT ✿ *Korean*

02-56 Parkway Parade, 80 Marine Parade Rd. Off map **4B6** ☎345-1338/9 ▭
AE ◉ ◯ VISA MRT: Kembangan or Bedok.
This cheery place has a section for dining Korean-style, seated on the floor. Good value in a do-it-yourself barbecue, with beef, chicken, squid, vegetables, mushrooms and more. For lunch you can eat all you want for an hour at a fixed price; try the crispy-skinned bean curd, king oyster fried in egg, Korean ginseng chicken soup.

SUMMER PALACE *Chinese*

The Regent, 1 Cuscaden Rd. Map **3B2**
☎733-8888 ext. 2148 ▭ AE ◉ ◯ VISA
MRT: Orchard.

This is a Chinese grand imperial eatery in a luxury hotel, splendidly regal, with superb food and service: *the* place for a celebration feast. The Cantonese chefs, brought over from Hong Kong, set the highest of standards. There's a set lunch and an extremely extensive *à la carte* menu.

THE TANDOOR ✿ *Indian*

Holiday Inn Park View, 11 Cavenagh Rd.
Map **3B3** ☎733-8333 ▭ AE ◉ ◯ VISA
MRT: Somerset.

North Indian and Kashmiri cuisine in a Moghul garden with a pool, which doesn't leave a lot of room for the restaurant, although it's cozy. The chefs are on display, tending a glassed-in *tandoori* oven.The specialties are *tandoori* kebabs (marinated overnight in a mix of yogurt and spices), pomfret, lobster, chicken, prawns; a good range of breads; fragrant, subtle curries with spices such as saffron and cardamom rather than fiery chili.

TRADEWINDS BAR AND FOOD STALLS ♣ *Indian/Malay*
Hilton International Hotel, 581 Orchard Rd. Map **3**B2 ☎737-2233 ▥ ≪ ▣ ▣ ▣ ▥ MRT: Orchard.

A great place to spend an evening, with thatched roofs, a tropical ambience and cool breezes at the poolside, nightly entertainment and a full-length movie every Sunday night. The food includes local Malay and Indian specialties and barbecue fare.

VICTORY and ZAM ZAM *South Indian*
701 and 699 North Bridge Rd., opposite Sultan Mosque. Map **4**B5. Both ▭ No cards. MRT: Bugis.

These two restaurants are neighbors, with men outside who will beckon you to enter. They wear white shirts, checkered sarongs and the white skullcaps that mark them out as having gone on the *hajj* (pilgrimage) to Mecca at least once in their lives — a dream of all Muslims. Inside, both of these establishments offer a simplified South Indian hybrid of North Indian Mughal cuisine, such as *biryani* with chicken, mutton or fish-head curry, *prata* and *murtabak,* Indian crepes that are hand-patted, swirled, twirled, stretched and smoothed before being seared on a hot griddle and dipped into or stuffed with spicy fillings. They both have seating upstairs from where, on a Friday afternoon, you can watch the faithful respond to the *muezzin's* call to prayer.

The row of shophouses that contains these non-airconditioned eateries is strung with the similar **Singapore**, **Jubilee**, and **Islamic** restaurants, like prayer beads, along North Bridge Rd. *(#697, 771 and 791-797 respectively)* opposite the SULTAN MOSQUE). Together, they make what is arguably the most successful "conservation" site in Singapore, having escaped redevelopment by government planners for almost a century (**Zam Zam** was born in 1908, **Victory** in 1910, **Singapore** in 1911). Enjoy them *in situ* while you can.

Singapore: nightlife and entertainment

Singapore after dark

Singapore does not spring into frenzied life after dark in the way that Bangkok does, but the many redevelopment areas have greatly expanded the variety of bars, nightclubs and discos. TANJONG PAGAR, EMERALD HILL, with nearby PERANAKAN PLACE at its base, and BOAT QUAY are restored districts of 19th century shophouses and residences that are already awash with trendy bars, pubs and restaurants. The new CLARKE QUAY, with 60 late 19thC and early 20thC godowns (warehouses) and shophouses along River Valley Rd. converted into shops and restaurants, pubs and discos, has been a welcome further injection of life into the city's nights.

Those in search of the naughtier forms of nocturnal prowls will still find succor in the red-light alley that runs from Jalan Besar to Serangoon Rd., the Malay Geylang district or the "massage" parlors in some of the shopping complexes, but such opportunities are much scarcer here than in other cities of the region.

The city is far from devoid of life after dark, but like the architecture in the redevelopment areas that have spawned them, bars and discotheques have become gentrified for the casual-smart set of a "Chuppy" nation (the still-prominent Chinese answer to those 1980s fossils of the West, the Yuppies). Most indicative are the places at **Boat Quay** and in the **Tanjong Pagar Conservation Area**.

Nightclubs and discos in hotels offer an array of evening entertainments, but freestanding operations have overtaken hotels to provide dance, *karaoke,* and live sessions from jazz to punk music to good old rock'n'roll. Strip shows have moved offshore N across the causeway to Johor Bahru, but there are still full-scale floor shows, often with a national motif.

A case in point are the Chinese nightclubs, such as: **Dallas Theatre Lounge and Nite-Club** (in the Amara Hotel), **Lido Palace Nite-Club** (in the Concorde Hotel), **Golden Million Deluxe Nite-Club** (in Singapore Peninsula Shopping Centre), **Kabuki Deluxe Nite-Club** (Orchard Bldg.), **Regent Night Club** (Cuppage Plaza), **Oasis Theatre Restaurant** (50 Kallang Park) and NEPTUNE THEATRE RESTAURANT.

There are also a number of English-style pubs, often with a disc jockey who will play favorites on request. Some bars in the redeveloped districts focus on specific kinds of music (see **Elvis' Place**, Tanjong Pagar Conservation Area).

CONCERTS: Regular performances by the 72-member **Singapore Symphony Orchestra** take place at the VICTORIA THEATRE. Smaller sections of the orchestra also perform regularly at lunchtime in various auditoria in the commercial district. There are also frequent concerts of **Chinese music**, which are performed at a number of different locations around the city by the **Singapore Broadcasting Corporation Chinese Orchestra** and the **People's Association Orchestra**.

Band concerts are held on Sundays *(5.30-6.30pm)* in the BOTANIC GARDENS, an oasis of lush greenery and well-trimmed lawns, which makes a pleasant spot for listening to military, classical and pop music.

DISCOTHEQUES: Discos are alive and well. Four of the city's largest are **The Warehouse** in a converted godown at River View Hotel, **Fire** at Orchard Plaza, **Khameleon** at Marina Village and **Zouk** in Jiak Kim St. **Fire** and **Zouk** are actually multipurpose centers with discos, separate bars, "KTV" and restaurants on premises.

Most of the others are in upmarket hotels and pride themselves on gadgetry or yuppie snob appeal. One such is **The Library**, opened in the 1980s at the MANDARIN SINGAPORE HOTEL to replace the raunchier and wilder **Boiler Room**, which opened in its basement in the pre-*karaoke* days of the late 1970s, when the world was awash with the polyester of *Saturday Night Fever*. **Xanadu** at the SHANGRI-LA is of the same genre.

FESTIVALS: The **Singapore Festival of Arts**, the biggest single performing and visual arts event held in Singapore, hosts a number of international concert stars and has a fringe theater festival too. This biennial extravaganza, and the many **religious festivals**, which are exciting to witness, are detailed in SINGAPORE'S CALENDAR on pages 49–53.

"INSTANT ASIA" SHOWS: First-time visitors could do worse than see one of these colorful variety shows, which give a taste of the traditional performing arts of the Chinese, Malay and Indian cultures. Good examples are offered by the **Pasir Panjang** restaurant *(265 Pasir Panjang Rd.* ☎*235-2102)* and by **Bibi's** restaurant *(Peranakan Pl.* ☎ *732-6966),* and by certain hotels such as the Instant Asia luncheon and the Lion City Review dinner at the **Cockpit**, ASEAN Night at the **Mandarin Singapore** and Malam Singapura dinner at the **Hyatt Regency**. Instant Asia is performed over dinner at the **Singa Inn Seafood Restaurant**.

KARAOKE: As elsewhere in Asia, the Japanese-style *karaoke* bar, where would-be Sinatras and Madonnas sing along to a video disc, is still going strong. **Gazers** on Armenian St. and **Java Jive** in Holland Village are typical of the type. **Novotel Orchid (Limelight)** and **Plaza Hotel (Singsation)** are more elaborate.

MOVIES: Local cinemas show movies in English, Malay, Tamil and Chinese. New Hollywood releases are usually first screened at Orchard Rd. theaters. Tickets for weekend screenings should be bought in advance (two days' advance purchase allowed).

THEATER: On stage, there is a fair amount of **English-language drama** at the **Victoria Theatre**, which also hosts musical comedies, ballet and classical Chinese operas. The **Hilton** hosts **dinner-theater** in its grill room at various times of the year, performed by troupes brought out from London's West End.

113

ALL-PURPOSE LOCATIONS

BUGIS STREET
Bounded by Victoria St., Queen St., Rochor Rd. and Cheng Yan Pl. Map 4B5.
MRT: Bugis.

For British servicemen stationed in Singapore while fighting Communist insurgents in Malaysia, and those Americans on "R&R" from Vietnam made famous in Paul Theroux's novel, *Saint Jack,* the most "all-purpose" entertainment venue in this town was Bugis Street.

This was where they went when everywhere else closed at night — a sleepy residential district that, phoenix-like, underwent a midnight transformation into the wildest kind of pedestrian promenade. Somewhere between a beer garden and hawker center, the street was notorious for another kind of bird — its transvestite prostitutes. It was named for Indonesian seafarers and former flesh traders of the Celebes Islands who reputedly traded slaves on the Singapore River and gathered here to party and count their cash. Everything about Bugis Street was fable and street theater, including the tall tales brought back to barracks by visiting troops.

For years this area remained the one great blight on Singapore's otherwise squeaky-clean reputation, much to the delight of the country's detractors. Then, in 1985, the street was shut down to accommodate the MRT Bugis Street Station.

Not even the profane is sacred to Singapore's urban redevelopment planners, however. As part of its effort to salvage something of old (and touristically appealing) Singapore, the government appointed a British architect, Christopher Carlisle, to help reconstruct a new Bugis Street. Carlisle was attached to British military forces in Singapore during the street's heyday in the 1960s and '70s and has struggled to salvage original artifacts and re-create the original ambience.

Just 120m (130 yards) from its progenitor, at a cost of US$6.8 million, the tattered old shophouses of Bugis Street have been re-created in a tarted up form, with the usual assurance of hygienic hawkers' stalls. As the original tourist bumf had it, 850 people could "party the night away" on the street; the original hawkers had been invited back; the new, period-costume shophouses offered private, upper-story, air-conditioned dining for more than 2,000 diners who wanted to "observe the fun but not necessarily take part" (voyeurs?); and a special platform was being prepared for "the more colorful performers whose early morning antics made the street so attractive" (presumably not the servicemen, but the otherwise unmentionable transvestites — who, like the former hawkers, had already removed themselves to new digs, now in the areas of Johore and Desker Roads.).

Middle-aged veterans of jungle warfare in Malaya and Vietnam would marvel to find that the planners have restored the centerpiece of the old Bugis St. bustle — the public toilet building (*sans* plumbing) on the roof of which transvestites performed until the wee hours. But today's Bugis St. is just another sedate evening beer garden and hawker food center that, as a historical re-creation, has something in common with that toilet-cum-stage: it wasn't built to be what it appears.

THE SUBSTATION

45 Armenian St., behind the National Museum and National Library ☎ *337-7800. Map 4C4. MRT: City Hall Station and walk, or bus nos. 7, 14, 16, 124, 167, 171, 173, 174, 179, 182 to National Library.*

A former power station, built in 1928, this three-story building was renovated and refurbished in 1985 as a community arts center, largely at the instigation of local playwright and theater critic, Kuo Pao Kun. There is a 200-seat multipurpose hall, art gallery, dance studio, arts bookstore, classrooms and a U-shaped, open space "Kopi Garden," which is used as an outdoor performance area. This is a good place to plug into what currently electrifies Singapore's young talents.

VICTORIA THEATRE AND MEMORIAL HALL

Empress Place. Map 4D4 ☎ *338-1230* 🆎 💿 💿 📼 *MRT: Raffles Place.*

Home of the Singapore Symphony Orchestra and location for stage performances in a variety of genres including Chinese Opera, Indian classical dance and English drama.

BARS

Sink into a rattan chair, sip a Singapore Sling and imagine that you're Somerset Maugham; quaff a hearty pint or two in a pub with a nautical flavor, or go the whole hog with an organized crawl round the Tanjong Pagar Conservation Area, where you can drink in the architecture and a unique ambience, complete with Singapore's very own Elvis.

BRANNIGAN'S

Hyatt Regency Hotel, 10–12 Scotts Rd. Map 3B2 ☎ *733-1188. MRT: Orchard.*

Captain David Brannigan, an adventurous British seafarer, chose to settle down in Singapore, and he opened this pub with a nautical-theme interior meant to reflect his life's travels. It has since become so popular as a singles bar that, when the Hyatt planned its recent renovation, specific instructions were given that Brannigan's was to remain, well, Brannigan's. If you like live music and tipping a pint or two amidships, among antique guns, masks, musical instruments, ship's wheels and cartwright's barrels for tables, this is indeed your port of call, matey.

FRONTPAGE PUB/THE NEXT PAGE PUB

#9 and 15 Mohamed Sultan Rd. (off River Valley Rd. near Oberoi Imperial Hotel and Clarke Quay) ☎ *235-7013/734-0721. Map 3C3* 🎵 ➡ 🆎 💿 💿 📼 *MRT: Dhoby Ghaut.*

Apart from the manual typewriter tucked between bottles at the end of the bar, framed "front pages" on the walls and a makeshift bookshelf for borrowers, the **Frontpage Pub** might be any one of the many that have been nipped and tucked into converted shophouses. The difference is that its owners are mostly newsfolk, including the convivial managing partner, Peter Lim, formerly a well-known local newshound. There's a darts room at the rear and inscribed black tee-shirts on sale at the bar.

For those who prefer billiards, the sounds of Sofia singing that she's a "One-man Woman" and cozy nooks in which to eat, such as canopy beds or private rooms with an Arabesque of cushions for seats, Lim's group has opened **The Next Page Pub** a few doors down the way. Truck drivers are known for frequenting the best lunch stops on the road, journalists for having a nose for news of the best bars in town. Those politically incorrect few who still like to imbibe in accompaniment to the art of conversation (and who have not succumbed to the moral superiority of designer water) should follow their noses to both of these stops on their next Singapore pub crawl.

HARRY'S

28 Boat Quay (near Cavanagh Bridge)
☎ *538-3029* ☏ *538-0365. Map 4D4*
Ⓐ Ⓞ Ⓒ Ⓥ *Live music Wed–Sat
9–11.30pm; Sun Jazz 5–8.30pm and Blues
9–11.30pm. MRT: Raffles Place.*

Proprietor Jim Gelpi waited two years to lease the right location for the launch of his rendition of a "Harry's Bar," known to Americans in Paris (and Parisians) since 1911. Even though there are now "Harry's" bars in New York, Italy and other places, there is no international franchise. It is only the efforts of the original Harry and his like-minded progeny that keeps this particular "expatriates welcome" kind of wateringhole alive and kickin'.

Since July 1992, there has been one in Singapore, opposite the Singapore River from EMPRESS PLACE, among the redeveloped shophouses at Boat Quay. Its number, 28, is a pun for "easy prosperity" in the tonal Chinese language, according to Jim, and here's where he hopes to find it. The music is good and so is the atmosphere, so lend him a hand your next time round, pilgrim.

If you are in the neighborhood, recommended eateries include the PASTA FRESCA DA SALVATORE Italian pasta house next door (see EATING AND DRINKING, page 109), **Kinara** North Indian cuisine *(57 Boat Quay* ☎ *533-0412)* or **Sushi Do-**

koro Yoshida Japanese restaurant *(58 Boat Quay* ☎ *534-1401),* just down the quayside.

MUSIC ROOM

Hilton International Singapore, 581 Orchard Rd ☎ *737-2233. Map 3B2* Ⓐ Ⓞ Ⓒ Ⓥ
*Open Sun–Thurs 3pm–2am; Fri, Sat
3pm–3am. MRT: Orchard.*

Deep-cushioned rattan and leather chairs beckon guests to relax and be entertained. The atmosphere and the music are perfect for English afternoon tea (served daily), pre-dinner cocktails and late-night dancing. The lounge bar in the Hilton's lobby is another relaxing place for drinks and conversation, with a resident band that provides nightly entertainment.

RAFFLES' LONG BAR

Raffles Hotel Arcade, 328 North Bridge Rd
☎ *337-1886. Map 4C5. MRT: City Hall.*

Ease back into old Malaya, mate, by sinking into a rattan chair in the same Long Bar that was the birthplace of the "Singapore Sling" cocktail in 1915. For the uninitiated, it's a planters' punch with a slow gin kick.

SOMERSET'S BAR

Westin Plaza, 2 Stamford Rd ☎ *338-8585.
Map 4C4* Ⓐ Ⓞ Ⓒ Ⓥ *Open 5pm–2am.
MRT: City Hall.*

Named after Somerset Maugham, this bar evokes the elegance of the Maugham era with its wicker chairs and wall murals of old Singapore. Jazz bands from the US are a regular feature, and the Sunday jam sessions for local musicians are popular.

TANJONG PAGAR CONSERVATION AREA *(Map 4E4)*

This area has become so much a center of "easy listening" deejay bars that the **Singapore Trolley** sightseeing company, which makes 22 stops in the city, offers an unlimited all-day ticket culminating in a special "pub crawl" to the district seven times daily *(4.35-9.35pm, except before and on holiday evenings* ☎ *227-8218* ☏ *227-0802).*

The trolley ticket (S$9) offers "Happy Hour" prices all day at three pubs: **The Third Man**, the **Flag and Whistle** and **Our Pub**, and until 6pm at **JJ Mahoney**. This is not quite as exciting as it sounds, however, since most pubs in the area have Happy Hours that run as late as 8.30pm anyway.

The five roads of the vaguely triangular district bounded by Tanjong Pagar, Craig and Neil Rds., with Duxton and Duxton Hill Rds. slicing through, offer rows of brightly restored shophouses chock-a-block with bars, restaurants, some offices and trendy shops. **Emmerson's**, run by the ubiquitous Raffles Company, which recalls its 1866 origin in name only, is a popular stop within the large **Crafts Centre** complex (where there is a pictorial **Tanjong Pagar Heritage Exhibition**) *(51 Neil Rd.* ☎ *227-7518* Fx *227-9735).*

Flanagan Jukebox Bistrotheque prides itself on its restored Wurlitzer jukebox, framed in what looks like an outsized fireplace mantle, and a DJ who brings back the late 50s and early 60s with sentimental spins from Connie Francis, Pat Boone and other croon-along friends *(54 Tanjong Pagar Rd* ☎ *225-5844).* **Unchained Melody Jukebox Bistrotheque** is a "sing-along pub" owned by the Flanagan group and so popular that it has two adjacent locations here *(52 and 54 Tanjong Pagar Rd.* ☎ *227-7466)* and another branch, by the name of **Pub KG**, at 546 Macpherson Rd. *(* ☎ *743-0093).*

Best-loved of the period Rock-n'Roll pubs is **Elvis' Place**, run by Elvis and Lily Wee. This former building contractor has a personal collection of about 300 records from his namesake, "the King," and 3,000 from His Majesty's era. With two years of success ("You'd be amazed how many Elvis fans there are in Singapore!" exclaims Elvis, still seeming a bit stunned by his own popularity), the Wees have now opened **Elvis II**, which shares quarters with American Express offices at the new Duxton Concourse on Beach Rd. *(1-A Duxton Hill* ☎ *227-8543 or 224-1228).*

Nothing about **Duxton's Chicago Bar and Grill** *(6&9 Duxton Hill* ☎ *222-4096 or 222-9556)* says "Chicago," but who cares, when you are on a tropical pub crawl less than 160km (100 miles) from the equator?

DINNER SHOWS

The performing arts of Singapore are so endlessly various that it would be a pity not to have even the briefest taste. Happily, it is possible to do so on even the shortest visit. Excellent, authentic performances can be seen over dinner at some of the city's finer hotels and restaurants.

ASEAN NIGHT

Mandarin Hotel, Orchard Rd. Map 3B3
☎ *737-4411* AE CB DC VISA *Closed Mon. Dinner 7pm, show 7.45pm. MRT: Somerset.*
An engaging miscellany of songs and dances from the six member countries (Brunei, Indonesia, Malaysia, the Philippines, Singapore and Thailand) of the Association of Southeast Asian Nations (ASEAN).

BIBI'S RESTORAN

Peranakan Pl., 180 Orchard Rd. Map 3B3
☎ *732-6966* AE CB DC VISA *Dinner show*
every Tues and Thurs. MRT: Somerset.
Bibi's is the perfect place in which to sample the Peranakan (Straits Chinese) culture, along with its unique and delicious cuisine. The dinner show features a 45-minute traditional wedding in full ceremonial dress, as well as a nine-course meal.

MALAM SINGAPURA

Hyatt Regency Hotel, Scotts Rd. Map 3B2
☎ *733-1188* AE CB DC VISA *Open Mon, Wed, Fri. Dinner 7pm, show 8pm. MRT: Orchard.*

117

Dinner followed by 45-minute South-east Asian cultural show.

NEPTUNE THEATRE

Overseas Union House, Collyer Quay. Map 4D3 ☎ *224-3922* ⒶⒺ ◉ ⒸⒹ 𝚅𝙸𝚂𝙰 *Open daily. MRT: Raffles Place.*

A theater restaurant serving Cantonese food, with a live extravaganza of song and dance, with up to 60 performers on the stage at any one time. Popular, so always reserve ahead.

PASIR PANJANG PARADISE RESTAURANT

265 Pasir Panjang Rd. Map 1E3 ☎ *336-0288* ⒶⒺ ◉ ⒸⒹ 𝚅𝙸𝚂𝙰 *Open from 11.30am. MRT: Buona Vista and taxi.*

The show here includes dances from all over Asia, beginning with a spectacular and traditional Chinese lion dance to the clash of cymbals and gongs, and progessing through a Malay harvest dance to a mesmerizing Indian snake charmer's act.

NIGHTCLUBS

Variety is the spice of life in Singapore, and nowhere more so than in its nightspots. The full spectrum, from old-time Oriental elegance through laser-lit hi-tech and hard rock to the best Country and Western that Southeast Asia can offer, is there for the taking.

APOLLO NITE CLUB

Apollo Hotel, 405 Havelock Rd. Map 3D3 ☎ *235-7977* ⇒ ⒶⒺ ◉ ⒸⒹ 𝚅𝙸𝚂𝙰 *Open nightly. MRT: Outram Park.*

In this Chinese nightclub, the old-fashioned custom of paying a hostess to dance with a patron is still observed.

BLACK VELVET

Century Park Sheraton Hotel, Nassim Hill. Off map 3B1 ☎ *732-1222 ext. 1584* ⒶⒺ ◉ ⒸⒹ 𝚅𝙸𝚂𝙰 *Open Sun–Fri 9pm–2am; Sat, hols 9pm–3am. MRT: Orchard.*

A striking place, with gold decor, laser light shows, special smoke effects and a sophisticated sound system.

EUROPA LOUNGE AND RESTAURANT

Europa Hotel, 10 Anson Rd. Map 4E4 ☎ *225-3668* 🖷 *226-0686.*

The fortunes of Matthew and the Mandarins have fallen with the price of oil. The scores of highly paid oil-rig workers and rig-supply employees from Jurong who once followed the band are not all gone, but mostly forgotten. Forgotten also is "Matthew's," the lead singer's former bar. The band are now the big attraction at this bar near the Shenton Way business district. If you like Country and Western music, you'll warm to the strummin' and singin' of Singapore's very own "cowboy," Matthew Tan, who has actually recorded in Nashville and who has his own performing group. He ain't no "Okee from Muskogee," but he'll do real fine until one comes along.

FABRICE'S WORLD MUSIC BAR

Dynasty Hotel (basement), Orchard Rd. Map 3B2 ☎ *738-8887* 🖷 *294-7505* 𝚅𝙸𝚂𝙰 ⇒ ⒶⒺ ◉ ⒸⒹ 𝚅𝙸𝚂𝙰 *Music weekdays 11.30pm–2am; weekends 12am–2.30am. MRT: Orchard.*

"A World In Your Ear" promises Fabrice de Barsy, the Belgian owner of this remarkable cavern decked out in terracotta tiles, with shields and rugs from the tribes of Irian Jaya, Africa and almost everywhere on earth. Fabrice, who bills himself as "the *enfant terrible* of funk and fun," means it. He opened with a Brazilian *Samba* band, followed by an African *Soukous* band from Zaire. Others have included a Spanish group, combining Iberian Rock with something close to Spanish *Flamenco* and Portuguese *Fado* music, and a Cuban combo with *salsa* and *reggae* sounds.

It is formally a club, with hotel guest memberships. Dues are S$1,000 a year, which entitles you to four bottles of complimentary champagne (the house tipple) and four $125 vouchers for meals with up to four guests at SAXOPHONE (see page 119), which de Barsy also owns.

HARD ROCK CAFE

#02-01 HPL House, 50 Cuscaden Rd. Map
3B2 ☎235-5232. ⊠235-7398 ▥≡≋
🅰 💽 💿 ▥ Open weekdays 11am–2am,
weekends to 3am. Food served until
10.30pm. MRT: Orchard.

Third in the line of famous franchised
bars with the same name. Like its
cousins in New York and London, this is
a two-story eatery chock-a-block with
rock'n'roll memorabilia. It specializes in
nonstop (and very loud) music from the
1950s onward, and in importing traveling talents of the era, such as the Blues-
Great John Hammond, for spot concerts.
The daddy of them all was created in
London, in 1971, by two Americans in-
tent on educating Europe in the joys of
"down-home" cooking and culture. New
York's branch of the HRC opened in
1984 with the first musical memorabilia
collection.

The Singapore branch, which opened in 1990, houses over 275 items —
autographed guitars, album covers (remember *albums*, folks?), letters, hand-
bills and posters. "Rock the World, Save
the Planet" and "Love All, Serve All" are
the chain's rather wacky marching mot-
toes. Their "Pig Sandwich" (of hickory-
smoked ham) and hamburgers haven't
yet saved the planet, but their presence
has done an "awesome" job of rocking
the world, as a noisy archive of their
parents' adolescence, aimed at the adult
progeny of the 60s "love children." (Sad
but true, boomers: a child born in the
mid-1960s is now almost a "thirty-some-
thing.")

A guide to *The Hard Rock Cafe Self-
motivating, Non-nuclear Powered
Memorabilia Tour of The World's Fore-
most Rock'n'Roll Museum* is available,
gratis, at the entrance. A separate counter
deals in various peace, love and earth-
first variations on the prized Hard Rock
Cafe tee-shirts, shorts, sunglasses and
other wonders of the merchandiser's
art. Reservations are recommended for
dinner.

LIDO PALACE

Concorde Hotel Shopping Centre, 317
Outram Rd. Map 3D2 ☎732-8855 ≡≋ 🅰

💽 💿 ▥ Open till 2am. Shows at 9pm
and midnight. MRT: Tiong Bahru.

Elaborate Eastern cuisine and Chinese
cabaret show featuring stars from Hong
Kong and Taiwan.

MYSTERY DISCOTHEQUE

Hotel New Otani, 177A River Valley Rd. Map
4C4 ☎338-3333 🅰 💽 💿 ▥ Open
8pm–2am. MRT: Dhoby Ghaut.

A good place to dance to the latest hits.
Unusually spacious dance floor, crisp,
shiny decor and friendly service.

SAXOPHONE

23 Cuppage Terrace (behind Holiday Inn
Park View). Map 3B3 ☎235-8385
⊠294-7505 ≡≋ 🅰 💽 💿 ▥ Music from
10.30pm–1am. MRT: Somerset.

Saxophone has an elevated stage behind its ground-floor bar that somehow
squeezes three musicians and a vocalist
into a space so tiny that you need a
drink to overcome the fear of them all
toppling off. A lively and popular jazz
bar and restaurant (upstairs and outside), Saxophone has a mediocre back-
up band whose shortcomings are made
up for by the high-quality foreign Jazz
and Blues singers that it manages to
import — Lady Rebecca, from the
United States, has been the vocalist for
the past two years. You can eat *al fresco*
on Cuppage Terrace, or tucked in as
tightly as the band in a tiny mezzanine.
Reservations are recommended if you are
dining late in the evening, when the
best music is played.

Saxophone is owned by the self-
proclaimed *"enfant terrible"* from Belgium who operates FABRICE'S WORLD MUSIC
BAR at the Dynasty Hotel (see page 118).
Both places have an outstanding anom-
aly in their interior decor: large photographs of the king of Belgium over the
door. The gregarious *patron,* Fabrice de
Barsy, likes to dine *al fresco* here with
friends, then drive over to the other
property in his classic Jaguar sedan
(painted in tiger's stripes). Both of de
Barsy's places are all about teaching
party people the meanings of *joie de
vivre* and *savoir faire*— with a distinct
Belgian accent.

SCANDALS
Westin Plaza, 2 Stamford Rd. Map **4***C4*
☎338-8885 AE DC MC VISA *Open 9pm–2am. MRT: City Hall.*
One of Singapore's most startling discos. Features include an overhead helicopter that twirls around shooting off laser beams. Lights and sound effects are all state-of-the-art. Attracts a suitably way-out crowd.

STUDIO M
Hotel Plaza, Beach Rd. Map **4***B5*
☎298-0011 AE DC MC VISA *Open Sun–Thurs till 2am, Fri, Sat till 3am. MRT: Bugis.*
Fast, furious pace and sophisticated gadgetry such as computer-synchronized lighting and sound.

T.G.I.F. (THANK GOD IT'S FRIDAY)
04-44-50 Far East Plaza, Scotts Rd. Map **3***B2* *☎235-6181* ═ ▥ AE DC MC VISA *Open noon–2am. MRT: Orchard.*
A lively disco on weekends, combined with a laid-back bistro offering a good pub-style menu, at reasonable prices. Popular with offduty Filipina domestics and foreign sailors. The presence of so many Filipinas taking their leisure on weekends has turned Scotts and Orchard Rds. into lively pedestrian promenades on Sundays, the domestics' day off — to the extent that a proposal has been drawn up to close Orchard Rd. to traffic altogether.

TOP TEN
Orchard Towers, 400 Orchard Rd. Map **3***B2* *☎732-3077* AE DC MC VISA *Open Mon–Fri till 2am, Sat, Sun till 3am. MRT: Orchard.*
Sophisticated disco, lounge and theater all in one. Three-level decor with Manhattan backdrop. Includes live shows by international and local performers and bands. Lively, casual atmosphere.

XANADU
Lower Lobby, Shangri-La Hotel, 22 Orange Grove Rd. Map **3***A1* *☎737-3644* AE DC MC VISA *Open 9pm–3am. MRT: Orchard.*
A place where guests can relax for an evening and enjoy the occasional dance. Away from the dance floor the music is soft enough to allow an easy flow of relaxed conversation. The decor is elegant, and the nightly laser show is spectacular laser.

Singapore: shopping

A shopper's paradise

Shopping centers in Singapore are education and entertainment islands and must be seen as such to be truly appreciated. There is yet to be an adequate study of their social importance to modern Asia, but a famous comment attributed to Sukarno, the first president of an independent Indonesia — Singapore's neighbor to the south — held that it is refrigerators, meaning the aspiration to possess them, and not ideologies, that make revolutions. If so, Singapore's consumer outposts are to modern Southeast Asia what *The Communist Manifesto* was to followers of Karl Marx.

Take refrigerators, owned by 85 percent of Singapore's householders but only 36 percent of those in Jakarta, Indonesia's capital city. To the other 64 percent, refrigerators are the stuff of dreams. Shopping centers titillate the imagination with symbols of all the lives that are possible to any man with a bank account or credit card. And they make the idea of a global village tangible, in the form of things from everywhere on earth that people can touch, try out or try on, and even own if they so wish.

Far East Plaza on Scotts Rd., for instance, has a MacDonald's, the Bintang Timur Malaysian restaurant, Japanese and Indian restaurants, and a mini hawkers' food area in which to eat. For nightlife it has the T.G.I.F. ("Thank God It's Friday") pub and bistro, a *karaoke* bar and a massage parlor. And, should you want to shop in this shopping center, there are dozens of outlets with hundreds of products — and money changers in case you run shy of local currency.

It has been in shopping centers such as these that, over the past 25 years, average Singaporean families have had their first experience of air conditioning, color televisions, escalators and the other marvels of our times.

The STPB's *Singapore Shopping* brochure, available free of charge, lists 33 different highrise shopping complexes in the major urban areas. Besides this, it has shoppers' maps and "A Guide to Honest, Reliable and Courteous Shops" — meaning some 450 shops that carry the "Merlion" seal of approval, issued by the STPB and the Consumers' Association of Singapore.

Newest of Singapore's emporia is **Lau Pa Sat** (formerly **Telok Ayer Market**), reopened at Raffles Quay in early 1992 after extensive renovation. The former wet market, within the financial district, housed in what is Southeast Asia's largest remaining Victorian cast-iron structure, has been transformed into a consumer goods market with a permanently festive feel. Beneath its unique clock tower, mime artists entertain crowds of shoppers looking for crafts and souvenirs, and diners in self-consciously "quaint" restaurants. Evenings feature live performances centered on the market's history.

Given the sheer range of both native and imported goods on offer, the highly competitive prices and the long opening hours, it is clear that shopping amounts to a national pastime in Singapore. And although veteran shoppers will spot many international designer shops familiar to any cosmopolitan center, much remains that is special to Singapore: 22- to 24-karat gold jewelry, silk, Far Eastern antiques, *objets d'art* and curios, hi-tech electronic equipment, Oriental carpets, pewterware, basketwork and many other treasures.

BARGAINING AND PRICES

Singapore has many large department stores where prices are *strictly* fixed, in addition to a vast number of shops within the shopping center complexes, where bargaining is the traditional *modus operandi*. Tactful bargaining is usually acceptable even in elegant establishments (at jewelry stores, for example), but more aggressive bargaining is expected in markets, street stalls and in places that are obviously designed to attract the tourist trade.

Before bargaining, it is always advisable to shop around and note the range of prices available. If you are looking for an item that you can also get at home, such as a camera, it's also important to know the selling price of the item in your own country — it may not always be so different. In addition, keep away from "touters" — people who solicit in the street for your business at certain stores. It's illegal.

Although discouraged by the government, a black market still exists in Singapore. Therefore, beware of name-brand goods offered by roadside vendors at low prices — they are almost always inferior imitations. If the time has come to give in to the urge to buy a Gucci wallet, be sure to do it at a reputable department store or at a shop that is an authorized distributor. Most shops are happy to accept major charge/credit cards and travelers checks, and do *always* remember to get a proper receipt. Further, don't forget to obtain a guarantee card when purchasing a camera or electronic goods.

WHERE TO GO

Singapore has a number of major shopping districts. Two distinctive examples are the **Orchard Rd.** area, featuring many upmarket, exclusive shops, malls and department stores, and **Change Alley** *(between Raffles Place and Collyer Quay),* which is a stall-filled bargainer's delight. There are also several sections of Singapore that specialize in ethnic goods.

The region in and around **Serangoon Rd.**, known as "Little India," is brimming with saris, jewelry, carved wood items and much more, while **Arab St.** offers an array of prayer rugs, baubles and basketware, and **Chinatown** has a wide variety of fine crafts for the discerning shopper.

Finally, farther toward the outskirts of the city are other shopping complexes, where many Oriental curios and other items are sold at quite reasonable prices. One such is **Holland Village** *(just a short taxi ride from MRT Buona Vista Station, or about a 15-minute walk).* This western suburb is a favorite haunt for European expatriates living in Singapore. The main building in the area has a large supermarket on the ground floor and, more interestingly, several more floors that are chock-a-block with shops selling everything from home sewing sets to reproductions of Dutch colonial artifacts from Indonesia.

The area around the shopping plaza was formerly a tumbledown collection of shophouses selling everything from basketware to rabbit food. These shops have now been gentrified out of existence in favor of about a half-dozen fast-food outlets, from Kentucky Fried Chicken to Milano's Pizza shop, and other shops selling clothes, cameras, batik, ceramics, curios and anything else in which any Westerner living in the neighborhood has ever expressed interest.

Holland Village is also the home of the well-known shop, **Lims Arts and Crafts**, a favorite haunt of locals and seasoned tourists, who love to browse and buy inexpensive, fun gifts and knicknacks.

STPB offers a free booklet, *Your Guide to Good Bargains in the Suburbs,* which reviews a dozen suburban areas for sights, food and drink as well as creative shopping excursions.

ANTIQUES AND HANDICRAFTS

Antiques, handicrafts, curios and *objets d'art* are on sale in such profusion throughout Singapore — in modern shopping complexes, in special night markets, in small shops that line a street specializing in a particular craft or ware — that there is little point in listing individual outlets here. Instead, here are some general guidelines.

An excellent place to begin is the **Singapore Handicraft Centre** *(between Grange Rd. and Tanglin Rd. off map 3 B1).* Here there is an array of antique and handicrafts shops featuring everything from Malaysian silk to inlaid lacquer screens. Reviving an old tradition, the **Pasar Malam** (Night Market) is also held here four nights each week *(Wed 6-10pm, Fri-Sun 4-10pm).*

The **Tanglin Shopping Centre** and the **Holland Road Shopping Centre** are excellent places for ferreting out antiques, curios and all types of folk art. A trip down **Orchard Rd.** or the nearby **Cuppage Rd.** can lead to similar "finds."

Boat Quay has a few shops among its renovated shophouses (most are restaurants and bars), such as **Chiao Yi**, which offers an eclectic tumble of items, ranging from antique lacquerware to old electric table fans *(60 Boat Quay, map 4 D4 ☎ 534-2483 Fx 533-8247).*

Visit **The New Ming Village** *(32 Pandan Rd., map 1 E3 ☎ 265-7711 Fx 266-2465, open daily 9am–5.30pm, MRT: Clementi or Jurong East)* to see craftsmen reproduce the finest porcelain and ceramic works of China's great Ming and Qing dynasty eras, which are available for sale. The **Thong Chai Medical Institute** (a.k.a. **Seiwan Arts Centre**) now houses a large shop with Chinese curios.

The **Mint Coin Gallery** *(249 Jalan Boon Lay Rd., Jurong, map 1 D2, open Mon-Fri 9.30am-4.30pm, MRT: Clementi or Jurong East)* caters to collectors of coins and medallions as well as displaying its own unique collection.

Handicrafts

Evocative of languid colonial elegance, **Rattan and cane furniture** are ideal for the summer house, conservatory or garden porch, and the best place to find it is all along Joo Chiat Rd. In addition to selling stock items, many shops will also create furniture to order. A seemingly endless choice of wickerware can be found along Arab St., with baskets, chests, hampers, totes and much more in every size and style.

For unique reproductions of colonial-era furniture in Indonesian hardwoods, try **Heritage Handmade Antiques**, which offers everything from miniatures at a few hundred dollars to full, four-poster bedroom sets for S$36,000. Their showrooms are at Tanjong Pagar Conservation Area, at 6 Raffles Blvd. in Marina Square and at 51 Neil Rd. *(factory and office* ☎ *368-0088* ℻ *368-1101).*

Pewterware is another specialty of Singapore. **Selangor Pewter** *(02-00 Thongsia Building, 30 Bideford Rd., map 3 B3 and 02-12 Singapore Handicraft Centre)* has been famous for quality and attractive designs since its founding in 1885. Or visit what is reputed to be the world's first **Pewter Museum** *(49A Duxton Rd. in Tanjong Pagar Conservation Area, map 3 E3* ☎ *221-4436* ℻ *224-2231, open daily 9am-5.30pm),* in two restored shophouses. Here you can see century-old samples of pewterware as well as daily demonstrations of the traditional pewter-making process, and purchase reproductions.

Traditional **Indian jewelry** can be picked up on Serangoon Rd. and **Malaysian jewelry** on Arab St. Another "take-home" item that is popular here is Indonesian and Malaysian **batik cloth**, which can be found in countless shops and department stores, as well as at the Singapore Handicraft Centre.

Good buys in **Oriental carpets** can also be found. Local reproductions of costly Chinese carpets are on sale at **Singapore Carpet Manufacturers** *(Haw Par Centre, Clemenceau Ave., map 4 C4).* Other locations for Persian, Turkish, Indian, Chinese and Afghan carpets and rugs are shops along Orchard Rd. and Arab St., carpet stores in the Tanglin and Lucky Plaza Shopping Centres and at the Singapore Handicraft Centre.

The elegant implements used for the traditional Chinese art of **calligraphy** are available at the **Chung Hwa Bookshop** *(71 South Bridge Rd.).* Here you can purchase delicate brushes, special paper, seals, inks — all beautiful to display if not to try your hand at; the shop also sells fine art work by contemporary Chinese painters, in addition to calligraphic scrolls and hand-painted fans.

If **Chinese goods** are a particular interest, try one of the emporiums — for example, the **Overseas Emporium** *(People's Park Complex, New Bridge Rd., map 4 D4);* the **Chinese Emporium** *(International Building, Orchard Rd., map 3 B2);* and the **Oriental Emporium** *(People's Park Centre, New Bridge Rd).* These are department stores filled with a large selection of reasonably priced Chinese items such as carved wooden chests and other handicrafts, silks, traditional brocade jackets, enameled jewelry, pottery, china and so on.

For **crocodile-** and other reptile-skin products, visit one of the CRO-CODILE FARMS listed on page 68.

DEPARTMENT STORES

Department stores are another popular attraction in Singapore. Like all their worldwide counterparts, these also sell a very expensive range of items. However, with each store there is a somewhat different emphasis. For example, the native **Metro** and the **C. K. Tang's** stores, the Japanese-owned **Yaohan** (all of which have a number of branches), and the French-owned **Printemps** are all known for very good prices on zingy women's fashions and trendy casual wear. **Metro Grand** is a posher, more upmarket version of its Metro relation.

English-owned **Robinson's** is Singapore's oldest department store, now with an updated and very fashionable image, selling high-quality goods. The **Chinese Emporium**, **Overseas Emporium** and **Klasse** are all particularly well known for their excellent prices on Chinese clothing, carved wood items, handicrafts, china, home furnishings and so on.

The Japanese department stores **Isetan** and **Daimaru** feature a special selection of interesting items and attractive ladies' fashions, both budget and designer range, especially from Japan.

Virtually all of the big department stores accept major charge/credit cards. Shopping hours are long, with an average daily opening time of 9.30–10am and a closing time of 9–10pm, generally all through the weekend as well.

- **C.K. Tang's Superstore**   320 Orchard Rd. Map **3**B2 ☎737-5500.
- **Chinese Emporium**   02-00 International Building, 360 Orchard Rd. Map **3**B2 ☎737-1645.
- **Isetan Havelock**   02-00 Teck Suat Chambers. Map **3**D3 ☎732-8866.
- **Isetan Katong**   Parkway Parade, 80 Marine Parade Rd. Map **2**D6 ☎345-5555. MRT: Paya Lebar.
- **Isetan Orchard**   Wisma Atria, Orchard Rd. Map **3**B2 ☎733-7777.
- **Klasse**   Centrepoint Complex, Orchard Rd. Map **3**B3.
- **Metro Grand**   7500 Beach Rd., The Plaza. Map **4**B5 ☎297-2388.
- **Metro Orchard**   Holiday Inn Royal Building, Scotts Rd. Map **3**B2 ☎737-1966.
- **Overseas Emporium**   420 People's Park Complex, 02-70. Map **3**D3 ☎535-0555.
- **Printemps**   100 Orchard Rd., 01-01 Meridien Shopping Centre. Map **3**B3 ☎235-7542.
- **Robinson's**   Centrepoint Complex, Orchard Rd. Map **3**B2 ☎737-9000.
- **Singapore Daimaru**   Liang Court Complex, 177 River Valley Rd. Map **3**C3 ☎339-1111.

- **Yaohan Orchard**   Plaza Singapura, Orchard Rd. Map **3**B3
☎337-4061.

FABRICS
Reams of dazzling silk are at your fingertips in Singapore. Magnificent Indian silk from Kashmir and Benares can be bought at any of the numerous sari stores in the Serangoon Rd. district at excellent prices. Thai silk is best found at **Design Thai** in the Tanglin Shopping Centre.

Perhaps the finest Chinese silk in Singapore is sold at **China Silk House** *(four branches: 02-77/78 Lucky Plaza, map **3**B2 ☎235-3528; 02-11/13 Tanglin Shopping Centre, map **3**B1 ☎235-5020; 02-01 Centrepoint Shopping Centre, map **3**B3 ☎733-0555; 01-03 Scotts Shopping Centre, map **3**B2 ☎235-4696)*. The Tanglin branch also incorporates a tailoring service.

FASHION AND TAILORING
Although the boutiques of international *haute couture* designers such as Chanel, Yves St. Laurent and others can be seen in the more elegant shopping centers and hotel arcades, Singapore does have a few of its own leading designers, whose luxurious fashions, especially in silk, should most definitely be sought out.

Custom tailoring is yet another specialty of Singapore, and many tailoring shops can create attractive, well-priced fashions for women and men in a relatively short time.

Tailors
- **Benny Ong**   Featured at China Silk House, 02-77/78 Lucky Plaza (and at all other China Silk House shops). Map **3**B2 ☎235-3528 [AE] [◆] [CD] [VISA]
- **Mohan's Custom Tailors**   14 Scotts Rd., 02-81 Far East Plaza. Map **3**B2 ☎732-4936.
- **Nath and Co.**   02-37 Tanglin Shopping Centre, Tanglin Rd. Map **3**B2 ☎734-6355.
- **Rewas**   Specialists Shopping Centre, Orchard Rd. Map **3**B3.

Women's fashions
- **Tan Yoong**   02-50 Lucky Plaza, 304 Orchard Rd. Map **3**B2 ☎734-3783 [AE] [◆] [CD] [VISA]

JEWELRY
Shops displaying rich 18-, 22- and 24-karat gold jewelry and dazzling stones are a common sight in Singapore. Many shops will be happy to mount unset precious and semiprecious stones (yours or theirs), with their in-house designers translating your ideas into a unique piece of jewelry. As they are used to working with time-pressed tourists, made-to-order items can usually be fashioned without delay in their own workshops. In addition, there is always a wide choice of ready-made pieces.

The Chinatown area, South Bridge Rd., New Bridge Rd. and People's Park are all good places to explore, especially for jade, pearls, precious stones and gold, in addition to the jewelry stores in the Orchard Rd. area. Don't be surprised if you see gold jewelry being sold by weight — that is standard procedure in some stores.

Jewelry prices are *extremely* competitive in Singapore, so don't forget to insist on a large discount (up to 50 percent) on the first quoted price (and progress from there . . .), even in a very upmarket shop.

*   **C.T. Hoo**   01-22 Tanglin Shopping Centre. Map **3**B1 ☎235-9343 AE ⊕ ⊙ VISA
*   **Je T'aime**   120 Oxley Rise. Map **3**C3 ☎734-2275 AE ⊕ ⊙ VISA
*   **Lai Loy Jewelry Co. Ltd**   01-28/29 Specialists Shopping Centre. Map **3**B3 ☎737-8248 AE ⊕ ⊙ VISA
*   **Madras Goldsmith**   154 Serangoon Rd. Map **4**A5 ☎291-2898 AE ⊕ ⊙ VISA
*   **Singapore Gems and Metals Co. Ltd**   7 Kung Chong Rd. ☎475-9733 AE ⊕ ⊙ VISA MRT: Redhill.

SHOPPING CENTERS

Shopping arcades and malls are everywhere in Singapore. Locals and tourists alike seem to greatly favor these air-conditioned, multilevel "mini-cities" of shopping, which feature shops of all kinds, boutiques, snack bars, restaurants, and usually a large department store or two.

Lucky Plaza is considered by many to be *the* bargainer's paradise, while **The Promenade**, full of ritzy, upmarket shops, is indeed designed for strutting. The following are the main shopping centers:

*   **Centrepoint**   Orchard Rd. Map **3**B3.
*   **Liang Court**   River Valley Rd. Map **3**C3.
*   **Lucky Plaza**   Orchard Rd. Map **3**B2.
*   **People's Park**   Eu Tong Sen St. Map **3**D3.
*   **The Promenade**   Orchard Rd. Map **3**B3.
*   **Scotts**   Scotts Rd. Map **3**B2.
*   **Shaw Centre**   Scotts Rd. Map **3**B2.
*   **Tanglin Shopping Centre**   Orchard Rd. and Tanglin Rd. Map **3**B2.

Finally, there is **Changi Airport**, with 94 shops in Terminals 1 and 2, as well as the **Singapore Showcase** *(Changi Airport, Terminal 2, Departure/Transit Lounge),* a spacious showcase for Singapore-made products. Fashion labels on display include Rest & Relax denim, Chomel ladies' executive wear, Estabelle for casuals, Mido silk lingerie, Hilly Creations and Bonia Fashion for leather goods and accessories. There are also electronic products, perfumes and jewelry.

At the airport's departure lounges, pick up a copy of the free *Shopping and Eating* guides to Changi, published by the Civil Aviation Authority of Singapore (CAAS).

Singapore: recreation

Sports and activities

The **Singapore Sports Council** (*☎345-7111 ext. 399*) is a state body responsible for promoting fitness, sports and physical recreation. It operates a range of public sports facilities, and provides useful information on badminton, cricket, golf, gymnasiums, netball, rugby, soccer, squash, swimming, tennis and track and field.

For spectator sports, the **Singapore Cricket Club** (*The Padang, map 4D4 ☎338-9271*) has cricket matches (*Mar-Oct Sat from 1.30pm, Sun from 10.30am*) and rugby matches (*Sept-Mar Sat at 4pm and 5.15pm*).

GOLF
Among Singapore's 17 golf courses are some of the finest in Southeast Asia, designed by such luminaries as architects Robert Trent Jones, Jr. and Ronald Fream. Full membership can be prohibitive, but visitors need only pay green fees, which range from S$50 on weekdays to $120 on weekends. The Singapore Tourist Promotion Board has created a six-day golfing tour package that includes sightseeing, golf clinics and plenty of time on the greens.

Golf courses
- **Changi Golf Club**   Netheravon Rd. ☎545-5133 Fx 545-2531, 9 holes, par 68
- **Jurong Country Club**   Jurong Town Hall Rd., map **1D2** ☎560-5655 Fx 567-1900, 18 holes, par 71, recently remodeled by Max Wexler to include night golfing
- **Keppel Club**   Bukit Chermin, map **2E4** ☎273-5522 Fx 278-1448, 18 holes, par 71, founded in 1904, 9 holes, recently redesigned by Ronald Fream
- **Raffles Country Club**   Jalan Ahmad Ibrahim, map **1D2** ☎861-7655 Fx 861-5563, two 18-hole courses, par 72, designed by Robert Trent Jones
- **Seletar Country Club**   Seletar Airbase, map **2B5** ☎481-4745 Fx 481-3000, 9 holes, par 70, 18-hole course under construction
- **Sembawang Country Club**   17km Sembawang Rd., map **2B4** ☎257-0642, 18 holes, par 72
- **Sentosa Golf Club**   Sentosa Island, map **2F4** ☎275-0022 Fx 275-0005, two 18-hole courses, Serapong par 72 and Tanjong par 69

- **Singapore Island Country Club**   Upper Thomson Rd., map 2C4 ☎459-2222 Ⓕⓧ458-3796, four 18-hole courses, par 72 for Bukit and New, 69 for Island and 70 for Sime
- **Tanah Merah Country Club**   East Coast Parkway (Garden Course) ☎ Ⓕⓧ545-1731; (Tampines Course) ☎ Ⓕⓧ542-4256, two 18-hole courses, par 72
- **Warren Golf Club**   Folkestone Rd., map 1D3 ☎777-6533 Ⓕⓧ778-5502, 9 holes, par 70

There are also golf driving ranges at **Marina Bay Golf and Country Club** *(Marina South, map 2E5 ☎221-2811)* with driving range, 150 bays, 230m (250-yard) landscaped fairway, 9-hole putting green, and at **Parkland Golf Driving Range** *(East Coast Parkway, map 2E6 ☎345-1111)* with 60 bays and a 200m (220-yard) driving range. STPB and Franco–Asian Travel offer a golfing vacation for about US$2,000, inclusive of five hotel nights in the Sheraton Towers or Omni Marco Polo hotels and all green fees.

HORSE-RACING
The **Bukit Turf Club** *(Bukit Timah Rd., map 1D3 ☎469-3611)* has a showpiece of a racecourse, set in 40ha (96 acres) of beautifully landscaped grounds. Its gigantic 18 by 6-meter (57 by 19-foot) "Diamond Vision" color video screen provides close-up television viewing of the horses even when they are on the far side of the track, and also relays coverage of races in neighboring Malaysia. The first race of a typical eight-event Saturday afternoon meeting begins at noon.

RACQUETBALL
There are public courts at the **East Coast Recreation Centre** *(Off map 2E6 ☎449-0541, open 7.30am-11.30pm)*.

RIDING
There are two grounds for riding horses: the **Saddle Club** *(behind the Turf Club ☎469-3611 ext. 295 for information and reservations Mon-Fri 9am-4pm; Sat 9am-noon)* and the **Singapore Polo Club** *(Thomson Rd., map 2D4 ☎256-4530)*.

SQUASH
There are public courts in most community centers. Among the most popular are: **Ang Mo Kio Squash Centre** *(204 Ang Mo Kio Avenue 9, map 2C4 ☎482-4980)*; **Clementi Recreation Centre** *(12 West Coast Walk, map 1D3 ☎778-8966, MRT: Clementi)*; **East Coast Recreation Centre** *(East Coast Parkway, off map 2E6 ☎449-0541)*; **Farrer Park** *(Rutland Rd., off map 4A4 ☎251-4166)*; **National Stadium** *(Kallang, map 2E5 ☎348-1258)*. Hours vary between 7–8am and 10–11pm. Some hotels have courts, too.

TENNIS
For a full list of courts open to visitors, call the **Singapore Sports Council** *(☎345-7111 ext. 399)*. Some hotels have tennis facilities,

notably the HYATT REGENCY, and the SHANGRI-LA and the BEAUFORT on Sentosa Island. Popular courts include: **Clementi Recreation Centre** and **Farrer Park** (see SQUASH, page 129); **Singapore Tennis Centre** *(East Coast Parkway* ☎ *442-5966);* **Tanglin Tennis Centre** *(Minden Rd., off map 3 B2* ☎ *473-7236).* Hours are from 7am to 10-11pm.

WATERSPORTS

Waterskiing is best off the N coast, around Coney Island, Sembawang Island and in the Kim-Kim River. **Punggol Boatel** *(Punggol Point, map 2 B6* ☎ *282-6879)* rents boats, skis and boatmen. **East Coast Sailing Centre** *(1210 East Coast Parkway* ☎ *449-5118, MRT: Bedok)* has rental equipment and also offers a windsurfing package that includes instruction, full equipment and a meal.

Singapore has no fewer than 26 public swimming pools. Contact the **Singapore Sports Council** *(* ☎ *345-7111 ext. 399)* for details. Visitors with children will almost certainly want to check out the boisterous wave pools and water slides at **CN West Leisure Park** *(9 Japanese Garden Rd., map 1 D2* ☎ *261-4771, MRT: Lakeside)* and at **Big Splash** *(East Coast Parkway, map 2 E5* ☎ *345-1211, MRT: Paya Lebar),* which boasts the longest slides in Southeast Asia and a children's pool, too. Great family fun.

Singapore: excursions

Short hops from Singapore

Surrounded by two of its most fascinating nations, Singapore is an ideal jumping-off point for exploring the Southeast Asian region. If you have a few days to spare, it's a short hop to peninsular Malaysia or Indonesia, to the north and south respectively.

The contrast between Singapore and surrounding countries highlights how far the city–state has progressed in terms of infrastructure and facilities. It also gives a glimpse of Singapore in the old days.

But Malaysia and Indonesia are to be considered not only in relation to their tiny, wealthy neighbor. Both countries offer a vast range of opportunities for the traveler, from Hindu festivals to Dayak villages, from heavenly beaches to mock-Tudor and cream teas in the hill resorts.

Malaysia

Peninsular Malaysia lies to the N of Singapore, so close that it is linked to Singapore by a 1km ($\frac{1}{2}$-mile) causeway. Small wonder, then, that many Singaporeans hop across to shop, have a seafood meal, or relax on one of Malaysia's superb beaches. Depending on the extent and duration of your visit, you can travel by road, rail or air.

When time is limited, a good idea is to join any of the organized tours starting from Singapore that offer either a few days at a specific destination, or a wider exploration of Malaysia in seven days.

Malaysia has four major areas of interest for tourists: **West coast** towns, much influenced by Portuguese, Dutch and English colonialists as well as Overseas Chinese immigrants, and the inland hill stations; **East coast** beaches, and the centers of indigenous Malay culture; **Malaysian coastal islands** in the South China Sea, for water sports; and **East Malaysia**, which comprises part of East Kalimantan (the former island of Borneo), shared with Indonesia and the sultanate of Brunei.

HILL RESORTS
Among Malaysia's most popular tourist destinations are its hill resorts, which offer a welcome respite from heat and humidity, amid some spectacular scenery.

Cameron Highlands

Reached by **bus** *or* **taxi** *from Tapah, 200km (125 miles) N of Kuala Lumpur.*
The three separate hillocks comprising the Cameron Highlands, **Brinchang**, **Tanah Rata** and **Ringlet**, are uncannily English in landscape, with rolling green hills and picturesque cottages. There are plantations and vegetable gardens to visit, waterfalls to swim in, an 18-hole golf course, badminton and tennis courts. For the more adventurous, there are jungle walks and mountain climbing. Caution: go into the jungle only with a guide or someone who knows the area well.

For accommodation, any of the following hotels should be reliable: **Foster's Lake House** *(Ringlet* ☎ *05-948680);* **Garden Hotel** *(Tanah Rata* ☎ *05-941911);* **Ye Olde Smokehouse** *(Tanah Rata* ☎ *05-941214)* and **Hotel Merling** *(Tanah Rata* ☎ *05-941205).*

If you prefer to stay in a bungalow, the choice is between the **Golf View Villa** *(Tanah Rata* ☎ *05-941624)* and **Rose Cottages** *(* ☎ *05-941173).* After walking in the hills, try **Ye Olde Smokehouse**, famous for its Devonshire teas, with delicious hot buttered scones.

Fraser's Hill

Altitude: 1,524m (4,983ft) above sea level. **By car:** *2hrs-plus from the Malaysian capital of Kuala Lumpur.*
A nature-lover's delight, Fraser's Hill offers wooded surroundings, cool, crisp air, waterfalls and a bird sanctuary. It also has a golf course, tennis courts, pony rides, skating rinks and some good restaurants. A sports complex in town has a gymnasium, squash courts and saunas. There's also a mini-zoo and children's park.

Accommodation can be found in resthouses, many of which are rambling, colonial bungalows. **Fraser's Hill Development Corporation** has bungalows for rent *(for reservations* ☎ *093-382201).* There is also the **Merlin Hotel** *(* ☎ *093-382279).* **Foster's Steakhouse** is a recommended restaurant, serving sizzling steaks at moderate prices.

EAST COAST

Malaysia's E coast is a lovely resort area with superb beaches, particularly in the states of **Kuantan**, **Terengganu** and **Kelantan**. Kuantan can be reached either by a brief plane trip or by an all-day bus ride from Kuala Lumpur. Terengganu is also served by bus.

As well as beaches, the E coast offers charming fishing villages, caves, markets, local festivals and handicrafts.

For accommodation in **Kuantan**: choose between the **Hyatt Kuantan** *(Telok Chempedak* ☎ *09-525211);* the **Merlin Inn Resort** *(Telok Chempedak* ☎ *09-522388);* the **Chendor Motel** *(29th milestone, Kemaman Rd.* ☎ *09-591369);* or the **Club Med Cherating** *(29th milestone, Kemaman Rd.* ☎ *09-7377397).*

In **Terengganu**, hotels include: the **Tanjong Jara Beach hotel** *(8th mile off Jalan Dungun, Dungun* ☎ *09-841801);* the **Rantau Abang Visitor Centre** *(13th milestone off Jalan Dungun, Dungun* ☎ *09-841533);* or the **Pantai Primula Hotel** *(Jalan Persingghan, Kuala Terengganu* ☎ *096-622100).*

There are many open-air eating houses, coffee shops and restaurants along the coastline. Many of them are unpretentious, but don't be put off by their appearance. Often they serve a delicious feast of seafood freshly hauled from the sea, and local Malay dishes.

Coffee shops at Telok Champedak, on the way to **Hyatt Kuantan**, serve lobster, crabs, prawns and other seafood, steamed, grilled or fried with chili. **Budaya Restaurant**, in the heart of the state capital **Kota Bharu**, serves authentic Thai-influenced Kelantan cuisine.

PENANG

An island off the NW coast of peninsular Malaysia, Penang is a popular resort and can be reached by plane from Singapore. For those with more time to spend, there is a 13-hour train journey from Singapore to **Butterworth**, followed by a brief ferry ride.

In addition to its idyllic beaches, Penang is famous for its Chinese pagodas, Indian temples, historic churches and its unique cuisine. Of particular interest are the **Snake Temple**, where poisonous snakes live amid the temple carvings, **Penang Hill**, the historic **Fort Cornwallis** and the **Botanic Gardens**.

Penang has a large range of accommodation to choose from, either in the city (**Georgetown**) or in resort hotels along the beaches. Any of the following is worth a try: the **Rasa Sayang Hotel** *(Batu Ferringi Beach* ☎ *04-811811);* the **Casuarina Beach Hotel** *(Batu Ferringi* ☎ *04-811711);* or the **Golden Sands Beach** *(Batu Ferringi* ☎ *04-811911).*

Penang has plenty of seafood on offer along the beaches of **Tanjong Tokong**. To sample a variety of Penang cuisine — basically Chinese in style but with the addition of local spices and flavor — visit any of the open-air stalls along Gurney Drive or at the Esplanade in the capital, **Georgetown**, and try *Penang Laksa, Goo Bak Kway Tewo* or *satay.*

EAST COAST ISLANDS

A number of delightful small islands stand in the South China Sea off peninsular Malaysia's E coast: **Pulau**, **Rawa**, **Babi**, **Babi Besar**, **Tioman**, **Berhentian** and others. The waters around these coral-fringed islands teem with rich underwater life, and they provide a perfect setting for camping and relaxation. On Pulau, Tioman and Rawa, accommodation is available in hotels, chalets or in local villages.

These islands are accessible from the town of **Mersing**, where you board a hovercraft or ferry. Mersing is a three-hour drive from Singapore and can also be reached by bus.

To visit the largely uninhabited islands that have no scheduled boat services, it is best to charter a fishing boat, which will cruise around the various islands and stay with you for the entire trip. Remember to bring your own food supplies and camping equipment. Boats may be rented from the Mersing jetty, a short walk from the Mersing Tourist Centre. **Resort Cruises** *(* ☎ *278-4677)* operates to Tioman from the Singapore Cruise Centre.

MALACCA

Malacca is an historic town dating back to the 15thC, with many medieval buildings and streets. It is a short flight from Singapore and can also be reached by bus. Malacca was first visited by the Chinese in 1409, and later by the Portuguese, Dutch and British, all coveting its port and strategic location. It is a charming town in which to browse through antique stores and explore such sites of historic interest as its **fortress**, the **Malacca Museum**, and the old **Portuguese quarter**.

✥ Try: **Malacca Village Resort** *(Air Keroh* ☎ *06-313600)* with a mini-zoo and children's park; **Wisma Hotel** *(114A Jalan Bendahara* ☎ *06-228311);* **Palace Hotel** *(201 Jalan Munshi* ☎ *06-222282).*

═ Restaurants in the Portuguese settlement are renowned for their hot Portuguese curries and tidbits. Malacca is one of the strongholds of the Straits Chinese and has many restaurants serving the spicy Nonya cuisine.

SARAWAK

For a complete contrast, travel across the Borneo Straits to **Sabah** and **Sarawak** in East Malaysia, a trip to attract those with a spirit of adventure. The state has numerous wildlife parks, and offers safari trips up-river by boat to a Dayak longhouse. Kuching, Sarawak's capital, is only one hour's flying time from Singapore.

Sarawak's indigenous tribes include several groups: Dayaks, Ibans, Kayans, Kenyahs, Bidayuh and others. Traditionally they live communally in stilted longhouses, usually near a river. Until recently, the Dayaks were headhunters: captured heads can still be seen hanging in the longhouses. Now the tribes are peaceful, and welcome visitors for overnight stays. Visitors are lodged in separate huts a short distance from the longhouse, with separate, modern conveniences. They are invited into the longhouse to meet the Dayaks and to see their way of life.

There are other off-the-beaten-track destinations and sights in Sarawak. Prehistoric paintings have been found in the **Niah** caves. But the caves' main claim to fame are the prized birds' nests to be collected there, considered a delicacy in local desserts and soups. Nearby **Bako National Park**, a treasurehouse for botanists and nature lovers, is worth a few days' stay, as there is so much to explore. The park is best known as the home of such exotic flora as the carnivorous Pitcher Plant. It also has a coastline indented by sandy bays and marked by steep cliffs that make the park appealing to hikers.

Kuching, the capital of Sarawak, lacks chic but is brimming with charm. The sleepy riverine town evokes the days of the White Rajah: the English adventurer James Brooke, who established a dynasty there in the 19thC. The capital has an old-world flavor, and many colonial buildings survive. One day is sufficient to get a feel of Kuching, whose most outstanding attraction is the **Sarawak Museum**, containing excellent collections of archeological and cultural artifacts. Fishing villages and upriver boats are other sightseeing diversions on offer.

Trips upriver, visits to a **Dayak longhouse**, and other excursions are best arranged through tour operators. Tours are well organized, and guides speak the local Dayak dialects. For information contact the **Tourist Development Corporation of Malaysia** *(#01-03 Ocean Building, Collyer Quay, Singapore 0104, map 4 D4 ☎ 532-6351).*

✿ For accommodation in **Kuching**, try the **Holiday Inn** *(Tunku Abdul Rahman Rd. ☎ 423111)* or **Aurora Hotel** *(Macdougall Rd. ☎ 20281).*

SABAH

Sabah, Sarawak's neighbor in East Malaysia, is equally alluring, with lush jungles and Southeast Asia's highest mountain, **Mt. Kinabalu,** 4,905m (16,039 feet) high. Sabah is a two-hour flight from Singapore.

The Kandazans form a third of Sabah's one-million population. Once headhunters, they are the largest indigenous group, and many hold high government positions. The Bajaus, or Sea Gypsies, are the second largest group. Found mainly along the coast, they are now expert pony and buffalo rearers. Sabah also has Malay, Chinese, Indian, and small indigenous tribal groups.

Kota Kinabalu, the capital of Sabah, is spread out along the coast and lacks a focus. Some new office buildings and shopping complexes dominate the skyline against the backdrop of the Crocker Range of mountains, but it has little to offer the tourist. It is primarily a business and administrative capital, and you must get out into the countryside to really appreciate Sabah.

Tanjong Aru Beach, a popular resort located just 5km (3 miles) from the city center, is the best area close to the capital for swimming. It is a great spot too for windsurfing, scuba diving and snorkeling, and there are offshore islands for undisturbed swimming. Boats can be chartered from the Tanjung Aru Beach Hotel. Close by is **Prince Philip Park**, with a children's playground, skating rink and fish pond. The resort offers diving lessons, fishing and other boat trips.

On the outskirts of Kota Kinabalu is the **State Mosque**, a fine example of contemporary Islamic architecture. The **Sabah Museum** features exhibitions on natural history, the prehistory of Sabah and contemporary handicrafts and artifacts, including an enormous collection of Chinese trade porcelain. **Signal Hill** is the place to go for a panoramic view of the city, while at **Tun Faud Stephens Park**, close to the town center, you can rent fiberglass rowboats to take onto the lake there.

A trip to Sabah is incomplete without a visit to **Mt. Kinabalu National Park**. There are many trekking routes inside the park, and guides are available. The more athletic can explore on their own, and the really fit can try climbing Mt. Kinabalu, a favorite for novice climbers as it can be scaled in gradual stages.

Kundasan is a pleasant mountain resort on the outskirts of the National Park and a great place to get away from the lowland heat. It is noted for its alpine scenery and its delicious asparagus, strawberries and local dairy products.

Kota Belud is more than two hours' drive from Kota Kinabalu. It is popular for its lively *tamu,* or Sunday market — a burst of vivid color and activity filled with tobacco, fruit, vegetables and local cakes for sale, and a buffalo auction that takes place nearby.

On the way to Kota Belud is **Tuaran**, which has a bustling *tamu* and Sunday horse races. **Pantai Dalit** is a quiet beach close by, with clear, calm water.

Tenom is the gateway to the interior. Some of Sabah's remaining longhouses can be found here, notably in **Kampong Marais**. In **Kampong Kalibatang**, blowpipes are still made.

Close to **Sandakan**, on the E coast, the **Sepilok Nature Reserve** features an orangutan sanctuary. The **Gomantang Caves** are s of Sandakan and are accessible by boat. The caves are noted for birds' nests and a multitude of bats. Overnight camping nearby adds a touch of adventure.

Semporna, also on the E coast of Sabah, is a colorful, lively town famous for delicious seafood. Its coral-rich waters and offshore islands are perfect for underwater exploration. The clear waters and sandy beaches of the **Turtle Islands** — Pulau Selingan, Pulau Bakungan Kecil and Pulau Gulisan — off the coast from Sandakan, are two to three hours away by boat. Chalets are available on Pulau Selingan for overnight stays.

❧ If you do choose to stay in **Kota Kinabalu**, try the **Hyatt International Kinabalu**, which is located in the center of town. For accommodation close to the **Mt. Kinabalu National Park**, contact **Sabah Parks (Reservation)** *(P.O. Box #626, Kota Kinabalu, Sabah* ☎ *211585)*. If you are thinking of staying in **Kundasan**, try the **Kundasan Resort Hotel**.

Indonesia

Accessible by air or sea from Singapore, Indonesia is its second closest neighbor: an archipelago of 13,677 islands scattered in a convex curve south of Singapore, as far as the western coast of Australia. Indonesia is the fifth most populous and the largest Muslim nation on earth. It has a rich dynastic history, with cultural legacies from as far afield as India — which is how Bali came to remain an island steeped in an ancient Hinduism.

There are actually many tribal cultures and languages scattered across this massive archipelago. This means it has much to offer, from temple ruins to beach resorts, and from lively cities to distant islands only marginally affected by the 20th century.

ISLANDS NEAR SINGAPORE

Indonesia's **Batam** and **Tanjong Pinang** islands are popular excursions out of Singapore and are suitable for weekend breaks. Batam is a half-hour ferry ride from Singapore. For tickets, contact **Inasco Enterprises** *(Counter 10, PSA Finger Pier Building, Prince Edward Rd., map 4F4* ☎*224-0698)*. It has quiet beaches, clear waters and good seafood at Nong Sa. The **Batam Island Country Club** offers a wide range of facilities including golf, waterskiing and sailing.

Tanjong Pinang, two hours by boat from Batam, has a former Chinese trading town built largely on stilts; its major street is lined with seafood restaurants and shops. The ferry zigzags through everglades scenery, moving past the various islands and fishing villages that dot the coastline. Ferry services depart regularly from the **Singapore Cruise Centre**. The main operators are **Dino Shipping** *(* ☎*270-0311)*, **Auto Batam Ferry Services** *(* ☎*271-4866)*, **Indo-Falcon Shipping Pte. Ltd.** *(* ☎*270-7100)* and **J&N Cruise** *(* ☎*270-7100)*.

Another short excursion is to **Medan**, one hour's flying time from Singapore. The capital of the province of Acheh, Medan is the gateway to N Sumatra. Its attractions include the mountain resort of **Brastagi**, just over one hour's drive away. Home of the *marquisa,* or passion fruit, the resort is a pleasant retreat.

Prapat, the main tourist town, lies on the shores of **Lake Toba**. The large lake is in the crater of a volcano. Today, it is a popular resort where visitors can swim, water-ski and go boating among scenic surroundings. **Samosir Island**, reached in half an hour by motorboat from Prapat, is the center of the tribal Batak culture and houses several villages of historical interest.

BALI

Known as the "Island of the Gods," Bali is to many people still a magical place of colorful dances, festivals and temples. It can be reached by a direct flight from Singapore.

Despite a rather crass commercialism fed by tourists, hotels and resorts, Bali merits a visit, if only to discover the secret of the island's famed enchantment. Once away from Denpasar, the beaches of Sanur and Kuta, and the route that most tourists take through some of the island's villages, you can still find the kind of pristine beauty that characterized all areas of Bali only three decades ago.

Dotting the island are 20,000 Hindu temples, and every day seems to be a festival day. Festival processions are spectacular, as are the various ceremonies and dances that the Balinese so enjoy. **Ubud** is a painter's colony, with spectacular scenery nearby of terraced rice fields, a monkey forest and a gorge. **Mas** is a wood-carving village, famous for Topeng masks. There is a holy spring in **Tampaksiring** within the inner courtyard of a temple where many Balinese come for healing. **Kintamani** is a mountain resort with orange and passion fruit orchards and panoramic views, and **Sangeh** is famed for its sacred nutmeg forest inhabited by monkeys. There is a spectacular coastal view from the rock of **Tanah Lot**, which stands like a sentinel guarding the southern tip of Bali's coast.

Kuta, **Sanur** and **Denpasar** are the more heavily visited areas. Kuta, once known as the "hippies' beach," has the best sunsets in Bali and ideal waves for surfing. Sanur is the most commercialized section of Bali, since most of the hotels are located here. Colorful outriggers moored here may be rented for sea trips. Denpasar, Bali's capital, is hot and dusty. Its **museum** and **Kokar** (Conservatory of the Performing Arts) are worth a visit, as are the restaurants along **Jalan Gajah Mada**, the main street.

❧ *Losmans,* which are rather like *pensions,* provide the least expensive accommodation in Bali. However, there is no shortage of deluxe hotels, with all amenities available. Many hotels have developed into self-contained resorts offering a wide range of facilities for sailing, windsurfing, waterskiing, bowling and golf.

EAST KALIMANTAN (BORNEO)

On the former island of Borneo, **East Kalimantan** is being opened up to tourism. The main town is **Balikpapan**, largely an oil base, which can be reached by plane from Singapore. The chief attraction is to visit Dayak country, whose people were once famous as fierce headhunters. The two-day trip up the Mahakam River is a memorable one, as the boat passes through rural villages rich in local arts, culture and customs, and then farther on to the longhouses of the Dayaks. Along the route lies the ancient capital of **Tenggarong**, where the former sultan's palace, now a museum, still stands.

The journey goes as far as **Lamin Mancong**, a magnificent two-story longhouse built by the Benuaq tribe and now being restored as a museum to house old Benuaq artifacts. A regular tour up the Mahakam River is offered by **Hotel Benakutai**, the only international hotel in Balikpapan. The tour takes four days, with an overnight stay at Kotabangan.

JAKARTA

The capital and main gateway of Indonesia, Jakarta is easily accessible from Singapore. The city is hot, dusty and congested, but the suburbs, with their spacious, tree-lined boulevards and Dutch-style bungalows, can be a delight.

The **Ragunan Zoo** has a wide variety of Indonesian fauna such as the rare Komodo dragon (a type of monitor lizard) and orangutans, all in their natural habitat. Just 45 minutes' drive from Jakarta is **Bogor**, whose famed Botanic Gardens are considered to be among Asia's finest, housing some 4,000 species of plants.

Yogjakarta is noted for the famous **Borobodur** Buddhist temple complex located 40km (25 miles) outside the city. Built in the 18thC, Yogjakarta town is the undisputed Javanese cultural heartland; it has been a center of civilization for hundreds of years. The **sultan's palace**, **Plaosan** and **Prambanan** Hindu temples and **batik factories** are other attractions here. There are no direct flights from Singapore to Yogjakarta, but you can fly to Jakarta, and from there take a train or a domestic flight.

NIAS

Those looking for an out-of-the-way spot in Indonesia should head for the island of **Nias**, off the coast of Sumatra. Just across from **Telok Dalam**, the capital of Nias, is **Lagundri Beach**, a great spot for surfing. Beach cottages and hotels have transformed this area into a mini-vacation center. However, most visitors to Nias go to the ancient villages of **Bawomataluo** and **Hilisimaetano** to view the "stones": giant *menhirs* with beautiful carvings. Jumping over them is part of a rite of passage for young males in the village as they reach adulthood.

THE THOUSAND ISLANDS

For those who are fond of beaches and swimming, Jakarta's **Thousand Islands**, or **Pulau Seribu**, in the bay of Jakarta are worth a visit. Fishing, diving and sailing are all available. Nearby is **Pulau Rambut**, with a lively Sunday market and a bird sanctuary. Sail to the offshore islands by boat from Ancol Marina or from the harbor of Tanjong Priok. For visits to Pulau Rambut, permits must be obtained from the Indonesian Nature Conservation and Wildlife Service head office in Bogor.

Getting there

For tours to Indonesia, contact **Scenic Travel** *(110 Killiney Rd., #01-02, Singapore 0923, map 3 C3* ☎ *733-8688)* or **Jetabout** *(#07-05/06 The Promenade, 300 Orchard Rd, Singapore 0923, map 3 B2 (* ☎ *734-1818).* For trips to Tanjong Pinang and Batam, contact **Trident Travel** *(* ☎ *336-2233).*

Bangkok

Bangkok: color, chaos, culture

Superficially, Bangkok invites comparisons with many Western cities. In its pulsating cosmopolitanism it is reminiscent of New York; in its network of crowded canals it has something of Venice; and with its filigreed skyline, pierced by the innumerable spires of *chedis* and steeply pitched temple roofs, it is suggestive of Paris. Yet no Western city can prepare the visitor for the sheer color, vibrancy and essentially Oriental vitality of Bangkok.

Capital of a country slightly smaller than France, Bangkok has a population of more than seven million and is home to one in every eight Thais. As the country's political center, the city is the base both for Thailand's much-respected constitutional monarch, His Majesty King Bhumibol Adulyadej (Rama IX of the Chakri dynasty), and the government, along with the military and the many divisions of the enormous civil service.

Not merely a secular seat of power in Thailand, Bangkok also serves as an artistic and spiritual focus; it is the crucible of modern Thai history, art and culture — both high and low — and of Buddhism, the faith of 94 percent of the population. More prosaically, as home to thousands of prostitutes of both sexes, the city is a center of vice; it is also a cauldron of traffic congestion and those fellow evils of air pollution and noise.

THAILAND: AN UNCONQUERED KINGDOM

Unlike Singapore, Bangkok is the seat of a long-established civilization and not a product of colonial administration. It is in fact the capital of the only country in the region that never succumbed to Western colonial rule. To celebrate that phenomenon, in 1949 the nation's leaders changed their country's name from Siam to Thailand (Muang Thai) — "land of the free."

Today, Thailand is one of the most prosperous and stable countries in Southeast Asia, although it has not escaped political turbulence in recent years. Since a bloodless revolution in 1932 changed the absolute monarchy to a constitutional one, Thailand has experienced almost 20 military coups and attempted coups, as well as a spate of guerrilla insurgencies and student revolts.

The leaders of the most recent coup overthrew a civilian government and held power, with the promise of impending free elections, for about a year. They then created revulsion around the world, as well as in Thailand, when troops under their command fired indiscriminately on demonstrators at the country's Democracy Monument, in May 1992.

This led to the downfall of the military government and a general decline of the military's prominence in Thai political life, formalized with the passage of constitutional reforms under a newly-elected civilian government. Prime Minister Chuan Leekpai, in his mid-50s, is Thailand's 20th premier and only the third to be elected from a coalition of civilian political parties, rather than those controlled by the military.

This period of political turbulence has not prevented Thailand from becoming the fastest-rising economic star of the Southeast Asian nations, with annual economic growth rates running at between seven-and-a-half and eight percent. Despite the tragic events of May 1992, Japanese investors ranked Thailand as the most attractive Asian nation.

A worldwide survey of countries' economic performance in 1992 ranked Thailand seventh in the world (after Taiwan, Singapore, Luxembourg, Japan, the Netherlands and Malaysia). Countries with the biggest investments in Thailand in 1991 were Japan, with more than 30 percent of direct investment; followed by Hong Kong, with almost 25 percent; then Singapore, the United States and Taiwan.

BANGKOK: SOMETHING FOR EVERYONE

Like other great capitals, Bangkok has something to offer all tastes. Somerset Maugham praised its temple architecture. Joseph Conrad stayed at its riverfront Oriental Hotel. Groups of businessmen in search of sexual titillation are reputedly met at the airport by busloads of young women. Art collectors flock to marvel at the cultural treasures of the National Museum, and students come to learn the mysteries of Buddhism in one of its great centers. Anthropologists and missionaries pass through the city on their way to the 20 or so distinct hill tribes in the north, and UN volunteers come en route to the refugee camps in the northeast at the Cambodian border.

As Thailand's capital, Bangkok has everything to do with determining the quality of life in the rest of the country and virtually nothing to do with the way in which life is lived there. It is about 40 times larger than Thailand's second city, Chiang Mai, to the north. It is a city of civil servants, with 15 percent or more of its workforce serving assorted virtually autonomous divisions of government authority. And it is the rush-hour traffic caused by such workers, traveling to lunch or commuting from their suburban housing estates, that chokes the overcrowded arteries of the city three times a day.

Bangkok's influence extends beyond Thailand's political boundaries. It is the regional headquarters for more than a dozen United Nations agencies, an air transport gateway between Southeast Asia and the rest of the world, the shipping center from which flow most of the country's gemstones and jewelry, garments, computers and agricultural exports (mainly rice), and the financial center to which foreign exchange returns.

The core of the city is a man-made island the shape of a mango, enclosed by the Chao Phraya River and a canal. Most of the rest of the city was assembled after the late 1950s; a ramshackle collection of low-rise shops, houses and office buildings in a style often referred to as "egg crate architecture."

Navigating Bangkok can offer a considerable challenge. Until 1960, when American consultants made the first-ever planning maps of the city, no records existed of such fundamental indicators as the administrative divisions of the metropolitan area, the distribution of population, traffic characteristics, or the location of basic facilities such as schools and markets.

Most of the population of Bangkok is ethnic Thai and, like those of their traditional enemies, the Burmese, their cultural origins owe much to India. Indian cultural antecedents are responsible for the presence of Buddhism and of Brahmanistic traditions that survive in such practices as the King's annual Plowing Ceremony to plant the first rice seeds and so placate the rice gods; and various rituals are used to determine the sites of buildings and "spirit houses."

The rest of the population consists predominantly of Chinese, Malays, Khmers and Vietnamese. The Chinese are the largest single minority group and have traditionally controlled the country's commercially important rice-milling sectors. Despite their obvious economic power, however, they do not encounter the kind of animosity that their business acumen often arouses in other Southeast Asian countries.

Bangkok's Chinatown feels a little like such enclaves elsewhere in the world, but the Chinese have been intermarrying for so long that they are now well integrated into the Thai community. Many Thai families have a Chinese ancestor tucked away in their family tree; it has been estimated that at least half of Bangkok's population is of Chinese descent. Indeed, the offspring of mixed marriages, the *luk-chin,* are respected in Thai society for their reputed mental alertness.

Although Thailand is sometimes called "the land of smiles," there is a violent side to Bangkok society. Most murders in the city are crimes of passion. Tour books may extol the demure Thai women, but they rarely point out that Bangkok also has probably the only clinic in the world that is reputed to specialize in patching up dismembered males attacked by jealous females.

In recent years there have been some well-publicized cases of attacks on tourists, but these are mostly associated with drugs or with those areas in which drugs are trafficked, in the so-called "Golden Triangle" of the northwest border with Burma and in the far south. Yet more than five million tourists a year spend on average one happy week in Thailand wandering all over the country, and mishaps are noticeable only because they occur so rarely. Most foreigners *(farangs)* will be aware only of the splendor and beauty of a friendly and colorful city and its surrounding countryside.

"It makes you laugh with delight to think that anything
so fantastic could exist on this sombre earth."
(Somerset Maugham, on Bangkok)

Bangkok: culture, history and background

A brief history of Thailand

An outpost of Bronze Age civilization flourished around Ban Chiang in NE Thailand about 3500BC. Before the arrival of the first Thai people in the 12th–13thC, Indo-Javanese, Khmer and Mon ethnic groups inhabited areas of what is now Thailand.

The Thais themselves originated on the Yunnan plateau in SW China. They and their ethnic and linguistic cousins — the Shan, or "big Thai" — moved S, into N Thailand and N Burma respectively. One theory holds that the Yunnan kingdom of Nanchao (7th–13thC) was Thai, and that its people were driven S by expansionist Han Chinese. Another, now winning wider acceptance, is that the Thai were sent S to stabilize disruptive border regions.

Certainly, by the **early 13thC** Thais had settled in the areas of modern-day Laos and N Thailand, establishing small city-states and cultivating rice. By mid-century they had displaced the Khmer and the Mon as the dominant ethnic group. In **1238** the Khmer were expelled from Sukhothai (which means Dawn of Happiness) and the first independent Thai kingdom was founded there.

Farther N, Thai chieftain Mangrai conquered the Mon kingdom of Hari Haripunjaya, and in **1296** they founded a second Thai state, Lannathai (Land of a Million Rice Paddies), with its capital at Chiang Mai. By **1351** a third kingdom, Ayutthaya (named after the legendary Hindu city of Ayodhya), had emerged in the S on the lower reaches of the Chao Phraya River.

The three states competed with each other for control of the rich wet-rice lands of the central plains, while resisting the encroachments of Burmese and Mon rivals to the W and Khmers to the E. Nonetheless, the period from the founding of Sukhothai until its abandonment 140 years later in **1378** saw the emergence of a distinctive Thai cultural identity.

Sukhothai's greatest monarch, Ramkamhaeng, inherited a small city-state. By the end of his reign (**1318**), his political, administrative and military skills had extended its power into Laos, Burma and the southern peninsula. He is popularly believed to have invented the Thai script, and he popularized the Theravada form of Buddhism.

Ramkamhaeng's descendants were less adept. By the mid-14thC Ayutthaya had imposed its suzerainty on them. The kings of Ayutthaya were aggressively expansionist. They rapidly extended their rule across central Thailand and into the southern peninsula. In **1431** the kingdom's armies drove the Khmers from their capital at Angkor Wat. From the Khmers they inherited a tradition of absolute monarchy and Brahmanistic Hindu rituals, some of which still survive today. In **1545** they subdued Lanna Thai in the N and set up ministries to administer the kingdom.

But war had weakened Ayutthaya. In **1558** Burmese invaders took Chiang Mai, and until the late 18thC much of N Thailand remained a vassal of Burma. In **1569** the Burmese took Ayutthaya itself. They were finally expelled in **1592**, and King Naresuen the Great restored the Thai kingdom and ushered in the longest period of peace they had yet known.

With the Thai states united, Ayutthaya grew into a powerful maritime nation. They traded profitably with the East, and opened their doors to European commerce also. The Europeans were bedazzled by the city of palaces and temples: "I have never seen anything fairer," wrote the French envoy Abbé de Choisy of his visit to King Narai's court in **1685**.

Many Western business adventurers and mercenaries were active in Asia at the time. Two of them, who had served in the British East India Company, became legendary figures in the court of King Narai: Constantine Phaulkon, a Greek who for a time became Thailand's effective foreign minister (and who had arranged for the French delegation that brought de Choisy); and the Englishman Samuel White, who ran Thailand's extensive trade with India under Phaulkon, from a base in Mergui, near modern Phuket.

The "Golden Age" lasted until **1760**, when a newly vigorous Burma invaded once again. In **1767**, after a 14-month siege, the Burmese captured the city and razed it. No less than 417 years of Thai history were devastated — an act of vandalism that the Thais have still not forgiven. It is said, in Thailand, that the gold that gilds the famous Shwedagon Pagoda, which towers over the Burmese capital, Rangoon, was made from that which was looted by melting off the statuary and temples of Ayutthaya. In 1950, Burma formally apologized and contributed to the building of a temple in Ayutthaya as a form of reparation.

A young Thai general, Taksin, expelled the Burmese from Ayutthaya seven months later, then immediately abandoned the city. Taksin moved his capital s, to Thonburi at the mouth of the Chao Phraya river. His years as king (**1767–82**) saw a reassertion of Thai power.

The Burmese were ousted from N Thailand and Chiang Mai, while Laos to the N and Cambodia to the E were reduced to vassal status. One of Taksin's victorious generals, Chao Phya Chakri, returned from Laos with the Emerald Buddha, the country's most revered Buddha image. When an increasingly autocratic and unbalanced Taksin was removed by palace officials in 1782, they offered the throne to General Chakri (**1782–1809**) — the first king of the dynasty that still reigns today.

It was Chakri, Rama I, who moved the capital across the river to the E bank village of Bangkok, displacing a community of Chinese traders, who were relocated to what is now Chinatown. Craftsmen from Ayutthaya built his Grand Palace, along with a Chapel Royal to house the Emerald Buddha.

Rama I christened his new capital "city of angels, abode of the Emerald Buddha, impregnable city of the God Indra, the grand capital of the world endowed with nine precious gems, the happy city . . . . " and so on and so forth. This is the longest name of any capital city in the world, but Thais generally abbreviate it to "Krung Thep." Foreigners invariably call the city Bangkok, which the Thais do not mind.

Ramas I, II and III consolidated their kingdom and returned to the splendors of the Ayutthaya period. Monasteries and temples (including Wat Arun) were built, the arts were encouraged, and relations with Western powers resumed. But it was the coming to power of King Mongkut, Rama IV (**1851–68**), that heralded Thailand's entry into the modern 19thC world.

Mongkut — misrepresented by the late Yul Brynner in the movie *The King and I* — was an educated and thoughtful man. He spent 27 years as a monk, read English and Latin, studied history and the natural sciences, and derived much enjoyment from peering at the stars through a telescope. He recognized that Thailand's continued independence, faced with the seemingly insatiable appetites of Western colonial powers such as Britain and France, depended upon modernization. Mongkut opened his markets and granted extra-territorial privileges to Western nations. Anna Leonowens was brought in to teach English to his children.

Still, the real revolution was left to his son Chulalongkorn, Rama V (**1868–1910**). Chulalongkorn's sons and promising young aristocrats were sent to study overseas. The first nonreligious schools were established, the armed forces were modernized, work began on railroads, the country's first hospital was opened, and government ministries were expanded and staffed with a civil service. Social reforms included the abolition of slavery, serfdom and forced labor.

Diplomatic relations proved trickier: from their bridgeheads in Burma, Malaya and Vietnam the British and French forced territorial concessions from Chulalongkorn. But Thailand maintained its independence even as all its Asian neighbors fell under colonial rule.

Vajiravudh, Rama VI (**1910–25**), Chulalongkorn's Oxford-educated son, continued the modernization process. Chulalongkorn University, the country's first, was founded. Compulsory primary education was introduced, and a sense of Thai nationhood was popularized. Vajiravudh replaced the traditional national flag — a white elephant on a red background — with the red, white and blue design that still flies today.

Rama VI was succeeded by Pradjadhipok, Rama VII (**1925–35**), a frugal, hardworking old-Etonian whose short reign coincided with the end of the absolute monarchy.

One consequence of social change was an increasingly assertive Western-educated elite demanding a bigger voice in government, but Pradjahipok refused to give ground. Budget cuts forced by an economic crisis in **1931** fed discontent, and in **1932** a bloodless coup ended the monarchy's absolute rule. Pradjahipok abdicated in **1935**. Soldiers and civilian politicians have dominated Thai politics ever since, with varying degrees of success.

After the "democratic coup" the military and the civilians vied for power. Under the leadership of Captain Luang Pibulsongram ("Pibul"), the military triumphed, and government became increasingly authoritarian and nationalist. It was Pibul who changed the country's name from Siam to Thailand in 1939. In World War II Pibulsongram collaborated with Japan, and when the war ended he was replaced by leaders of the "Free Thai" resistance movement.

Their tenure of office was brief. Ananda Mahidol, Prajadhipok's nephew, was proclaimed King in 1935 while at school in Switzerland. He finally returned to Thailand in 1945, and a year later died of gunshot wounds in circumstances that to this day remain a mystery. The civilian government collapsed, and in 1947 the military regained control. Pibulsongram, by now a Field Marshal, held power for the next decade.

With Communist insurgencies taking off throughout Southeast Asia and the Communist victory in China in 1949, Thailand tightened its economic, political and military ties with the United States. 1957 saw another military coup and another authoritarian leader, Field Marshal Sarit Thanarat.

Sarit's six-year rule was marked by the opening up of the Thai economy to foreign investment and the tourist industry. His chosen successors, Generals Thanom Kittikachorn and Prapas Charusathien, took Thailand into the Vietnam war, trading Thai combat troops and US air bases for massive US economic aid.

The US presence enormously stimulated the economy. The Americans built major highways throughout the country, created employment for hundreds of thousands of Thais, and laid the basis for the country's infamous sex-for-sale industry. But like others before them, they failed to make a lasting impression on the 800-year-old Thai culture.

Thanom and Prapas were toppled in 1973 after a series of bloody clashes between police and student activists at Bangkok's Thammasat University. During the three years of often chaotic democracy that followed, Thailand watched nervously as the American forces were driven out of Vietnam, and Communist regimes took power in Cambodia, Vietnam and Laos.

In October 1976 the military seized power again. The arrival in Thailand of hundreds of thousands of refugees from Indo-China undermined the appeal of Communism. Fears that Thailand would be the next Southeast Asian "domino" eased, as a mix of rural development schemes and counterinsurgency operations whittled away the indigenous Communist Party of Thailand (CPT).

Support from post-Mao Zedong China, and fellow members of ASEAN (the Association of South East Asian Nations), along with a prosperity fueled by its strong agricultural base and new manufacturing industries, boosted the country's self-confidence in its complex relationship with a Hanoi-dominated Indo-China.

Cautious moves toward democracy began in 1979. Taking over as Prime Minister in 1980, Prem Tinsulanonda survived two attempted military *coups d'état* to lead a multiparty coalition of elected civilian politicians until 1988. He was defeated by Chatichai Choonhavon. His government was overthrown on February 23, 1991 in a bloodless coup led by General Sunthorn Kongsomphong, whose junta created a "National Peacekeeping Council" that promised a new constitution by 1992.

The efforts of the military government to hold power led to violent street demonstrations. In May **1992**, troops fired into crowds near the Democracy Monument, creating such revulsion among the Thai people that the promised elections were held, and won by a coalition of civilian political parties. By mid-**1993**, Thailand was again stable and on track to become the next economic "tiger" or "little dragon" of Southeast Asia, after Taiwan, Singapore and Hong Kong.

Three distinct power bases make up the Thai political establishment: the armed forces, especially the army; a shadow government of civil servants, Western educated, often of noble lineage with a disdain for commerce; and political parties, not one of which has ever won an outright parliamentary majority. These in turn are influenced by three strands of opinion: that of the much respected King Bhumibol, the growing middle class, and the working people. Chaotic though this form of governance may seem, by April **1982** Bangkok was able to celebrate its 200th anniversary as the nation's capital.

The unifying and stabilizing thread running through Thailand's often confused postwar history has been King Bhumibol Adulyadej, Rama IX, who came to the throne after his brother's death in **1946**. Although no longer an absolute monarch, he is seldom out of the public eye and is revered by the Thai people for his piety and his tireless efforts to improve the lot of the small farmers, who constitute the majority of the population. Together with the Buddhist religion and a universal pride in the country's independent identity ("Thai" means "free"), the monarchy continues to underpin the lives of today's 58 million Thais.

Thai architecture

The architecture of Bangkok is a reflection of centuries of influence and borrowings from other civilizations: India, China, Cambodia, Sri Lanka and, more recently, the West. Almost without exception, the most significant and distinctive buildings throughout Thailand are religious structures, built for the monarchy by the finest craftsmen. Their stylistic evolution can be traced from the civilizations that, for centuries, held sway over Thailand.

The **Dvaravati period** (7th–11thC) reached its zenith in the 7th–8thC, when India was the prime influence on Thailand's architectural style. These earliest Buddhist structures in Thailand are characterized by the *stupa,* a tall, many-tiered pyramid-form on a square base, with Buddha images housed in alcoves on each terrace. One example of the genre is **Wat Kukut** at Lamphun in N Thailand.

The **Sri-Vijaya period** (8th–13thC) was dominated by the Sumatran empire, which introduced to Thailand the Mahayana school of Buddhism with its pantheon of deities and vibrant iconography. The Sri-Vijaya period's greatest legacy is the Borobodur temple in central Java (part of modern Indonesia), but some examples remain in S Thailand, notably **Pra Barom That** at **Wat Phra Mahathat** in Surat Thani province, featuring a chamber to house the Buddha image and a five-towered, terraced *stupa.*

The period of Khmer rule of central, N and NE Thailand, which brought the style of monumental stone architecture seen at Angkor Wat and Angkor Thom in modern-day Kampuchea, is known as the **Lopburi period** (11th–13thC). Until the 10thC the Khmers embraced Hinduism, and even after the rise of Mahayana Buddhism in the 11thC, their sanctuaries remained very much in the tradition of Indian Brahmanism, with only an overlay of Buddhist influence.

The best Khmer monuments are pre-Buddhist, identified primarily by chunky stone towers (known as *prang*). Usually there are three towers ranged along one side of the temple, representing the Hindu trinity of Vishnu, Shiva and Brahma. The building's structure is organized in a series of concentric squares, with the most sacred sanctuary at the center. The stone temple at **Pimai** in Nakhon Ratchasima Province is a fine example of this style.

The **Chiang Saen period** (12th–15thC) is the first era of what can accurately be called "Thai" architecture, the earliest examples of which are found in Chiang Mai in the N. Borrowing remained extensive: for example, **Wat Chet Yot** (Seven-spired Temple) is thought to be an imitation of a temple in Myanmar (Burma), which is, in turn, a copy of a Buddhist monument in Bihar, India.

But new features did emerge, notably the multilayered, sloping, slightly concave roofs of the *bot* — the rectangular temple building. The horn-shaped finials (*chofa* or "bunch of sky") are thought to be a relic of animism, designed to repel evil spirits.

Unlike the Khmer, the Thais built in wood, brick and stucco; however, the Thai *chedi (stupa)* continued to echo the Khmer-style: square-cornered and topped by a bell-shaped dome. The best examples are **Wat Phra Singh** and **Wat Chet Yot**, both in Chiang Mai, and **Wat Mahathat** in Phitsanulok, which has a fine Khmer *prang*.

Sukhothai (13th–14thC), the rival kingdom in N Thailand, created a "Golden Age" that established the firmest foundations of a distinctly Thai architectural style, although Khmer and Sri-Vijayan influences still enjoyed periods in vogue.

For example, Thai *chedis* of this period cover the entire range of foreign styles, but they also refine them. **Phra Prang** of **Wat Sri Sawai** is a good mix of Khmer style with Thai innovations.

To the *bot* (the main temple building), Sukhothai invention brought a large main door that opened to bathe in natural light the Buddha image situated at the far end of an avenue of supporting pillars.

From its earliest years the architecture of the **Ayutthaya period** (14th–18thC) was also an imitation of its predecessors. The central monument of most Buddhist monasteries at this time was a Khmer-style *prang,* but in the course of the 16thC the popularity of this feature gave way to bell-shaped *chedis* of Sinhalese-influenced Sukhothai design, topped, however, by a tall, narrow spire. The best of these is to be seen at **Wat Pra Sri-Sanpet** in Ayutthaya.

Replica of a **royal palace** from the Ayutthaya period, at Ancient City

By the mid-17thC the Khmer *prang* had a brief resurgence of popularity. After a successful campaign against the Khmers, King Prasat Thong (1630–55) built **Wat Chaiwatanaram**, in unashamed imitation of Angkor Wat.

Later, contact with Western countries influenced King Narai (1656–88) in the construction of religious buildings and of his own palace at Lopburi. For the first time Thai architecture featured soaring Gothic-style roofs and Rococo wall and ceiling decorations.

The familiar porch and gallery that surrounded temple buildings were abandoned, and windows were cut into the walls. In the final years before Burmese armies sacked Ayutthaya in 1767, temple pillars topped with the **blooming lotus** design were introduced, and for the first time plain terracotta roofing tiles were replaced by glazed tiles.

Replicas of distinguished Ayutthaya-period buildings, such as the **Royal Palace**, illustrated on page 151, can be seen at ANCIENT CITY, 33km (21 miles) SE of Bangkok (see DAY TRIPS FROM BANGKOK, pages 251–2).

Initially, the goal during the **Ratanakosin (Bangkok) period** (since 1782) was to re-create an architectural inheritance devastated by the razing of Ayutthaya. At first there was little innovation, but soon architects were able to draw liberally from all the styles that had gone before. What emerged was an often ill-coordinated, sometimes whimsical mix of architectural features, but with more color, ornamentation and variety than any single preceding period.

For example, the collection of buildings known as the **Grand Palace**, begun in 1782 by Rama I, the founder of the Chakri dynasty, and added to by his successors, is a rich potpourri of Thai architectural history, bristling with all manner of gilded spires, *chedis*, Khmer-style *prangs*, sweeping, brightly tiled roofs and lavish ornamentation.

Within the compound, the **Dusit Maha Prasad**, with a four-tiered roof rising to a nine-tiered spire, and **Wat Phra Keo** (illustrated on page 192), home of the Emerald Buddha, are perhaps the ultimate distillation of all that came before .

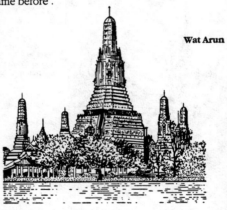

Wat Arun

Across the river in Thonburi, at **Wat Arun** (Temple of Dawn), Rama II (1809–24) and his son Rama III (1824–51) raised **Pra Prang**. At the time, the 79m (259-foot) spire, encrusted with multicolored shards of Chinese porcelain, was the tallest structure in the kingdom. It remains the finest example in Bangkok of Thai variations on a Khmer theme.

Toward the end of the 19thC, Western influence began to make itself felt in religious and royal architecture. The throne room in the **Grand Palace**, **Chakri Maha Prasad**, built from 1876–82 to mark 100 years of the dynasty, was designed by British architect John Chinitz and is essentially a Victorian building topped with a Thai roof and three pagoda-like spires. **Wat Benchamabophit**, which was begun in 1901, introduced Carrara marble, enclosed courtyards and convex Chinese roof tiles (illustrated on page 199).

Certainly Bangkok's temple architecture is the city's unique and most striking feature. But the 19th and 20thC saw the construction of many other notable buildings, some of which have survived the rapid modernization of recent years.

"Colonial" architecture is best represented by embassies and diplomatic residences. The oldest is the **Portuguese mission**, built on riverside land in the early 19thC. The **French embassy** (mid-19thC), the Edwin Lutyens-designed **British residence** (1920), the **Dutch embassy**, and the **US Ambassador's** ante-bellum-style **residence** all have a graceful, anachronistic charm.

Government ministries, particularly the **Ministry of Defense** opposite the Grand Palace, reflect the growing European influence in Bangkok at the turn of the century. **Government House**, originally built by Rama VI (1910–25) for a favored courtier, is in Western "wedding cake" style, as is another of his projects, **Ban Phitsanuloke**, which now serves as the Prime Minister's residence. A nearby government house, **Seri Manangasila**, is improbably mock-Tudor.

Given the large Chinese presence, there is surprisingly little **Chinese architecture** in Bangkok. A few examples have survived, notably the rows of two-story **Chinese shophouses** on Lang Krasuang, behind the Foreign Ministry, and a private residence, the **Hok Lok Siaw house**, built in 1813 on the Chao Phraya River and moved to Sathorn in 1892. Among its *Chinoiserie* delights is an inner courtyard overlooked by a four-sided gallery.

In the precincts of the **Bang Pa-in palace** (see DAY TRIPS FROM BANGKOK, page 255), visitors can see a reconstruction of a Chinese-style palace and a Chinoiserie guesthouse.

Typical **waterside dwellings**, Bangkok

Traditional Thai houses on stilts are almost as rare and are usually inaccessible. Exceptions include the former home of vanished silk entrepreneur and architect **Jim Thompson**. This teak house is actually built from six houses, transported to Bangkok from country areas in the N, dating from between 1800 and 1900. **Ban Kamthieng**, in the grounds of the Siam Society, is considered among the finest extant examples of 19thC Northern Thai architecture.

Contemporary Thai architecture has less to recommend it. Much of it is either "poured-concrete utilitarian" or unesthetic, Post-Modernist style. A distinctive exception is the **Siam Inter-Continental Hotel**, which succeeds in marrying classic Thai design with modern construction methods.

In the 1980s the most popular architectural embellishment was Greco-Roman columns fronting steel and glass towers. The two best examples are the **Amarin Plaza** at Ratchaprasong, and the **Wall Street Tower** near Patpong, on Surawong Rd. The Thai architect of the newer **Grand Hyatt Erawan Hotel** brought his columns inside, behind the glass facade of the atrium lobby.

But the prize for the wackiest design must go to the **"robot" building** on Sathorn Rd. Modeled on a Japanese-style robot toy, it has "eyes," "arms," and a giant steel bolt through its "neck" — an example of the Thai talent for imitation, taken to the extreme of what the Japanese adoringly refer to as *"kawai"* or "cuteness."

Thai art

Historically, the artistic talent of Thailand has found its most frequent expression in the creation of religious art. It is in this field that the Buddhist tradition has been most eloquently conveyed, through a multitude of sculptures, paintings, amulets, illuminated manuscripts and various ceremonial objects.

Like that of its close relative, architecture, the history of art in Thailand also involves much stylistic borrowing and inspiration from the other cultures that ruled Thailand over many centuries. Beginning in the 6thC (known as the **Dvaravati** period), the influence of Indian culture can be seen in Thai art, as evidenced by Gupta-inspired Buddhas in simple, diaphanous drapery with large, broad-featured faces and a head of tightly coiled curls.

During the same era, a Sumatran (Indonesian) influence is seen in the art of southern Thailand, giving rise to the artistic period that is called **Sri-Vijaya**, characterized by Buddha figures sculpted with intricately carved adornments.

The Khmer (Cambodian) invasion of Thailand in the 11thC resulted in the popularity of their artistic style. During this period, known as **Lopburi** (11th–14thC), depictions of the Buddha exhibit sharp noses, prominent chins and a highly stylized *ushnisha,* the elaborate top-knot characteristic of the Buddha. Overlapping with the Lopburi period is the **Chiang Saen** era (12th–15thC), during which time the Chinese esthetic influence also began to be seen in northern Thailand.

It was not until the 13thC that the Thais themselves began to translate and refine these multicultural currents into their own artistic style. At this time, bronze replaces stone as the favored material for sculpting, and we see Buddha images with highly emphasized almond-shaped eyes, arched brows, a sharp nose and a more delicate mouth, a style that was later simplified in the **Sukhothai** era (13th–15thC) and softened during the **Ayutthaya** period (15th–18thC).

Since the 18thC, the art of the **Bangkok** (or **Ratanakosin**) period has produced rounder-faced sculptures, decked out in highly elaborate Thai costumes.

Throughout these eras, artistic depictions of the Buddha show him in postures of meditation, preaching, or bestowing grace, or illustrate an aspect of his extraordinary life: emerging at birth from the side of his mother, Queen Maya; seeing the four sorrows of the world while still a young and sheltered Indian prince; renouncing the comforts of his privileged life to find "the middle way" to salvation; reaching enlightenment under the Bodhi tree; expounding upon the Four Noble Truths, the cornerstone of the Buddhist teaching; and, finally, entering *nirvana* at his death. Thailand also created its own unique "Walking Buddha" figures.

Thailand possesses many exquisite **sculptures** of the Buddha, which were created by monks or craftsmen, and often commissioned by the monarchy. Some of the best examples are: the Buddha Sihing in the National Museum; the Buddha images at Wat Benchamabophit, especially the replica of Phitsanulok's Phra Buddha Chinaraj; the five-ton solid-gold Sukhothai Buddha at Wat Traimitr; the enormous Buddha at Wat Po, covered in gold leaf (the largest Buddha in Thailand); and the magnificent Emerald (jasper) Buddha at Wat Phra Keo (in the Grand Palace compound), Thailand's most revered Buddha image.

Painting, particularly **temple murals or friezes**, has provided Thai artists with yet more ways of depicting the life and message of the Buddha. Wat Phra Keo features restored murals, dating from the first half of the 19thC. Other fine examples include the early 19thC murals of the life of the Buddha, the *Jataka Tales,* which can be seen in the **Buddhaisawan Chapel** in the National Museum, and the murals in Wat Suthat, which were created slightly later. Along the balustrades of the main chapel at Wat Po is a characteristic frieze of scenes from the *Ramakien,* the Thai version of the Hindu epic, the *Ramayana.*

Illuminated manuscripts, with paper from pressed bark of the *khoi* tree, tell the story of Thai culture and religious tradition in a different form. One of the finest examples was commissioned by King Taksin in 1776 and is on view at the National Museum.

Craft, **drama** and **dance** are all art forms that have long been employed to express not only the religious stories but also the more secular folk tales of Thailand. Examples of shadow puppets, masks for *khon* (classical masked dance-drama) and marionettes can be seen in the National Museum.

For centuries, court dance was considered "high art" in Thailand, with each elegant and exotic gesture, movement and costume replete with meaning. In order to keep this magnificent tradition alive, the Thai government maintains a school for training dancers, and public performances are held regularly.

The **contemporary art** scene in Thailand has been quite varied over the past half century. In the 1930s, Thai artists sought to deal with secular themes utilizing techniques of Western-style realism. Later, many Thai artists went abroad to study, returning home much influenced by trends in Abstract Expressionism.

Later still, in the 1970s, a period of civil unrest in the country prompted some artists to explore sociopolitical themes. However, a number of them went underground when restrictions were placed on their freedom of expression, and consequently their work soon ceased to have any impact.

In the 1980s, many Thai artists again turned to the religious images that inspired their ancestors, revitalizing them with contemporary interpretations. There are several galleries that exhibit such works, and there is also a modern art museum and school under royal patronage. An excellent and representative collection of contemporary Thai artists can be seen at the **National Gallery**.

Many traditional **folk crafts**, such as the creation of nielloware (silver filigree against a blackened background), lacquerwork, mother-of-pearl inlay and wood carving, continue to flourish in Thailand, still mostly under royal patronage, as they have for centuries.

Bangkok:
practical information

This chapter is organized into seven sections:
- **BEFORE YOU GO**, below
- **GETTING THERE**, page 160
- **GETTING AROUND**, page 161
- **ON-THE-SPOT INFORMATION**, page 166
- **BUSINESS IN BANGKOK**, page 172
- **USEFUL ADDRESSES**, page 173
- **EMERGENCY INFORMATION**, page 176

Each section is organized thematically rather than alphabetically. Summaries of subject headings are printed in CAPITALS at the top of most pages.

Before you go

TOURIST OFFICES OVERSEAS
Tourism Authority of Thailand (TAT) offices:
- **New York**   5 World Trade Center, Suite #3443, New York, NY 10048 ☎(212) 432-0433 [Fx](212) 912-0920.
- **Los Angeles**   3440 Wilshire Blvd., Suite 1100, Los Angeles, CA 90010 ☎(213) 382-2353 [Fx](213) 389-7544.
- **London**   49 Albemarle St., London W1X 3FE ☎(071) 499-7679 [Fx](071) 629-5519.

Thai Information Attaché's Office (for general, not tourist, information):
- **Washington, DC**   Royal Thai Embassy, 4250 Connecticut Ave. NW, Suite 260, Washington, DC 20008 ☎(202) 667-3108 [Fx](202) 537-3630.
- **London**   Royal Thai Embassy, 28 Princes Gate, London SW7 1QF ☎(071) 584-5421 [Fx](071) 581-0122.

DOCUMENTS REQUIRED
British, Commonwealth and US citizens arriving in Thailand with **confirmed onward tickets** will be granted 15-day transit visas at the airport, but these cannot be extended. **Tourist visas**, obtained at the Thai embassy or consulate in your home country before you leave, are valid for 60 days and can be extended by 15–30 days at the Immigration Department in Bangkok (see USEFUL ADDRESSES on page 173).

All visitors must carry identification, preferably their **passports**. Foreigners staying longer than 90 days at a time are liable for local income tax and cannot leave without first obtaining a tax clearance certificate, which is a long and time-consuming exercise.

Health documents are not required unless you have visited an infected area. However, before leaving home inquire at the Thai embassy or consulate or consult a doctor, especially concerning vaccinations against cholera and hepatitis.

An international **driver's license** is required if you wish to drive in Thailand; US, UK and other licenses are often not accepted.

TRAVEL AND MEDICAL INSURANCE

It is advisable to have a valid travel and medical insurance policy. American Express provides comprehensive worldwide travel and medical coverage, which includes 24-hour emergency assistance anywhere in the world. Contact **American Express Travel Service** for details. **Extrasure** sells a comprehensive package that provides on-the-spot emergency assistance. Be sure your insurance company has a reciprocal arrangement with companies in Thailand for refund of medical expenses.

The **IAMAT** (International Association for Medical Assistance to Travelers) is a nonprofit organization that has a directory of English-speaking doctors who will call, for a fee. It has member hospitals and clinics throughout the world, including several in Thailand. Membership is free and other benefits include advice on health risks overseas. For further information, and a directory of doctors and hospitals, write to IAMAT headquarters in the US or Europe *(at 417 Center St., Lewiston, NY 14092, USA or 57 Voirets, 1212 Grand-Lancy, Genève, Switzerland).*

MONEY

The unit of currency is the **baht** (B). The baht floats against a basket of currencies, but its value follows the US$ closely; at the time of writing, the rate has been fairly constantly pegged at US$1 to B25–30.

The baht is divided into 100 *satang.* "Copper" coins are valued at 25 and 50 *satang,* and "silver" coins are in denominations of 1, 2 and 5 baht. Paper money consists of bills for 10 baht (brown), 20 baht (green), 50 baht (blue), 100 baht (red) and 500 baht (purple).

There is no restriction on the amount of **foreign currency** visitors can bring into the country, but it should be declared on a customs form issued on arrival. Restrictions exist for taking foreign currency out of the country, but this concerns Thai citizens more than the average tourist. Avoid problems by declaring foreign currency on arrival.

Travelers checks issued by American Express, Barclays, Thomas Cook and Citibank are accepted at first-class hotels, restaurants and shops that are accustomed to dealing with tourists. Major international charge and credit cards (American Express, Diners Club, MasterCard and Visa) are accepted, but some shops levy a surcharge of as much as six percent on credit card transactions, often springing it on you after the deal has been struck.

There may, on the other hand, be a generous "cash price" discount. Ask before buying. It is a good idea to carry some local currency to use at small, family-run shops and restaurants outside the city and main tourist areas.

Be sure to read the instructions included with your travelers checks. It is important to note separately the serial numbers of your checks and the telephone number to call in case of loss. Specialist travelers-check companies such as **American Express** provide extensive local refund facilities for lost checks through their own offices or agents.

CUSTOMS ALLOWANCES
Standard allowances for consumer goods apply. One still camera or one movie camera can be brought in duty-free; unused film limits are five and three rolls respectively. Thai Customs conduct thorough inquiries into intended use of hi-tech electronic and computer equipment brought into the country, as these are heavily taxed and are expensive items on the local market. Leave them at home or, if you must have them, insist that the equipment is for your personal use and will leave the country with you. There is no duty on precious stones, gold or platinum jewelry on departure.

There are prohibitions against commercial trade in religious artifacts and the export of items of national cultural value: Buddha statues and other religious artifacts are illegal exports unless accompanied by permits issued by the **Department of Fine Arts** offices at the national museums in Bangkok, Chiang Mai or Songkhla *(call Bangkok National Museum ☎ 224-1370, 1402 or 1396 for information)*. Most arts and antiques dealers will arrange licenses and transport for you.

Import and export of pornography is also forbidden. For information on customs prohibitions, call the **Customs Dept.** *(Sunthornkosa Rd. ☎ 249-0431)*, the **Immigration Office** *(Soi Suanphlu, Sathorn Tai Rd. ☎ 287-3101)* or the **Revenue Dept.** *(Chakkapong Rd. ☎ 281-5777, 280-0140)*.

NARCOTIC DRUGS
Travelers are warned against carrying drugs in any circumstance. In Thailand, the maximum penalty for trafficking opium or heroin is death. The alternative is life imprisonment.

You are strongly advised:
- **NEVER** to agree to carry any amount of drugs;
- **NEVER** to check in baggage on behalf of someone who claims to have excess baggage;
- **NEVER** to carry packages or baggage for anyone unless you are absolutely sure they don't contain drugs.

TIME ZONES
Bangkok and all of Thailand is 12 hours ahead of US **Eastern Standard Time** and 13–15 hours ahead of other US time zones. It is seven hours ahead of **Greenwich Mean Time** and one hour behind Singapore and Sydney.

CLIMATE AND CLOTHES

The climate is tropical, with three seasons: dry (March to May), wet (June to November) and cool (November to February). The average annual rainfall is 1,500mm (59 inches), and the average temperature 28°C (82°F). During April (the cruellest month), temperatures in Bangkok reach 36–38°C (96–100°F), with an average dry-season temperature above 34°C (92°F); at night it remains above 25°C (79°F), with humidity over 70 percent. In the wet season, humidity is over 80 percent. In the northern city of Chiang Mai, dry-season temperatures can reach 40°C (104°F) and in the cool season can fall to 8°C (46°F) at night.

The best time to visit is the cool season when the weather is pleasant with a balmy wind in the evenings, but even then some visitors find the heat hard to bear. The weather is often too hot for formal attire, although the Thais maintain their own version of casual chic. A sun hat is essential.

Men should bring light cotton clothes, lightweight socks and comfortable walking shoes that are easily removed for visits to temples, and light jackets or sweaters to counteract air-conditioning overkill. Some upmarket restaurants require a jacket and tie. Women too should bring light cotton clothes, a sweater or casual jacket to fight off the air conditioning, easily removed shoes for day wear and a pair of casual evening shoes, and short-sleeved dresses (not sundresses) for visiting temples.

Keep shorts for the resorts; if improperly attired, you may be denied entry to temples. A sweater is needed for Chiang Mai in December.

Getting there

BY AIR

Bangkok's **Don Muang Airport** is easily accessible. Some 50 airlines land at Bangkok, at Chiang Mai in the N and at Phuket, a resort island in the SW. **Thai Airways** is the national domestic carrier, flying to most cities within the country; **Thai International** operates worldwide.

BY RAIL

There is a regular train service between Bangkok and Singapore. Passengers from Singapore change trains and stay overnight at Butterworth in Penang, Malaysia. Three trains a week leave Butterworth early in the morning *(Mon, Wed and Fri),* arriving in Bangkok the next morning. Passengers pass through Thai immigration in Bangkok, which takes a long time and often requires standing in line in the sun.

For rail buffs on a generous budget, the **Eastern and Orient Express** (details on page 34) is the perfect mode of transport between the two centers. If money is limited and time is not, the **People's Express** (see page 35) is another option.

BY SHIP

A number of luxury cruise liners call at the southern resort town of Pattaya, about 160km (100 miles) from Bangkok.

Getting around

FROM THE AIRPORT TO THE CITY

Don Muang Airport is 25km (15 miles) from the city. If you have not arranged for a hotel representative to meet you with a car, there are several choices. The simplest and fastest way to arrange transport to the city is to approach Thai Airways International's counter in the arrival lounge, where transport by **car**, **bus** or **train** is available.

If you choose to take a **private air-conditioned sedan** to your hotel, buy your ticket and tell the attendant your destination; part of the ticket will be taken, and when the name of your hotel is called, acknowledge the call; someone will carry your luggage to the car. The **airport shuttle bus** is less expensive, but only stops at the Asia Hotel; then you have to find your way.

Minibuses are available. Budget travelers can cross a pedestrian overpass to the public bus stop on Vibhavadi Rangsit Highway and take an **air-conditioned bus** (nos. 4, 29, 10, 13). Although inexpensive (the fare depends on distance), they may be crowded and have no luggage facilities. Fares are collected on board. Frequency can be erratic, so brace yourself for a long wait in the heat.

There are also **taxis**, both licensed and unlicensed, whose drivers will approach you. Taxis are not metered, so the fare must be negotiated before you get in: be firm in your bargaining. Fares vary, depending on your destination and bargaining prowess. Unlicensed taxis may cost marginally less than those licensed, which are identifiable by their yellow license plates and the "taxi" dome sign lighted on the roof. Buses, cars and taxis direct to nearby Pattaya beach resorts are also available at the airport.

The State Railway of Thailand offers a special **Airport Express** train service, which traverses the distance from Don Muang airport to **Bangkok Station** *(Rama IV Rd.)* in 35 minutes, with one stop at **Samsen Station** *(Rama VI Rd.)* en route. You can choose from air-conditioned, or non-air-conditioned coaches. Tickets also include passage on an air-conditioned shuttle bus that ferries passengers the short distance from both international and domestic airports to Don Muang Railway Station.

The train departs from the airport six times a day: 8.55am, 12.10pm, 2.35pm, 4.55pm, 7.20pm and 9.40pm. Departure times from Bangkok Station: 7.35am, 10.35am, 1.35pm, 3.45pm, 5.55pm and 8.45pm. Tickets are sold at four locations: at the international airport, at Thai Airways International's limousine counter (#7) in the arrival hall; at the domestic airport, at the Thai Airways counter in the arrival hall; at Bangkok Railway Station, platform 12 and at Don Muang railway station.

LIGHT RAPID TRANSIT

Bangkok's **Light Rapid Transit** system, which was expected to help solve the city's stifling traffic congestion problem, was scheduled for completion in 1994. Unfortunately, for the present it remains mired in wrangling between the Hong Kong developer and various government agencies.

BUS SERVICES

Touring the city by public bus is inexpensive but requires considerable spare time: schedules are misleading because of the congestion, which lasts as late as 8.30pm, routes are complex, and it is easy to miss your stop. Only the most stalwart backpackers need even consider anything but the air-conditioned bus system, the routes of which are shown on the *Latest Tour Guide to Bangkok and Thailand* map in English or *The Tru* (sic) *Bangkok Map*, with legend in Thai, on *Walking Tours Bangkok* and (selected routes) on *Nancy Chandler's Map of Bangkok*.

Special air-conditioned buses travel to the resort areas and serve many out-of-town beach spots. Reservations can be made at hotels and travel agents, or at the following bus terminals: **Eastern Bus Terminal** *(Sukhumvit Rd., opposite Soi 63, see map on page 187* ☎ *392-9227, 391-9829)* serves Pattaya beach resort; **North and North-Eastern Bus Terminal** *(just across from the weekend market on Phaholyothin Rd.* ☎ *279-4484);* **Southern Bus Terminal** *(Pin Klao-Nakhon Chai Si Rd.* ☎ *435-1199).* Note that telephone numbers listed are for air-conditioned bus counters.

TAXIS

Bangkok must be one of the few cities left in the world where, on most days, you can flag down a taxi at any time of the day with ease. Taxi travel is relatively cheap, but the problem is agreeing on a price: there are 13,500 taxis serving the city, most with meters that are never used. You must therefore bargain with the driver.

Taxi drivers generally don't speak English: many of them are rural truck drivers who have migrated to the big city. It's no use showing them your destination on English-language maps: ask one of the hotel staff or a Thai friend to write the address in Thai. Most Thais are literate, so if your taxi driver still looks puzzled, he probably doesn't know the place you want to go to. Wave him on and wait for another one. If he nods his head, he knows where it is; the next step is to negotiate the fare.

Using sign language, offer half the driver's initial asking price and settle somewhere in between. Tourists pay more than locals. Drivers will say the traffic's bad today (it's bad every day) and the price is up, but don't succumb: be firm and say no, smile, shake your head, and if all else fails, walk away. They often change their minds and call you back — they just wanted some "face."

Above all, don't get angry. Once the price is agreed, even if the driver takes a circuitous route or gets lost, he'll seldom demand more when you finally arrive. You may pay more if it's raining — prices can double or even triple within minutes as the rain turns Bangkok into a city of slippery, flooded, pot-holed streets. Numbers of passengers and distance can be less important cost-factors than congestion: an extra fee may be charged because of long waits at jammed intersections.

There are few cab stands in the city, and you cannot book a taxi by telephone. Taxis that cluster near hotels are more expensive: a walk around the corner can mean a lower fare. No tip is necessary, but carry small change with you: most drivers will not have change for large notes.

The dome light on top indicates legal taxis — "illegals" are private cars. It's difficult to see whether a taxi is free, as most cars have tinted windows. New cars tend to be cleaner and have air conditioners that work, for which you pay more. Drivers of old taxis sometimes wind the windows up, deceptively implying that their car is air-conditioned: check before entering. If it is not, smile, shake your head and decline, or fan your face with your hand to show it's too hot. Seating space is small, and so is luggage space, since most taxis run on bottled gas installed in the trunk (boot). If you're lucky you may get a driver who speaks English, and he'll probably chatter away throughout the journey. Avoid discussions on Thai politics and the Royal Family.

Most large hotels have their own limousines, with flat rates charged hourly or daily.

SAMLORS *(TUK-TUKS)*

Bangkok's unique *tuk-tuks* (pronounced "tuke-tuke"), gaily decorated open carriages on three wheels, are a quick method of short-distance travel. Open on three sides, with a plastic-wrapped bench for passengers and a canvas roof with a dome light on top, their name is onomatopoeic with the sound their gas engines make as they slow down at intersections: "tuk, tuk, tuk." However, they seem to speed up more than they slow down — sedate they're not. They seat two or three people behind the driver. Negotiate the fare before you get in, and avoid them on rainy days.

RIVER AND CANAL *(KLONG)* TRANSPORT

One of the coolest ways to see Bangkok is on the water. The **Chao Phraya Express River Ferries** (☎ *465-3836)* travel the Chao Phraya River from Krung Thep Bridge to Nonthaburi and back, taking in the Grand Palace. There are about 16 major stops between the Taksin and Krungthon bridges, and express boats are identifiable by their comparatively large size and a number on the roof. Prices depend on distance.

Cross-river ferries operate from almost every boat landing. "Long-tailed taxis" ply the smaller canals *(klongs):* negotiate the price first, and choose a boat with an awning against sun and rain. Their name comes from the very long propeller shafts extending into the water from the car engines they use as outboard motors, which create a spectacular effect as they pull off.

The most famous landing is at the Oriental Hotel. On Wednesday evenings its private yacht, *Oriental Queen,* tours the city (☎ *236-0400),* with dining and dancing by candlelight. The hotel also arranges boat tours to the nearby sites of AYUTTHAYA and BANG PA-IN (see DAY TRIPS FROM BANGKOK, pages 252 and 255).

GETTING AROUND BY CAR

Although still only 28 percent of Bangkok's householders own cars, prosperous urbanites are currently registering new cars at a rate of 400 a day. Traffic is heavy and parking is a problem. Streets are often under repair — or should be. Thais are reckless drivers, speed limits are often ignored, and there are few pedestrian crossings and many jaywalkers.

It is inadvisable for visitors to drive in Bangkok, although most major road signs are marked in Thai and English and are likewise indicated on maps. Cars drive on the left. Some one-way roads have special bus-only lanes that run in the opposite direction, presumably to discourage lane poachers. The language barrier compounds the crisis of an automobile accident.

Avoid unpleasantness: don't drive. Cars with drivers cost only marginally more to rent than those without. Drivers will take care of the car and local directions, and can even be good company.

Car travel on country roads is somewhat less chaotic. Thailand has a good road network and traffic is relatively light. Country road signs are usually written only in Thai, rarely in English. The roads are narrow — "freeways" are usually two-lane thoroughfares with traffic in both directions. Country traffic includes motorcycles, bicycles, pedestrians, animal-drawn carts and animals. The most dangerous vehicles are ten-wheel trucks: the drivers work on incentives contingent on speedy deliveries, and they tend to drive accordingly.

RENTING A CAR

Avis operates in Bangkok, as well as local car-rental companies. Both self-drive and chauffeur-driven cars are available. A valid international driver's license is required for self-drive rentals; the minimum age is 21. It's wise to shop around: smaller companies offer lower rates, but it may prove costlier if the car isn't properly serviced. While smaller companies may ask for cash deposits, the following major firms accept charge/credit cards and offer 24-hour service:

- **Avis**   Central Reservation at 2/12 Wireless Rd., map 7D7 ☎255-5300 Ⓕ253-3734, with reservation desks at four hotels: Dusit Thani ☎238-0032; Royal Princess ☎281-3088; Grand Hyatt Erawan ☎254-1234 and Sukothai Bangkok ☎287-0222
- **Klong Toey Car Rent**   1921 Rama IV Rd., beside Bangkok Bank Lumphini Branch, map 7E6 ☎250-1141/1361 Ⓕ252-3566
- **Krung Thai Car Rent**   233–5 Asoke-Dindaeng Rd., map 7B7 ☎246-0089, 246-7508 Ⓕ246-8478
- **Petchburee Car Rent**   2371 New Phetburi Rd., Huaykwang, map 7C7 ☎318-1752, 319-7255 Ⓕ319-1394

RAIL SERVICES

A cheap and efficient **rail service** links the capital with the rest of the country. Express trains go N to Chiang Mai and S to Malaysia. Cars have sleeping berths: **first-class** (air-conditioned and often very cool) is best for hot-season travel (March to June); **second-class**, with ceiling fans, is adequate in the cool season (November to February). Express trains have dining cars offering a surprisingly wide range of food and drinks.

Touring by train can be done with a **Rail Pass**, discounted for nonresidents of Thailand, with a special rate for children. Typical itineraries include Chiang Mai, Phitsanulok, Lopburi, Ayutthaya, Bang Pa-in and Ko Samui *(from Surat Thani station in the s)*. Passes are valid for 20 days for second- and third-class buses.

All trains leave from Bangkok's **Hua Lampong Station** *(Rama IV Rd., map 6 D5 ☎ 223-0341, open Mon-Fri 8.30am-6pm; weekends and hols 8.30am-noon)*. Reservations can be made at the station and at travel agents up to 90 days before departure *(advance booking office ☎ 223-3762/224-7788)*. There is a surcharge for express trains. Schedules and fares are available at the **Rail Travel Aids** counter in the station, from the **Tourist Authority of Thailand (TAT)** or from travel agents. Trains leave on time but may be delayed en route.

WARNING: The Tourism Authority of Thailand advises all tourists, while traveling by bus or train, **never to accept any foods, drinks or snacks** from strangers, no matter how friendly they may seem. You might be drugged and robbed of your belongings. For information, contact the **TAT service center** *(Ratchadamnoen Nok Ave. ☎ 282-8129, 281-5051)* or the **Tourist Police** *(509 Vorachak Rd. ☎ 221-6206)*.

WALKING IN BANGKOK

With increasing population and prosperity since the 1950s, Bangkok has grown rapidly into a confusing city that lacks any obvious urban plan. But, armed with a decent map and a good sense of direction, you can — for a while — tour parts of the city on foot, until the heat, noise and air pollution drive you indoors or into an air-conditioned car.

For the hardy and adventurous, a number of rewarding walks are suggested in SIGHTS AND PLACES OF INTEREST.

DOMESTIC AIRLINES
Thai Airways

Thai Airways, the domestic airline, has its terminal beside the international airport. It flies Boeing 737 jets and serves 17 provincial capitals and tourist resorts, five in the N, five in the NE and seven in the S. For less busy routes, Shorts 330 commuter aircraft are used. There is a small departure tax, sometimes included in the ticket price.

The domestic terminal has a limousine service that tends to close early, but hotels will send cars if you make reservations.

*   **Head office:**   89 Vibhavadi Rangsit Rd. ☎ 253-1681 Ⓕ 253-1629
*   **Booking offices**: 485 Silom Rd. 7, map 7E6 ☎ 233-3810 Ⓕ 237-6124; Yaowaraj, 45 Anuwong Rd., map 5D4 ☎ 224-9602; Lan Luang, 6 Lan Luang Rd., map 6C4 ☎ 280-0070 Ⓕ 280-0735; Charn Issara, 4th Flr., Charn Issara Tower ☎ 235-4588; Asia Hotel, 296 Phyathai Rd., map 7D6 ☎ 215-2020.

Other domestic airlines

Bangkok Airways *(Pacific Place Bldg., 140 Sukhumvit Rd., see map on page 187 ☎ 253-4014, 253-4004 Ⓕ 253-8400)* flies to Ko Samui and Krabi.

Yellowbird (Tropical Sea Airlines) *(office at the airport, Bldg. 302 ☎ 535-3466 Ⓕ 535-3470)* fly 20- and 28-seater seaplanes to and from

Pattaya twice a day. They also run a service to Phuket *(office at Phuket Airport, 3rd floor, Passenger Terminal ☎ (074) 311-511 ext. 2182)*.

On-the-spot information

ADDRESSES
In almost every respect, getting around in Bangkok is a challenge requiring a healthy sense of adventure. It might just be of some help to know that houses are numbered according to when they were built, rather than in a sequence, going along the street. The first house in a road *may* be #1, but its neighbor may be #23, and so on.

New complexities arise when you are trying to find your way around Sukhumvit Rd., Bangkok's up-and-coming neighborhood. An attempt to guide you through this minefield, with an explanation of how the *sois* (lanes) off Sukhumvit are numbered and/or named, is on page 186, along with a map on page 187.

The best advice in all cases is to establish, perhaps with the help of the English-speaking concierge at your hotel, where you are going before you set off, and to go armed with a decent map.

LANGUAGE
Like many Eastern tongues, the Thai language is tonal, and thus difficult for Westerners to learn. A mispronunciation of a diacritical tone mark in a word could alter its meaning entirely. Most people employed in the tourist industry speak English, and visitors are not expected to speak Thai. Avoid misunderstandings by sticking with English; or carry a good phrasebook.

PUBLIC HOLIDAYS
Religious events are determined by the lunar calendar and fall on different dates every year. Years are numbered according to the Buddhist Era, which began in 543BC; AD1992 was the year BE2535 in the Thai calendar. If an official holiday happens to fall on a weekend, the following Monday becomes a public holiday. Chinese New Year, between late January and early February, is not a public holiday in Thailand, but many shops and restaurants owned by Chinese or their descendants close for three to four days.

Dates of public holidays alter according to the lunar calendar. Magha Bucha Day, for instance, can fall on any date between February 25 and March 12.

Holidays in 1994 and 1995 are:

New Year's Day, January 1; **Magha Bucha Day**, between February 25 and March 12; **Chakri Day**, April 6; **Songkran** (Water Festival), April 12–14; **Labor Day**, May 1; **Coronation Day**, May 5; **Royal Plowing Ceremony**, mid-May; **Visakha Bucha Day**, between May 13 and 24; **mid-year holiday**, July; **Asalha Bucha Day**, between July 11 and 22; **Khao Phansa Day** (first day of Buddhist Lent), between July 12 and 23;

H.M. Queen Sirikit's Birthday, August 12; **Chulalongkorn Day**, October 23; **H.M. The King's Birthday**, December 5; **Constitution Day**, December 10; **New Year's Eve**, December 31.

SHOPPING AND BUSINESS HOURS

Department stores are open daily from 10am to 8pm (until 9pm on Friday and Saturday). Smaller shops often open seven days a week, 9am–8pm or later. Businesses and government offices work a five-day week (assume 8.30am–4.30pm) with a noon–1pm lunch break.

Street stalls selling imitation designer-label gear, positioned near the bar and hotel areas and at major intersections, stay open well into the night; the center of Patpong 1 Rd. turns into a gaily-lit street bazaar from 7pm to 3am, brimming with knock-offs of designer shirts (e.g., Benetton, Boss, Polo) and wristwatches, as well as many Thai handicraft products.

RUSH HOURS

Bangkok has three rush hour periods: 8–9.30am, 11.30am–2pm and 5–8.30pm. Buses are packed with people, cars stand motionless at jammed intersections. Traffic is at its worst on Friday evening and on the evenings before public holidays. Lunchtime and shopping crowds are heavy between 11am and 3pm.

BANKS AND CURRENCY EXCHANGE

Banks are open Monday to Friday 8.30am–3.30pm and close on weekends and public holidays. Some large banks have currency exchange counters that are open until 8pm on weekdays, half-days, on Saturday and some public holidays. All banks and money changers charge a commission on travelers checks unless the checks were issued by the same bank or by an overseas partner bank.

Money changers are to be found all over the city and are open on weekends and into the night. Always check the exchange rates and commissions first. Hotels also change foreign currency, but the rates are always lower. There are foreign exchange counters in the airport arrival and departure lounges. You will need your passport.

American Express has a **MoneyGram**® money transfer service that makes it possible to wire money worldwide in just minutes, from any American Express Travel Office. This service is available to all customers and is not limited to American Express Card members.

The Communications Authority of Thailand offers three money services through all post offices. **International Money Orders** operate with 27 countries. The **International Telegraph Money Order Service** has a reciprocal arrangement with seven countries. Amounts received are payable in Bangkok within a day and in up-country post offices within two to three days, following the day of issue. It also has an emergency program.

The **Postcheque Service** allows Postgiro account holders from six other countries to cash up to 10 checks of up to 5,000 baht at a time.

For information on each of these services, call the **Monetary Services Division** (☎ 573-5466/573-0099, ext. 3483 or 3590).

DISABLED TRAVELERS

There are few facilities for disabled travelers. Arrangements should be made in advance to alert airlines and hotels. It is best to travel around the city by limousine, avoiding public transport.

MAIL AND TELEPHONE SERVICES

The **General Post Office** (GPO) is at 1160 New Rd. *(map 6 F4 ☎234-4893/234-5586; open Mon-Fri 8am-8pm; Sat, Sun, hols 8am-1pm for postal services and Mon-Fri 8am-5pm; Sat 8am-noon for monetary services)*. Some English is spoken. There is a good packing service for small parcels. All other post offices are open Monday to Friday 8.30am–12pm, 1pm–4.30pm; Saturday, Sunday, holidays 9am–12pm for postal services and Monday to Friday 8.30am–12pm, 1pm–3.30pm for monetary services. All have express mail and telegram services. The airport has two post offices, one in the departure lounge, the other outside.

There are two **special package services**: SAL (Surface Airlifted Mail Service) is a discounted service to nine countries: England, France, Germany, Indonesia, Japan, Netherlands, Philippines, Singapore and Switzerland. Maximum weight to most of these countries is 2kg for letter-post, 20kg for parcels.

EMS (Express Mail Service) covers all of Thailand and more than 50 countries. Maximum EMS weight in Thailand is 10kg; to most other countries serviced, it is 20kg. Delivery is made within 24 hours between Bangkok and Thai provinces, within 48 hours between provinces and within one to three days to other countries.

Overseas telephone calls can be made at the **Overseas Telegraph Office**, and telex services are available at the **International Telecommunication Centre**; both are beside the GPO, in the Nava Bldg. on New Rd. *(map 6 F4)*, and provide a 24-hour service.

For telephone information operators ☎13 in Bangkok, **183** up-country, **100** for operator-assisted long distance calls. To make overseas calls direct ☎001 plus the country code and area code. The enquiries numbers are ☎235-0030 for operator-assisted calling, **234-3016** (24-hour) for technical inquiries on international subscriber dialing.

Bangkok telephones are notorious for being more out of order than in, and it is not uncommon for numbers to change overnight without warning. Public telephones, which take 1-baht coins, can be found in shops, in restaurants and on the streets, but are not always reliable, and there are some districts in the city not yet on the telephone exchange. Red public booths take only local calls; blue booths provide both local and long distance services. Private premises charge as much as 5 baht for use of their telephones and hotels add a surcharge ranging from 10–20 percent above normal rates.

Lines in the city are often overloaded and connections can be poor. There are only about three telephone lines per 100 people in all Thailand, and although most are in Bangkok, the telephone service is at best erratic. The government means to multiply the number of telephone lines ninefold by 1995, but meanwhile it's best not to rely on the efficiency of the phone service.

TIPPING

Tipping is a matter of discretion. Expect to give a tip where you are pleased with a service, except, of course, if you have fixed the price in advance. Cab drivers are not usually tipped, except if they have been acting as a private driver. Hotel porters should get a minimum of 20 baht, and other hotel staff receive tips at your discretion. Tip 10 percent in restaurants where no service charge has been added to the bill.

ELECTRIC CURRENT

Current is 220V 50-cycles AC, and plugs are two-pronged. Power outlets are not grounded (earthed).

LOCAL PUBLICATIONS

The city has two English-language daily newspapers: *The Bangkok Post* and *The Nation*, published in the morning. Tourist publications such as *Thaiways, Tourist's Handbook, Tourist Authority of Thailand Official Shopping Guide, This Week Thailand, Angel City, Look* and *Where* are available at TAT offices or in lobbies of the major shopping complexes and hotels.

LOCAL RADIO

There are two daily tourist assistance radio programs broadcast in English: *Travel Thailand* is aired each morning at 6.30am (FM 97 MHz) and *Welcome to Thailand* each evening at 8pm (FM 95.5 MHz).

LAWS AND REGULATIONS

Although Thais are known for their tolerance, they draw the line at tourists climbing on statues of Buddha to take photographs; the sanctity of the Buddha is protected by law, and offenders are prosecuted. Likewise, the royal family is highly venerated. Tourists can and *will* be arrested for making disparaging remarks or showing disrespect toward photographs or symbols of royal family members.

The export of religious artifacts and objects of cultural value is controlled; obtaining the necessary permits is best left to experienced antique dealers (see CUSTOMS on page 159). Import and export of narcotics and pornography (see page 159) are also strictly prohibited, and penalties are harsh.

When visiting temples, dress neatly and conservatively, remove your shoes at the door, and behave with due decorum — remember you are at the gates of heaven, and a foreign heaven at that. Religious practice prohibits women from touching monks.

CUSTOMS AND ETIQUETTE

Thai life is a continuous ceremony of symbolic gestures and deference to social rank. Initially, trying to understand the nuances of Thai social protocol is rather like trying to remember which fork goes where at your first formal dinner. In the time between the first welcoming *wai* — the hands pressed palms-together with the fingers up and head bowed to meet you — and the revelation that Buddha images are objects of veneration rather than decoration, any reasonably sensitive Western traveler will invariably begin to feel inept and clumsy as he or she realizes that movements of the eyes, hands, head and feet all have potential meaning in Thai daily interactions.

The protocol becomes all the more comprehensible if you remember that Thailand is an agricultural society. Three-quarters of the population are farmers who spend their lives at ground level: "Our backs to the sky, our faces to the ground . . . forever," as the Thai farmers say. The people of the great central plain of Thailand support the court and urban life of Bangkok, and look up to it for leadership.

On the plains, height indicates power: that which is good, desirable, superior, strong and valuable is elevated. So, Buddha figures are built on platforms or to gigantic proportions; temple spires pierce the flat sky of the plains; the King sits high on his throne; monks and figures of authority are bowed to; maids serve beer to their master on their knees so as not to rise above his seated level; the head is to be respected, and the feet are not to be lifted nor pointed toward other people unless an insult is intended. It is usual to remove shoes when entering a private home.

Often, this ritual behavior alternately embarrasses and irritates Westerners, who may tend to confuse deference with servitude. But, as any resident can tell you, however deferential a Thai maid may seem, she is rarely servile.

Two other aspects of Eastern Asian culture that Westerners often fail to understand are the pleasures of **accruing merit** (derived from Buddhist ethical canons), and the social requirements of **conflict-avoidance**. The host gains status (merit) by paying for the guests he has invited to a dinner. Don't deny him by fumbling for your "share" of the bill.

The social extension of Buddhism's concept of merit-making in this life in order to be more advanced on the wheel of rebirth in the next, expresses itself in mutual benefit for gift-giver and recipient. Merit and social status are gained by generosity, and are increased commensurately by a gracious recipient.

The dominating national characteristic of conflict-avoidance means that "constructive criticism" does not exist in the Thai social lexicon. Criticism is seen as a threat to social cohesion, and, like juvenile delinquency or drunken disorder in the West, is something to be avoided. Differences of opinion are not aired: the quickest way to offend a Thai is to challenge or criticize him openly. This social inhibition has made Thais, and Asians generally, masters of subtle solutions to conflict.

Robert and Nanthapa Cooper provide a good illustration of indirect criticism in their excellent survey of Thai social mores, *Culture Shock Thailand . . . and how to survive* (Times Books International Singapore, 1982), concerning **white elephants**, which are symbols of national peace and prosperity. The current King has at least six. Any white elephant that is found is traditionally presented to the King and looked after (at DUSIT ZOO) according to an established and expensive procedure.

In the past the King would often honor an especially favored noble by giving him a white elephant. The problem of the expense of maintaining the beast in the manner to which it was accustomed was solved by including a gift of land. The noble's status was greatly enhanced. A noble who had somehow gained the King's displeasure might also be sent a white elephant — but without any land. The "honor" could not be refused, the elephant would do no work and could not be sold or given away, and the noble's purse would be drained. He would thereafter take care to adjust his behavior in order to avoid any further such "honors."

People call each other by their **first names**; with adults, the name is always preceded by *Khun* (the Thai version of Mr.) or by a single-syllable nickname. This is helpful: most Thai surnames are multisyllabic and hard for Westerners to pronounce.

BUDDHIST MEDITATION CENTERS

As the canons of Buddhism grow in popularity — there are now Thai Buddhist temples in the United States and United Kingdom, for instance — its meditation practices have become popular with Westerners. The following are places where foreigners can learn more about or practice this unique form of religious contemplation.

- **World Fellowship of Buddhists** Thailand Meditation Center, 33 Sukhumvit Rd. (between Soi 1 and Soi 3), off map **7D7**, see map on page 187 ☎251-1188. English meditation class first Sunday monthly 2–6pm. Lectures on Buddhism third and last Sunday monthly 2–6pm. For information call in the mornings Monday–Friday.
- **Wat Mahathat** Facing Sanam Luang, near the Grand Palace, map **5C2**. This temple houses one of the two most important schools for monks in Thailand, Maha Chulalongkorn Buddhist University, and a Sunday school for children. This huge facility is divided into 29 quarters *(khana)* and classes are held daily at Khana 5.

There are more than half a dozen temples or centers where foreigners can attend meditation classes or practice. For a complete list, contact the Tourism Authority of Thailand or the World Fellowship of Buddhists.

HEALTH AND HYGIENE

Most **water** in Southeast Asia is badly polluted. Thailand is no exception. Tap water in Bangkok is treated, but it's safer to drink bottled Artesian water or mineral water, of which there are several brands. Most hotels supply bottled or boiled drinking water. The safest fruit juice to drink is coconut served straight from the shell. Other fresh fruit juices are often diluted with water and ice, and not all restaurants are careful about boiling the water.

Be wary of eating **shellfish**, which can be a common source of hepatitis and acute dysentery, and avoid raw fish and oysters.

If you become briefly ill, you may be simply acquiring "local immunity"; if it seems serious, consult a doctor (see EMERGENCY INFORMATION on page 176).

PUBLIC LAVATORIES (BATHROOMS)

Bangkok has no public lavatories. Use those in hotels, restaurants, coffee shops and department stores. Squat toilets are flushed by tipping a bucket of water into the bowl. Bucket and water are supplied, but not tissues, so carry your own.

Business in Bangkok

A rising star in the dynamic Asian-Pacific business scene, Bangkok is a major commercial center with facilities to match.

USEFUL BUSINESS ADDRESSES
Business organizations
- **Bangkok Shipowners and Agents Assn.**   227 Sunthornkosa Rd. ☎249-2601
- **Board of Trade of Thailand**   150 Ratchabophit Rd., map **5D3** ☎221-0555, 221-1827
- **Federation of Thai Industries**   394/14 Samsen Rd., map **5B3** ☎280-0951, 281-5980
- **Lapidaries Assn.**   406 Soi Talard Lertbuasin, Taksin ☎466-4209
- **Marketing Assn. of Thailand**   1221/11-8 Sukhumvit Rd. Soi 61, see map on page 187 ☎390-1264
- **Trade Assn. for Electronics**   660 Rama IV Rd., map **6E5** ☎233-1790
- **Thai Bankers Assn.**   302 Bangkok Insurance Bldg., Silom Rd., map **7E6** ☎234-1140 ext. 380
- **Thai Hotels Assn.**   Bangkok Airport Bldg. ☎523-8556
- **Thai Merchant Assn.**   150 Ratchabophit Rd., map **5D3** ☎221-3300

Chambers of Commerce
- **American Chamber of Commerce**   7th floor, Shell House, 140 Wireless Rd., map **7D7** ☎251-9266, 251-1605 [Fx]255-2454
- **Australian–Thai Chamber of Commerce**   163 Surawong Rd., map **7E6** ☎226-5562 [Fx]235-7166
- **British Chamber of Commerce**   54 Sukhumvit Rd., Soi 21, see map on page 187 ☎260-7288
- **Chambre de Commerce Franco-Thai**   9th floor, Shell House, 140 Wireless Rd., map **7D7** ☎251-9386
- **German–Thai Chamber of Commerce**   6th floor, Kong Bunma Bldg., 699 Silom Rd., map **7E6** ☎236-2396 [Fx]236-4711
- **Italian–Thai Chamber of Commerce**   Ital–Thai Bldg., 2013 New Phetburi Rd., map **7C7** ☎247-1558
- **Thai Chamber of Commerce**   150 Ratchabophit Rd., map **5D3** ☎225-0086, 225-4900 [Fx]225-3372

QUEEN SIRIKIT NATIONAL CONVENTION CENTER
The builders of this massive yellow, cream and blue complex have succeeded in creating a modern national monument, worthy to host international or local events and to honor Thailand's much-revered queen.

The center, which cost US$90 million to build, opened in August 1992, in time to host the 46th annual meetings of the boards of governors of the World Bank Group and International Monetary Fund — some 10,000 leaders of world finance from 154 countries.

The center is the largest open-floor exhibition facility in Southeast Asia, with 64,665 sq.m (691,915 square feet) of space. Its multipurpose Plenary Hall can seat 5,200 at a conference or almost 2,000 at a theatrical performance. It can accommodate 7,000 guests at a cocktail reception or transform itself into an ice hockey surface, six competition tennis courts or the venue for a trade fair for bulldozers.

Set on 8ha (20 acres) beside a lakeside park, on land donated by the Thai Tobacco Monopoly, the QSNCC is also one of the largest repositories of Thai art and crafts in the world, with some 1,500 items drawn from throughout the kingdom, mainly via the Queen's own Foundation for the Promotion of Supplementary Occupations and Related Techniques (SUPPORT) (see SHOPPING, page 233), an organization created to provide sources of secondary income to rural families.

This superb facility was built and is owned by the Thai Ministry of Finance. For detailed information contact the Sales Manager, N.C.C. Management and Development Co. Ltd. *(New Ratchadapisek Rd., Klong-toey* ☎ *229-3000* Fx *229-4253).*

ONE-STOP EXPORT SHOWCASE

The Department of Export Promotion (DEP), in the Ministry of Commerce runs these three 4,000sq.m (428,000-square-foot) halls of permanent exhibition space. About 10,000 items are on show, with displays from about 250 vendors rotated each month.

DEP will arrange appointments, arbitrate disputes and provide meeting rooms without charge to interested buyers. Contact the **Thai Trade Center** at the Royal Thai Embassy's Commercial Counsellor's Office in your own country, or the DEP directly *(Ratchadapisek Rd.* ☎ *511-5066* Fx *512-1079, 513-1917).*

Useful addresses

TOURIST INFORMATION

- **Tourist Authority of Thailand (TAT)**   Head Office, 372 Bamrung Muang Rd. Map 5C3 ☎226-0060, 226-0072, 226-0085 Fx224-6221
- **American Express**   11th floor, Bangkok Bank Building, 333 Silom Rd. Map 7E6 ☎273-0033
- **American Express Travel Service**   c/o **Sea Tours Co. Ltd,** 4th floor, Siam Centre, 965 Rama I Rd. Map 7D6 ☎251-4862
- **Immigration Office**   Soi Suanphlu, Sathorn Tai Rd. Off map 7F6 ☎285-7003
- **Tourist Police** and **Tourist Assistance Centre (TAT)**   Ratchadamnoen Nok Ave. Map 6C4 and map 6B4 ☎281-5051. Open

8am–midnight. Special department to assist tourists; English spoken.

TOUR OPERATORS
Most hotels have tour desks operated by travel agents who run bus tours round the city.
- **Diethelm Travel**   Kiangwan Bldg. II, 140/1 Wireless Rd., map 7D7 ☎255-9150 Ⓕⓧ256-0248, 254-9018
- **Dits Travel**   Kian Gwan House, 140 Wireless Rd., map 7D7 ☎255-9205 Ⓕⓧ255-9216
- **Sea Tours Co. Ltd**   See **American Express Travel Service**, page 173.

Five Kings Media and Advertising Co. Ltd. *(Klaosiam Condominium, 2nd flr., 560/38–40 Dindaeng Rd., Phyathai* ☎ *246-0370* Ⓕⓧ *246-4513)* produces a monthly *Air-Sea Guide* with extensive listings of air passenger and cargo routes, a shipping guide and lists of Bangkok travel and other transport agencies.

EMBASSIES AND CONSULATES
- **Australia**   37 South Sathorn Rd., map 7E7 ☎287-2680
- **Canada**   12th floor, Boomitr Building, 138 Silom Rd., map 7E6 ☎234-1561
- **New Zealand**   93 Wireless Rd., map 7D7 ☎251-8165
- **United Kingdom**   1031 Wireless Rd., map 7D7 ☎253-0191
- **United States**   95 Wireless Rd., map 7E7 ☎252-5040/252-5171

AIRLINES
- **British Airways**   Charn Issawa Tower, 942/136 Rama IV Rd. map 7E6 ☎236-8655
- **Cathay Pacific**   5th floor, Charn Issawa Tower, 942/136 Rama IV Rd. map 7E6 ☎233-6105
- **Singapore Airlines**   2 Silom Rd., map 7E6 ☎236-0303
- **Thai Airways** (domestic)   6 Lanluang Rd. map 6C4 ☎280-0070
- **Thai International**   138 Silom Rd., map 7E6 ☎234-3110
- **United**   183 Ratchadamri Rd., map 7D7 ☎253-0559

PLACES OF WORSHIP (Non-Buddhist)
Roman Catholic
- **Assumption Cathedral**   23 Oriental Lane, map 6F4 ☎234-8556, Sunday English sermon at 10am.
- **Deutscher Katholische Gemeinde**   St. Louis Hospital, South Sathorn Rd., off map 6F5 ☎286-2002. (Inquire at this number for times of services.)
- **Holy Redeemer Church**   123/19 Ruam Rudi Lane (Off Wireless Rd., behind US Embassy), map 7E7 ☎253-0505, Sunday English sermons at 8.30am, 9.45am, 11am and 5.30pm.

Protestant
- **Bangkok Eakamai Church**   (Seventh Day Adventist) 57 Soi Charoenchai, Ekamai Rd. ☎391-3593, Saturday English Sabbath

School at 9.30am; worship service 10.45am; Wednesday prayer meeting at 7.30pm; Friday vespers at 7.30pm.

- **Calvary Baptist Church**   88 Sukhumvit Rd., Soi 2, off map **7D7**, see map on page 187 ☎251-8278, Sunday school at 9am; Sunday English service at 10.15am and 7pm.
- **Christ Church**   11 Convent Rd., map **7E6** ☎234-3634, Sunday English service at 8 and 10am and 6pm.
- **International Church**   67 Sukhumvit Rd., Soi 19, see map on page 187 ☎252-0353, Sunday English service at 8am.

Jewish

- **Jewish Association of Thailand**   121/3 Sukhumvit Rd., Soi 22, see map on page 187 ☎258-2195, Friday services at 6.30pm, Hebrew school 3.30pm.

Islamic

- **Darool Aman Mosque**   Phetburi Rd. map **7C6** (near Ratchatevi Circle), *Kootbah* 12.15–1.15pm, *Jamat* 1pm.
- **Haroon Mosque**   Charoen Krung Rd. (New Rd.), near GPO, map **6F5**, *Kootbah* 12.15–1.15pm, *Jamat* 1pm.

RIVER AND *KLONG* TOURS

- **Chao Phraya Express Boat Co.**   Royal Orchid Sheraton Hotel, 2 Captain Bush Lane, off New Rd., map **6E4** ☎465-3836.
- **Globe Express Travel Co. Ltd.**   301 Tadmai Rd. ☎233-7852.
- **World Travel Service**   Oriental Hotel, 1053 New Rd., map **6F4** ☎233-5900.

Tours up and down the Chao Phraya River on the *Oriental Queen* can be reserved through the **Oriental Hotel** *(☎ 236-0400 or 0420)*.

ENGLISH-LANGUAGE BOOKSTORES

- **Asia Books**   221 Sukhumvit Rd. (see map on page 187) and three other locations.
- **The Bookseller**   81 Patpong Rd., map **7E6**.
- **D. D. Books**   32/9–10, off Soi 21, Sukhumvit Rd. See map on page 187.
- **Patpong University Books**   109 Surawong Rd. (beside D.K. Kitchen), map **7E6**.
- **Robinson Book City**   222 Siam Sq.
- **Yajimaya**   1037/3B, Ploenchit Arcade, Ploenchit Rd.

Emergency information

EMERGENCY SERVICES

- **Police** ☎191 or 123 or 246-1338
- **Highway Police** ☎193
- **Tourist Police** ☎195 (and see below)
- **Tourist Assistance Centre** ☎281-5051, 282-8129 or Don Muang Airport Desk ☎523-8972. Regional desks are in **Pattaya** ☎(038) 419-371, **Chiang Mai** ☎(053) 222-977, **Phuket** ☎(076) 212-213, **Hat Yai** ☎(074) 246-733 and **Ko Samui** ☎(077) 421-281.
- **Fire** ☎199 or 246-0199
- **Ambulance** (with English-speaking staff) ☎252-2171 or contact one of the hospitals below.

HOSPITALS (WITH ENGLISH-SPEAKING STAFF)

- **Bangkok Nursing Home** Convent Rd., map **7F6** ☎233-2610
- **Bumrungrad Hospital** Soi 3, Sukhumvit Rd. See map on page 187 ☎251-0415
- **Samitivej Hospital** 433 Soi Klang, Sukhumvit Rd., see map on page 187 ☎392-0010

PHARMACIES

Medicines can be bought across the counter without a prescription. Buy only from the larger pharmacies and always check the date stamp. There are no 24-hour pharmacies, but the following are open long hours: **S. V. Dispensary** *(between Sois 15-17, Sukhumvit Rd., see map on page 187)* and **Phuket Dispensary** *(383 Sukhumvit Rd.* ☎*298-3749)*. In emergencies the hospitals listed above have pharmacies.

LOST PASSPORT

Contact the police and your embassy immediately.

LOST TRAVELERS CHECKS

Contact the police and the issuing bank immediately. Report stolen **American Express** travelers checks and cards at 11th floor, Bangkok Bank Building, 333 Silom Rd., map **7E6** ☎235-0990.

LOST PROPERTY

If you have lost something on public transport, contact the Tourist Police.

TOURIST POLICE

The tourist police force was established in 1982 to coordinate with the Tourism Authority of Thailand (TAT). Some 500 more or less bilingual police are attached to TAT offices in Bangkok, Pattaya, Chiang Mai, Hat Yai, Phuket and Kanchanaburi.

An alternative emergency number is the **Tourist Police Centre** (Section 4), Crime Suppression Division *(509 Worachak Rd.* ☎*221-6206)*.

Bangkok:
planning your visit

When to go

The best months to visit Bangkok are November to February. Predictably, these are also the peak tourist months, and most hotels are fully booked. If you are willing to brave intense heat and unpredictable weather, visit between April and September, when many of the city's hotels offer low, offseason rates to tourists.

If you go in the peak season, try early December — the best time to avoid both heat and excessive crowds. Christmas and Chinese New Year are popular times with regional travelers, who combine leave time with Christmas/New Year public holidays.

Events in the Thai calendar

The Thai national creed of *sanuk* (pleasure), mixed with strong religious beliefs, is reflected in the large number of festivals that take place each year throughout the country. Try to plan your tour of Thailand to coincide with at least one of these festivals. The Tourism Authority of Thailand has an annual publication with a colorful list of the dozens of festivals. Obtain a copy before you go. The following abbreviated list gives just a taste of what there is to see. Refer also to PUBLIC HOLIDAYS on pages 166–7 and the SPORTS CALENDAR on pages 248–9.

JANUARY
January 10–11, **Chaiyaphum Elephant Round-up**. Smaller than the more celebrated Surin round-up in November, but still an exciting display of these magnificent animals' skills as log-haulers and of their bravado as machines of medieval Asian warfare. January 17–19, **Bo Sang Umbrella Fair** is a celebration of the village near Chiang Mai that is the center for one of Thailand's most famous handicrafts — the making of handpainted paper umbrellas. While villagers vote for their next "Miss Bo Sang," tourists are offered a selection of the country's best umbrellas.

End January or early February, **Chinese New Year** celebration. Shops and restaurants close down so that Thai–Chinese residents can watch, or join in, Dragon and Lion Dance parades. One of the most popular of many celebrations in various places around the country is Nakhon

Sawan's annual **Dragon and Lion Parade**, but most market- or rice-milling towns in Thailand have Chinese populations who make up with fireworks and fervor what they lack in numbers. Other annual fairs in January include those at Suphan Buri and Ayutthaya, at the Bang Sai Arts and Crafts Center.

FEBRUARY

February 3–9, birdwatchers will delight in Chai Nat Bird Park's annual **Straw Bird Fair**, in which the more than 85 species in the park are celebrated with a parade of large straw reproductions, accompanied by displays of local handicrafts and a food festival.

First weekend in February, **Flower Festival** in Chiang Mai, the city known as "The Rose of the North," with floral floats and beauty contests. "The Rose" is capital of the only area in Thailand where the climate is cool enough for roses to grow, and is also believed by Thais to spawn the nation's prettiest women. Mid-February, annual **Prison Crafts Exhibition** in Bangkok, with a wide range of goods notable for both quality and fair price.

Late February or early March, **Makha Puja Day** is an important Buddhist holy day and a national holiday. Temples are alive with merit-makers and candlelit processions circle three times around monastery chapels at night. Annual fairs are held to honor **Chao Mae Lim Ko Nieo**, a Chinese goddess, in Pattani, Phetchaburi, Lampang, Phitsanulok, Nakhon Phanom and Nakhon Si Thammarat (often timed to coincide with Makha Puja Day).

MARCH

First week in March, the **ASEAN Barred Ground Dove Festival** in Yala draws participants from the entire Southeast Asian region. The highlight is a dove-cooing contest that may strike foreign ears as funny but, typically, attracts around 1,500 Asian competitors. First week in March, wildlife enthusiasts gather for the **Setting Free of Young Turtles** in Phang-Nga.

Around March 10 and in mid-September, the **Bangkok Gems and Jewelry Fair** at Queen Sirikit National Convention Center is the biannual showcase for the gemstone and jewelry trade, employer of around one million Thais. Thailand ranks in the top three of the world's exporters of gems and finished jewelry. Other annual festivals in March are held in Si Sa Ket, Chumphon and Nakhon Ratchasima.

APRIL

April 6, **Chakri Day**. The pantheon at Wat Phra Keo (Temple of the Emerald Buddha) is opened to the public. Mid-April, **Songkran Festival** (the old solar **Thai New Year**). This is a day of purification at the *wat,* of housecleaning and colorful parades culminating in cheerful water-splashing. It is seen at its best in Chiang Mai, but celebrated throughout the country. Notable in and around Bangkok are events in Wisutkasat district and at Phra Padaeng, in the large Mon community of Samut Prakan, s of the city. Wherever you witness this festival, expect to get wet. Late April or early May, annual **Raek Na Ceremony**. Ritual first plowing in Bangkok, presided over by the King.

Other annual fairs in April are the **Pattaya City Festival**, the **Sweet Grape Fair** in the Damnoen Saduak floating market area of Ratchaburi, the **Poi San Long** ordination ceremony of the Yai tribal group in Mae Hong Son and the **Phanom Rung Fair**, held at the town's ancient Khmer temple.

MAY

Mid-May, a **Rocket Festival** in Yasothon is the way in which villagers of the NE encourage plentiful rains in the coming **rice-planting** season. There is much merriment, with dancing, stage shows, parades and, of course, a host of rather extraordinary rockets, some of which are several meters long, to rouse support from the heavens. Late May, **Visakha Puja Day**. Buddha's day of birth, enlightenment and death, is marked by a very solemn ceremony in Bangkok in which the King distributes fans to monks and novices at the temple of the Emerald Buddha. In the evening, there are processions with flowers and candles around the main monastery buildings.

Other events this month include **Fruit Fairs** in the eastern seaboard provinces of Rayong, Chanthaburi and Trat and the **Chao Mae-To-Mo Fair** in Narathiwat, which honors a Chinese goddess.

JUNE

The **Phi Ta Khon** festival in Loei derives from a story from the life of the Buddha (*Jataka Tales*) in which Prince Vessandorn, his penultimate incarnation, is welcomed back to his home city. Young men dress as spirits and parade the streets in rituals reminiscent of Halloween or Mardi Gras in the West. Early June, the **Chanthaburi Fruits and Gems Fair** celebrates the abundance of both riches in this SE province. Local fruits include rambutan, durian, jackfruit and pomelo. Local gems include rubies and sapphires.

JULY

Mid-July to early August, **Asanha Puja Day** (also **Khao Phansa Day**) begins the Buddhist Lent or "Rains Retreat." For Buddhist monks, a three-month period of meditation and confinement begins. Related events are the **Candle Festival** in Ubon Ratchathani, featuring magnificent sculpted wax candles, some of which are many meters tall, and **Tak Bat Dok Mai (Merit-making Festival)** in Saraburi, with a spectacular procession to its Shrine of the Holy Footprint.

AUGUST

August 1–2, the **Longan Fair** in Lamphum, about half an hour to the s of Chiang Mai, is a harvest festival for lovers of this fruit (known in Thai as *lamyai*), complete with an annual "Miss Lamyai" beauty contest. August 12 is the **Queen's Birthday**, when H.M. Queen Sirikit is honored with magnificent celebrations in the grounds of the Grand Palace. Bangkok's public buildings are garlanded with colored lights to make the route along Ratchadamnoen Ave., from the old palace to the new royal residence at Chitrlada Palace, a blaze of beautiful lighting effects.

SEPTEMBER

Mid-September, the **Bangkok Gems and Jewelry Fair** (see MARCH). Late September, the **"Sat Thai" Merit-Making** in Kamphaeng Phet is a must for "sweet-tooths." It features contests for the best *Kluai Khai,* the nationally-renowned banana-and-rice dessert from this N province. Late September to early October, **Chinese Lunar Festival** in Songhkla (and elsewhere in Thailand) features lantern-making contests, processions and the mandatory lion and dragon dances.

Other events this month include a **Food and Fruits Fair** in Nakhon Pathom, the **Festival of the 10th Lunar Month** in Nakhon Si Thammarat, for 15 nights of the waning moon, featuring cultural shows, exhibitions and contests, and **Boat Races** in Phichit, Narathiwat and Bangkok (see the SPORTS CALENDAR on page 248)

OCTOBER–NOVEMBER

October–November, **Vegetarian Festival** in Phuket, 900km (559 miles) s of Bangkok. The Chinese community parades through the streets to honor Chinese legendary gods and heroes who allegedly enter the bodies of those in a trance, causing them to pierce their cheeks with skewers and perform other theatrics.

Late October to early November, **Thot Kathin Festival**, marking end of Buddhist Lent and of the rainy season. **Loi Krathong Festival**. Thais around the country float lanterns in rivers, lakes and canals under the full moon, in a festival that started more than 700 years ago in Sukhothai. Other notable locations include Nakhon Phanom, Chiang Mai and Ayutthaya.

Mid to late November, **Elephant Round-up** in Surin Province, 454km (282 miles) NE of Bangkok, where more than 100 trained elephants are put through their paces in an internally famous event.

Late November to early December, **River Kwai Bridge Week**. Archeological and historical exhibitions, folk culture performances and rides of World War II vintage steam locomotives at River Kwai, Kanchanaburi Province.

Late November to early December, **Silk Fair** in Khon Kaen, a traditional production center of the famed lustrous fabric that has become an emblem of Thai culture. Other events in this period include the **Chak Phra and Thot Phapa Festival**, in which sacred Buddhist images are pulled around the town of Surat Thani and the **Tak Bat Devo** festival in Uthai Thani, where monks descend from the hilltop temple to receive alms, amid folk theater performances and other entertainments by the local populace.

There are many **country fairs** at this time of the year, as well as sporting events such as boat racing, buffalo races, game fishing tournaments and the **Bangkok Marathon**. See also the SPORTS CALENDAR (page 249) for details.

DECEMBER

Tourism Festival and **National Identity Exhibition**. A nine-day festival to promote Thai tourism takes place at Amporn Garden, Bangkok. Cultural performances, firework displays, handicrafts sales and exhibitions. December 3, **Trooping of the Colors**, in Royal Plaza, Bangkok. Given the prominence of the military in ancient Thai lore and modern Thai governance, it is small wonder that the annual swearing of allegiance to the King by H.M.'s elite Royal Guards is a major event, and a very colorful one too. December 5, the **King's Birthday** and **National Day** are celebrated throughout the country with colorful pageantry.

December 10, **Constitution Day**. Other events related to Thailand's martial history at this time include: **Prince Chumporn Commemoration**, in Chumporn, home of the modern Thai navy's patriarch; and **King Taksin the Great Memorial Fair** in Tak, commemorating the warrior hero who drove out the Burmese after the fall of Ayutthaya.

Early December, the **Rose Festival** in Chiang Mai celebrates the horticulture of the N (including the rose), and one of Thailand's newest agricultural exports, the *bonsai* tree. There are several major sporting events: the **Siam Windsurf World Championship** in Pattaya, the **Phuket King's Cup Regatta** in Phuket and the **I-San Kite Festival** in Buri Ram. (See also the SPORTS CALENDAR on page 248.)

Bangkok: orientation

Bangkok, home to about 7.6 million of Thailand's 54 million people, is the center of Thailand's political, intellectual and commercial life. The city sits at the apex of the Gulf of Thailand, sprawling across pancake-flat land on the E of the country's major transport link, the Chao Phraya River. All roads lead to Bangkok, quite literally. Imports, exports, ambitious country people hoping to make good, foreign visitors — all pass through Bangkok.

The country's prosperity still depends heavily on the agricultural abundance of the Central Plains — Thailand's "rice bowl," with Bangkok on its s lip — and 75 percent of Thais still live in the countryside. Between 5 degrees and 21 degrees N of the Equator, it stretches 1,640km (1,330 miles) from N to S, 800km (497 miles) from E to w, sharing borders with Laos to the N and NE, Cambodia (Kampuchea) to the E, Burma (Myanmar) to the w and Malaysia to the S, and embracing a rich diversity of terrain and people.

Thailand's 73 provinces include tropical rainforest in the s peninsula, semi-arid plateau in the NE, rugged mountainous areas in the N, and the flat Central Plains, the heartland that unites all this topographical, ethnic, religious and linguistic variety.

Wet rice cultivation, mostly by small tenant farmers, is far and away the biggest industry. But the country also produces large exportable surpluses of tropical fruits, maize, tapioca, jute, hardwood timber, natural rubber and palm oil. The more temperate N cultivates commercial crops of coffee, strawberries and peaches. Tin and wolfram are mined in the s, and nitrates in the NE. In the Gulf of Thailand significant deposits of undersea natural gas are being tapped. Coastal communities around the Gulf, and along the Andaman Sea to the w, form the basis of a large fishing industry.

In addition to ethnic Thais, the population includes Chinese, Moslem Malays, and smaller minority groups of Lao, Mon, Khmers, Vietnamese, Burmese, Indians and more than 20 hill-tribe groups of Sino–Tibetan stock. All are to be found in the Bangkok melting pot.

When the first king of the ruling Chakri dynasty chose the site in 1782, defense against Burmese attack from the w was his prime concern. He succeeded: the Chao Phraya River and manmade canals rendered the city almost impregnable. Although lately many canals have given way to modern roads, plump rice barges still carry the countryside's wealth to Bangkok. But there is a price to be paid. As a growing population drains Artesian wells beneath the city, Bangkok is steadily sinking. Every fall, monsoon rains and rising river inundate the city, turning it briefly into what it once was — "the Venice of the East."

Bangkok's neighborhoods

Bangkok lies about 24km (15 miles) N of the Gulf of Thailand, most of it on the E bank of the Chao Phraya river. The core of the city is the man-made **Ratanakosin island**, in the shape of a mango, enclosed by the river and a canal. This is the historic center and the site of many important buildings.

Bangkok is not a planned city. Most of it has simply grown haphazardly, especially during the period of prosperity following World War II, and adding, in the late 1950s, a ramshackle collection of low-rise shops, houses and office buildings. Most of Bangkok's many canals were filled in during the 1960s, but several of them still crisscross the city.

The areas listed below are most visited by foreign tourists.

THE INNER CITY *(map 5 C2-3 & D2-3)*. This is the original site of Bangkok, where the first king of the Chakri dynasty founded his kingdom. The GRAND PALACE, Sanam Luang (Royal Field), WAT PHRA KEO (Temple of the Emerald Buddha), WAT PHO (or Wat Phra Chetuphon: Temple of the Reclining Buddha), Wat Ratchabophit, WAT SUTHAT and the Giant Swing are here; also WAT MAHATHAT (Temple of the Great Relic), the NATIONAL MUSEUM, NATIONAL ART GALLERY, National Theatre and two national universities, Silapakorn and Thammasat. See INNER CITY AREA on pages 192-3.

DUSIT AREA *(map 6 A4-5 & B4-5)*. This is a later development of Royal Bangkok; Chitralada Palace (home of the present king), WAT BENCHAMABOPHIT (the Marble Temple), WAT SAKHET (Temple of the Golden Mount), Parliament and DUSIT ZOO are all situated here. The area's most distinctive feature is the Western-style architecture (ca. 1930s/1940s) lining both sides of the regal, six-lane, Ratchadamnoen Nok Ave., between the Democracy Monument and Parliament. Most of the buildings today house government offices — including the Tourism Authority of Thailand headquarters.

OLD TOURIST BANGKOK *(map 6 E4-5 & F4-5 and page 196)*. Also the Chinese, Indian and Muslim parts of town. The General Post Office is here, on New Rd. (Charoen Krung), and along the river are a clutch of hotels: Oriental, Royal Orchid Sheraton and Shangri-La. On Lower Surawong Rd. and Silom Rd. are some of the city's best-known antique stores. See OLD TOURIST BANGKOK AND PATPONG on pages 195-6.

CHINATOWN *(map 6 D4)*. In the environs of Yaowaraj Rd. and encompassing Pahurat (cloth market), an Indian area. At Nakhon Kasem (Thieves' Market), musical instruments, new and old antiques, curios and bric-a-brac line the streets. See CHINATOWN on page 189.

NEW TOURIST BANGKOK *(map 7 E6-F6)*. This begins around Upper Silom Rd. and Surawong Rd., where Jim Thompson's silk store, the Montien and Dusit Thani Hotels are located. Nearby are the Siam Inter-Continental and the Rajdamri, Regent Bangkok and Grand Hyatt Erawan hotels. The President Hotel is in the Gaysorn area, the Hilton International on Wireless Rd., and in recent years many new department stores have opened temptingly nearby. See NEW TOURIST BANGKOK, page 195.

PATPONG ROAD *(map 7 E6)*. This is the major bar and nightlife district of Bangkok, about six square blocks sandwiched between Silom Rd. and Surawong Rd. and at the juncture of old and new tourist areas, where Rama IV Rd. meets Silom Rd. During the day it is a sleepy place of airline offices and small office buildings with only a few bars open for the lunch crowd. At night it jumps, with X-rated sex shows, hundreds of go-go-dancers and dozens of bars. See OLD TOURIST BANGKOK AND PATPONG on pages 195–6.

SUKHUMVIT ROAD *(off map 7D7; see map on page 187).* A new residential area with modest hotels and many freestanding restaurants; some cater mostly to Middle Eastern visitors and others to budget travelers. Due to the press of shopping center and hotel developments and related rent hikes, this area has supplanted both the OLD and NEW TOURIST BANGKOK areas as the premier district for conversion of private residences into cozy restaurants. At the Eastern Bus Terminal, *(Sukhumvit Rd., opposite Soi 63),* air-conditioned buses leave for the southern beach resort of Pattaya.

LARD PRAO/PHAHOLYOTHIN *(off map 7A7).* The newest residential area, on the way to Bangkok's international airport. The Hyatt Central Plaza Hotel is here, trains to the northern city of Chiang Mai pass through, and the Weekend Market at Chatuchak Park is nearby.

Organizing your time

Despite the interminable traffic jams, related air pollution and oppressive heat that prevails for most of the year, the relative compactness of Bangkok's historic area, government and business districts makes sightseeing easier to plan than in many other cities. Here are suggested agendas for two- and four-day visits.

TWO-DAY VISIT
- **Day 1**   Spend the morning visiting the GRAND PALACE and its environs, including WAT PHRA KEO. In the afternoon, visit the NATIONAL MUSEUM and WAT MAHATHAT.
- **Day 2**   In the morning take a boat tour of the Floating Market and the Chao Phraya River, including a view of the ROYAL BARGES. In the afternoon visit CHINATOWN and WAT TRAIMITR with its Golden Buddha.

FOUR-DAY VISIT
- **Days 1–2**   As for 2-day visit.
- **Day 3**   In the morning visit WAT BENCHAMABOPHIT and DUSIT ZOO. See JIM THOMPSON'S HOUSE in the afternoon.
- **Day 4**   Make a day excursion to the ancient capital city of AYUTTHAYA (see DAY TRIPS FROM BANGKOK).

Bangkok: sights and places of interest

Introduction

Thailand is a Buddhist country and a monarchy that has only in this century become a parliamentary democracy. Its greatest manmade splendors are all expressions of devotion to these two forces that have most shaped the Thai identity.

It says something for the magnetism of Thai culture and its artifacts that Thailand's tourism authorities have felt no need to invent tourist attractions within the city of Bangkok. Even those that have sprung up on the outskirts of the city, such as the Rose Garden or the Ancient City (both covered in DAY TRIPS FROM BANGKOK), are designed to be microcosms of Thai social life and architectural splendor, rather than adventure playgrounds or artificial theme parks.

Attractions such as the Dusit Zoo, the Weekend Market and the Pasteur Institute Snake Farm, which are all in the city, are places designed to serve the needs of Thai citizens, that happen also to be fun to visit.

DISTRICTS

The four districts described in this section are not pedestrian "neighborhoods" as such, save for Chinatown. The Inner City is a mango-shaped island of monuments and *wats* (temples), between which one travels by motorized vehicle.

Bangkok's old tourist district is a sea of virtually unrelieved storefronts, commercial buildings and hotels, pedestrian-friendly because it is compact and a wonderful place to buy the artifacts and souvenirs of Thai culture. New tourist Bangkok is a district of highrise shopping centers and hotels, with wide divided highways — built for the movement of cars rather than easy pedestrian access.

THE GREAT WATS (TEMPLES)

This section includes entries on the seven great temples of Bangkok, but there are hundreds of others. Wat Mahathat and Wat Pho are also Buddhist museums and universities, centers for the study of traditional medicine, massage and meditation.

Wat Benchamabophit (The Marble Temple) offers an education in the styles of Thai Buddhist sculptural art through the ages. Wat Sakhet (The Golden Mount) offers a splendid view of the city and Wat Suthat is dominated by the anomalous presence of the Giant Swing outside its walls. Wat Arun (Temple of Dawn) is an architectural delight across the river from the Grand Palace, with its tower of ceramic shards and gleaming mirror fragments. Wat Traimitr is a humble neighborhood place of prayer — with one exception — its centerpiece of devotion is a massive, solid gold figure of the Buddha.

CULTURAL TREASURES
With the single exception of the Jim Thompson House and Museum, all of the ten great secular architectural wonders and museum collections included are the products of direct or indirect royal patronage. First, there is the walled city of the Chakri dynasty kings that is the Grand Palace/Wat Phra Keo (Temple of the Emerald Buddha) complex. The Vimanmek Throne Hall and the berths of the Royal Barges are other royal properties thrown open to public view.

Hindu influences
The Erawan Shrine and Lakmuang Shrine show how closely Hindu influences have become enmeshed in the popular culture of Thailand. State events such as the annual Royal Plowing Ceremony, overseen by Brahmins, and the Spirit Houses found in the courtyards of every Thai building to placate earth spirits disturbed in the building process, reflect how very deeply the Indian culture that created Buddhism permeates Thai life.

National collections
The National Museum is a teaching institution designed to display works of the eight great periods that comprise the history of Thai culture and its direct antecedents, from the Dvaravati, beginning in the 6th century, to the Ratanakosin or Bangkok period, covering the last 200-year period under the Chakri dynasty.

Secular painting is new to Thai culture, perhaps only 100 years old. All art before that was devoted to Royal or Buddhist subjects. So, quite understandably, the National Art Gallery is most interesting for its large contemporary art wing.

Northern Thai architecture
Ban Kamthieng ethnographic museum (in the grounds of the Siam Society), the Suan Pakkard Palace garden, designed for a Thai princess and the home of the American "silk king," Jim Thompson, offer the best examples of Northern Thai architecture open to the tourist in all of Thailand.

SUKHUMVIT RD.
The map on the opposite page should help you navigate your way around Sukhumvit Rd., a maze to be approached with a sense of adventure, caution and patience. It can hardly be avoided, however, as it contains many excellent restaurants and fashionable shops.

Addresses on Sukhumvit are confusing and may not always follow a consistent pattern. They are based on the *Sois* (lanes) into which the road is divided, and the *sois* leading off them. *Sois* all have numbers, and some, not all, have names. This applies to the offshoot *sois* as well as the main ones. A standard Sukhumvit address might be: 22 Soi 11 (Chaiyos), Sukhumvit Rd. (22 is the street number, on Soi 11, which is also known

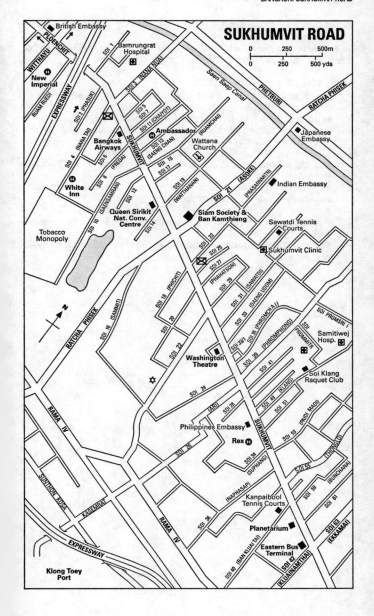

as Soi Chaiyos). But there are many permutations. Some *sois* are not named, for example.

Before setting out for a location on Sukhumvit, it is always best to get directions, perhaps from the Thai concierge at the hotel.

HOW TO USE THIS A TO Z SECTION

- The alphabetical listings use English or Thai names according to common English-language usage.
- **Bold type** generally indicates major points of interest.
- Cross-references to other entries or to other sections of the book are printed in SMALL CAPITALS.
- The ★ symbol identifies the most important sights.
- The ▥ symbol indicates buildings of considerable architectural interest.
- The ◁€ symbol is used to indicate places from which the view is especially panoramic or picturesque.
- Places of special interest for children (✿) are also indicated.
- For guided tours, look for the ✗ symbol: details follow this symbol where appropriate.
- **For a full explanation of all the symbols used in this book, see page 7.**

Bangkok's sights A to Z

BAN KAMTHIENG (Kamthieng House) ▥ ★
Siam Society Grounds, Soi Asoke 131, 21 Sukhumvit Rd. ☎*258-3494. Travel section* ☎*260-2831* ☒*258-3491* ▨ *⥓ ✹ Open Tues–Sat 9am–noon, 1–5pm. Buses 38, 98, 136. No cards accepted at gift center.*

Built of solid teak, this house on stilts was dismantled at its original site in Chiang Mai, N Thailand and moved to Bangkok, to the headquarters of the Siam Society, to which it was bequeathed in 1963 by the Nimmanhaeminda family. Grants from the Asia Society and Rockefeller Foundation financed its relocation and establishment as an ethnological museum.

Ban Kamthieng is considered to be one of the finest surviving examples of Northern Thai architecture of the 19th century. The house is more than 160 years old and its shape resembles a buffalo — the outward sloping sides of the house are the buffalo's shoulders and its sturdy pillars are the animal's legs. The interior of the house is dark, spacious and sparsely furnished. Apart from the main living area, there are five other units.

The museum has a fascinating collection of household artifacts, especially strong on basketware, kitchen utensils and textiles — the tools and products of tribal women's work. The beautifully patterned embroideries, which formed part of bridal dowries, bear the stories of their creation, thus acting as the holy books of their peoples.

One example is that of the Yao, a hill people originating from Guizhou province in China. Their story of Faam Tah and Faam Kah, the first sister and brother, tells much about the central role of mountains, sewing and weaving, and women, in their world. It seems Faam Kah was too lazy and small to make much of a world, so sister Faam Tah took up needle and thread and sewed the land together, pulling it up into mountains. Yao girls ever since have known the importance of embroidery and begin learning their skills from ages five or six.

Be sure to see the display of inlaid architectural friezes, farm equipment and the impressive *klong-ee* waist drums, below the house. They look like cannons on caissons, ranging in length up to 3.5m (11$\frac{1}{2}$ feet) and 50cm (1$\frac{1}{2}$ feet) in diameter. In N Thailand, they are used as lunch and dinner gongs to signal monks back from the fields for meals twice a day and as community alarm systems.

Unfortunately, there is no guide on the staff, and no English-speakers, but there are good bilingual (English–Thai) written descriptions to individual exhibits.

CHINATOWN
Map 6D4. Air Buses 1, 7.

Chinatown lies just to the SE of the Inner City, sprawling over three major streets, Charoen Krung (New Rd.), Yaowaraj and Sampeng Lane. The district is famous for its gold stores, jewelers, fortune tellers, herbalists and cinemas showing *kung-fu* movies from Hong Kong. Sampeng Lane is a good place for household goods, with everything from sewing needles to kitchen equipment. Worth visiting is **Leng Nuei Yee**

(Dragon Flower Temple), a Chinese Buddhist temple located on Charoen Krung, between Mangkon Rd. and Itsaranuphap Lane.

A pedestrian walkway links Chakraphet Rd. and **Pahurat Cloth Market**, where you will find Indian Sikhs selling linen and materials for *saris* and *sarongs*. Also on sale are Indian costume jewelry and accessories for weddings and Thai dancing.

Nakhon Kasem (Thieves' Market) is situated on the corner of Boriphat Rd. and Yaowaraj Rd. This was once a place where thieves went to sell their booty, a practice remembered in the name only. Nowadays the shops are legitimate and sell everything from musical instruments to fake antiques and from coffee grinders to wooden animals.

DUSIT ZOO

Rama V Rd., Dusit district, between Chitrlada Palace and National Assembly Building. Map 6A5 ☎281-2000 ▭ ✳ Open 8am–6pm. Air Bus 10.

Established in 1938, this 19ha (47-acre) zoological park features a children's playground, a lush botanical garden, and a fine collection of animals, including kangaroos, leopards, black panthers, snakes, deer and crocodiles. The rare **white elephants**, long associated with royalty and sacred in the Buddhist tradition (explained on page 170), are a special attraction.

In all, about 350 mammals, 900 birds and 250 species of reptile are housed on the grounds. There is also a lagoon with paddle boats and a small, open eating area facing it that makes a lovely and inexpensive location for lunch or a snack. The tiny **natural history museum** in the grounds is also worth a visit.

Just walking through this park is a delight, as it easily ranks amongst the world's most beautifully designed, largely because its original purpose was to serve as the private gardens of King Rama V, attached to the Royal Dusit Garden Palace. In effect, the zoo was tastefully integrated with a botanical garden well and truly "fit for a king" to enjoy. The national Zoological Park Organization operates this zoo and two others in Cholburi Province and Chiang Mai.

A small circus performs here on weekends and public holidays.

ERAWAN SHRINE ★

Junction of Ploenchit Rd. and Ratchaprasong Rd. (Ratchaprasong intersection) in front of Sogo Department Store and Grand Hyatt Erawan hotel. Map 7D7 ▭ ◁≣ Open 6am–11pm. Air Buses 4, 5, 11, 13.

This Hindu shrine of the four faces of Brahma, San Phra Prom, is revered throughout Southeast Asia for fulfilling the wishes of the faithful. Fully trussed traditional Thai dancers and musicians are on hand and can be hired for impromptu performances to please the god (payment is made according to the number of dancers and the duration of their dancing), garlands of jasmine and incense sticks and tiny candles are on sale, and there is never any shortage of worshipers, at this shrine of the god responsible for people's destinies.

A small herd of teak elephants, another expression of supplicants' pleas or gratitude, helps furnish the small, fenced enclosure. The miracle that gave this shrine its special powers is said to have happened in 1956, when it appears to have put a stop to a series of inexplicable accidents and delays in the building of the original Erawan Hotel, near this corner. Spirit doctors diagnosed the problem as stemming from tree spirits made homeless when their abodes were chopped down to make the hotel's foundation beams.

Earth spirits, such as those meant to be appeased by the "spirit houses" seen in front yards of every Bangkok household, are related to Hindu rather than Buddhist deities. A similar Brahman shrine resides at Wat Khaek, near the Narai Hotel, but no other has the same mystique and magnetism for Asians.

GRAND PALACE AND WAT PHRA KEO (Temple of the Emerald Buddha) ★
Naphrathat Rd. Map 5C2 ☎*222-8181 ext. 40* 🍴 💺 *Open daily 8.30–11.30am, 1–3.30pm. Admission includes tickets to* VIMANMEK THRONE HALL *(see page 197) and a Coin Pavilion in the grounds. Proper dress essential. Guides recommended. Air Buses 8, 12.*

To call this compound by a single name suits the convenience of travel agents, but it is a monumental misnomer. It is the centerpiece of **Rata-nakosin Island**, the old **Royal City**, on a mango-shaped bend in the Chao Phraya River severed from the rest of Bangkok at the back by Klong Lawd (a large canal), and actually a small walled city, like the Kremlin in Moscow. As in the Kremlin, one must allow time to see it at least twice within the same visit: once to absorb the grandeur of its external architecture and again to sort out the staggering assortment of details that each building contains.

The **Grand Palace** itself was built by Rama I in 1782, and additional buildings in the compound were erected by subsequent monarchs. Its four walls, built in 1783, total 1,900m (6,232 feet) in length. There are now about 35 buildings on the site, and some dozen enormous *stupas*. Currently used for state occasions and royal functions, certain sections of the palace remain on public view. Visitors can tour the spacious rooms adorned with art objects and royal memorabilia.

Also to be seen is the **Dusit Maha Prasad**, a classical Thai palace built in 1789, which features the king's mother-of-pearl throne; note the nine-tiered spire surmounting a four-tiered roof.

One of the most elegant structures, the elevated **Royal Dressing Hall** *(Aporn Pitmok Maha Plasan)* seems badly named, at least if one associates dressing with privacy — it is an open building supported by elegant pillars, a kind of Thai Parthenon. Like so much on these grounds, it is modeled on an Ayutthaya original and is used after coronations for a new king to don the royal robes, which he does very publicly.

Many of the buildings are only opened on special occasions. The **Library Hall** is only open on the Buddha's birthday, which coincides with the first full moon in May. Buddhist services can be seen at the **Montien Chapel** on Sundays *(8.30-9am)* and on special Buddhist days that coincide with moon cycles four times a month.

The **Royal Pantheon**, a beautiful blue building where statues of former kings are kept, is open only three times a year: 6th April, during

191

the Songkran or Water Festival (which marks the old Thai New Year), from 12th–14th April and on the King's birthday, 5th December.

The small **Pla Kantara** hall, with diamond-shaped tiles in green, blue and yellow, houses the farmers' Buddha and is visited by the King on 9th May as part of the Plowing Ceremony rituals.

Wat Phra Keo is the royal temple that houses the 15thC **Emerald Buddha** (actually jasper or jadeite), brought to this site in the latter part of the 18thC. This small sculpture (about 75 by 45cm/30 by 18 inches), drawn from a single piece of semiprecious stone, is the most important symbol of dynastic inheritance in the kingdom.

Wat Phra Keo

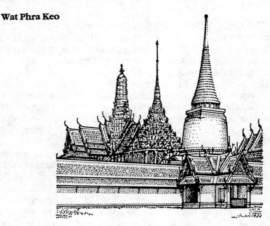

The story of its original discovery in Chiang Rai (in AD1434), its capture by various kingdoms, and its loss and recapture, has come to be viewed as an allegory for the destiny of the Thai kingdom: initially glorious, then fallen, and finally rebuilt by the Chakri dynasty. In this sense, it is more precious than the solid gold Buddha of Wat Traimitr and is worthy of its precious "emerald" attribution.

At the beginning of each season, the king performs a sacred ceremony during which he changes the robes of the Buddha. The ceremony coincides with full moons; in July, the body adornment is most ornate with belts, bracelets, and so on; in March, one shoulder is draped in a saffron robe; and in November, a full cloak is worn.

The temple precinct contains many other striking Thai buildings, including a **hall for sacred objects**, a **library**, a **mausoleum** and a magnificent **scale model of Angkor Wat**, the old Khmer capital in Kampuchea (Cambodia).

INNER-CITY AREA (Ratanakosin Island) ★
Map 5C2–3 & D2–3.
This is the historic heart of Bangkok. Here, on a small sliver of land,

protected by the river on one side and a moat on the other, King Rama I established his capital in 1782. The fairy-tale GRAND PALACE complex is here, as well as many temples, the NATIONAL MUSEUM and other sights.

It is possible to view the outstanding buildings of the Grand Palace area in a three-hour walk, beginning at the LAKMUANG SHRINE, then visiting the GRAND PALACE itself, WAT PHRA KEO and WAT PHO. If you have more time, however, continue NE and visit Wat Ratchabophit, WAT SUTHAT and the **Giant Swing**.

A separate three-hour walk, taking in the N part of the inner-city district, would include the NATIONAL MUSEUM, the NATIONAL ART GALLERY and WAT MAHATHAT.

JIM THOMPSON'S HOUSE ▥ ★
End of Soi Kasemsan 2, off Rama I Rd., opposite the National Stadium. Map 7C6 ☎ *251-0122* ▨ ✗ *Open Mon–Fri 9am–5pm. Volunteer English-language guides on site. Air Bus 8.*

Visitors are drawn to this house partly because of its traditional Thai construction, but largely because of the legend of Jim Thompson, the American who used to live in it and who revived Thailand's silk industry after World War II. Architecturally, it is a collection of seven Thai-style houses from various parts of Thailand, brought down to Bangkok and assembled to make one large teak house.

Besides his interest in the local silk industry (see SHOPPING, page 236), Thompson was an avid art collector, and displayed in the teak-paneled rooms are hundreds of pieces of Chinese blue-and-white export ware and Bencharong ("five colors") porcelain, wooden Burmese statues, and Khmer and Thai stone images.

Thompson, an architect by profession, came to settle in Thailand after the war. He took it upon himself to revitalize the ailing Thai silk industry, which would have been enough in itself to turn him into a legend. But the romance of his life-story was secured by its mysterious ending: Jim Thompson vanished mysteriously on vacation in Malaysia at the height of his career as a silk manufacturer and exporter.

Thompson's house is set in a luxuriant garden with the Maha Nag *klong* running by it. Across the *klong* are the homes of some of the silk weavers who used to row across to visit Thompson with their bales of brilliantly colored Thai silk.

LAKMUANG SHRINE
Junction of Ratchadamnoen Nai Rd. and Naphrathat Rd. Map 5C3 ▣ ◀€ *Open 5.30am–7.30pm. Air Buses 2, 8.*

In a location that is well-trafficked by local people and a good place for visitors to begin their tour of the old part of the city, this shrine stands just across from the entrance to the **Temple of the Emerald Buddha** (see GRAND PALACE), the home of the city's guardian spirit.

It was erected by Rama I (1782–1809) as the foundation of his new capital, but unlike the magnificent and rather awesome architectural complex next door, this small enclosed enclave has an appealing intimacy and informality about it.

In the main building, floral offerings deck the pillar, and the smell of burning incense surrounds the shrine, which is believed to have the power to grant wishes. Inside is a *lingam,* the phallic stone power symbol of the Hindu god Shiva.

Between the two small buildings on the site is a covered shrine to the spirits of Thonburi, the neighboring town to Bangkok. Inside, suppliants can purchase performances of Thai classical dance and music as tokens of appreciation for favors granted.

The second building contains a row of images, with a seated Buddha figure, salvaged from the destroyed city of Ayutthaya (see EXPLORING THAILAND), in the center. On the right is an interesting array of collection boxes for each day of the week and on the left you will often see a kneeling man trying to lift a small but heavy Buddha figure up above his head, usually cheered on by accompanying family members (a ritual called *Para Sientai).* This is physically harder to do than it looks or sounds. The belief is that if the person succeeds in doing this twice, they will have success in life.

Helping to set the location's cozy feel is a third structure in which folk theater is performed throughout the day. These are usually satires of Thai domestic life, analogous to TV "sitcoms."

NATIONAL ART GALLERY ★
Chao Fa Rd. (opposite National Theatre). Map 5B3 ☎*281-2224* ▨
Open Wed–Sat 9am–4pm. Closed Mon, Tues, hols.
Thailand's national art gallery has three wings, the most interesting of which is the second, housing an excellent selection of contemporary Thai art. The first, and arguably less interesting, contains historical and what might be termed "patriotic" works. The third is a sales gallery that rotates shows every month.

The **national film archive** is also housed on the grounds, mostly of interest to Thai-language movie buffs and students.

NATIONAL MUSEUM ★
4 Naphrathat Rd. Map 5C2 ☎*224-1333/234-1396* ▨ ✗ *Open 9am–noon,*
1–4pm. Closed Mon, Tues, hols. Air Buses 3, 11.
The National Museum was converted from an 18thC palace to a museum by King Chulalongkorn in the latter part of the 19thC, with further buildings added in 1926 and 1966. The museum, which today is claimed to be the largest in Southeast Asia, features a collection of prehistoric artifacts from the Ban Chiang civilization (around 4000BC), as well as an excellent array of Buddhist icons from various periods. Other displays include royal regalia, costumes, weapons and coins, masks and porcelain.

The **Buddhaisawan Chapel**, on the museum grounds, was built in 1795 for the private use of a prince. It houses the 15thC image of the **Phra Buddha Sihing**, the second-most-revered religious icon in Thailand, after the Emerald Buddha (see GRAND PALACE above). Its murals are the oldest extant works of their kind in Bangkok (make special note of the foreigners shown as demon troops in the panel depicting Buddha subduing

Khon mask of **Hanuman**, the monkey warrior from the *Ramakien,* National Museum

the demon king, Mara). The steps and unusually constructed red poles in front of the chapel are a *howdah*-mounting platform, used by royalty to mount elephants.

Free English-language, 90-minute tours of the museum are given three days a week, covering different topics such as Thai culture, Thai art and Buddhism. The tours start from the information desk at 9.30am.

Thai art is usually discussed in terms of the stylistic techniques that were developed in the course of the following eight historical epochs: Dvaravati (6th–11thC), Sri-Vijaya (8th–13thC), Lopburi (11th–14thC), U Thong (12th–15thC), Sukhothai (13th–15thC), Chiang Saen (12th–15thC), Ayutthaya (15th–18thC), and Ratanakosin or Bangkok (18th–20thC). For a full account of the history of Thai art, see pages 154–6.

NEW TOURIST BANGKOK
Map 7C6–D6. Air Buses 1, 8.

This is the area surrounding Siam Sq. and the Siam Inter-Continental hotel. Behind the hotel is the **Srapathum Palace**. It is the home of the mother of the reigning king of Thailand.

In the same compound as the hotel is the **Siam Centre**, a multistory, air-conditioned commercial complex with many shops selling expensive imported clothes, and a favorite place for local Thais.

Opposite, across the pedestrian walkway, is **Siam Sq.**, which is divided into more than ten lanes, with Thai and Chinese restaurants and fast-food outlets, three movie theaters, shoe stores, bookstores, boutiques, curio places, dentists and clinics.

OLD TOURIST BANGKOK AND PATPONG
Map 6 & 7E & F5–6. Air Buses 2, 4, 5.

This area runs E and W between the river and Rama Rd. At the W side, along Charoen Krung (New Rd.), near the Oriental Hotel, are many antique stores selling Burmese lacquerware and tapestries, Thai *objets d'art*, Cambodian silver animals, jewelry and gems. To the s on New Rd. is **Bungkrak**, one of the busiest fresh-food and flower markets in Bangkok.

To the E, between Surawong Rd. and Silom Rd., is the **Patpong** area (in fact three streets called Patpong 1, 2 and 3; see NIGHTLIFE on pages 224–5). This is an area that is best explored at the twilight hour when bored dancing girls can be seen sitting outside bars in skimpy costumes, some putting on their makeup while others eat or chat and wait for the witching hour to start.

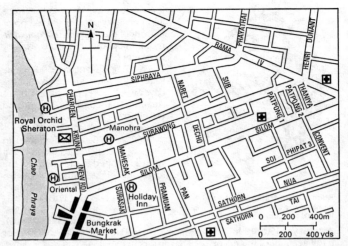

Besides bars to suit all kinds of drinkers, some reputable restaurants and fast-food places, there are three kinds of sex shows on sale here: loud bars with friendly go-go girls to ogle; flauntingly obscene stage shows wherein women insert all manner of foreign objects into places they don't belong; and "full body" massages performed in private rooms by numbered men or women (depending upon the parlor) chosen from a holding pen viewed through two-way mirrors.

PASTEUR INSTITUTE SNAKE FARM

Junction of Henri Dunant Rd. and Rama IV Rd. Map **7**E6 ☎ *221-0161 ext. 306* ▥ *Open Mon–Sat 8.30am–4.30pm; hols 8.30am–noon. Snake-venom extraction: 10.30am–2pm weekdays; 10.30am hols. Air Buses 2, 7.*

A wide variety of poisonous and nonpoisonous snakes can be seen here, including kraits, vipers and enormous cobras. Located in pits within the Red Cross Compound, the snakes are milked daily to extract their poison for use in serum production.

When not entertaining tourists, this is actually a working medical facility, where one can obtain inoculations for cholera, smallpox, typhoid and rabies.

ROYAL BARGES ★

Klong Bangkok Noi, off Chao Phraya River. Map **5**F2 ☎ *424-0004* ▥ *Open 8.30am–4.30pm.*

These beautifully carved boats were once used by Thai kings for special occasions and religious festivals. The oldest and biggest barge, which is reserved for the king's exclusive use, is called the **Sri Supannahong**. Richly carved, its prow is decorated with a gilded bird's head, representing a *hansa,* or sacred swan.

The full-scale Royal Barge ceremony happens only rarely, normally in October, in connection with the Buddhist Kathin ceremony, which marks the end of the "Rains Retreat" (i.e., Buddhist Lent) and presentation by the king of new saffron robes to the monks at Wat Arun. A fleet of more than 50 barges carry king and robes across the river. Only three such ceremonies have been held since 1967, the last of which was in 1987.

SUAN PAKKARD PALACE 血 ★

353 Si Ayutthaya Rd. close to Victory Monument. Map 7C7 ☎245-4934. Open Mon–Sat 9am–4pm. Buses 17, 58, 72.

This was the home of the late Princess Chumbhot of Nagara Svarga, a devoted art connoisseur who was legendary within her generation for her sharp wit — expressed even in the naming of her "lettuce patch" *(suan pakkard)* palace, which commemorates what was on the land when her family bought it. At that time, the surroundings were rural. Now only the serene gardens around her home remain green. All else is part of urban Bangkok.

Overlooking beautifully landscaped gardens are five traditional teak houses, each displaying a carefully chosen, fine collection of antiquities and art objects such as Khmer statues, porcelain, Thai furniture, Buddha images and musical instruments used at the Royal Court.

Situated in the palace gardens is the splendid 17thC **Lacquer Pavilion**, brought from the Ayutthaya region and lovingly restored. Inside are murals executed in gold leaf illustrating scenes from the life of the Buddha and from the Hindu epic, the *Ramayana*.

VIMANMEK THRONE HALL (Phra Thi Nang Wimanmek or The Celestial Residence) 血 ★

Entrance at Suan Puttan Gate, Ratchavithi Rd., near National Assembly Hall. Map 6A4 ☎281-4715/281-1518 ☒281-6880 ☎ ✗ Free English-language tours conducted every half-hour from 11.15am–3pm. Open 9.30am–4pm. Closed Mon, Tues. Bus 70. Tickets to Grand Palace compound include entrance ticket for this location. Tickets sold on site until 3pm.

This four-story, octagonal palace was built in 1900 for King Chulalong-korn (Rama V), who lived here for five years. The largest construction of golden teak in the world, it contains 31 display rooms filled with art objects and memorabilia that were collected by the widely-traveled monarch.

Rama V was the first Thai king to travel to Europe, twice, in 1897 and 1907. It was after his European experience that he started a fashion trend by allowing his wife to wear her hair long. Before that time, Thai women had worn close-cropped hair to disguise them from the hated and feared Burmese. (Looking like men, they also fought beside them in the defense of their cities. Numerous warrior heroines are honored in Thai history.)

Rama V introduced many technical and social innovations, this last including the abolition of slavery and, by his marriage to a commoner and habit of disguising himself as one, so as to go out and see how his people actually lived, the erosion of a vast gulf that had hitherto divided the king from his people. In consequence, he easily ranks as the most-revered and best-loved of all former Thai monarchs.

From 1955 to 1982, the building was used as a warehouse. At the instigation of H.M. Queen Sirikit, it was restored and opened to the public as part of the Bangkok bicentennial celebrations. There is an interesting collection of European porcelain, glass-paneled cabinets display a half-dozen full sets commissioned by King Chulalongkorn, painted in different colors for each day of the week — which stemmed from the Thai belief that each person has an associated color that matches the day they were born.

There are also portraits of Queen Victoria in both youth and old age, hunting trophies and other amazing Asian and European bric-a-brac in this eclectic Oriental potentate's palace.

English-language tours of the wooden wonder are conducted every half-hour. Transport buffs will enjoy the **Royal Carriage Museum** on the grounds, where they can see 13 well-polished and historic horse-drawn carriages used during the reign of Rama V.

WAT ARUN (Temple of Dawn) ▥ ★

West Bank of Chao Phraya River. Map 5D2 ▦ ◁ *Open 8.30am–5pm. Water taxi from Tha Tien jetty. See illustration on page 152.*

Aruna is the Indian god of dawn, from whom this "Temple of Dawn" takes its name. Its central spire *(prang),* which stands 79m (270 feet) high, is one of the most photographed sites in Bangkok, perhaps because it is so well placed across the Chao Phraya river from the Grand Palace compound. Its unique profile even features in the corporate logo of the Tourism Authority of Thailand (TAT). At dawn its shadow is cast across the river and its fragments of mirrors and porcelain gleam resplendent in the buttered light of dusk.

Wat Arun must be approached by water taxi, and the walk up from the jetty then offers a carnival atmosphere of fortune-tellers, touts ped-dling rides up the *klongs* in long-tailed boats, vendors of cold drinks, and an endless stream of dumbstruck tourists standing in awe of this magnificent structure, as well as several others of a lesser scale.

On the site of an older temple built as part of King Taksin's palace compound when Thonburi was Thailand's interim capital, Wat Arun was enlarged by King Rama II (1809–24) and completed by his son, Rama III (1824–51). Its impressive Khmer-style spires are encrusted with glittering mosaics composed of Chinese porcelain shards, colored glass and mirrors. Climb one of the tower staircases to enjoy a breathtaking view of both the Chao Phraya River and the temple compound below, which is dotted with many lovely pavilions.

WAT BENCHAMABOPHIT (Marble Temple) ▥

Si Ayutthaya Rd. Map 6B4 ☎281-2501 ▣ *Open 8am–5pm. Air Bus 3.*

One of Bangkok's most recent temples, constructed of creamy-white Carrara marble imported from Italy (hence its colloquial English-lang-uage name), this is also one of its most admired. Built on the site of earlier monasteries around the turn of the 20thC, during the reign of

King Chulalongkorn, its interior, with lacquered and gilded beams, matches the outside in magnificence.

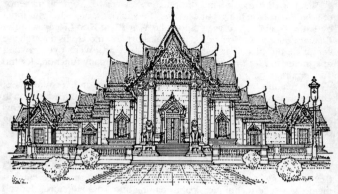

A gallery behind the temple *bot* displays more than 50 images of the Buddha, most of which are reproductions, intended to show the evolution of Thai religious art. The lovely grounds, which include a turtle-filled moat, are a relaxing oasis in the middle of the city. The best time to visit is in the morning, when monks are at prayer in the main chapel.

WAT MAHATHAT (Great Relic Monastery)
Naphrathat Rd. (Between grounds of Silpakorn and Thammasat universities).
Map 5C2 🔳 *Open 9am–5pm.*
One of the oldest monasteries in Bangkok, the original temple burned down in 1782 and has twice been rebuilt since, most recently in 1844. This large but austere center of Buddhist medicine and meditation is the home of one of the two major Buddhist seminaries in Thailand, Mahachulalongkorn Buddhist University, which is run by the Mahanikal monastic sect.

It is an important teaching institution, which specializes in meditation practice *(vipassana)*, and English-language instruction is often available. There is an open-air market for medicinal herbs and tonics on Buddhist holy days *(wan phra)*, on the full and new moons every two weeks.

WAT PHO (Wat Phra Chetuphon) 🏛 ★
Chetuphon Rd. Map 5D2 ☎222-0933 🔳 *Open 8am–5pm. Children's Sunday school for playing traditional music at a small bot, Pharalai Badilhu 9–11am. Bell Tower in courtyard sounds the call to prayer at 4.30am and 4.30pm daily. Massage school open 8.30am–6pm. 24hr hotel service* ☎587-9345.
English-language student guides from Chulalongkorn University are available on the grounds and highly recommended. Air Buses 6, 12.
Thailand's largest temple complex, also known as Wat Phra Chetuphon, is spread about an 8ha (20-acre) site. Wat Pho (pronounced po) was founded as the royal temple of Rama I, about 200 years ago.

Several of the country's monarchs have augmented its buildings and fine collection of art objects.

Wat Pho, the temple's most popular name, derives from the presence of a *bodhi* tree on the grounds (*"pho"* tree in Thai), brought from India by Rama IV about 120 years ago. Like **Wat Phra Keo** (Temple of the Emerald Buddha), also favored by Chakri dynasty monarchs through the centuries, the place has the feel of an elderly art lover's overcrowded apartment and for the same reason: it serves so many functions for the Thai community.

The result is an eclectic melange of artifacts and architectural styles, either salvaged from elsewhere or custom-built, offering an education in Thai Buddhism in their own right or squeezed in to fit the requirements of Thai numerology (eg. 99 *chedi*). Additions have been made during different stylistic periods, before and since the city's founding in 1782, by nine different Chakri dynasty monarchs.

The temple compound features a library, a college for the study of the Pali language, and a center for traditional Thai medicine. It was Thailand's first university campus, with a curriculum that still features herbal medicine, massage techniques, palm reading and Thai literature, derived from Sanskrit and published in unusual pandanus leaf books bound with painted boards strung together like venetian blinds.

There are 99 spired *chedi* surrounding the temple, each a columbarium of ashes of deceased devotees, sometimes with photographs as death masks on their markers. Their shape is derived from India's *stupa*.

The four very large pagoda-shaped monuments formerly held the ashes of Thai kings, and each is colored in the hue associated with a given monarch's day of birth: Rama I (green), Rama II (yellow), Rama III (orange) and Rama IV (blue). Thais believe that every day of the week has an associated color. The royal ashes have been removed to the GRAND PALACE complex.

The main attraction for visitors is the huge sculpture of the **Reclining Buddha**, 46m (153 feet) long, 15m (50 feet) high and covered in gold leaf. The soles of its feet are inlaid with mother-of-pearl designs depicting the 108 auspicious signs of the Buddha, which encircle the "disk of life" or *mandala*.

This figure displays all of the characteristics associated with the Buddha's physiognomy in Thai iconography: he rests in what is held to be his final posture before his death, at 80 years of age. He has a hooked nose, extended earlobes, arms that hang to his knees, golden skin, four fingers on each hand and four toes on each foot, all of the same length.

Built in the reign of Rama III, more than 160 years ago, the original sculpture was *al fresco*. The brick and stucco building was constructed 10 years later. The gilt of his golden skin was resurfaced in 1992, at a cost of three million baht. One charming way to make an offering is to fill the 108 bronze alms bowls along the wall facing the Buddha, corresponding to the auspicious signs. One buys a 10 baht bowl of 25-satang coins to drop into them, one coin at a time.

Finely carved teak doors, with mother-of-pearl inlay on the main temple *(bot)*, were created under Rama III and are considered artistic masterpieces. The 154 marble friezes that surround the temple exterior tell the story of the *Ramakien* (the Thai version of the Hindu epic, the *Ramayana*). The painted surfaces of the carvings have long since been worn away, and the high relief marble sculptures are the original source of the many rubbings of *Ramakien* scenes now sold in printed and colored reproductions in all tourist gift stores.

In the temple grounds, near the main entrance is a Sala tree, the flowers of which are considered lucky and to bring good health, as the Buddha was born near such a tree. Among the rocks behind it is an assemblage of *yogi,* masters of medicine sculpted in different postures from a mixture of clay and tin. They date from the reign of Rama III and each represents the special ailment for which he has the power of cure (toothache, back and shoulder pain, etc.). The ill come to make offerings each morning by pasting small squares of gold leaf (on sale at all temples) on affected body parts.

All about the grounds, gaudy green and gold architectural details of buildings peep out from behind dull gray giants in the form of standing Chinese sandstone soldiers or mythical animals that together make of the place an irresistible magical mystery tour. There are Chinese lions sculpted in lava that were given to Rama I, with magnificently detailed tails and, elsewhere, 3-meter-tall (9-foot) entrance guardians in sandstone, that had been used for ballast in the Chinese trading ships calling at the port and later presented to Rama III by local traders.

The Thai bestiary is represented by the Singha, from whence Thailand's most famous brand of beer takes its name. Its full name is Singha Samprang, an entrance guardian with the head of a serpent and a lion's body (those at Wat Pho date back to the reign of Rama III). At the entrance gate to the hall that contains the Reclining Buddha stand four giant, identical figures dressed as the same Chinese businessman, believed to represent Marco Polo.

Do not make the average tourist's error of seeing only the Reclining Buddha. There are about 1,000 Buddha images in the temple compound. In one courtyard beside the main chapel, there are 394 seated bronze Buddha figures covered in gold leaf, salvaged from the old capital city of Ayutthaya by Rama I, all of which are approximately 500 years old (see DAY TRIPS FROM BANGKOK).

One must also make time to see the most famous school of traditional massage in Thailand. There are two school buildings, each with tables for 22 patients. As with Chinese acupressure, they massage more than 100 nerve points. Also preserved on the grounds are stone slabs with recipes for herbal medicines. Mixtures include up to five different herbs and sometimes bits of animal bones and sugar cane.

Anything up to 20 palmists or face readers occupy pitches on the temple grounds, advertising themselves with delightfully constructed English-language solicitations, such as the following: "All kinds of Astrology which concern the 6th sense I can forecast or predict your cycle of life. Your girlfriend or boyfriend will be congenial with you or not and will be good or bad. You will be rich or poor in the future. You will succeed or collapse in your business."

WAT SAKHET AND THE GOLDEN MOUNT (Phu Khao Thong) 🏛

Junction of Ratchadamnoen Ave. and Klong Banglampoo. Map 6C4 📷 ◁€
Open daily: no official hours. Air Buses 11, 12.

Constructed during the 19thC, the man-made Golden Mount makes an excellent lookout point for surveying Bangkok. At its 79m (261 feet) summit, reached by a 300-step ascent, Wat Sakhet houses relics from Nepal believed to be those of the Buddha, given to the Thais by the British government in the late 19thC

Originally intended by Rama III (1824–51) as the site for a large shrine beside one of Bangkok's canals, the project was given up when the structure collapsed while under construction due to a shift in the soft earth beneath it. His son, Rama IV (1851–68) solved the problem through a major engineering feat of its time: he had 1,000 teak logs sunk into the ground as a foundation and then built the hill on top. A raucous fair held each November at this site features crafts, stage shows and candlelit processions.

WAT SUTHAT 🏛 ★

Bamrung Muang Rd. at Sikak Sao Chingcha (Giant Swing Sq.). Map 5C3 📷
Open 9am–5pm. Air Bus 8.

King Rama I's builders took 27 years to complete this temple's *viharn* (hall for sacred objects), designed to house a fine 14thC bronze statue of the Buddha (Phra Sri Sakyamuni Buddha), which stands 8m (26 feet) tall and is surrounded by many smaller images of Buddha. Stone figures of Chinese military heroes and Confucian scholars in the temple courtyard were originally brought to Thailand as ships' ballast and gifts to Chinese merchants, who later donated them to the area's temples. This is also how WAT ARUN (illustrated on page 152) came to have Chinese porcelain shards decorating its towers.

In the temple precinct is the **Giant Swing**, an elaborately constructed device upon which acrobatic feats were once performed to entertain the Hindu god Shiva during his brief visit to earth each winter. It was constructed during the reign of Rama I, in 1784.

Bags of gold were set at the top of 15m (50-foot) poles on each side of the swing and four young Brahmans called *naciwan*, after the sacred *naga* (the snake who spread his hood over the Buddha to protect him from the elements while he meditated), would stand in pairs at each end and work the swing into motion, until the bags could be snatched from each pole. The poles symbolized mountains on either side of an ocean.

As there were no safety nets, sudden slips often proved fatal, and the ceremony was suspended in the 1940s. Today, only the swing's giant frame remains as a grim reminder of those devotional daredevils. Photos of the swing in action are on display in one of VIMANMEK THRONE HALL's many rooms.

WAT TRAIMITR (Temple of the Golden Buddha) ★

Traimitr Rd. (where Yowarat and Charoen Krung Rds. intersect near Hualamphong rail station). Map 6D4 📷 *Open 9am–5pm. Air Buses 1, 7.*

While being moved to this temple in 1957, a huge plaster sculpture of the Buddha cracked open to reveal a stunning image of solid gold, weighing more than five tonnes. The 3m (10-foot) Golden Buddha is thought to have been created during the Sukhothai period (AD1238–1378) and later covered in plaster so as to conceal it from Burmese invaders.

Wat Traimitr is, except for its Golden Buddha, an otherwise very ordinary neighborhood house of worship, and even the giant gold figure is of no real esthetic consequence, perhaps proving that "all that's golden does not glitter."

WEEKEND MARKET ★

Chatuchak Park, Phahonyothin Rd. opposite Northern Bus Terminal. Off map 7A7. Open Sat and Sun 7am–6pm. Air Buses 3, 9, 10, 13.

Located in a northern suburb, at the junction of Phaholyothin Rd. and Lard Prao Rd., the Weekend Market in Chatuchak Park should be considered a must on any itinerary. It should be explored in the morning, before the day gets too hot.

The divisions of the market are not clearly marked, but visitors can spend a whole morning there, looking at sections selling house pets, Siamese fighting fish, birds, plants, pythons, vegetables, "new" and old antiques, ceramic ware, hill-tribe handicrafts, old and new clothes, cooked and fresh food, pirated cassette tapes, army-surplus equipment and much else. This market was relocated here from the grounds outside the GRAND PALACE compound, which were cleared to celebrate Bangkok's bicentennial in 1982.

Bangkok:
where to stay

Bangkok's hotels: bouncing back

Bangkok in the mid-1990s is one of the tourist hubs of Southeast Asia, outstripping its most glittering neighbors, Singapore and Hong Kong, in the number of long-haul passengers who arrive there, and the quantity of hotel beds needed to accommodate them. Its success in attracting tourists — both from within Southeast Asia and from farther afield — came on the heels of the sea-change of the early 1980s, when massive construction and renovation was undertaken in the run-up to a decade of tourist promotion that began with the Bangkok bicentennial celebration in 1982.

Big international hotel chains took over a number of hotels (the Stock Exchange of Thailand today lists 12 hotel companies that have long been open to foreign investors), and prices ratcheted upward accordingly. Grand-luxe rates of US$100 or more a night became common, and moderate "rack rates" doubled in the period between 1988 and 1992.

The hotel boom almost came to an untimely full stop with an unholy alliance of the Gulf War in Kuwait, economic slump in the West, and the Thai military coup in 1992. In the demonstrations that followed this upheaval, troops fired indiscriminately into protesting crowds, and some tourists were caught up in the imbroglio.

To these sobering events were added complaints about environmental degradation and a growing undercurrent of fear about the prevalence of the AIDS pandemic in the Thai sex industry (and the repercussions for foreign tourists).

Tough times have led to the postponement of most major new hotel projects in Bangkok, and also to extensive price discounting for rooms. The dream of six million arrivals by 1991 was shattered with an actual decline against the previous year, down to 5.1 million. Improvements in the second half of 1992 only inched visitor arrivals back to the level recorded in 1990.

These setbacks are unlikely to be permanent. Just as the country bounced back from military rule with an elected civilian government and major constitutional reform, there is still every reason to believe that the Tourism Authority of Thailand's target of 12 million visitors by the year 2000 can be met. The appeal of Thailand is as constant as its people remain remarkably resilient to change.

More than 60 percent of Thailand's tourists are other East and Southeast Asians, mostly from Malaysia, Japan, Hong Kong, Singapore and

Taiwan. Substantial numbers of Europeans (about 25 percent of the total traffic) also visit, mostly from Germany, France, the United Kingdom and Italy.

MAKING YOUR CHOICE

Before you choose your hotel, decide your location according to what you will want to see or do, or you will spend a lot of time bargaining for taxis and being stuck in traffic jams while crisscrossing the city.

There are three popular areas:

- **THE OLD BUSINESS OR TOURIST AREA** *(map 6 & 7E-F5-6)* This is the location for the famous riverside **Oriental Hotel**, as well as many newer hotels such as the **Royal Orchid Sheraton** and the **Shangri-la**.
- **THE NEW TOURIST AREA** *(map 7C6-D6)* This covers a larger area, including **Upper Surawong**, **Silom**, **Ratchaprasong** and **Ratchadamri Roads** — the **Narai**, **Mandarin**, **Montien**, **Dusit Thani**, **Regent Bangkok**, **Grand Hyatt Erawan**, **Le Meridien President**, **Hilton International** and pioneering **Siam Inter-Continental** hotels are all there.
- **SUKHUMVIT ROAD** *(off map 7D7, see map on page 187)* Bangkok's new residential area has several medium-priced hotels, notably the **New Imperial** and the **Ambassador**.

RESERVATIONS, SEASONS AND PRICES

Bangkok has any number of first-class hotels with impeccable service, big rooms — and prices to match. If all you seek is a clean place to stay with the minimum of ceremony, numerous other hotels offer mid-priced accommodation, and cater to visitors with small children.

The top hotels are often fully booked months in advance for the tourist season (October to March), so it is advisable to have a confirmed hotel room before you start your trip. December is the coolest, driest and busiest month of the year. During the off-season, between April and September (also the rainy season, and very hot with it), many hotels offer generous discounts and special weekend packages, some including the 10-percent service charge and seven-percent government tax.

Make sure before you start that the price quoted includes everything — a surprise 17-percent addition puts a large dent in anyone's budget. Unless they are part of a tour package, room prices do not generally include breakfast.

FOOD AND DRINK

Hotel breakfasts are substantial continental and American affairs, with the delightful Southeast Asian addition of a wide variety of fresh fruits. Order room service or have breakfast in the hotel coffee shop until you are familiar with the city; it may be difficult to find a nearby café offering Western-style breakfasts at lower prices than your hotel offers.

If you are staying in the old tourist area, try **Maria's Bakery** on either Surawong or Charoen Krung (New Rd.) for pleasant Western or Thai-style breakfasts, with local newspapers provided for reading.

HOW TO USE THIS CHAPTER

- **Symbols**:   See the KEY TO SYMBOLS on page 7 for an explanation of the full list.
- **Prices**:   The prices corresponding to our price symbols are based on average charges for two people staying in a double rooms with bathroom/shower. For this purpose, breakfast and tax are not included. Although actual prices will inevitably increase, our relative price categories are likely to stay the same. **Thai baht** are quoted here.

Symbol	Category	Current price
▨▨▨▨	very expensive	over B4,000
▨▨▨	expensive	B2,800–4,000
▨▨	moderate	B1,100–2,800
▨	inexpensive	under B1,100

THE ORIENTAL — BANGKOK'S LANDMARK HOTEL ♣
48 Oriental Ave. Map **6**F4 ☎236-0400 ▨TH 82997 ▨236-1937 ▨▨▨▨
394 rms, 34 suites ▨ ▨ ▨ ▨ ▨ ▨ ▨ ▨ ▨ ▨ ▨ ▨

Location: By the river in the old business area. It seems that every city in Asia has at least one hotel that has transcended the commercial concerns of hostelry and become part of the city's cultural life. In Bangkok that hotel is the Oriental.

Much has been written about the Oriental Hotel, and it's all true. This is the best that Bangkok has to offer and, in the view of many businessmen and independent travelers, quite simply the very best hotel in the world. Reserve well in advance, especially if you're visiting Bangkok during the peak season. You will lack for nothing if you stay here.

Rooms are spacious and the ones in the new wing have verandas — the better to contemplate the wondrous view of the Chao Phraya River, which runs right past the hotel. There is a superlative restaurant, **Le Normandie**, offering French *haute cuisine* of an unforgettable standard. There are also 34 majestically appointed suites, which are named for the many literary luminaries who have either visited the region or used it as a setting — names such as Graham Greene, Barbara Cartland, Joseph Conrad, John le Carré, Gore Vidal, James Michener, Noel Coward, Somerset Maugham.

Tea or cocktails are served in the **Authors' Wing**, the old part of the hotel, built in 1886, where Maugham and Conrad stayed when they visited the "City of Angels." Sip a drink on the veranda and watch the sun set over the river, or relax in the lobby, where a tuxedoed quartet plays chamber music till dinner time.

Brilliant use of very constricted space has been made by acquiring land on the opposite river bank in Thonburi. The hotel's own water-taxi runs guests across to the **Sala Rim Naam** Thai food restaurant, where food is served in a traditional setting and is accompanied by court and folk dancing.

Also here is the **Rim Naam Thai Cooking School**, where you can take a course over five half-days (it costs about US$1,000 but can be taken in units). The hotel also boasts good athletics facilities, the **Oriental Health Spa** and **Thai Herbal Treatment Centre**. A regular series of lectures, by prominent Thai academics, on all aspects of Thai culture and arts, make this center of cultural activities a Thai version of Colorado's Aspen Institute.

The search for space also led to the renting of a private 19thC European-style residence behind the hotel. Now restored, it must be the world's most dignified Cantonese restaurant, **The China House**, with six large private dining rooms and a kitchen staffed by Hong Kong master chefs. Behind the hotel is a six-story shopping mall.

As if all these extra facilities were not enough, the hotel runs its own daily cruises upriver to the ruins of AYUTTHAYA and BANG PA-IN SUMMER PALACE (see DAY TRIPS FROM BANGKOK, pages 252 and 255) on its private yachts, *The Oriental Queen I* and *II*.

HOTELS CLASSIFIED BY PRICE

VERY EXPENSIVE ▥
Arnoma Swissôtel
Dusit Thani
Grand Hyatt
  Erawan
Oriental
Regent Bangkok
Siam Inter-Continental

Royal Orchid Sheraton
Shangri-La

MODERATE ▥
Airport
Ambassador
Manohra
Narai

EXPENSIVE ▥
Central Plaza Bangkok
Hilton International
Holiday Inn Crowne Plaza
Le Meridien President

INEXPENSIVE ▥
New Trocadero
Royal
Siam Orchid Inn
White Inn

Bangkok's hotels A to Z

AIRPORT HOTEL ♣
333 Cherdvuthakart Rd., Don Muang
☎566-1020-1 ✆TH 87424 ⊠566-1020
▥ 300 rms ═ 🖭 ⊙ ⊚ 🖾 ❧ ≈ ♈
✔ nearby.
Location: five minutes from the airport.
Offers good value for money, especially if you're in transit. The hotel provides free transport to and from the airport, to which it is actually connected by a long, air-conditioned walkway.

AMBASSADOR
171 Sukhumvit Rd., Soi 11 and 13. Off map

7D7. See map on page 187 ☎254-0444
✆TH 62910 ⊠253-4123 ▥ 1,000 rms
═ 🖭 ⊙ ⊚ 🖾 ❧ ♈
Location: In the busy residential area of Sukhumvit Rd. A particularly good place for families; the hotel features an aviary and a mini-zoo for children, plus a large, serve-yourself cafeteria offering ten different types of cuisine.

ARNOMA SWISSÔTEL
99 Ratchadamri Rd. Map 7D7 ☎255-3410
✆21212/21233 ⊠255-3456/8 ▥
403 rms 🖭 ⊙ ⊚ 🖾 ≈ ♈ ♨ ☞

Location: Just opposite the World Trade Centre and beside Ratchadamri Arcade (between Ploenchit and New Phetburi Rds.). An elegantly appointed hotel set in what is destined to become as close as Bangkok is likely ever to get to a central business district, with the World Trade Centre commercial complex right across the street and Amarin Plaza just around the corner, on Ploenchit Rd. The decor is first-class functional — that is, smallish rooms in crisp combinations of Thai hardwoods and pastels, made to soothe rather than attract the eye. Public areas are built around an emphasis on conference and banquet facilities (they can hold up to 1,000 banqueters). Not a place to brag or complain about, just steady and reliable as the Swiss franc.

CENTRAL PLAZA BANGKOK

1695 Phaholyothin Rd., Chatuchak
☎541-1234 ⊠TH 20173 ⊠541-1087
▥ 1,214 rms ⧫ ◉ ◖ ▨ ☙ ⇌ ◡/
▽ ⛴

Location: Within Bangkok Convention Centre complex. This is an island of business services and meeting venues about midway between the airport and the central business areas of the city. There's an 18-hole golf course across the street and Thailand's largest shopping mall, with more than 200 shops and a six-story department store, Central Lard Prao, next door. The Weekend Market is held in Chatuchak Park, just a block away. There is a free shuttle bus to the city center throughout the day.

DUSIT THANI

*946 Rama IV Rd., Saladaeng Circle. Map
7E6* ☎238-4790 ⊠TH 81170/81027
⊠236-6400 ▥ 520 rms ⧫ ◉ ◖
▨ ☙ ⟨⟨ ⇌ ♫ ⛴ ◉ ⟲

Location: In the new business/tourist area. This was the first Thai-owned and -operated hotel to attain international stature; it has been a favorite location for Thai banquets and weddings for more than 20 years. Some rooms have a view of the city and of Lumphini Park. An area set aside for the Foreign Correspondents Club of Thailand means that the hotel is frequented by the foreign press, but it also has a good reputation as a businessmen's hotel — averagely luxurious, with excellent service and amenities.

GRAND HYATT ERAWAN

494 Ratchadamri Rd., Pathumwan.
Map 7D7 ☎254-1234 ⊠TH 20975
⊠253-5856 ▥ 400 rms ⇌ ⧫ ◉ ◖
▨ ☙ ⇌ ♫ ▽

Location: In the new business-tourist area, next to Erawan Shrine. The original Erawan was torn down in 1989 and replaced in late 1991 by this 22-story executive palace. Designed to be the location of choice for businesspeople and diplomats, it offers two Presidential Suites (and they *do* cater to heads of state), six Diplomatic Suites and 30 Executive Suites. There is also a Regency Club, offering the usual "hotel-within-a-hotel" facilities.

The public areas are suitably grand. The four-story atrium lobby, under a stained-glass ceiling, is evocative of a traditional Thai tropical garden, complete with babbling streams. The hotel became a major collector of Thai contemporary art by decorating rooms and public areas with almost 2,000 original works, ranging from massive oil paintings to collages on rice paper.

The staff uniforms were created — exclusively in Thai silk and cotton — by Thailand's top clothing designer, Nagara, to compliment the unique textiles used to decorate the hotel's lobby and three of its restaurants. Note the waiters' trousers, the traditional Thai *chong kra bane,* an intricately twisted and knotted affair with a baggy flare at the hips, an art to put on in the mornings.

Visual splendors aside, every facility to pamper the business traveler is laid on, including a fifth-floor "oasis" sports area, featuring a jogging track.

HILTON INTERNATIONAL

Nai Lert Park, 2 Wireless Rd. Map 7D7
☎253-0123 ⊠TH 72206 ⊠253-6509
▥ 343 rms ⇌ ⧫ ◉ ◖ ▨ ☙ ⇌ ♫
▽ ⛴

Location: In the new business-tourist area. Set in an elaborately landscaped private 3.4ha (8.5-acre) park, the flower-filled walkways are lit by sunlight filtering in through three atrium lobbies. The low-rise, four-story building sprawls in three wings that form a U-shape so large that a small replica of a traditional Thai house sits like a curio-piece outside the main entrance. Rooms are spacious and modern, decorated in Thai and Italian styles, the service efficient.

HOLIDAY INN CROWNE PLAZA
981 Silom Rd. Map **6F5** ☎*238-4300*
📠*238-5289* 🏧 ⬛ ⬛ ⬛ 🔲 ≈ 🏖
Location: At intersection of Silom and Surasak Rds. at the edges of both the old and the new tourist areas. Location is the main attraction of this hotel, set at one of the main Silom Rd. intersections within walking distance of New Rd. and a short *tuk-tuk* ride from Patpong. Without any great architectural charm, it has a sun deck and its own arcade with no fewer than 88 shops.

MANOHRA
412 Surawong Rd. Map **6F5** ☎*234-5070*
📞*TH 82114* 📠*237-7662* 🔲 *250 rms*
⬛ ⬛ 🔲 ≈ 🏖 🚗
Location: Opposite the New President Hotel, a five-minute walk from Charoen Krung (New Rd.). A real butterfly has emerged from the extensive renovation that this hotel has recently undergone. The lobby is well appointed with discreet marble floors and walls; an enclosed sidewalk café, the **Buttercup Coffee House**, has a baby-grand piano set in the window. Its covered outdoor pool is set beside man-made waterfalls; the roof deck has colorful director's chairs. The gem-trading nature of the area is reflected in the names of nearby buildings: Jewelry Trade Center, Gems Tower, Silom Precious Tower and so on.

LE MERIDIEN PRESIDENT
135/26 Gaysorn Rd. Map **7D7**
☎*253-0444* 📠*253-7565* 🔲 ≈
⬛ ⬛ ⬛ 🔲 ≈ 🏖
Location: Off Ploenchit Rd., in the new business-tourist area. This is a quiet, efficient hotel, set nicely in a *cul de sac* and near shopping. It is currently build-

ing a new 400-room hotel in front of the current location, to open in 1994.

NARAI
222 Silom Rd. Map **6F5** ☎*237-0100*
📞*TH 81175* 📠*236-7161* 🔲 *500 rms*
≈ ⬛ ⬛ ⬛ 🔲 ◁€ ≈ ♈ 🏖
Location: In the new business-tourist area, about midway between the river and Patpong Rd. This is an unpretentious hotel, recently renovated. The old British Club is at its rear on Surawong Rd. There is a pool and jogging track on the third-floor Tropical Terrace. Its **Rabiang Thong** coffee shop is well-placed on the mezzanine for people-watching above Silom Rd. The hotel's restaurants are frequented by locals.

NEW TROCADERO ♣
343 Surawong Rd. Map **6F5**
☎*234-8920/9* 📞*TH 81061* 📠 *c/o New Peninsula 236-5526* 🔲 *140 rms* ⬛ ⬛
⬛ 🔲 ≈
Location: Close to the intersection with Charoen Krung (New Rd.) close to the river in the old business district. This five-story hotel is almost as old as its more dignified neighbor, that *grande dame* on the river, the **Oriental**, which is a five-minute walk away. It has for decades been a favorite with visiting journalists, for being inexpensive, clean, well-placed in the most interesting part of Bangkok for pedestrians, and with very friendly service. It also has a loyal South Asian clientele, due to the area being a gem and jewelry center and the location of an active Islamic community.

The only amenities are what must be Bangkok's smallest hotel swimming pool and a top-floor snooker room with ancient, massive tables. The lower rooms fronting Surawong Rd. can be noisy. The Trocadero has had a hike in rates after a renovation that seems more like a failed facelift. All the pieces are in place — hallways in wine-red carpets, French floral motifs on pastel blue and pink wallpapers and so on — but the carpets are a trifle lumpy and loose-fitting, the wallpaper's not always well-pasted. This is no *grande dame*. Like the old tart in *Zorba the Greek,* the lady's lipstick is smeared and rouge too red, but she pushes on with aplomb.

ORIENTAL   See entry on page 206.

REGENT BANGKOK
*155 Ratchadamri Rd. Map **7**D7*
☎251-6127 ℻253-9195 ▥ 400 rms
⇌ 🖭 🖸 🖂 🖩 《 ⇜ ♈ 🏌 ⚓

Location: In new tourist area, near Erawan Shrine, facing the Royal Bangkok Sports Club's race track and 18-hole golf course. Constructed like a series of interconnecting Thai houses, this top hotel has three blocks of rooms at seven, eight and nine stories in height. There are also seven "cabana"-style rooms whose patios overlook landscaped gardens with lotus pond and Bangkok's largest swimming pool. The hotel, one of Southeast Asia's largest, has won international plaudits for everything from its bathrooms to the friendliness of its staff, and has featured prominently in lists of the world's best. Be sure to visit its SPICE MARKET restaurant (see RESTAURANTS, page 221), and its elegant bar, with watercolors by one of Thailand's leading painters, Suchart Wongthong.

ROYAL
*2 Ratchadamnoen Klang Rd. Map **5**C3*
☎222-9111 ⓉⓍTH 87266 ℻224-2083
▥ 122 rms 《 ⇜

Location: At a corner of Sanam Luang, the huge royal field next to the Grand Palace. More than 50 years old, and perhaps a little frayed around the edges, this pleasant hotel is nonetheless a perfect base from which to visit the nearby temples, the National Museum and UN agencies. The Royal is one of only two hotels along the regal Ratchadamnoen Klang Rd., a divided, tree-lined, six-lane boulevard that runs majestically from the Grand Palace compound to the Parliament Building, with dark brick buildings in Western-style architecture, dating from the 1930s. It is making a valiant recovery from the unsought notoriety it gained when troops fired indiscriminately on the crowds in the May 1992

Democracy Monument protests, inadvertently hitting a number of tourists outside the hotel.

ROYAL ORCHID SHERATON
*2 Captain Bush Lane, Siphaya Rd. Map **6**E4*
☎234-5599 ⓉⓍTH 84491
℻236-8320/6656 ▥ 773 rms ⇌ 🖪
🖸 🖭 🖩 《 ⇜ ⅀

Location: In the old business-tourist district. Modern and opulent, this 28-story, Y-shaped hotel has a commanding view over the Chao Phraya River, with its own private pier. Connected by a covered walkway to River City, a large air-conditioned shopping arcade, the Royal Orchid is also within easy reach of many of the city's sights.

SHANGRI-LA
*89 Soi Wat Suan Plu, New Rd., Bangrak. Off map **6**F5* ☎236-7777 ⓉⓍTH 84265
℻236-8597 ▥ 697 rms ⇌ 🖪 🖸 🖸
🖩 & 《 ⇜ ⅀ ♈ 🏌

Location: The old business-tourist area. One of several newer hotels that have begun to line both sides of the waterfront, this one has a superb view of the Chao Phraya River.

SIAM INTER-CONTINENTAL ♣
*967 Rama I Rd. Map **7**D6* ☎253-0355
ⓉⓍTH 81155 ℻253-2275 ▥ 400 rms
⇌ 🖪 🖸 🖸 🖩 《 ⇜ ⅀ ✓ 🏌

Location: Opposite the Siam Centre and Siam Sq. This is a peaceful hotel with an unhurried atmosphere, set in 10ha (26 acres) of well-kept grounds. There's a small hornbill aviary along the path to the pool and a putting green and driving range for golfers. This was the first low-rise, self-contained resort complex in the city, intended to provide an island of serene sanity away from but handy for the sputtering *tuk-tuks* and stiflingly hot streets of the central city.

SIAM ORCHID INN
*109 Soi Ratchadamri, Ratchadamri Rd. Map **7**D7* ☎251-4416; 255-3140
℻255-3144 ▥ 40 rms ⇌ 🖪 🖸 🖸 🖩
Location: Sandwiched between the Arnoma Swissôtel and Le Meridien President, opposite the World Trade Center.

This new hotel is perfect for business travelers of moderate means. It has a 24-hour business center and room service, which offers Thai and Western cuisines. The best bet, however, would be to use some of the savings on room rates to eat at the fine hotel restaurants surrounding it, including those of the two above and those of the Grand Hyatt Erawan, less than a block away.

WHITE INN ♣
41 Soi Nana Tai, Sukhumvit Rd. Off map **7**D7. *See map on page 187* ☎252-7090 ☒254-8865 ▥ *27 rms* ⬛ ◉ ◎ ▨ ⚶ ⛟

Location: Close to Sukhumvit's department stores. One of Bangkok's best-kept secrets, the White Inn is small, intimate, and very cozy — like a British country inn.

OTHER GOOD CHOICES

- **Asia Hotel**   296 Phyathai Rd. Map **7**C6 ☎215-0808 ☒215-4360 ▥ ⬛ ⒶⒺ ◉ ◎ ▨ ⚶ ⛟ Located close to Siam Sq. shopping and entertainment district. Clean and unpretentious. Thai International's City Terminal ticketing counter in lobby.

- **Mandarin Bangkok**   662 Rama IV Rd. Map **7**E6 ☎234-1390 ☒237-1620 ▥ ⒶⒺ ◉ ◎ ▨ ⚶ ⛟ Near intersection of Rama IV and Siphaya Rds. A central, strictly business facility catering to small conferences and business travelers. No connection to the more illustrious Mandarin Oriental Hotel Group, which operates a property of the same name in Hong Kong.

- **Menam**   2074 New Rd., Yannawa ☎291-1717/289-1148 ☒291-1048 ▥ ⒶⒺ ◉ ◎ ▨ ⟨⟨ ⚶ ⛟ ⌂ On Chao Phraya River s of Taksin Bridge and just s of old tourist area. Very pleasant, well-run hotel with 14 acres of terraces and gardens.

- **Montien**   54 Surawong Rd. Map **7**E6 ☎233-7060/234-8060 ☒236-5218 ▥ ⬛ ⒶⒺ ◉ ◎ ▨ ⚶ ⛟ In the new business-tourist area, a short walk to shops and nightlife on Patpong and Surawong Rds. Elegant, modern hotel with spacious rooms.

- **New Imperial**   Wireless Rd. Map **7**D7 ☎254-0023/0111 ☒253-3190 ▥ ⬛ ⒶⒺ ◉ ◎ ▨ ⚘ ⚶ ⤴ ⛟ In E part of city, near business-tourist area, very near to embassies, banks, department stores and arcades. Landscaped grounds. Rather "no-frills." Restaurants popular with locals.

- **Novotel**   Soi 6, Siam Sq. Map **7**D6 ☎255-6888 ☒255-1824 ▥ ⒶⒺ ◉ ◎ ▨ ⚶ ♈ ⛟ ⬠ In one of the major shopping districts across from the Siam Inter-Continental. Standard fare in its class.

Bangkok:
eating and drinking

Thai cuisine

The Thais are justifiably proud of their cuisine. Through the centuries they have adopted dishes from China, India, Indonesia and Malaysia and made them uniquely Thai. To Westerners the cuisine is highly exotic, not only in style and the indecipherable Thai names of the dishes, but also literally — many of the spices, herbs, vegetables and fruits used are unobtainable or unheard of in the West.

Curry dishes form only a small part of the Thai cuisine: they have also made good use of spices and herbs such as coriander, different types of basil, garlic, pepper, chili, lemon grass, ginger, cardamom, cinnamon, tamarind (especially in sauces and marinades) and aniseed, blending them into four basic tastes — sour, hot and spicy, pungent, and very sweet. Instead of salt, fish sauce (or *nam pla*) is used. Many dishes have a coconut milk base.

The staple is rice, but Thais also love noodle dishes of all kinds, which they usually season by sprinkling sugar, dry chili flakes, a few spoons of vinegar and fish sauce on top. A Thai meal typically comprises five or six dishes of curry, soup, omelette, vegetables, fish, etc. with rice or noodles.

Thai food can be very hot: beware the volcanic *phrik lueng*, a lovely yellow-orange chili, and the tiny red and green chilies, called *phrik kee nu*. A single inadvertent bite can easily burn those whose mouths aren't cauterized by long use, and no amount of cold water or beer will quench the blaze. However, most larger restaurants have bilingual menus often stating the degree of hotness of each dish — usually by the handy device of a visual "chili rating" that runs up a scale of one to four. Few tourists will want to venture above two.

Restaurants catering to tourists often tone down the spicier dishes; so when ordering the meal, tell the waiter how hot you want any particular dish. Beware too of the artificial seasoning monosodium glutamate, which some restaurants tend to add too liberally.

MENU GUIDE
The usual practice and the best way to experience Thai food is to select several dishes — say, a pork, beef, chicken or vegetable dish, perhaps a soup, along with plenty of aromatic white rice — which everyone at the table shares. The following list will help the daunted diner to identify key ingredients and order accordingly. Whatever one chooses, Thai food is delicious, and surprises are usually pleasant ones.

Drinks
Thais drink hot and cold coffees and teas, fresh milk, iced fresh lime juice with or without salt, fresh orange and coconut juice. All wine is imported, and prices are high. A local brew, Mekhong whisky, mixed with lime and soda, goes well with Asian food, as do the local beers (Kloster and Singha). Always be certain that the water that was frozen for ice has been boiled first.

Staples
Aromatic or sticky (glutinous) boiled or fried rice predominates, but bread is also served. Recommended: fried rice with prawns and vegetables *(kow pat gung),* with pork *(kow pat muu),* or with egg *(kow pat ky dow raat nad).*

Sauces
The key ingredients in Thai sauces are butter, ginger, salt, sugar, vinegar, chili, soy, lemon, coconut, fish, black pepper, tamarind and other spices.

Appetizers and light dishes
The following is a short selection of recommendations: sautéed cashews *(met mamuang Kimmapan),* sweet crispy noodles *(mee krob),* barbecued pork *(muu satay),* spring rolls *(poh pia),* fried noodles with egg and bean sprouts *(kwit teo pat ty),* or vermicelli with pork, mushrooms, dried prawns and lemon *(yam woonsen).*

Soups *(tom)*
Popular choices include rice congee with meat, prawn or egg and seasoned with ginger, as well as many combinations of meat, egg, fish and vegetable soups. Try lemon prawn soup *(tom yaam gung),* for a hot and sour dish, or coconut milk and chicken soup *(tom kah guy),* for a hot and sweet flavor.

Main dishes
These are based on chicken *(guy),* beef *(nua),* pork *(muu)* and duck *(ped).* Meat curries are flavored with coconut milk *(gaeng pah)* and sometimes fresh coriander leaves *(gaeng keow wahn).* Try: barbecued chicken *(guy yaang),* deep-fried chicken *(guy tort),* fried chicken with *toey* herbs *(guy hor buy toey),* dry chicken curry *(penang guy),* fried sliced beef with oyster sauce *(nua pahd nahm hoy),* and fried sliced beef or chicken with shredded ginger *(nua/guy pat king).*

Seafood
Fish *(pla)* or shellfish *(hoi)* is usually fried, steamed, grilled or cooked in a pot *(garm poo ohb mor din).* Recommended: fried butterfish *(pla jaramed),* fried sea bass served with sauce and green vegetables *(pla kapong tord grob nahm dang),* crab claws hot pot with soy sauce, peppercorns and herbs *(garm poc ohb mor din),* mussels steamed in a pot *(hoy mang poo ohb mor din),* squid, mussels and prawns fried

with basil and chili *(pahd gra prou aharn ta le)*, freshwater lobster and herbs hot pot *(goong ohb mor din)*, and curried crab fried with spring onions.

Vegetables *(pak)*
A very wide variety is available. Try peppered eggplant with garlic and lime *(yam ma keu keow)*, stir-fried morning-glory *(pakboon pad)*, broccoli *(pakarna pad)* or mixed vegetables *(pad pak lai yang)*.

Desserts *(kanom)*
Thais have a sweet tooth, and most desserts are cooked in coconut milk and sweetened with palm sugar. From March–June try sticky rice in coconut milk with mango *(kow neo manmuang)*. Some less seasonal recommendations include banana fritters *(gluay tawt)*, egg custard *(kanom maw gang)* and coconut ice cream *(ice cream krati sohd)*.

Fruit *(poolamai)*
Bangkok offers a cornucopia of tropical fruits — with strawberries in the "winter." The papayas *(malako)* are the best in Asia and available, like many other fruits, all year round. Several kinds of banana *(kluai)*, many types of mango *(mamuang)*, all-year oranges *(som)* and pomelos (*som-o* — similar in size and taste to a large, sweet grapefruit).

Try a sapodilla *(lamoot):* peel the green or brown skin and slice the flesh lengthwise; it is very sweet, with a taste faintly like figs. But show restraint: the Thais say more than one may give you wind and quicken your heartbeat.

Also available year-round are guava *(farang)*, watermelon *(taengmo)*, pineapple *(sapparot)*, and young coconut *(maphrao-on)* — the juice of which is highly recommended to accompany Thai meals, or as a safe and healthy alternative to canned soft drinks). Less familiar to Westerners are jackfruit *(khanun)* and green plum *(phutsa)*. From April to September, mangosteens *(mangkut)* are delicious: the skin is deep purple, the flesh red and white, and the taste is like lychee with a touch of lemon.

Mangkut ripens at the same time as and is often eaten with durian *(thurian)*, which the Thais and other Southeast Asians term the "king of fruits." Again, beware; despite its delectable taste, the durian has such a potent aroma (redolent of *extremely* old cheese) that airlines and many hotels have banned it. The size of a football and covered in menacing thorns, this fruit has a creamy-caramel, custard-like flesh.

Seasonals include lychee *(litchi* — April to June), *(langsat* — May to July), longan *(lamyai* — July to October), three kinds of rose apple *(chom phu* — April to June), custard apple *(noi na* — July to September) and rambutan *(ngo* — May to July). The Tourism Authority of Thailand (TAT) offers a useful descriptive brochure free of charge. See page 215.

DINING OUT IN BANGKOK
In addition to the complex and unique Thai cuisine available (each region — central, northern, southern and northeastern — has its own specialties), Bangkok also offers a wide variety of other ethnic foods

such as Vietnamese, Indian, Chinese (Cantonese, Peking and Shanghai), Japanese (about 75 restaurants in town) and Middle Eastern. Specific European cuisines include French, German, Hungarian, Italian and Scandinavian.

Bangkok is unique among Southeast Asian capitals in its large number of freestanding restaurants serving European and other Asian cuisines. Only at the very top of the market can hotel restaurants be said to reign supreme. To give some indication of the variety on offer, the *Greater Bangkok Telephone Directory* has 13 pages of freestanding restaurants.

This happy situation is largely the result of so many foreigners marrying Thai women and settling in Bangkok. No other city in Asia is so varied in its numerous independent restaurant operators. The Thais have also taken to fast food in a big way, and all the major internationally franchised hamburger, fried chicken and pizza chains are well represented.

Local people are more interested in the quality of the food than in the décor of their restaurants. Dining outside is very popular; if you plan to eat under the banyan and palm trees, don't forget the mosquito repellant. For those interested in being entertained by Thai classical dance troupes while dining, the Tourism Authority of Thailand's free *Where To Eat in Bangkok* brochure lists a dozen restaurants featuring dance. Among our selection, see BAAN THAI, ORIENTAL RIM NAAM, PIMAN, TUMPNAKTHAI below and RUEN THEP in Silom Village (see SHOPPING on page 238.)

USEFUL TO KNOW

- **Opening hours**: Lunch often starts at 11.30am. Most people dine early, with restaurants opening at 6pm, and many establishments tend as a result to close early. Call ahead if you plan to dine late, especially in larger groups. Light snacks are available in Patpong, the nightlife and bar area, where eateries tend to stay open later.
- **Taxes and surcharges**: Eating out is relatively inexpensive, although in hotels and major restaurants, you should expect a 10-percent service charge and seven-percent government value-added tax on the bill. There are bistros, cafés and local establishments away from the hotel areas, where there are no surcharges.

HOW TO USE THIS CHAPTER

- **Symbols**:   See the KEY TO SYMBOLS on page 7 for an explanation of the full list.
- **Prices**: The prices corresponding to our price symbols are based on the average price of a meal (dinner, not lunch) for one person, inclusive of house wine, tax and gratuity. Although actual prices will inevitably increase after publication, our relative price categories are likely to stay the same. **Thai baht** are quoted here.

Symbol	Category	Current price
▨▨▨	very expensive	over B1,200
▨▨	expensive	B800–1,200
▨	moderate	B350–800
▯	inexpensive	under B350

Bangkok's restaurants A to Z

ABU KHALIL *Middle Eastern*
Nana Plaza shopping area, Soi 4, Sukhumvit Rd. Off map **7**D7. *See map on page 187*
☎251-0038 ▥ ▣ ⊙ ▣ ▥
One of the best Middle Eastern restaurants in the city, with a fantastic array of starters, special dishes of the day at fixed prices and good desserts. Go early, because it tends to close if business slows down.

AMBASSADOR HOTEL
Thai/Chinese/Japanese/European
171 Sukhumvit Rd., Soi 11 and 13. Off map **7**D7. *See map on page 187* ☎254-0444
▣259-0970 ▥ *to* ▥ ▣ ⊙ ▥
Dozens of restaurants are huddled under one hotel roof, serving Thai, European, Chinese and Japanese food. The **Asian Food Fair** is on the ground floor. Buy coupons first (prices vary widely) to pay for your selection *(no cards)* of: fried noodles, curries, seafood, raw fish, Thai dishes, Western dishes, desserts, fresh fruit. It is a good place to take children, with an aviary (of a sort) in the parking lot. The other restaurants in the hotel accept charge/credit cards.

AVENUE ONE *French*
Siam Inter-Continental Hotel, 967 Rama I Rd. Map **7**D6 ☎253-0355, ext. 7545
▣253-2275 ▥ ▣ ⊙ ⊙ ▥
This is *nouvelle cuisine* with an Oriental touch, served in a modern, pastel-shaded setting in the grounds of the first hotel that was built as a self-contained garden resort in the city. Reservations recommended.

BAAN THAI ("Thai House") *Thai*
7 Soi 32, Sukhumvit Rd. (adjacent to Rex Hotel). See map on page 187
☎258-5403/258-9517 ▥ ◀◀ ⊙ ▥
Open daily 7pm–10pm. Show starts 9pm. Closed lunch.
Thai food has been served for more than 25 years in this rambling, old Thai-style wooden house, set in a lovely garden compound with a lotus pond. There are three stages, one upstairs and two downstairs, upon which about 20 students from the government's Fine Arts Department perform a selection of six different traditional dances to accompany dinner — which is served to as many as 350 people at a sitting. This is one of about a dozen restaurants featuring Thai entertainment and ambience, most commonly in converted private mansions or on the grounds of hotels. Be forewarned that food quality is not the main reason for dining in freestanding restaurants such as this, or **Tumpnakthai**. They are usually designed to cater to mass tourism with canned entertainment and architectural ambience — and care in food preparation may bear an inverse relationship to the high-season press of guests.

BOBBY'S ARMS ♣ *Pub food*
114/1–2 Patpong 2, 2nd floor of parking lot, off Silom Rd. Map **7**E6 ☎233-6828
▥ ▣
A congenial place for a pub lunch, with a fine selection of homemade pies. Features Dixieland Jazz on Sundays. This is a popular place for overseas tourists to tank up in, before venturing off to carouse in Patpong's go-go bars.

LA BRASSERIE *French*
Regent Bangkok Hotel, 155 Ratchadamri Rd. Map **7**D7 ☎251-6127 ▣253-9195
▥ ▣ ⊙ ⊙ ▥
Good French street food — at fairly steep prices — served in the pleasant surroundings of a quiet, open-air courtyard.

BUSSARACUM *Thai*
35 Soi Pipat 2 (off Convent Rd.)
☎235-8915 or 233-5152. *Also at 425 Soi Pipat 2 (Trinity Complex), map* **7**F6
☎234-2600 or 234-4519 ▥ ▣ ⊙
⊙ ▥
Hard to beat for elegantly presented Thai food in agreeable surroundings, the Bussaracum is often ranked among the best restaurants in Bangkok. It formerly conducted a Thai cooking school similar to that at the Oriental's **Sala Rim Naam**.

CABBAGES & CONDOMS *Thai*

8 Soi 12, Sukhumvit Rd. See map on page 187 ☎*251-5552* ▨ ▣ ▣ ▣ ▨ *Open daily 11am–10pm.*

Only something dreamed up by an organization associated with the legendary Mechai Viravaidya could create a restaurant with such a name. The Population and Community Development Association (PDA), founded by him, runs this restaurant as a fundraiser — along with a handicrafts shop (see SHOPPING). Both are on the grounds of the PDA office complex. Unbelievably, the restaurant is decorated with all manner of birth control devices. Like the organization itself, this eatery is earnest about controlling population, about eradicating AIDS . . . and about serving above-average Thai food at moderate prices. Small souvenirs from the restaurant are available in a gift case at the cash register — such as a sample of its table bouquets in monographed blue-and-white porcelain vases, with multi-colored condoms cleverly fashioned into stemmed flowers. Not for everyone, but given the impact of the AIDS pandemic on international awareness of condoms, these may become the next century's collectors' items. See fuller explanation on page 223.

CAFE INDIA ✿ *Indian*

460/8 Surawong Rd. Map 6F5 ☎*233-0419* ▨ ▣

A very small Indian restaurant with a great selection of vegetarian dishes. The house specialty is butter chicken, which is always tasty, as is the bread.

CAPTAIN BUSH GRILL ✿ *English*

Royal Orchid Sheraton Hotel and Towers, 2 Soi Bush Siphya (off New Rd.). Map 6E4 ☎*224-5599* ▨*236-8320 or 236-6656* ▨ ▣ ▣ ▣ ▨

Named for a 19thC British adventurer who eventually worked as a mercenary for the Thai throne, settled in Bangkok and — as they say in the storybooks — lived happily ever after. Victorian-style furniture and décor and dark wood-paneled walls give the impression of an English gentlemen's club. The food is in

keeping, with fine roast beef, Yorkshire pudding and roast potatoes, and a good range of desserts; wine is expensive. Reservations are recommended.

LE CHANCELIER *Vietnamese/French*

70/1 Soi 1, Sukhumvit Rd. See map on page 187 ☎*251-8933* ▨ ▣ ▣ ▣ ▨

This is a townhouse converted into a restaurant. The decor is European, the menu (Vietnamese and French) is extensive, although the wines are sometimes overpriced.

THE CHINESE RESTAURANT *Cantonese*

Grand Hyatt Erawan, 494 Ratchadamri Rd. Map 7D7 ☎*254-1234* ▨*254-6243* ▨ ▣ ▣ ▣ ▨

The decor is as stunning as the food is delicious in this *nouveau Chinois* restaurant in the hotel's basement. Its main dining room is divided into a series of seating niches by a network of cracked glass partitions, indirectly lit in such a way as to suggest ice walls. These are set off by black marble walls and a teak floor. Highly inventive and beautifully presented variations on a Cantonese theme are meant to appeal to the growing numbers of well-heeled business travelers from Hong Kong and Taiwan, and succeed admirably. Chefs are from Hong Kong. Highly recommended are the steamed *garoupa* (grouper-fish), minced pigeon and stuffed *tofu* (beancurd) with shrimp. Chinese food *aficionados* will enjoy *pang mein*, a variation on the Chinese *dim sum* dish known as *har gau* (a shrimp dumpling). There is a daily *dim sum* and set luncheon. Ask for assistance from the Chinese floor captain, Mr. Meechai Pornrattahanawanarom ("Khun Meechai" will do). Adjoining the main area, there are seven private dining rooms, which are clearly intnded to appeal to the "power lunch" set.

LE DALAT *Vietnamese*

Soi 23 (Prasarnmitr), 51 Sukhumvit Rd. (opposite Indian embassy). See map on page 187 ☎*258-4192/260-1849* ▣ ▣ ▣ ▨ *Open daily 11.30am–2.30pm, 6pm–10pm.*

This stylish "home made Vietnamese cuisine" restaurant is set in the garden of the private residence of Madame le Camy, herself Vietnamese. As with most Vietnamese restaurants, entrées here are helpfully shown in small photo albums. There is no set menu. Chef's choices are *chaoton* (shrimps laced around sugar cane stalks and grilled), *Bo Nuang Vi* (barbecued prawn and beef) and *Gou Ca* (sliced raw fish "cooked" in lime juice). There are two other branches of Le Dalat, at the following addresses: 2nd floor, 1 Patpong Bldg., Soi Patpong 1–2, Surawong Rd. (☎ *234-0290*) and 104/30–31 Chaengwatana Rd., Donmuang (☎ *573-7017*).

D'JIT POCHANA ♣ *Thai*
Three locations: 1082 Phaholyothin Rd., Ladprao, map 7B6 ☎ *279-5000/2; 62 Sukhumvit Rd., Soi 20, off map 7D7, see map on page 187* ☎ *391-3846; 26/368-380 New Phaholyothin Rd., off map 7B7* ☎ *531-1644 or 531-2716* ⅢⅢ ♥ 🆔 🔟 🎫

Good Thai food at reasonable prices has been on offer here for more than 40 years. Beer is served, but no wine. You can dine outside in the attractive gardens at the Phaholyothin branch, but beware of mosquitoes.

FIREPLACE GRILL *European*
Le Meridien President Hotel, 135/26 Gaysorn Rd., Ploenchit Rd. Map 7D7 ☎ *253-0444* 🖷 *253-7565* ⅢⅢ 🆔 🔟 🎫

As you'd expect from a hotel whose management group is owned by Air France, the Meridien has a good Continental restaurant, with its own brick oven and an extensive European menu that has made it a popular rendezvous for lunch and dinner in the city for more than 25 years. The bread is commendable. Reserve ahead.

GRAND SHANGARILA *Chinese*
58/4–9 Thaniya Rd. (off Silom Rd.), map 7E6 ☎ *234-0861/6; 154/4–5 Silom Rd., map 6F5* ☎ *234-9147/9* ⅢⅢ 🆔

This restaurant is recommended for Chinese food, Shanghai-style, with such dishes as Peking duck, fried prawns in chili sauce and *ma po tao fu* (bean curd in chili sauce). Décor is in the ornate Chinese idiom, with dragons and phoenixes aglow in bright reds and golds.

HAMILTON'S *English*
Dusit Thani Hotel, 946 Rama IV Rd. Map 7E6 ☎ *236-0450/9* 🖷 *236-6400* ⅢⅢ 🆔 🔟 🎫 🔟

An English club atmosphere, all Chippendale and silvered mirrors. In every way, this steak house is designed to be a London "Beefeater's" delight. The dress code is formal, and reservations are recommended.

HIMALI CHA CHA *Indian*
1229/11–12 Charoen Krung (New) Rd. (near Oriental Hotel). Map 6F5 ☎ *235-1569* ⅢⅢ 🆔 🔟 🔟 🎫

This can be easy to miss — look for the big green and yellow sign bearing the likeness of Cha Cha, who once cooked for Lord Mountbatten. It is a small Indian restaurant, decorated with Mughal prints. Dishes include lamb brains curried or fried, spinach and cheese, mutton curry and fish *tikka*. The *tandoori* dishes are always good. Dinner reservations are advisable.

HOI THIEN LAO RIM NAM ♣ *Chinese*
1449/1 Lardya Rd., Klong Sarn, Thonburi ☎ *434-1121* ⅢⅢ 🆔 ⮘ 🆔 🔟 🔟 🎫

The oldest Chinese restaurant in Bangkok, originally located in Chinatown. It now overlooks the Chao Phraya River from the Thonburi side. The food is Cantonese, with a lunchtime *dim sum* that is good value. Dinner is twice the price.

KHUN CHERIE *Vietnamese*
593/13 Soi 33/1, Sukhumvit Rd. (in front of Villa Theatre). See map on page 187 ☎ *258-5058 or 258-5060* ⅢⅢ 🆔 🔟 🔟 🎫

Delicious Vietnamese food at reasonable prices. Order several dishes and share.

LEMONGRASS *Thai/Malay/Chinese*
5/1 Soi 24, Sukhumvit Rd. See map on

page 187 ☎*258-8637* ▥ ▣ ▣ ▣ ▥
Open 11am–2pm, 6pm–11pm.
Good Thai food served in a four-room
wooden house surrounded by greenery, in its own walled compound in an
alley off busy Sukhumvit Rd. The dining
room is decorated with an eclectic assortment of Thai and Khmer *objets d'art,*
hard-backed wooden booths, marble-
topped tables and an enormous curio
cabinet full of colored and cut glass
pitchers, bowls and vases. The main
dining room looks out onto the garden
through a picture window. A good range
of wines, from Mumm Champagne to
Italian Soave, is on offer, or for a small
fee you can bring your own (this also
applies to beer). Unusual in that it specializes in the cuisine of the South (where
the chief chef was born), rarely found
in Bangkok. Malay and Chinese dishes
are also found on the small menu of
about 30 entrées and 20 appetizers.
Some of the chef's recommendations
are *Goong Penang* (Malaysian Penang-
style prawns); *Goong Som* (marinated
shrimps in coconut milk); and *Yam
Som-o* (pomelo salad), a mix of roast
coconut, chili, lime, coconut milk and
sugar. By Thai standards, the food tends
toward the sweet and mild. The menu
is the same for lunch and dinner.

LORD JIM'S SEAFOOD *Seafood*
*Oriental Hotel, 48 Soi Burapa (off New Rd.).
Map 6F4* ☎*236-0400, ext. 32–2 to 4*
▣*236-1937/9* ▥ ◀€ ▣ ▣ ▣ ▥
The decor simulates the interior of a
schooner, and the buffet lunch offers a
wide range of seafoods. Dinner is à la
carte. There's a fine view of the Chao
Phraya River.

MA MAISON *French*
*Hilton International Hotel, Nai Lert Park, 2
Wireless Rd. Map 7D7* ☎*253-0123 or
253-6470* ▣*253-6509* ▥ ◀€ ▣ ▣
▣ ▥
Very pricey French *nouvelle cuisine,*
with a limited menu. The restaurant is a
magnificent creation of wood panels in
various harmonizing shades, meant to
evoke the charm of Thai architecture. It
overlooks the Hilton's private park,

viewed through a massive picture window. Reservations are recommended.

MAYFLOWER *Chinese*
*Dusit Thani Hotel, 946 Rama IV Rd. Map
7E6* ☎*236-0450* ▣*236-6400* ▥ ▣
▣ ▣ ▥
This smart Chinese restaurant is considered by many to be the city's premier
Chinese eatery. The food is Cantonese-
style and always well presented. No
wine served. Reserve ahead.

LE METROPOLITAIN *French*
*74 Sukhumvit Rd., Soi 63 (Ekamai). See
map on page 187* ☎*391-3331*
▣*391-1527* ▥ ▣ ▣ ▣ ▥
Good French cuisine in a bistro atmosphere with lots of wrought iron, large
heart-shaped mirrors and scenes from
Can-Can. The pâtés are delicious, and
on Friday there's *bouillabaisse,* a meal
in itself. The rabbit in mustard sauce is
a strong point, as is the chocolate soufflé,
which must be ordered 20 minutes in
advance. Established in 1968 and formerly near the President Hotel.

MITZU'S KITCHEN *Japanese*
32 Patpong 2 Rd. (off Silom Rd.) Map 7E6
☎*233-6447* ▥
A Japanese restaurant serving delicious
grilled fish and deep-fried oysters. They
also serve steaks and curries. No wine.

NEIL'S TAVERN ✿ *American*
*58/4 Soi Ruam Rudi, Vithayu Rd. (behind
Wireless Rd. near U.S. Embassy). Map 7E7*
☎*256-6874 to 6* ▣*256-6603* ▥ ▣ ▣
▣ ▥ *Lunch 11.30am–2pm, dinner
5.30–10.30pm. Closed Sun.*
Western food in a grillroom atmosphere.
The steaks are good, as is the combination of steak and seafood ("surf n'
turf"), and there is a fair wine list. They
have their own bake shop *(open 10am–
7pm),* and the cheesecake is the best in
the city. Very popular: reservations are
a must.

NICK'S NO. 1 HUNGARIAN INN
European
*17 Soi 16, Sukhumvit Rd. See map on page
187* ☎*259-4717* ▥ ▣ ▣ ▣ ▥ *Open*

11am–2pm, 6–11pm weekdays; weekends 6–11pm.

European cuisine once served on Sathorn Rd., in a lovely old house said to be haunted by the ghost of a Thai princess. The new location is just off the Asoke Rd. extension and no longer has the spooky feel of old. It is now haunted only by the memories of those who knew Nick Jero, its owner and operator for 40 years, who has since passed away. The menu has not changed, however, and the place is run by Nick's widow, Renoo. The quality of the food fluctuates, but prices are moderate and the wines are well kept. Reserve.

LE NORMANDIE French
Oriental Hotel, 48 Soi Burapa (off New Rd.) Map 6F4 ☎236-0400 ext. 3380–1 ▥ ◀€ ⒜⒠ ⒝ ⒟ ▥

French *haute cuisine* par excellence, by some of France's best chefs, on the top floor of the old wing of the Oriental Hotel, with a fine view of the city and the Chao Phraya River, all of which is breathtaking at night. Previous visiting chefs have included the Brothers Troisgros and Louis Outhier. The consulting chef is Louis Outhier, one of France's finest chefs, with his long-time associate, Julien Bompard, as resident chef. Jacket and tie are required. Food, service and prices are all breathtaking.

OAM-THONG 3
Vietnamese/Thai/Chinese
33 Sukhumvit Rd. (Soi Daeng Udom). See map on page 187 ☎258-0668 ▥ ⒜⒠ ⒝ ⒟ ▥ Open 11am–11pm.

When it was launched in late 1992, replacing a French restaurant called White Rabbit, this restaurant inherited a delightful imitation of a small, two-story French provincial château, set in a large courtyard. Small groups of 15 to 20 can eat in private rooms upstairs, the two main dining rooms can hold 20 and 50 people, and there are outside tables where you can eat fresh, grilled seafood. The bright château features large windows and walls covered with cheerful drawings and prints of herbs. There are two other locations: at **Oam-Thong**

1 *(Phaholyothin 11* ☎279-5958) and at **Oam-Thong 2** *(Laksi Plaza, ground floor* ☎576-0222), with live music.

L'OPERA (Girarrosto Ristorante) Italian
53 Soi 39, Sukhumvit Rd. See map on page 187 ☎258-5606 ▣261-4706 ▥ ⒜⒠ ⒝ ⒟ ▥ Open daily 11.30am–2pm, 6pm–11pm.

Simple décor and good Italian food, with a limited wine list. Pizzas are baked in brick ovens on the premises, but everything from a simple *pasta* dish to rich and unctuous *gnocchi al Gorgonzola* is well prepared. Don't let the simplicity deceive you; this eatery has won four awards in different annual reviews. There are regular barbecue evenings and daily specials — call to find out when. Reservations essential.

PAESANO ✿ Italian
96/7 Soi Tonson, Ploenchit Rd. Map **7**D7 ☎252-3592 ▥ ◀€ ⒜⒠ ⒝ ⒟ ▥ Open 10.30am–11pm.

This small Italian restaurant offers good food at reasonable prices, along with a casual atmosphere. The chef, who hails from Montreal, takes great pride in their thin-crusted pizza. The desserts are also especially tasty. Located close to the Central Department Store, between Ploenchit and Sarasin Rds.

NEW PAN PAN/CAPRI ✿ Italian
New Pan Pan: 591 Sukhumvit Rd. (corner of Soi 33). See map on page 187 ☎258-5071 (near **Renoir** and other bars named for Impressionist painters, see NIGHTLIFE, pages 225–6); Capri: 45 Soi Langsuan (off Ploenchit Rd.), map **7**D7 ☎252-7104. Both ▥ ⒜⒠ ⒝ ⒟ ▥

A pair of small Italian restaurants under the same ownership, which serve good homemade pasta, passable pizza and an excellent selection of ice creams and desserts. The atmosphere is informal: a reliable place to take the family. A third branch is in Pattaya (see EXPLORING THAILAND, pages 266–7).

PIMAN THAI THEATRE Thai
46 Sukhumvit Rd., Soi 49. See map on page 187 ☎258-7866 or 258-7861 ▥

◄ *Closed lunch. Shows nightly*
8.45–9.30pm.
Local food in a Thai house decorated in the style of the Sukhothai period. Dinner is accompanied by Thai dancing and music. No wine served.

RIVER CITY BAR B-Q Thai
River City Shopping Centre, 5th floor (opp. Royal Orchid Sheraton). Map 6E4
☎237-0077 ext. 240 ▥ ⊙ ⟨VISA⟩
Cook for yourself on the roof of a shopping center looking out over the river. Guests grill meats and vegetables over their own *hibachi*. Try for a table at the riverside.

SCALA ♣ Chinese
218/1 Siam Sq., Soi 1, Rama I Rd. Map 7D6 ☎254-2891 or 251-4799 ▥ ⟨AE⟩
A Chinese restaurant serving Peking-style food, with evening entertainment — smart, but good value. They claim to have the best Peking duck in Bangkok. The pot-stickers and fried noodles are recommended. No wine.

SEAFOOD MARKET Seafood
388 Sukhumvit Rd. (Corner of Ratchaphisek Rd. and Sukhumvit Rd.). See map on page 187 ☎258-0218 ▥ ⟨AE⟩
This restaurant offers a colorful selection of fish, prawn, mussels, clams, crabs and lobsters, plus meats and vegetables, all of which you purchase supermarket-style, in a trolley, which is wheeled to a table where a waiter comes to ask how it should be cooked. No wine.

SHIN DAIKOKU ♣ Japanese
32/8 Soi 19 (Wattana), Sukhumvit Rd. See map on page 187 ☎254-9981 ▥ ⟨AE⟩ ⊙ ⊙ ⟨VISA⟩
Not only one of the best Japanese restaurants in town, but excellent value as well — the set lunches are a bargain. Most of the private dining rooms look out on a Japanese-style garden.

SINGHA BIER HAUS German
179 Soi 21 (Asoke), Sukhumvit Rd.
☎258-9713/4 and Welco Dept. Store, Pinklao ☎434-9036 ext. 116. For both, see map on page 187 ▥ ⟨AE⟩ ⊙ ⊙ ⟨VISA⟩

A pleasant beer garden atmosphere and architecture — all stucco and dark wooden beams evoking the feel of mountain cottages above Munchhausen — makes this an appealing place to have a bite to eat in after a visit to the Siam Society's **Ban Kamthieng** ethnological museum, about a block away on Soi Asoke.

SPASSO Italian
Erawan Arcade, Grand Hyatt Erawan Hotel, 494 Ratchadamri Rd. Map 7D7
☎254-1234 ⟨FAX⟩253-5856 ▥ ⟨AE⟩ ⊙ ⊙ ⟨VISA⟩
A wood-fired clay oven provides the pizza, the pasta is prepared right before your eyes in a glass-partitioned display kitchen and, in the evening, the place resounds to live Rhythm and Blues.

THE SPICE MARKET Thai
Regent Bangkok Hotel, 155 Ratchadamri Rd. Map 7D7 ☎251-6127 ⟨FAX⟩253-9195 ▥ ⟨AE⟩ ⊙
A good but small menu offers Thai food, heavily toned down for visitors — if you want it hot and spicy, tell the waiter in advance. The atmosphere is very pleasant: with its teak panels and sacks scattered about the floor, it resembles a spice warehouse.

THAI ROOM INTERNATIONAL CUISINE
Thai/Chinese/Mexican/European
37/20–5 Patpong 1 Rd. (off Silom Rd.). Map 7E6 ☎233-7920 ▥ ⟨AE⟩ ⊙ ⊙ ⟨VISA⟩
This is one of the oldest restaurants in Bangkok. The decor is simple, more like a café, but a wide range of food is offered: Thai, Chinese, Mexican and European. Guests order individual dishes or a selection to share.

THON TUM RUB Thai
115/7 Soi 8, Sukhumvit Rd. Off map 7D7
☎253-5145 ▥ ⟨AE⟩ ⊙ ⊙ ⟨VISA⟩
Thai food served on elegant crockery in an ornate Thai-style atmosphere, which helps to make it a popular tourist spot. There is live music in the evenings.

TRATTORIA DA ROBERTO Italian
Plaza Bldg., 33/9 Patpong 2 Rd. (off Silom

Rd.). Map *7E6* ☎234-5987 ⅢⅢ ᴀᴇ ⊙ ⊙
ᴠɪsᴀ *Open daily 11am–midnight.*

Enjoyable Italian food in an agreeable
setting. A good place to take the family
for lunch, although not dinner, when
it's expensive, as an entertainment surcharge is imposed for the privilege of
hearing one of the world's least interesting electronic piano players.

TUM NAK THAI *Thai*

131 Ratchadapisek Rd., off Sukhumvit Rd.
See map on page 187 ☎276-1810
ꜰᴀx248-0321 ⅢⅢ ᴀᴇ ⊙ ⊙ ᴠɪsᴀ

This Thai-style garden restaurant sprawls
across 4ha (10 acres) and is currently
the world's biggest restaurant, seating
3,000 guests, as confirmed by the *Guin-
ness Book of World Records*. It com-
bines a computer ordering system with
1,000 staff members, many of whom are
distinguished by their prowess on roller
skates, which is how they whisk the
orders around the grounds. This is all
very cute for a short while, until the
rattle of the skates across the wooden
floorboards of the restaurant begins to
wear on the nerves. There is a large
menu, but the food is undistinguished,
as is the Thai dancing *(Mon-Sat 7.30-
9.30pm)*. Near Robinson's department
store (see SHOPPING, page 237).

TWO VIKINGS *Scandinavian*

2 Soi 35, Sukhumvit Rd. See map on page
187 ☎258-8843/8846 ꜰᴀx258-8840 ⅢⅢ
ᴀᴇ ⊙ ⊙ ᴠɪsᴀ *Open 11.30am–2pm,*
6.20–10.30pm.

This is a Scandinavian restaurant tucked
into a converted private residence and
laid out in lodge hall style by its Danish
founders nearly 30 years ago. Mogens
Esbensen left for Sydney to open a restaurant and write a cookbook several
years ago, but his co-founder, Preben
Vinther, remains. Gravad laks or orders
from the herring cart are tempting starters, and the list of *entrées* includes veal
stuffed with crabmeat and breast of
duckling with green peppercorn sauce.
Taped classical music is played in the
evening.

WHOLE EARTH CAFÉ *Thai Vegetarian*

93/3 Soi Lang Suan, Ploenchit Rd. Map
7D7 ☎252-5574 ⅢⅢ ᴀᴇ ⊙ *Open*
11.30am–2pm, 5.30pm–midnight.

This is one of the few restaurants in
Bangkok that specializes in vegetarian
dishes. The cuisine is Thai, with dishes
such as vegetables served in a whole
pineapple, curried in coconut milk or
wrapped in fresh or fried Spring Rolls.
A good dessert menu features fried ba-
nanas and pancakes and there is a special *hors d'oeuvres* menu with a sampler
of three dishes. Live classical guitar
music provides dinner entertainment.
This location has been open for more
than 10 years. Another, in Chiang Mai
(see EXCURSIONS) has been operating for
nine years. A third, on Sukhumvit Rd.
(Soi 26 ☎ *258-4900, see map on page*
187), opened in early 1993.

Bangkok: nightlife and entertainment

Bangkok after dark

Bangkok's nightlife deserves its reputation. If anything, in the '90s the naughtiness has grown naughtier, with the city authorities disinclined to crack down for fear of discouraging the huge number of foreign tourists, Thailand's largest source of foreign exchange. For legions of Asian, European and American men, many of a certain age, waistline and wallet-size, after-dusk Bangkok provides a full menu of fleshly delights, from the cheeky and cheerful to the frankly evil, in go-go bars, gay bars, explicit "sexotic" cabarets and massage parlors.

No male tourist can escape the murmuring sirens of Bangkok nights: taxi drivers, bellhops, touts outside Patpong bars, hotel chauffeurs sitting out on sidewalks, all intoning the same chant — "Young girls, boys, sex show, massage . . . have a look." If you hesitate or show the slightest interest, a small photo album will be waved in your face, with a seductive selection of numbered young girls (or boys, as you like).

An irresistible aside. One character emerged during the 1980s, whose ideas on birth control have revolutionized the Thais. The legendary Mechai Viravaidya, founder of the Population and Community Development Association (PDA), employed comic and theatrical techniques; he won the following of farmers by paying them to paint family planning slogans on the backs of water buffaloes. He won the hearts and hygienic practices of Patpong Rd. ladies of the night by entering bars to give out colorful condoms and blow them up as balloons.

His idea was to break down the taboos about such devices with humor. It worked. His organization is an international success story, now studied by other nations as a model of population control. For a picture of CABBAGES AND CONDOMS, an extraordinary Thai restaurant that is also helping to put across the message, see page 217.

Caveat emptor

Mechai has convinced most of the city's prostitutes to insist on "safe sex" under the cover of what has become called a "mechai," but a killer stalks the streets in the form of the AIDS virus. A 1991 study concluded that, even using the most conservative estimate, at least a million Thais will die from AIDS by the year 2000.

Recent studies show the convergence of drugs and prostitution in Chiang Mai to have made it the epicenter of the AIDS pandemic in Thailand, but the incidence is high in all major tourist areas. No one has as yet ventured an estimate of how many tourists have been infected.

Nightlife

A TOUR OF PATPONG

Hard to avoid on the highest-minded trip to Bangkok are two garishly lit, raucous little streets named for their owner, Mr. Patpongpanich, a Thai–Chinese graduate of the University of Pennsylvania. Patpong Rds. 1 and 2 run parallel between Surawong and Silom Rds. *(map 7E6)*. A third street nearby is unofficially known as Patpong 3. Like the legendary American "Silk King," Jim Thompson, Mr. P. was parachuted back into his country's jungles by the O.S.S., in the closing days of World War II. The war ended before either of them could see action.

He inherited the land and a large, old teak house which, with astounding prescience, the Japanese had turned into a V.D. clinic for their troops. Patpong Rds., as they are called today, are products of the Vietnam War, when American troops on "R&R" flooded into Bangkok. Mr. Patpongpanich cut two roads through the lot, erected Bangkok's first custom-built office building, and later began to rent out space on the streets for bars and massage parlors.

In an interview in 1984, Mr. P. estimated that there were 50 bars and about one thousand girls working the strip, not including what he coyly described as "the loose ones," perhaps referring to those who do not wear the otherwise obligatory numbered badge pinned to what little material is available on their extremely scanty dancing gear.

In daylight hours the area is popular for its restaurants. From sundown (7pm) until the early hours (1 or 2am), the street becomes an open market, specializing in fake designer sports clothes, watches, etc. Inside the bars it pulsates.

The names of the bars can change overnight, but the action is always the same. Some screen videos, some serve food, some feature Thai boxing matches. These are but leitmotifs to the main events: loud disco-beat music, scantily clad young dancers (girls and boys) in high-heels and incongruous number badges on their chests, who hustle drinks and company between dance sessions on stages in go-go bars; upstairs sex-shows in which dancers from downstairs do unmentionable things with ping-pong balls, darts and balloons, burning candles, etc; "full body" massage parlors that do not engage in false advertising; sex for sale everywhere, all the time.

Nowadays, as many local Thais as tourists form the clientele (mostly male) and, unlike comparable "red light" areas in New York or Paris, the atmosphere is lighthearted and oddly innocent. The girls offer a convincing imitation of having a good time, given that they spend six or seven hours, seven nights a week on stage pretending to dance, or offstage pretending to dote on the whims of every client in valiant efforts at several assorted languages ("Whaaat you name? Where you cummm from? My name Nit. You buy me drink?" rendered in similarly feeble German, Italian, Japanese or Chinese), and the hustle seldom becomes aggressive.

There is a "bar fine" to pay if you take girls out before closing, and they are legally required to turn in their identification cards at hotel desks when they accompany clients back to their rooms Thanks to Mechai's efforts, they will virtually all be carrying spare condoms. For those who want a structured evening of mischief (massage parlor, go-go bar, erotic show) there's an 8–11pm **Bangkok Night Tour**. Hotels and travel agents have details.

CABARET

For supper-club-style cabaret with visiting Western singers or imported Parisian dancing girls, clubs within the major hotels, notably the DUSIT THANI's **Penthouse**, are about the only source.

There are a number of cavernous Chinese nightclubs featuring Taiwanese songstresses, acrobats and comedians, but they are usually extremely expensive and raucous: the **Galaxy**, with "no hands" dining (customers are fed by individual female hostesses), is probably the best. The **Pantip Theatre** brings in Chinese-language talents from Hong Kong and Taiwan and caters mostly to large tour groups and dinner parties.

BARS

Effortless elegance in a colonial setting, hot jazz in raunchy Patpong, groovy '60s retro, country 'n' western under the eyes of a Post-Impressionist: Bangkok's watering holes offer the full spectrum.

BAMBOO BAR

Oriental Hotel, Oriental Ave. Map 6F4
☎236-0400 AE ⬤ CB VISA *Open Mon–Sat till midnight.*
Elegant piano bar with live jazz on Monday nights. Setting for a Somerset Maugham story and popular with those who find life but a pale imitation of fiction.

BOBBY'S ARMS

1/F Patpong Carpark Building, Patpong 2. Map 7E6 ☎233-6828/234-1549
🍽 *Open 11am–1am: music Fri–Sat 8.30pm–midnight, Sun 8–11pm* AE CB
⬤ VISA
English-style pub featuring live Dixieland jazz on Sunday. Popular wateringhole with garrulous Brits and Aussies preparing for a night out in the raunchy world surrounding it. Opened in 1975 and now a senior citizen of Patpong, along with the *Trattoria de Roberto* nearby, which has been around as long and under the same management.

BOURBON STREET

29/4–6 Washington Sq. (behind Washington Theatre), Soi 22, Sukhumvit Rd. See map on page 187 ☎259-0328 AE ⬤ VISA

Open daily 7am–1am.
A popular spot with American expatriates due to the "cajun–creole" cuisine that owner Doug Harrison refers to as "cookin' with jazz." Darts and a Dixieland jazz band bring New Orleans to Bangkok, gumbo and all.

CAT'S EYE BAR

Le Meridien President Hotel. Map 7D7
☎253-0444. *Open Mon–Thurs till 1am, Fri–Sat till 2am* AE ⬤ CB VISA
Thai band and singers serving up jazz and pop music. No cover charge, but two-drink minimum on weekends. Expensive.

RENOIR

10/3–4 Soi 33 (Daeng Udom), Sukhumvit Rd. See map on page 187 ☎258-5720.
Open daily 4pm–2am. Happy hours 4–8pm
VISA
One of a number of bars concentrated in this lane, in the Sukhumvit Rd. area, that are named after French painters (others nearby are **P. Gauguin**, **Degas**, **Monet** and **Van Gogh**). They combine the concepts of local pub and scheduled disco theme party. And so one

Thursday a month you can have a drink in Tahiti, served by a girl in a grass skirt, another in the Caribbean with Calypso dancers, or perhaps American cheerleaders. This is the most popular of the genre. All seem to feature heroic sculpture in their inside foyers, very small framed prints of the namesake artists' paintings (perhaps an index of how small a role art plays in their proceedings) and a cozy mezzanine.

Of the others, **Degas** is the youngest, founded in 1992, and **Van Gogh** the oldest, founded in 1988. In the latter, a huge reproduction of a Van Gogh self-portrait overlooks a tiny bandstand where live "Country and Western" music

is played every night *(9pm-1am)*. The clientele comes mostly from the US, Hong Kong and Japan.

WOODSTOCK ROCK'N'ROLL BAR

2nd floor, Nana Plaza, Soi 4, Sukhumvit Rd. Off map **7D7**. *See map on page 187. Open daily 11am-1am; weekends till 2am* 🄰🄴 🅅🄸
This is the place to go if you're missing "the 60s" and their music. The decor features period posters of its namesake concert and forgotten, overdosed heroes of the "peace and love" era, such as Jimi Hendrix and Jim Morrison. A good place for drinks and nostalgia before a sumptuous Middle Eastern dinner at **Abu Khalil**, across the plaza.

NIGHTCLUBS

If wall-to-wall erotica fails to appeal, there are more restrained options. More circumspect nightbirds can listen to cool jazz or dance the night away at a disco, watch Thai dance or a transvestite revue, or take a trip down Mexico way.

BROWN SUGAR

231/19 Soi Sarasin (opp. Lumphini Park). Map **7E7** ☎*250-0103/250-1826* 🄰🄴 🄾
🄲🄳 🅅🄸 *Open Mon–Thurs 11am–1am; Fri–Sat 11am–2am; Sun 5pm–1am. Music daily 9pm–1am.*
A small jazz club that spills out onto the sidewalk on a street lined with other similar establishments. This, the pioneer on which others are modeled (opened March, 1985), fills a small space with very good sounds. Although it takes forever to arrive, food of a reasonable standard is served, ranging from a serviceable "Drunken Noodle" dish (fried egg-noodle with minced beef, basil and *lots* of chilies) to a mixed grill platter. As with many Bangkok restaurants, you can BYOB (Bring Your Own Booze) for a corkage fee; they will label and keep it on shelf for you. The credo is printed on the menu: "Blues is life, jazz is happiness. Brown Sugar is a house full of life and happiness." Dig it.

BUBBLES

Dusit Thani Hotel, Rama IV Rd. Map **7E6** ☎*236-0450* 🄰🄴 🄾 🄲🄳 🅅🄸 *Open Sun–*

Thurs 9pm–1am; Fri, Sat 9pm–2am.
This flashy videotheque disco with a British deejay is a vision in black, red and silver.

CALYPSO BANGKOK BROADWAY

Chokchai Bldg., 688 Sukhumvit Rd. (between Soi 24 and 26 beside Chokchai Bldg.). See map on page 187
☎*261-6355. Two shows nightly: 8.15pm and 10pm* 🄰🄴 🄾 🄲🄳 🅅🄸
La Cage Aux Folles had nothing on this place for costume and slick productions such as the "Holiday Fantasy" transvestite revue, with God knows how many lip-synch singers and look-alikes for Madonna, Marilyn and the rest. All of the tourist resorts in Thailand have a transvestite revue. This 720-seat theater has Bangkok's. The shows include Mandarin Chinese and Japanese numbers, as well as English.

DIANA'S

Oriental Plaza Shopping Centre, Chartered Bank Lane, off New Rd. Map **6F4** ☎*234-1320* 🄰🄴 🄾 🄲🄳 🅅🄸 *Open 8pm–midnight (weekends till 2am).*

A "Top 40" disco, popular with locals. Dimly lit red and black décor, full of alcoves and dim passageways. Artfully decadent for the "ever so naughty" set who probably spend their days shopping in the upmarket mall on top of which the club sits. Everything in this renovated 19thC bank building is a bit precious, and Diana's is no exception.

D'JIT POCHANA

48 Oriental Ave., New Rd. Map 6F4
☎*234-9920* ▭ AE ⊡ CD VISA
Open 7am–11pm.

Thai classical dance (episodes from the *Ramakien)* and dinner. Air conditioning and low tables.

THE GLASS

22/3–5 Soi 11 (Chaiyos) Sukhumvit Rd. See map on page 187 ☎*254-3566* AE ⊡ CD VISA *Open 6pm–1am, music from 9pm. Minimum charge on weekends and Mon.*

People lounge on the balconies and around the band, which plays in the center of the small club. The Glass is popular with the local glitterati, especially on "Beatles Night" *(Mon),* when it is *de rigueur* for customers to sit in with the band and belt out all those golden oldies.

EL GORDO'S CANTINA

Soi 8, Silom Rd. (opp. Bangkok Bank). Map 7E6 ☎*234-5470. Open daily 7pm–1am, weekends till 2am* AE ⊡ CD VISA

Besides having excellent Mexican and Tex-Mex food and a quasi-authentic Mexican ambience — with two *sombreros* slung about and some efforts at American Southwest-style furnishings — this happy little cantina set at the dead-end of an alley off Silom Rd. near Patpong has Freddie (a Filipino) and Levi (an affable American folksinger with a Thai wife). There's not a Mexican in the house. Both singers do a mean rendition of *Dueling Banjos* and other folk and country favorites. El Gordo's opened in 1989; given time it's likely to join the ranks of other *farang*- (foreigner) operated places that pepper Bangkok's modern history and tourist mythology. **Nick's Number One Hungarian** and

Two Vikings and now El Gordo's Cantina are typical of a type of place where aging adventurers go because they're just too stubborn to fade away. Long may they remain.

MONTIENTHONG

Montien Hotel, 54 Surawong Rd. Map 7E6 ☎*233-7060* ▭ AE ⊡ CD VISA *Open 7pm–midnight.*

This is a supper club frequented by locals, featuring live music and occasional dramatic performances. Popular on weekends.

PANTIP THEATRE RESTAURANT

604/3, 5/F, Pantip Plaza (entrance from parking lot, Phetburi Rd., Phyathai). Map 7C6 ☎*252-0141/7* ⚏*252-0148* ▭ AE ⊡ CD VISA *Open 11.30am–2pm, 6.30–10pm. Entertainment: 7.30pm featured pop singer, 8.30pm main floor show. Sun family show from 1pm.*

This mammoth restaurant and music hall stages live floor shows nightly, with Chinese-language singers and dancers hailing from Hong Kong, Taiwan and Singapore. The program changes fortnightly and there are seasonal extravaganzas (for example, for the Chinese New Year). There is also a Sunday "family show" featuring magicians and the like for children. A Cantonese *dim sum* lunch is offered daily. Up to 7,500 patrons can be accommodated. The main hall seats diners at tables for 10 people, with a rotating lazy-susan tray at the center. Private rooms overlook the stage and hall from a mezzanine.

The Thai chef of this eight-year-old pleasure center is current president of the city's chef's association, but its most notable feature is what is probably the least enticing entrance in Bangkok: from the fifth floor of the building's rather grimy parking lot, you enter a massive lobby that features a large glass case displaying assorted dried shark's fins, medicinal liquor bottles with strange things inside and other items delectable to the Chinese palate. English-speakers should ask for help from Khun Suda Thongphew, the assistant manageress.

SALA RIM NAM
Oriental Hotel, 48 Oriental Ave., New Rd.
Map 6F4 ☎*236-0400* 🚭 AE 💳 💳 💳
Open 7pm–11pm.
A good place to watch Thai dancing,
with an outdoor buffet dinner. Popular
with the hotel's guests, as well as out-
siders, so arrive early.

SILK'S
Royal Orchid Sheraton Hotel, 2 Captain
Bush Lane. Map 6E4 ☎*234-5599* AE 💳
💳 💳 *Open 9pm–midnight (weekends till*
2am).
A typical hotel disco, with lots of flash,
lots of decibels and a live deejay to
scrape the needle across the wax.

The performing arts

There are other, albeit perhaps tamer, forms of entertainment in Bangkok. A growing and increasingly cosmopolitan Thai bourgeoisie, together
with a sizeable foreign population, have pushed for striking improvements in the capital's cultural diet. That said, for the moment the performing arts are still only thinly served and there are few purpose-built
performance centers.

CINEMA
Cinema is scarcely more varied. Popular Thai movies usually focus on
adolescent romance and swashbuckling violence. Commercial theaters
showing Western movies stick closely to international blockbusters or
low-budget trash. A better selection is offered by various cultural missions
such as the **Alliance Française**, the **British Council** and the **Goethe
Institute**, but tickets can be hard to obtain.

CONTEMPORARY MUSIC
Inside or outside the big hotels, live modern music is to be found mostly
in bars and cocktail lounges (see our listings on pages 225–6). **Bobby's
Arms** pub has Dixieland ("Trad") jazz every Sunday afternoon; the
Oriental's Bamboo Bar has a full program of visiting performers; and
El Gordo's Cantina serves up banjo-pickin' country/folk singers with
its Mexican food.

   Brown Sugar offers the best contemporary jazz music in the city on
Soi Sarasin, opposite the entrance to Lumphini Park. Leading saxophonist
Thewan Subsanyakorn (a.k.a. "Tong") plays there on weekends. His
latest album, *Novel Jazz,* mingles musical styles and instruments from
both hemispheres with abandon.

   For **contemporary Thai music**, watch out for advertised concerts
by **Caravan**, the country's best rock/folk group. There are a number of
good **discos** where good local bands perform, again mostly in the major
hotels, although Bangkok's young glitterati gravitate to **Superstar Disco**,
above the bar of the same name on Patpong 1 Rd. Thai Yuppies prefer
Diana's in Oriental Plaza Bldg.; gays go to the **Rome Club** on Soi 4, off
Silom Rd.

CULTURAL INSTITUTES

- **Alliance Française**   29 South (Tai) Sathorn Rd. Map 7F6. ☎213-2122-3. Opening hours vary. Movies, plays and exhibitions from France. There is also a small restaurant.
- **The British Council**   428 Siam Sq., Soi 2. Map 7D6 ☎252-6136 or 252-6111. Opening hours vary. British movies, plays, ballet and music.
- **Goethe Institute**   18/1 Soi Ngarmduplee. Map 5B3 ☎287-1991 or 286-9002 to 4 Fx287-1829. Opening hours vary. Movies and other cultural events from Germany.
- **Siam Society**   131 Soi 21 (Asoke), Sukhumvit Rd. See map on page 187 ☎258-3491. Opening hours vary. Dedicated to the study of Thai history and culture. Stages movies, talks, musical evenings and trips up-country. Nonmembers welcome. See also BAN KAM-THIENG on page 189.

THEATER

Western theater is an exotic import and therefore poorly served. The **Bangkok Community Theatre** performs plays in English (usually at the American University or at the Alliance Française), small London West End companies take dinner dramas to the SIAM INTER-CONTINENTAL hotel, and modern Thai-language theater is sometimes staged at the MONTIEN hotel. **Chulalongkorn University** occasionally has visiting British troupes playing Shakespeare and other classics.

To keep abreast of the performing arts, consult the English-language newspapers, the *Bangkok Post* and the *Nation*. Most hotels stock free weekly guides such as *Bangkok This Week*.

TRADITIONAL THAI MUSIC AND DANCE

Nothing can compare with the performances staged by the **National Theatre** *(Na Phra Lan Rd., next to NATIONAL MUSEUM, map 5 C2 ☎224-1342 weekdays 8am-4.30pm for current programs; regular exhibition shows of dancing and music on last Fri and Sat of each month)*, usually with a cast from the dance school of the Department of Fine Arts. Clothed in rich brocade costumes and accompanied by an orchestra of xylophones, gongs, drums and wind instruments, the dancers act out episodes from the *Ramakien*.

A full show would take about 20 hours, so what's offered are highlights from the battle between the hero Phra Ram (the God Vishnu reincarnated as an Ayutthayan king) and the villain, King Thotsakan of Sri Lanka, who has abducted Nang Sida, wife of Phra Ram.

However, like those of the Khon masked dances derived from Indian temple rituals, shows are rare. Some major hotels, and a few specialty restaurants, have cultural shows on most nights that give a glimpse of the tale. See our listing of RESTAURANTS (pages 216–222) for some recommendations, or the Tourism Authority of Thailand's brochure *Where To Eat In Bangkok,* which lists a dozen locations.

One place for both traditional Thai, as well as Shan, Lao and Thai country dance, is at **Silom Village**, which is essentially a quiet, tree-shaded courtyard given over to food stalls, where the entertainment is free *(at Ruen Thep ☎ 233-9447 or 234-4448; shows nightly from 8.20-9.20pm)*.

WESTERN CLASSICAL MUSIC
The city now has two **orchestras**, the **Bangkok Philharmonic** and the **Bangkok Symphony**. Both are young and perform infrequently, but their string quartets can be heard most evenings in the lobby of smarter hotels such as the ORIENTAL, the GRAND HYATT ERAWAN and the REGENT.

Two talented amateur companies, the **Bangkok Music Society** and the **Bangkok Combined Choir**, stage occasional performances, and their mixed Thai and Western singers now have the confidence to tackle major productions such as *La Traviata* and the *Messiah*. Some foreign missions bring in chamber groups and contemporary dance companies, but there is no set pattern or location.

Bangkok: shopping

Where to go

As shopping in Bangkok is not concentrated in one particular area, the discriminating shopper must be prepared to scout around to find the best of what the city has to offer.

Thailand sells many first-rate goods, notably jewelry crafted from precious and semiprecious stones, silk and cotton garments and textiles, silver jewelry and tableware, nielloware, traditional handicrafts, wicker-ware, pottery, wood carvings, lacquerware (often with mother-of-pearl inlay) and bronze items.

Collectors of Asian *objets d'art* will also want to look out for five-color Bencharong porcelain, lacquered books of calligraphic scriptures, Khmer sculptures and Laotian textiles. Since it is very difficult to authenticate many of these pieces, and reproductions abound, the axiom *caveat emptor* always applies. If you don't mind well-made copies, say so from the outset — the price goes down, decorative value does not. Be on your guard if you are offered an "antique" piece at a low price — chances are it's a recently-made copy. Genuine antiques are costly, precisely because they are hard to come by.

Insurance is strongly advised if you are arranging for large items to be shipped home. Most shops will be able to arrange this. Customs documentation should also be arranged by the seller. Objects that are more than 100 years old must be licensed for release by the government's Fine Arts Department; it is not permitted to take religious icons out of the country.

Several large hotels have shopping arcades. However, many of the best department stores are located in modern shopping complexes where prices are fixed and shopping hours are long — generally 9am–9pm every day. In some of the big market areas of the city, opening hours are even longer and some bargaining is to be expected. Major credit cards are widely accepted in large stores, but some smaller shops may want to add a surcharge to the bill on these purchases even though this practice is not strictly legal.

WHAT TO LOOK OUT FOR

Thailand is a major exporter of indigenous **gemstones**: rubies, sapphires (especially the rare Chantaburi sapphires), garnets, zircons and "cat's eyes." Be aware that Sri Lankan sapphires are often artificially colored and resold in Thailand. Gem purchases should be made from a trader bearing the Tourism Authority of Thailand (TAT) logo; always ask for a certificate of authenticity.

Although many tourists come to Bangkok to buy **gold**, it is measured in *bhat,* a local unit of weight, and it can prove difficult to have a true value appraised back home.

Thailand produces high-quality **silverware**, which, according to government guidelines, is required to contain at least 92.5 percent silver. Except for antique silver jewelry crafted by the Thai hill-tribes, most silver items tend to be reasonably priced. Popular silver goods include bowls, boxes, trays, traditional and modern jewelry and flatware. Many of these things are engraved with attractive and mythological images or floral designs.

Thai **bronzeware** is noted for its quality, with tableware available in both modern and classical styles at reasonable prices. Cutlery handles are often made of teak, rosewood and black water-buffalo horn. Nickel-plated bronzeware, in addition to brass and copper items, is also sold.

Nielloware is said to have been introduced into the country by the Portuguese in the 16thC. The Thais call this durable alloy of silver, copper, lead and sulfur *thom.* Inlaid, its blue-black color is striking against a white or silver background. There are numerous items that feature niello: bracelets, cuff links, boxes, belt buckles and so on.

Bencharongware (five-color porcelain) originally came from China for use in the Thai court. Craftsmen here have continued to fashion these attractive pieces, which often include a touch of gold. **Celadon pottery** flourished in Thailand in the late Middle Ages and is still popular today, mostly in shades of green, blue and yellow-brown.

Thai **silk** has been world-famous ever since the industry was revived in the 1950s by the American entrepreneur Jim Thompson. It has a distinctive, unfinished texture and comes in a brilliant array of colors. A good test for pure silk is to burn a scrap of it — pure silk forms droplets, but synthetic mixtures vaporize.

Another kind of Thai silk, known as *Mud Mee,* is made by weavers in the NW. Intricate designs — mythical animals, flora and fauna — form the pattern on the fabric. In addition, locally produced cotton **textiles** come in many different weights and patterns and are also a good "find." If you have a bit of time, a Thai tailor can easily create a good copy of a favorite item of clothing out of one of these attractive materials. Although 24-hour tailoring services are a common sight, they should generally be avoided, as the final product looks like what it is: a rushed job.

The Hmon, Yao, Lahu, Lisu, Karen and Akha hill-tribes of northern Thailand are famous for their fine design sense and the durability of their work. They produce a wide range of brightly colored **handicrafts**, which include basketware, embroidered material, clothing, silver jewelry, and Thai dolls dressed in traditional costumes.

Thailand is a world center for the cultivation and export of **orchids**, and these lovely flowers are available throughout the city. Fragrant, colorful garlands called *malai,* composed of jasmine buds, roses and African daisies, are often used as offerings at shrines and can also be easily found for sale at street stalls in tourist areas.

ANTIQUES, ARTS AND CRAFTS

The tradition of Thai handicrafts and art objects is greatly admired, and a variety of appealing items is found in Bangkok's antique and craft stores. Some shops also feature works from neighboring countries. As always, a wide range of quality and price is available. Some of the best-known shops in Bangkok are in upmarket hotel shopping arcades, with prices to match. Besides **Monogram** *(Oriental)*, there are also **Chailai, Prasat Collection** *(Peninsula Plaza)*, **Art Resources, The Heritage, Lotus** and **House of Handicrafts** *(Regent)*, among others.

ART & ANTIQUE CENTRE
Captain Bush Lane, next to Royal Orchid Sheraton Hotel. Map 6E4 ☎ *236-8320*
🆎 💳 💳 💳
Located on the third and fourth floors of the River City shopping complex, these 40 shops specialize in antiques and *objets d'art.* An auction is held on the first Saturday of each month.

ASIAN GALLERIES
460 Surawong Rd. Map 6F5 ☎ *233-4014*
🆎
Buddhist icons of carved wood as well as bronze and stone figures are on sale here. Another branch is in the River City shopping complex.

CABBAGES & CONDOMS HANDICRAFTS
6 Sukhumvit Rd., Soi 12 (behind Sukhumvit Plaza). See map on page 187 ☎ *256-0080 or 256-0097* 📠 *255-8804. Open daily 11am–9pm* 🆎 💳 💳 💳
This unique collaboration has for six years provided a marketing outlet for the Population and Community Development Association (PDA) and the British aid and development organization, OXFAM, with support from Mobil Oil Thailand Co. Ltd. The shop may be small, but it has an excellent selection of crafts, apparel, textiles, silver jewelry and incised silver tableware — as well as what must be the world's largest collection of tee shirts sporting messages about AIDS and birth control. Prices are very modest and money goes to support PDA's rural development and AIDS education efforts.

CHITRLADA SHOPS
Chitrlada Villa, Dusit Palace ☎ *281-1111 or 282-1202* 🆎 💳 💳 💳

This is the fundraising outlet for SUPPORT, or Supplementary Occupations and Related Techniques, established in 1976 under the patronage of HM Queen Sirikit. Its mission is to help create cooperatives of Thai farmers, who comprise around 75 percent of Thailand's total population, and provide them with equipment and training in 21 distinct cottage industries. Today there are more than 90 such training centers spread throughout the country. SUPPORT also promotes and markets their work overseas and has branches at the Grand Palace, Oriental Plaza and Vimarnmek Mansion *(opp. Dusit Zoo)* in town and another in the Rose Garden Country Resort. Its airport shops are in Bangkok, Chiang Mai and Phuket. There are also shops in Bang Sai at Ayutthaya and in Pattaya.

HOUSE OF HANDICRAFTS
Sukon Court, 2nd floor, 46 North (Nua) Sathorn Rd. Map 7F7 ☎ *234-3021; Regent of Bangkok, 155 Ratchadamri Rd. Map 7D7* ☎ *250-0724, Amarin Plaza, Ploenchit Rd. Map 7D7* ☎ *256-9732* 🆎 💳 💳 💳
The stock concentrates on Burmese tapestries, *Mud Mee* silk, lacquerware, hill-tribe crafts, all said to be the work of some 7,000 native women. Featured on television and in craft fairs in Europe, Japan and the US.

MONOGRAM
Oriental Hotel, Menam Mall. Map 6E4 ☎ *235-2603* 🆎 💳 💳 💳
This well-known antique store was founded by Mrs. Connie Mangskau, a close friend of Jim Thompson, the American "silk king," who was one of the most highly regarded figures of Bang-

kok society. Along with Thompson, she was one of the first Bangkok residents to have a home built in genuine Thai country style. This has since become *de rigueur* for local intellectuals of means. Mrs. Mangskau is now deceased, but her daughter still runs the shop, which features a fine selection of Oriental art objects. Look out for the tapestries and rain drums from Burma and the silver animals from Cambodia.

NARAYANAPHAND PAVILION
127 Ratchadamri Rd. Map 7D7
☎252-4670 AE ◉ ◉ VISA *(second shop at Din Daeng, near Thai—Japanese Youth Center). Open daily 10am–8pm.*

This joint venture between the Thai government and a private businessman is the grand-daddy of Thai craft products stores, founded more than 50 years ago and formerly in a ghastly little lavender building on Larn Luang Rd. It has one of Bangkok's best selections of good quality handicrafts at fair prices on the ground floor and mezzanine and, quite literally, a "bargain basement," reached via a side entrance of the building. This is the most convenient mid-to-low-priced shopping arcade for a cluster of five-star hotels, including the GRAND HYATT ERAWAN, LE MERIDIEN PRESIDENT, the ARNOMA SWISSÔTEL and the REGENT.

PENG SENG
942/1–3 Rama IV Rd. at Surawong Rd. Map 7E6 ☎236-8010/234-1285 AE ◉ ◉ VISA

This Thai–Chinese family business is in its third generation and offers a good selection of porcelain items. Virtually next door to the **Jim Thompson Thai Silk Co**.

SAI JAI THAI FOUNDATION
Vocational Training Center, 306/1 Si Ayutthaya Rd., Phya Thai. Map 6B4 ☎246-5565 or 245-8703. Open Mon–Fri 8.30am–5pm; Sat 8.30am–noon.*

Since 1975, this organization has helped support the families of Thai soldiers maimed or killed in the ongoing skirmishes on Thailand's borders with Laos and Kampuchea. A leatherwork center

was established to train disabled veterans in 1980, and another for glass etchings was created in 1986. Women's purses and briefcases, as well as very finely etched vases and other glassware are typical of the items on offer. Their goods are also sold in CHITRLADA shops (see page 233). The foundation is under the patronage of H.R.H. Princess Maha Chakri Sirindhorn.

S. SAMRAN THAILAND
302–308 Phetburi Rd. Map 7C7
☎215-8941

This family business is one of many to have its own bronzeware factory, which has been selling teakwood boxed sets of flatware to tourists for about 40 years. It is best to buy from shops such as this with their own factories. Ask to see their export catalogs, as they will ship anywhere and you can create a starter set on your visit, which may be added to later by mail order.

THAI CELADON
Celadon House, 8/8 Sukhumvit Rd., Soi 16 (at intersection of Ratchadapisek Rd., near SEAFOOD MARKET *restaurant). See map on page 187* ☎259-7744/254-6033 FAX(662) 255-5298 AE ◉ ◉ VISA *Open Mon–Sat 8.30am–5.30pm. Closed Sun, hols. In Chiangmai: Thai Celadon Kilns, 62 Chotana Rd.* ☎213-541.

It is believed the celadon firing process came to the kingdom of Sukhothai from China in about the 14thC, but emerged in its own unique designs in the Thai "dragon kilns." Thai Celadon was founded more than 30 years ago.

A complete range of celadon tableware and decorative items is available in the traditional greens and browns and in a newly developed blue shade, from Thai Celadon's Bangkok shop, which has three floors of household goods (first floor), lamps and vases (second floor) and "seconds" (top floor). Lower-priced "seconds" shelves have many bargains and stock clearance sales are held in December, with 50–70 percent discounts. Catalogs are available for overseas orders. Ask for showroom manager Poonpon Dechakaisaya.

The Chiang Mai factory and show-room of this shop is a must if you travel N. There, some 90 potters turn out lovely reproductions and some new lines. Also in Chiang Mai is an even more unique shop, **Mengrai Kilns** *(37/1 Rasd Uthis Rd., near Gymkhana Club* ☎ *241-802)*, selling reproduction cela-don pieces made by Donald Gibson, crafted, using methods that are identical to those of the originals, in a 16thC brick kiln on the city's outskirts.

Mr. Gibson, a retired British civil ser-vant and devotee of Thai ceramics, was the founder of this business, producing new art objects using traditional methods, to make perfect replicas at affordable prices.

THAI HOME INDUSTRIES
35 Oriental Ave. Map 6F4 ☎ *234-1736*
AE CB DC VISA
This shop is housed in what appears to be an old *godown* (warehouse) just

behind the Oriental Hotel. Service is, shall we say, casual, and it is not air conditioned, so be advised to visit early or late in the day. There is an eclectic selection of handicrafts, but it is best known for its bronze flatware and bowls and, most recently, its unique hand-forged silverware, which was ex-hibited at the New York Museum of Modern Art. This is very pricey com-pared to the bronzeware and the selec-tion of actual utensils is rather limited, but it has a rough beauty that sits surpris-ingly well with the welded constructions and tactile montages of modern art.

YONG ANTIQUES
1320 New Rd. Map 6F5 ☎ *235-6199*
AE CB DC VISA
A wide array of items is on sale here, including lacquerware, silver jewelry, basketware, porcelain and ceramics, carved ivory, as well as a huge selection of wooden animals.

CLOTHES AND FABRICS
Thailand is known for its distinctively textured, colorful silk and cotton fabrics. Many shops sell both material and ready-to-wear clothing. Some shops also feature a made-to-measure tailoring service where your just-purchased silk can be transformed into a favorite garment, often within a relatively short time.

ANITA THAI SILK
294/4–5 Silom Rd. Map 7E6 ☎ *234-2481*
AE CB DC VISA
A large range of Thai silk and cotton plus home furnishings and gift items, all at reasonable prices. Anita Thai Silk de-signs have won a number of US and European awards. Its ready-to-wear collections are a regular feature in US and UK department stores.

ANONG GALLERY
Chartered Bank Lane. Map 6F4
☎ *235-7991* AE CB DC VISA
On the second floor of the Oriental Plaza complex, this shop offers hill-tribe clothing in pricey original designs.

ART'S TAILOR
62/15–6 Thaniya Rd., Silom. Map 6F5
☎ *234-9874* AE

Expensive made-to-measure clothes for men, skillfully crafted, imported fabrics. A second branch is located at the Orien-tal Hotel Arcade.

CHOISY
9/25 Surawong Rd. Map 7E6 ☎ *233-7794*
AE VISA
Run by an elegant French woman and her daughter, who offer French fashion designs in ready-to-wear and made-to-measure evening clothes, made from high-quality Jim Thompson Thai silk.

DESIGN THAI
304 Silom Rd. Map 6F5
☎ *234-2481/235-1553* AE CB DC VISA
The distinctive white Thai-style facade and lintel of this shop has been a Silom Rd. landmark for more than 20 years. It sells the same sort of silk clothing as

rivals such as **Anita, Jim Thompson Thai Silk, Kanitha** and many others, but, inexplicably, its prices have always been marginally lower.

HOME MADE (H.M.) THAI SILK
45 Prom Chai Prom Pongse, Soi 39, Sukhumvit Rd. See map on page 187 ☎*258-8766/8769* ⬛ ▦ *Open 8.30am–6pm.*
This is factory-outlet shopping, Bangkok-style. It stocks ready-to-wear clothes fashioned from *Mud Mee* silk, which is also sold by the meter, manufactured at an on-site factory that employs about 100 people. This family business began about 30 years ago, with four looms. After World War II, the patriarch worked for the Americans, who often complained of the poor quality of silk. So he decided to develop a better product. Today there are 25 looms, worked mostly by women brought down from NE Thailand, from where the silk originates, and where weaving skills remain high. This is not an easy place to find, buried in the great, walled backlanes off Sukhumvit Rd., but the reward is to buy items here at perhaps 35 percent less than you would pay at more conveniently located downtown outlets.

JAGTAR
137/3 Sukhumvit Rd., between Soi 9–11. See map on page 187 ☎*251-1984* ⬛ ⬛ ⬛ ▦
A specialty here is made-to-order, high-quality silk bedspreads, pillow covers and home-furnishing items.

JIM THOMPSON THAI SILK CO.
9 Surawong Rd. Map 7E6 ☎*234-4900* ⬛ ⬛ ⬛ ▦
Very high-quality Thai silk and cotton clothing and material. This popular shop, designed in the style of a Thai house, also has departments for home furnishings, accessories and exclusive jewelry. Expect to pay a premium for the name.

JOHN FOWLER'S
Ploenchit Arcade. Map 7D7 ⬛ ⬛ ⬛ ▦
Good value in casual clothes and beachwear. Another branch is at the corner of Silom and Convent Rds. Fowler made his name a byword on the beaches of Thailand with original designs and slogans on tee shirts.

KAI
257/23 Wireless Rd., Ploenchit Rd. Map 7D7 ☎*251-5441* ⬛ ⬛ ⬛ ▦
Elaborate evening wear by one of Bangkok's leading designers. Their other shop, in the Oriental Plaza mall, sells linen and silk day-wear.

KHOMAPASTR
52/10 Surawong Rd. Map 7E6 ☎*233-6825* ⬛ ⬛ ⬛ ▦
Hand-painted Thai cotton and attractive home-furnishing textiles from a family business that began in Hua Hin more than 30 years ago. Notable for successful translations of traditional Thai designs to modern uses.

LOTUS
155 Ratchadamri Rd. Map 7D7 ☎*251-6127* ⬛ ⬛ ⬛ ▦
Located in the Regent Bangkok Hotel Arcade, Lotus offers a small, splendid collection of antique Oriental textiles, Chinese mandarin gowns, Kashmiri wool shawls, Tibetan prayer rugs and attractive jewelry and accessories.

N & Y BOUTIQUE
11 Chartered Bank Lane. Map 6F4 ☎*233-0903.*
A small but good selection of clothes in Thai cotton, silk or a silk-and-linen blend. Can also tailor clothes to order.

NGOR BATIK STUDIO
11 Soi 30, Sukhumvit Rd. See map on page 187 ☎*258-4840.*
Run by a well-known artist, this shop sells hand-painted silk and cotton textiles and clothing. It also has a range of batik items.

PERRY'S TAILOR
60/2 Silom Rd. Map 7E6 ☎*233-9236.*
Made-to-measure clothes for women and men at very moderate prices. A good place to have a favorite item of clothing copied in Thai silk.

DEPARTMENT STORES, SHOPPING MALLS AND ARCADES

Bangkok's department stores, many of which are located in shopping malls, sell a wide range of Thai items. Imported items, however, are heavily taxed and therefore quite expensive. But this has not deterred a Japanese retail invasion, with six stores to date: Isetan, Jusco, Daimaru, Yaohan, Tokyu and Zen (the last a joint venture between Bangkok's Central group and Japan's Hankyu).

Most department stores have the convenience of a café, bakery, pharmacy and supermarket on the premises. One store (**Big Bell**) even has a small zoo on its top floor! The following is a sampler.

BIG BELL
*888 Ploenchit Rd. Map **7**D7* ⬛ ⬛ ⬛ ⬛
A shop selling mostly imported Japanese goods. The top floor boasts a mini-zoo and aviary.

THE BRITISH DISPENSARY
*109 Sukhumvit Rd. Off map **7**D7. See map on page 187* ☎252-8056.
An English-speaking, well-stocked pharmacy carrying prescription medicines, cosmetics and toiletries, including their own brand of "prickly heat" powder — excellent protection against the Bangkok climate — and Lomotil for upset stomachs. This shop is conveniently located beneath an office of British doctors. There is another branch at 1–5 Oriental Lane.

CENTRAL PLAZA
*1691 Phaholyothin Rd., Lard Prao (part of Central Plaza Hotel complex). Map **7**A7* ☎513-1240 ⬛ ⬛ ⬛ ⬛
Founded in 1928 by the Chirthivat family, in Thonburi, and now part of the largest department store chain in Bangkok, this location is claimed to be the largest shopping plaza in Southeast Asia. The group has about ten properties in the greater Bangkok area, with its headquarters in the Silom Complex on Silom Rd. It has now opened its first upcountry branch, in Chiang Mai, and plans another eight centers, spread throughout Thailand. Sells mostly imported clothes and other expensive items, but one can sometimes find good local products, especially ladies' shoes. On the upper floors is a section selling hill-tribe artifacts, and a well-stocked supermarket.

MAH BOONKRONG CENTER
*444 Phya Thai Rd. (Siam Sq. area, near the National Stadium) Map **7**D6* ☎217-9472.
This giant, seven-story arcade is a downscale shopper's dream and so a magnet for Thailand's teenagers. There are restaurants, a movie theater and concert hall and a large hawkers' food center on the premises. The only incongruous touch is a large Tokyu department store, which sits inside this buzzing indoor flea market like a man wearing a tuxedo to a garage sale.

ORIENTAL PLAZA
*30/1 Chartered Bank Lane. Map **6**F4*
☎234-1320/9 ⬛ ⬛ ⬛ ⬛
This colonial-style building converted into a shopping complex houses some of Bangkok's better antique stores. **Chitrlada**, which is under royal patronage, sells hill-tribe and handicraft items on the third floor, and **Kai**, a well-known Thai designer, has a small shop on the first floor.

RIVER CITY
*Captain Bush Lane, off New Rd. Map **6**E4*
⬛ ⬛ ⬛ ⬛
This shopping center has many outlets selling ready-to-wear clothes, gift items and much more. The top two floors have been turned into an antique arts center with more than 40 shops selling *objets d'art* and curios.

ROBINSON
*2 Silom Rd. Map **7**E6* ⬛ ⬛ ⬛ ⬛
A five-story department store: the top floor sells cooked food, coffee and ice cream, making it a good place to take children.

SIAM CENTRE
*Rama I Rd. Map **7**D6* AE CB CD VISA

The Siam Centre is a three-story shopping complex, selling local and Japanese designer clothes. A popular place with locals, with interesting shops and restaurants. Some shops deal in quality leather items. Across the street from the Centre is Siam Sq., where there are several fast-food outlets (**A and W**, **Kentucky Fried** and **Mister Donuts**). The area is not air conditioned, so it is difficult to cover much ground because of the heat. Several movie theaters are located here. Charge/credit card policy varies from shop to shop.

SILOM VILLAGE
*Silom Rd. near Narai Hotel. Map **6**F5*
AE CB CD VISA

This is a private estate converted to a mini shopping mall on two stories, with further shops in what was a courtyard. The seafood restaurants on the ground floor have Thai dancing nightly. The shops carry virtually everything for which Thailand is known by tourists — from leather goods to stylized wooden elephants in repose, and leaping ceramic fish for your garden. But don't let the stylish ambience bedazzle you. Bargain hard.

SOGO
*Amarin Plaza, 500 Ploenchit Rd. Map **7**D7*
☎256-9131.

Occupies a large portion of the four-story Amarin Plaza shopping mall. A fully-equipped model of what has become a commonplace in Asia — the Japanese department store. Sogo can be considered a prototype of the phenomenon, with 21 stores in Japan, another six in the rest of Asia and, opened just in time for the 1992 Olympics, a new outlet in Barcelona, Spain. The top floor has a good selection of Thai arts and crafts and a selection of Asian maps.

FLEA MARKETS
There are five "must" markets in Bangkok: **Pratunam**, which stretches in a ten-block tract along Ratchaprarop Rd., especially good for discounted clothing *(map **7**C7)*; the city's largest at **Banglampoo**, N of Ratchadamnoen Klang Rd. near the National Library *(map **5**B3)*, in the middle of cheap guesthouses and so a great world center for backpackers; **Chatuchak Weekend Market** (see page 203); the **Patpong 1/Silom Rds.** *(map **7**E6)* night markets *(after 7pm nightly)*; and Chinatown's **"Thieves' Market"** *(Nakhon Kasem) (map **5**D3)*.

This last is more fun to watch at work than to shop in, since it's mostly given over to housewares. There are some dubious "antique" shops true to the area's name, selling things such as bronze Laotian rain drums that are likely to be younger than the shopkeepers selling them.

FLOWERS
Fruit and flowers are two of the great natural wonders of Thailand. The latter, in the form of garlands of jasmine, roses and other flowers *(puana malai)* are wonderful daily reminders of this country's bounty, superstition and artistic temperament. Almost every traffic-choked intersection of Bangkok will have girls stringing together complex patterns of fragrant flowers. These are sold to drivers, who hang them from their rearview mirrors, and to passers-by with a ribbon for stringing them about the neck. They're meant to bring a daily dose of good luck.

Garlands also decorate "spirit houses" built in yards of homes and offices to appease earth gods who may have been disturbed when foundations were laid. Such floral tributes are also left as offerings in

Buddhist temples and at Hindu shrines (see ERAWAN SHRINE). This wonderfully exotic transcendence of tradition over concrete street life is no more remarkable to Thais than Americans having milk and eggs for breakfast. Regrettably, the fragile garlands don't travel well. They are part of the magical, everyday Thai world that is not exportable.

Fortunately, beautiful orchids, the Thai national flower, can be carried home with you — a pleasant compensation for the jasmine and ginger petals you left behind. Specializing in orchids, these and other shops can pack them safely for your return trip home.

- **Jane**   Soi 10, 430/29 Siam Sq. Map **7**D6 ☎251-3421.
- **Malaiwan**   854 Sukhumvit Rd. (opp. Soi 55). See map on page 187 ☎391-9808.
- **Orchid Silom**   387 Silom Rd. Map **6**F5 ☎233-0858.
- **Pen Flowers**   10/2 Decho Rd. Map **6**E5 ☎235-6110.
- **Phuang Thong Florist**   12/1 Convent Rd. Map **7**E6. ☎235-7003.
- **White Rose**   390 Sukhumvit Rd. Off map **7**D7. See map on page 187 ☎258-1929.

There are also four large street markets specializing in horticulture:

- **Bangrak**   On New Rd., between Silom and Sathon Rds. Off map **6**F5. Not large, but has a good variety of cut blooms (especially orchids).
- **Pak Khlong Talat**   Maha Rat Rd., near the Memorial Bridge. Map **5**D3. Wholesale market for cut flowers.
- **Thewet**   On the bank of Khlong Phadung Krung Kasem, just off Samsen Rd. Map **5**B3. Large market for potted plants.
- **Phahonyothin**   On the road of the same name. The city's newest and largest plant market, set in a row of small shops opposite the Northern Bus Terminal.

JEWELRY

Bangkok jewelry stores offer all manner of adornments at a range of prices. All feature ready-made items and most will also sell and mount stones. Many jewelry stores offer silverware too. Be aware that there is a racket in bringing gray Sri Lankan sapphires here and irradiating them so as to artificially turn them into the buyers' preferred blue color.

That is but one of many rackets in the gem trade. In 1990, the Tourism Authority of Thailand had 300 complaints from visitors who had been lured into shops by touts with "special deals," which they estimate covered only 60 percent of such rip-offs. They offer a free brochure, *The Gem Sting in Bangkok,* which describes these unsavory, but technically legal (which means no refunds, folks!) practices.

As a general rule, jewelry cannot be returned. Where refunds are given, there is often a 25- to 30-percent deduction, as damages to the shopowner. Be absolutely certain you have any promises of refunds *in writing* on your receipt, along with absolutely all details about the quality of your stones. Always insist on a certificate of authenticity that carries a full description of what your gems are purported to be.

239

In 1990, Thailand had 20 percent of the global market and was the number-two gem exporter in the world. Rubies and sapphires are the most common indigenous Thai stones. There is also a large intra-Asian trade, via Thailand, in Burmese jadeite. Indicative of the country's pre-eminence as a gem source, four high-rise gem and jewelry malls, ranging from 29 to 63 stories, are planned or under construction on Silom Rd., Bangkok's gem trading center. There are also plans for a gem bourse.

The **Thai Gem and Jewelry Traders Assn.** *(942/152 Charn Issara Tower, 15th flr., Rama IV Rd.* ☎ *235-3039* Fx *235-3040)* publishes a useful *Gem & Jewelry Trade Directory.*

The most authoritative source of advice or education about gems is at the **Asian Institute of Gemological Sciences**. This was founded in 1978 as Southeast Asia's first educational facility devoted exclusively to the study of gemology, and is now located in its own six-story building in Ratchadapisek district *(484 Ratchadapisek Rd., Samsennok, Huay-Kwang* ☎ *513-2112 or 513-7044* Fx *512-4097, open 8.45am-5pm)*. The institute offers a five-day "Introduction to Color Stones" course all year round, conducted in English and Thai *(3hrs a day, ask for the school registrar)*.

The school has opened a separate **AIGS Gem Laboratory**, which will grade gems, but not appraise them *(12/1 Surasak Rd., Silom, Bangrak* ☎ *238-4503 or 238-4532* Fx *238-3219, open weekdays 9am-5pm; Sat 9am-noon; takes 2 days-1wk)*. For those who want to make a more serious study of the gem business, it also conducts two-day tours to the Chanthaburi and Trat province ruby and sapphire mines, led by a gemologist.

There are more than 20 pages of jewelry stores listed in Bangkok's Yellow Pages. Shop around.

A.A.
104 Siam Centre, Rama I Rd. (opp. Siam Inter-Continental). Map 7D6 ☎ *251-7283*
AE 回 回 VISA
A good range of jewelry is stocked in this shop, which is particularly popular with Thais.

ALEX & CO
14/1 Oriental Lane. Map 6F4 ☎ *234-3908*
AE
A long-established jewelry store, selling good-quality pearls for necklaces, earrings and rings. It also sells precious stones in gold settings. Good workmanship.

ROYAL THAI GEMS
Oriental Hotel Arcade. Map 6F4
☎ *234-0130* AE 回 回 VISA
Reliable quality, excellent stones, exquisite settings. Very expensive.

SINCERE JEWELRY
Dusit Thani Hotel Arcade. Map 7E6
☎ *233-0643* AE
A range of expensive brooches, necklaces, bracelets and rings in exquisite settings and designs.

TOK KWANG
224–6 Silom Rd. Map 6F5 ☎ *233-0658*
AE 回 回 VISA
Gems and pearls of a very high quality are sold in this shop with its own resident gemologist.

UTHAI'S GEMS
28/7 Soi Ruamruedi, Ploenchit Rd. (near Holy Redeemer Church). Off map 7D7
☎ *253-8582* AE
Has a very good reputation with foreigners in Bangkok. The staff are willing to help and can copy designs of any piece of jewelry. Uthai and his wife are

always at the shop, and in the event of customer dissatisfaction, he will buy the purchase back at any time. A good selection of gems, especially rubies, sapphires and emeralds. Orders can be despatched to anywhere in the world.

TOYS

Well-crafted wooden toys and dollhouses are sometimes difficult to come by these days; dolls crafted to collectors' quality standards are even rarer. Both are still to be found in Bangkok.

AWE DESIGNS

591/10 Soi 33/1, Sukhumvit Rd. (near Villa cinema). See map on page 187. Open Mon–Fri 9am–5pm ☎ 381-3330 🆎

This delightful little shop is tucked above **Sally's Choice Irish Cafe**, on a lane chock-a-block with Middle Eastern carpet stores. Inside, its British proprietress, Kathy, has been selling a range of good, old-fashioned wooden toys, dollhouses and jigsaws for about ten years. This is an excellent place to buy gifts for children, from reasonably-priced dollhouses to individually illustrated and monogrammed boxes for keeping Lego pieces in. It is hard to find, but worth the search.

BANGKOK DOLLS

85 Soi Ratchatapan, (locally called Soi Mohleng) Makkasan ☎ 245-3008. No cards.

Tongkorn Chandavimol is to doll-making in Thailand what Jim Thompson was to the silk industry. Bangkok Dolls' products have won numerous international accolades. She has been crafting dolls for more than 35 years, mostly in four styles: classical and Khon Masked Dancers (her best sellers); people from Thai daily life, such as farmers and fruit vendors; hill tribe members; and stuffed "cuddly dolls."

Khun Tongkorn had been a teacher at Chulalongkorn University, but, on a visit to the United Nations headquarters in New York City, she saw how poorly made representative Thai dolls were and felt that someone should do better to represent her culture. In 1956, she accompanied her husband to Japan to attend a five-day dollmaking course. She never looked back. She conducts her own research into costume and makes all her own parts. In 1978, her work won first prize in the third International Folklore Dolls Competition.

More than 800 handmade dolls are displayed, traditional Thai figures and others. This museum and shop are as near to heaven as any doll collector may ever get.

Bangkok: recreation

Sports in Bangkok

Many sporting facilities in the city are for members only. Visitors must be invited or have reciprocal arrangements through clubs and associations in their own country of residence.

GOLF

Golf first came to Thailand in the 1920s, as part of the amenities of the Railway Hotel in Hua Hin, and today there are some 65 courses in the country. Most of Bangkok's larger courses are outside the city. Green fees are double on weekends. For details, see the English-language newspaper *The Nation*.

Thailand's most famous and most expensive championship course is **Navatanee** *(pass Hua Mark, turn off on Sukhumvit Rd., Soi 71 and cross Hua Mark bridge; 30mins from city center; par 72)*, venue for the 23rd World Cup Tournament in 1975 and designed by Robert Trent Jones. One unusual feature is the team of female caddies.

The **Railway Training Centre** *(Phaholyothin Rd., on the left-hand side of the superhighway toward Don Muang Airport; 15mins from city center; par 72)* has 18 holes and a driving range. The **Royal Bangkok Sports Club** *(Henri Dunant Rd., map 7 D6)* has a nine-hole course and is only open to members and nonresident guests.

Visitors are welcome to practice at the **Phetburi Driving Range** *(Soi Soonvijai, left of Phetburi Rd. extension toward Sukhumvit Rd., Soi 63, see map on page 187)*. The **Rose Garden** *(some 30km/20 miles w of Bangkok on Highway 4)* has an 18-hole course.

Muang Ake *(5mins drive N of airport, 40mins from city center; par 72)*, was the site of the 1987 Ladies Open on the Asian circuit. **Ekachai Golf and Country Club** *(in Samut Sakhon, some 40mins drive w of Bangkok; par 72)* has both 18- and nine-hole courses. It was designed by Gregory M. Nash of California.

Near the Thammasat University junior campus (at Putun Thani, on the outskirts of the city) is the **Pinehurst Golf and Country Club**, modeled on a North Carolina club of the same name. It claims to host Asia's first golf school, with classes conducted by professionals from the US namesake. **Krungthep Kritha** *(par 72)* and **Unico** *(par 72)* are next to each other and about 30 minutes' drive from the city center.

The **Royal Thai Army Golf Club** *(25mins drive from city center, off the airport highway; par 72)* is Thailand's first 36-hole course. **Panya**

Resort, with three par 72 courses, is the country's largest golf club *(on the Bang Na–Trat Highway, about 83km/52 miles from Bangkok)*. **Green Valley Country Club** *(on the main Bangkok–Pattaya highway, 25mins drive from city center; par 72)* was designed by Robert Trent Jones.

Bangphra *(par 72)* is an hour's drive from Bangkok, between Bang-saen and Pattaya on the Gulf of Thailand. There are also courses in and around Pattaya, Hua Hin, Chiang Mai and Phuket. Access to clubs can be arranged by the hotel concierge or through a specialist agent, such as **Paradise Golf Plus** *(37/88 Ladprao, Soi 101, Ladprao Rd., Wangthong-lang, Bangkapi ☎377-3522 ⨍ᴀ322-6983)*, which works with hotels such as the GRAND HYATT ERAWAN.

HEALTH CLUBS
Health clubs in **hotels** offer fitness facilities for the use of guests. Some of Bangkok's best are listed below, but see also individual hotel entries in WHERE TO STAY, pages 206-211.
* **Ambassador**   Aerobic and jazz dancing, gym and jogging track.
* **Dusit Thani**   Gym and jogging track, run by Fitness International.
* **Grand Hyatt Erawan**   Gym facilities, aerobic rooms, tennis courts, pools, in-house jogging track on the fifth floor.
* **Hilton**   Clark Hatch Fitness Center (part of a regional group run by an American bodybuilder), squash and tennis courts.
* **Oriental**   Aerobics classes, tennis and squash courts, a golf practice range, jogging track and gym.
* **Regent Bangkok**   Gym and squash courts.

HORSE-RACING
Horse-racing is held at the main racecourse at the **Royal Bangkok Sports Club** *(Henri Dunant Rd. ☎ 251-0181)*. Races are held on the second Sunday of every month. The **Royal Turf Club** *(Phitsanulok Rd., map 6 B5 ☎ 280-0020)* holds race meetings on alternate Sundays. Meets have up to a dozen races.

RUNNING
Runners looking for something a good deal more serious than a jog around the block should contact the **Hash House Harriers** *(☎282-9161)* and **Harriettes** *(☎258-5144)*. See Saturday's *Bangkok Post* for details.

Asia's own Hash House Harriers club is now a global phenomenon, some say the world's most popular running club, with membership in the thousands, hailing from every continent including Antarctica. It was founded by six British expatriates in colonial Singapore, in 1938. The inspiration was one A.S. Gisbert, who decided to work off an awful hangover by running round the sports field of the city's Selangor Club.

The idea spread to his drinking buddies, who all ate in the club's dining room (hence "hash house"). Their sporting activities were based around the consumption of beer and the loose emulation of harriers (hunting dogs, used to track and chase hares), with one runner playing the hare, leaving clues meant to confuse the hounds, played by fellow members.

The "Hashers" are legendary for their willingness to run over every conceivable terrain, no matter what the circumstances. In one famous exploit, a band of them stumbled upon Communist guerillas during the Malayan Insurgency of the 1950s, as they thrashed heedlessly through the jungle.

"On-on-on," the famous Hasher rallying cry, refers to the dinner and drinking bash that takes place after every sortie, the not-so-secret basis of their social success and the source of their self-descriptive sobriquet, "drinkers with a running problem."

TENNIS
Some of the best public courts:
- **Amom & Sons**   8 Soi Amom, 3 Sukhumvit 49 ☎392-8442–3
- **Bang Kun Non Court**   58 Soi Watanasuk Charansnidvongs ☎424-2391
- **Bangkae Tennis Court 53**   10/14 Soi 53 Phetkasem, off map **5E1** ☎413-0144
- **Bangna Tennis Court and Swimming Pool**   57/455 Soi Bangna Coml. Bangna-Trad ☎393-8276–8
- **Central Tennis Courts**   Soi Attakarn Prasit/Soi Jusmag, off South Sathorn Rd., map **7F7** ☎213-1909
- **Golden Golf & Tennis**   7 Soi Soonvijai, 1 New Phetburi, map **7C7** ☎318-1651
- **Kanpaibool Tennis Court**   10 Soi 40, Sukhumvit Rd. ☎391-8784
- **Ngarmvongvan Tennis Court**   60 Ngarmvongvan ☎588-3055
- **Sathip Swimming Pool-Tennis-Badminton**   140 Soi 56, Sukhumvit Rd. ☎331-2037
- **Sivalai Club House**   168 Soi Anantapoom Issarapharp ☎411-2649
- **Soi Klang Racquet Club**   8 Sukhumvit Rd., Soi 49 (Klang) ☎391-0936/392-8442

To locate tennis courts in the Sukhumvit Rd. area, see the map on page 187. The courts at the **Rose Garden** are available to visitors but are often fully booked on weekends.

THAI BOXING
Boxing (Muay Thai) is a popular spectator sport. Thais are such congenial hosts that it's easy to forget they are a martial people, whose heroes cut and hacked their way to power throughout their history. This may be "the land of smiles," but it was not charm and conflict-avoidance that kept Thailand "the land of the free." Their national sport is considered by many to be the ultimate martial art.

Thailand's traditional enemies, the Burmese, first commented upon this ferocious form of unarmed fighting, in a 15thC record noting that such trials by combat decided the fate of Thai kings against pretenders to their thrones. It is recorded that on one famous occasion in modern times, five of Hong Kong's top *kung-fu* masters were each knocked out in a total elapsed ring time of under $6\frac{1}{2}$ minutes. Thais have also floored

Asian contenders from China, Taiwan, Singapore, Korea and Japan and also those from Holland, Germany, France and the US.

Thai boxing must be seen to be appreciated. It is a unique combination of gymnastics, lightning *kung-fu* kicks and Western boxing techniques: fighters wear boxing gloves but use almost every part of the body — bare feet, elbows, knees and shoulders — to floor an opponent. Kicks and punches are actually disdained as mere softeners for more serious thrusts from elbows and knees. Thai boxers have won medals in past Olympics, and at home they are heroes.

Thai boxing is staged at **Lumphini Stadium** *(Rama IV Rd., map 7 F7, Tues, Fri, Sat from 6pm)* and **Ratchadamnoen Stadium** *(Ratchadamnoen Ave., map 6 B4, Mon, Wed, Thur from 6pm; Sun from 5pm)*. Ticket prices range from B150–500, and tickets are often sold out.

Sports in Thailand

Trekking in some of the country's 53 national parks, especially in the N Thailand hills, and water sports in the SE resorts on the Gulf of Thailand and the SW resorts on the Andaman Sea or in the environs of the hundreds of islands off the country's 2,400km (1,500-mile) coastline (many now protected in marine national parks), provide some of the kingdom's most appealing diversions. See also under individual destinations in DAY TRIPS FROM BANGKOK, pages 251-257 and LONGER TRIPS, pages 258–270.

SEA SPORTS
With its warm, clear seas and tropical-island beaches, Thailand is paradise for the watersports enthusiast. Some of the most breathtaking and unspoiled coral reefs left on the planet are an attraction for divers. Intrepid anglers can wrestle with marlin or stingray. Tourists can learn to parasail or windsurf in forgiving waters that do not require a wet suit. Or you could just float around the islands on a luxury liner . . . .

The Tourism Authority of Thailand has a free *Thailand Sea Sports* brochure that lists operators for all of the activities described below in Phuket, Pattaya, Chumphon and Ko Samui.

Cruising
Cruising to popular offshore islands from PHUKET, PATTAYA, HUA HIN or CHA-AM can be done on everything from converted Chinese "junks" to *Miami Vice*-style speedboats. You can also cruise in comfort on a small luxury liner, with onboard swimming pools and entertainment.

Diving
The warm, clear waters of the **Andaman Sea** near PHUKET make it a paradise for divers. The **Similan islands** (off the SW coast) were recently rated among the world's ten most beautiful locations for underwater scenery by *Skin Diving* magazine in the United States. This area

has coral reefs and stunning underwater life, with visibility up to 12m (40 feet) and water temperatures of 80–85˚F — no wet suits required for typical dives to depths of 70 or 80 feet (40m). Other first-class dive spots are **Ko Racha**, **Shark Point**, **Phi Phi** and **Elephant Rock**.

Most grounds can be reached within two hours on motorized craft, which converge on these areas daily. PATTAYA has war wrecks for extra thrills, in depths less than 28m (90 feet), with visibility up to 30m (100 feet) on good days. In short, the water is so clear and shallow, you can see the boat from the surface before diving to it.

Beginners go for shallow dives off the nearby islands of **Ko Lan**, **Ko Khrok** and **Ko Sak**, all less than an hour's ride from Pattaya. **Certificate courses** are offered in Phuket, Pattaya and Ko Samui from both **NAUI** (National Association of Underwater Instructors) and **PADI** (Professional Association of Diving Instructors). Courses usually take a week or less.

The best book on diving here is *Thailand: Kingdom Beneath the Sea*, by Ashley J. Boyd and Collin Piprell *(Artasia Press, Bangkok)* and there is a useful brochure offered free from the tourism authority.

If something goes wrong . . . .

Thailand's *only* recompression chamber is at the **Department of Underwater and Aviation Medicine** *(Somdej Pra Pinklao Naval Hospital, Taksin Rd., Thonburi, 24hr ☎ 460-0000 ext. 341; office hours ☎ 468-6100)*. The SE coast, on the Gulf of Thailand, is the only area with a diving physician, at **Apakorn Kiatiwong Naval Hospital** *(Sattahip, Chonburi province, about 26km/16 miles from Pattaya ☎ (038) 601-185)*. From other popular diving spots, such as the south water off Surat Thani or Songkhla or the southwest waters off Phuket, stricken divers must fly by civil aviation (in pressurized aircraft) to Bangkok for help.

Game-fishing

About a dozen major giant species, among them black marlin, barracuda, wahoo, sailfin, seabass, stingray and shark, are abundant in Thailand's warm waters, making game-fishing a popular sport. PHUKET, **Krabi** and the **Phi Phi islands** are centers in the Andaman Sea. On the E coast, in the Gulf of Thailand, the best spots are offshore from PATTAYA and nearby **Ranong**, HUA HIN, **Chumphon**, KO SAMUI and **Surat Thani**.

Fishing tackle is normally supplied on boats, while local shops and department stores are well stocked with gear for sale. Vessels also normally provide live bait, a fighting chair, flying gaff, gloves, harness, lures and knives as necessary. Spear guns are allowed but frowned upon.

Game-fishing excursions run from a single day to several. There are three fishing styles: **deep sea angling** using eight to ten lines, to catch bottom-feeders, **trolling** with two or three lines and **fast trailing**, using two or three lines, with surface bait. There is an annual competition (see SPORTS CALENDAR, page 249).

Parasailing

The best places for parasailing are PATTAYA *(platform in the sea near Ko Lan)* and PHUKET. Major centers will usually have several parasailing rigs and boats spread along the beaches.

Water scooters

It might be very tempting to rent a motorized **water scooter**, but be advised that these are prone to flip over if improperly driven and so can be dangerous to novices.

Windsurfing

Windsurfing on PHUKET is headquartered at **Patong**, **Karon** and **Kata** beaches and at **Jomtien** beach in PATTAYA, where there are many schools and several organized races each year. One of these takes place during the **Pattaya Festival** in April; the others are the **Thailand Open** (November) and the **Siam World Cup** (December). The best time of year for windsurfing is from mid-February to April *(winds around Beaufort 3-5, waves offshore up to 1m/3ft).*

Yachting

Yachting has become a popular pastime over the past five years, with most crafts dropping anchor off PHUKET island, before sailing among those nearby, either N to **Surin** and **Similan** or NE to **Phang-Nga Bay**, with the stunning limestone outcrops featured in the James Bond movie, *Man With the Golden Gun* (see illustration of **Nail Island** on page 264) or SE to the **Phi Phi islands**, recently voted among the world's most beautiful.

Rental yachts of 9–16m (30 feet to 50 feet) are available, chartered crewed or bareboat. All boats come equipped with snorkeling gear, with diving equipment available on request. Private boats call in **Chalong Bay** at the s tip of Phuket *(you must report to Immigration and Customs within 12hrs of arrival; a month or longer stay is normally granted).*

The best yachting season is from November to May (wind 20–25 knots, Beaufort force 3–4, mean temperature 27°C, seas light to calm).

A smaller yachting center is at **Jomtien Beach** in PATTAYA, where island-hopping to **Ko Lan** and **Ko Sak** is popular. A useful magazine-format guide with marine charts and anchorage information, *Sail Thailand,* was launched in 1991 *(Artasia Press Co. Ltd., PO Box 1996, Bangkok* ☎ *235-3379* [Fx] *237-3218).*

TREKKING

CHIANG MAI is the center for trekking in Thailand, with about a dozen standard tours available in **Doi Inthanon National Park**. As well as the country's highest mountain (2,565m/8,413 feet), the park's attractions include many hiking and elephant trails, waterfalls, nearby hill tribes, a wide variety of native birds and a cool climate in winter.

Treks among hill tribes N of the city should be preceded by a visit to **Chiang Mai University's Tribal Research Center**, which offers a useful booklet on the subject. *(For recommended guides, contact the local TAT office* ☎ *(053) 233-351).*

Other parks with marked trails include **Khao Yai** in the NE, **Phu Kradung** in Loei and **Nam Nao** in Phetchabun. Khao Yai National Park was Thailand's first and sprawls across four provinces: Nakhon Ratchasima, Nakhon Nayok, Prachin Buri and Saraburi. It was listed among the world's top five parks in 1971 and recently selected as an ASEAN Natural Heritage Site.

In **Sai Yok National Park**, through which flows the River Kwai, relics of human habitation dating back to the Old Stone Age have been found; it also has a seven-cascade waterfall. Near KO SAMUI (see PHUKET AND THE SOUTH, page 265) is **Ang Thong Islands National Marine Park**, with more than 40 pristine islands off the w coast of Surat Thani Province.

Hiring a guide

Trails in most parks are unmarked and it is inadvisable for even experienced trekkers to set out without renting a local **guide**. Park offices can usually secure guides for reasonable fees. In Bangkok, contact the **National Park Division** of the Royal Forestry Dept. *(Phahonyothin Rd., Bangkhen* ☎ *579-2791).*

Sports calendar

FEBRUARY
Kite fighting in Sanam Luang, Bangkok. A "battle of the sexes" is fought with kites as surrogates — the cumbersome male *Chula* tries to ensnare the more agile female, *Pakpao*, and drag her back to his turf, while she works to take the air out of his sail. This is also the season for *takro*, a game of putting a rattan ball through a hoop, and *krabi krabong*, Thai swordfighting.

MARCH
Marine Festival in Chumphon features scuba-diving excursions to coral islands, deep-sea fishing competitions, boating and marine rescue and salvage demonstrations.

APRIL
Volvo Women's Open competition, held at Dusit Resort in Pattaya, is Thailand's only World Tour Tennis event.

JULY
Phuket International Marathon, a world-class full- and mini-marathon with international and local runners.

SEPTEMBER
Phichit Boat Races is a regatta of rowed longboats held on the Nan River. • **International Swan Boat Races** are held on the Chao Phraya River after the annual rains in Bangkok. • **Korlae Boat Races** on the Bangnara River are held coincident with Narathiwat Produce Festival.

OCTOBER
Lanna Boat Races feature distinctive *Nan* boats — brightly-painted hollowed logs. • **Phitsanulok Boat Races** are held on the Nan River. • **Sakon Nakhon Boat Races** follow a Wax Castle Festival, wherein

Buddhist temples and shrines are cast in miniature from beeswax and paraded to the temples. • **Chonburi Buffalo Races**, which, like tractor races in the American Midwest, puts the plowmen's water buffaloes to more amusing uses.

NOVEMBER

Phimai Boat Races in Nakhon Ratchasima (Khorat) on the Mun River, near the ancient Khmer city of Phimai. The regatta features boats decorated to resemble the famous Royal Barges of Bangkok. • **Buri Ram Boat Races** are held on the Mun River in Satuek district.

• The famous **Elephant Round-up** takes place in Surin Province, where each year more than 100 trained elephants are put through their paces. • **Thailand Long-boat Races** in Phichit, part of the regional heats that help the Tourism Authority of Thailand to select the nation's best rowers to compete in Asia's regional "dragon boat" races championships, which now draw competitors from around the world.

• The Andaman Sea **Game Fishing Tournament** (see GAME-FISHING, page 246), held around the islands of Krabi, Phi Phi and in Phang-Nga Bay, attracts both local and foreign anglers. • Late in the month, the **Bangkok Marathon**, set mostly along the Chao Phraya River, which the course twice crosses: an international-ranked event.

DECEMBER

Phuket King's Cup Regatta, sponsored by the Phuket Yacht Club. Competitors from Singapore, Malaysia and elsewhere in the region take on Thai yachtsmen in their home waters of the Andaman Sea. • **Siam Windsurf World Championship** is held at Jomtien Beach in Pattaya and attracts internationally-ranked surfers. • **I-San Kite Festival** in the NE town of Buri Ram, features traditional kite fights in surrogate battles of the sexes, with *chula* (male) and *pakpao* (female) kites.

Day trips

Treasures of Thailand

Thailand's abundant attractions include mountain and marine parks, beach resorts, ruined cities, archeological treasures and superb scenery. Many can be reached on a single day trip; the following selection includes **Ayutthaya**, **Ancient City**, **Bang Pa-in**, the **Crocodile Farm**, the **Rose Garden**, **Samphran Elephant Ground and Zoo** and **Kanchanaburi Province**, where the bridge over the river Kwai is located. Descriptions of these can be found below, under DAY TRIPS FROM BANGKOK (pages 251–57).

Other destinations, such as **Phuket and the south**, **Pattaya** or **Chiang Mai and the north**, require — and merit — more complex advance arrangements. The mini-guides to these areas listed here under LONGER TRIPS (pages 258–70) should give you the information you need to plan your trip.

Our detailed **map** of Thailand (opposite) shows all the major places of interest listed in this section.

Day trips from Bangkok

A short distance from Bangkok lie a wide variety of places to visit. Some, such as the ancient city of AYUTTHAYA, require at least a full day's exploration. Others, such as the **Crocodile Farm** and the **Rose Garden**, can be seen in conjunction with others or as a short (half-day) trip.

ANCIENT CITY (Muang Boran)
33km (20 miles) from Bangkok, down the Sukhumvit highway, in Changwat Samut Prakan. 4hr tours (☎) can be arranged through the Muang Boran office on Ratchadamnoen Ave. in Bangkok (☎226-1936 or 224-1057, open 8.30am-5.30pm daily). Cars and vans are available for rent.
This is a kind of outdoor museum containing impressive replicas of ancient buildings (see illustration of royal palace, page 151). A walking tour at a comfortable pace will take about 1½ hours. There are waterside Thai restaurants and craft sales arcades within the grounds. The tours leave from **Democracy Monument**. Here a millionaire with a love of Thai history and architecture has landscaped 81ha (200 acres) of rice fields into the shape of Thailand.

Many of the monuments and buildings are exact replicas; others are miniatures, and some have been reconstructed from existing ruins. Of note is the **Si Sanphet Prasat**, a vast audience chamber rebuilt in such splendor and with no expense spared that it would do justice to the original, which once stood in Ayutthaya.

There is also a reconstructed **Thai fishing village** and several groups of Thai-style houses, all thoughtfully laid out with ponds, artificial waterfalls, wading birds and gibbons. There is a total of 89 different buildings or special sights on the grounds, carefully cataloged in a guide available for purchase on site, *Muang Boran, A City With a Cultural Conscience.*

AYUTTHAYA

Thailand's capital for 417 years, from 1350–1767, Ayutthaya was once one of the world's most magnificent cities. More than 100 temples, most in ruins today, bear witness to its past splendor. The site was carefully chosen at the point where three rivers meet, so that all that was needed to make it into an island was a small canal.

Unfortunately, such natural defenses did not save Ayutthaya from the Burmese, who invaded in 1767 and, not satisfied with merely conquering the city, set about looting it, destroying everything along the way. Left undisturbed for more than a century, the city sank into near-oblivion. Currently, an ambitious scheme to dig all the canals again and to reassemble many of the temples and palaces is underway.

The Chakri dynasty that followed the fall of Ayutthaya, and King Taksin's short reign preceding it in Thonburi, was built on the use of this once-great city and center of Thai civilization as a kind of literary allusion. It was regarded as a paradise lost and regained, on the banks of the Chao Phraya river in Thonburi and Bangkok. Its memory still evokes the full play of national emotions, much as "the glory that was Greece" does for the West.

At least until the reign of Rama V, in the 19thC, everything the Thai court did in Bangkok was meant to replicate or rival what had been cumulatively achieved by the 33 monarchs who had ruled before them in Ayutthaya.

Ironically, even the reconstruction of this once-glorious city has to rely upon outside sources. To study Ayutthaya, it is necessary to go to France, where the sketches of the famous embassy described by Abbé de Choisy (see page 146) are the most thorough extant records of what the city actually looked like in its prime.

GETTING THERE

This spectacular ruined city lies 86km (53 miles) to the N of Bangkok, an easy day's excursion. **Buses** leave the Northern Bus Terminal every ten minutes for the 1½-hour ride. **Trains** leave approximately once an hour from Hualamphong Station. By **boat**, it's a longer journey up the Chao Phraya River. Boats leave daily from Tha Thien pier, near Wat Pho. The *Oriental Queen,* operated by the Oriental Hotel, also makes the trip daily, serving lunch on board.

Special **tours** are available from most tour operators, most of which include a visit to BANG PA-IN (see page 255). The best plan is to travel, by air-conditioned bus, the 1½-hour trip to the first site at **Great Victory Stupa**, and return downriver by boat, which takes about four hours *(four cruise operators)*.

The Tourism Authority of Thailand (TAT) offers a useful **free brochure** on Ayutthaya, which includes guides to accommodation, eating and local transport.

Boat tour operators

- ***Ayutthaya Princess***   From Shangri-La Hotel pier ☎255-9200 Fx255-9216
- **Chao Phraya Express Boat**   Sunday cruise from Maharat pier, also stops at the Royal Folk Arts and Crafts Center in Bangsai; price of ticket depends on which deck you sit on ☎225-3002. All-day cruises leave at either 7.45 or 8am and return by 5 or 5.30pm.
- **Horizon Cruise**   From River City pier ☎538-3491, 538-0335 Fx538-2465
- ***Oriental Queen***   From Oriental Hotel pier ☎236-0400 Fx236-1939, attn: Oriental Queen
- **River Sun Cruise**   From River City pier ☎237-0077 ext. 333, 334 Fx237-7608

TOURING THE AYUTTHAYA AREA

En route to study Thailand's resplendent past, you encounter the makings of its future, on the bus ride upcountry through the suburb of **Patun Thani** or "Lotus City," so called because it is very fertile, and the center of a province within which much fruit is grown. Today, Patun Thani is populated by textile factories and rows of townhouses in massive tract developments. The bus also passes the junior campus of **Thammasat University**.

The **Great Victory Stupa** is the first stop on the bus tour, on the outskirts of Ayutthaya. Built in 1592 to celebrate the defeat of a Burmese army in 1588, the *stupa* is notable for the 108 figures of the Buddha that were once assembled in line around its inner walls. The figures that you will see are reproductions, the originals having been moved to the NATIONAL MUSEUM (see page 194). The *stupa*'s design was influenced by Sri Lankan religious architecture (the Sri Lankan Sinhalese follow the same school of Buddhism as the Thais).

In a small modern shrine nearby is a massive **mural** depicting the famous battle. It also provides some interesting lessons on male bonding in the classical Thai style (on elephant-back). The resident monk at the shrine explains that the army's supreme commander commonly rode to war on the same elephant as his king, carrying signal feathers with which he commanded the movements of his troops from the back of their *howdah* (elephant seat).

The custom was that the supreme commander must never return from battle without his leader, which assured the commander's loyalty and concentrated his mind on keeping his king out of harm's way.

The **Phra Nakhon Si Ayutthaya Historical Park**, a large site in the center of the ancient city, has been included in the UNESCO list of World Heritage Sites since late 1991. The whole of Ayutthaya covers about 2,560sq.km (988 square miles), administratively divided into 16 districts *(amphoes)*.

One temple that managed to escape the attentions of the Burmese relatively unscathed is **Wat Pramane**, across the river from the Royal Palace. The remarkable interior, recently restored, has a wooden ceiling with richly ornamented panels supported by rows of eight octagonal columns.

A fine Ayutthaya-period Buddha sits on the altar, but the most famous Buddha, **Phra Kanthararat**, is in the *viharn,* seated on a throne. This stone Dvaravati Buddha is an excellent example of *Mon* art, which archeologists believe originally came from Wat Pramane in Nakhon Pathom, to the s.

Wat Mahathat

Also important are **Wat Raja Burana** and **Wat Mahathat**. Both were vast, imposing complexes built opposite one another. Wat Raja Burana is surrounded by a wall with monumental gateways and openings, some of which still stand. In the center of the compound is a most impressive *prang* with round *chedis* at the corners.

Wat Mahathat is believed to have been built around 1374; its *prang,* the tallest and most ambitious of its kind, fell down when it reached 46m (150 feet). It was later rebuilt to 50m (164 feet), but only the huge base remains today.

Also worth a visit is the **Chao Sam Phraya National Museum** *(near the junction of Rojana Rd. and Si Sanphet Rd. and opposite the City Hall ☎ open Wed-Sat 9am-4pm)*. It contains many beautiful relics from Lopburi, U-Thong and Ayutthaya.

The museum is administered by the **Ayutthaya Historical Study Center**, also on Rojana Rd. Here are exhibited reconstructions from the city's past and there is a **library** for more serious study *(☎ (035) 244-769 ☎ open daily 9am-4pm)*.

A proper viewing of Ayutthaya takes more than a day; the determined visitor should seek out one of the small hostels for basic but inexpensive accommodation. If you have only a day, either rent a car, or rent a boat and circle the "moat."

BANG PA-IN PALACE

*Tambon Ban Len, Amphoe Bang Pa-In, 40km (25 miles) s of Ayutthaya township.
58km (36 miles) N of Bangkok* **by rail** *and 61km (38 miles)* **by road**. *From
Ayutthaya, take Phahonyothin Rd., turn right at the Km 35 marker for another
7km* 🚌 **Open** *daily 8.30am–12pm, 1–3.30pm* ☎(035) 261-004 or 224-3273.

Most organized trips to AYUTTHAYA (see page 252) include this nearby
country estate, which was built in 1632 as a retreat on the family
property of King Prasat Thong (1630–55) and used by every Ayutthayan
monarch from then on.

The king had the **Chumphon Nikayaram Temple** built on the
grounds, as well as a small palace that sits like a wedding cake on a raised
platform in the middle of the estate's long, narrow lake (400m/1,312 feet
long and 40m/131 feet wide). Both buildings still stand, and there would
be no more to see had not King Mongkut (1851–68) taken an interest in
what had, by the time of his reign, become a deserted ruin unoccupied
for 80 years.

The King made of it a playground for his children and the base for
constructing an eclectic array of small architectural follies for his own
pleasure. There is a **lighthouse-style building** from the top of which
he viewed the stars, the **Wehat Chamrun Palace**, in Chinese style, as
well as a number of European-style buildings and a Chinoiserie guesthouse, recently renovated.

Adding to the whimsical environment is a delightful wooden **gazebo**
where Rama V read Shakespeare to his children (his sons were sent off
to school in England, creating a short line of "old Etonian" monarchs),
with heroic Italian nude sculptures on its main bridge and a family of
eight elephants carefully sculpted from large bushes.

KANCHANABURI PROVINCE

Kanchanaburi City is 120km (75 miles) NW of Bangkok, approximately 2½hrs by
bus. *Air-conditioned buses leave from the Southern Bus Terminal on
Charansamitwong Rd. every 15mins from 5am–7pm (reservations* ☎414-4978).
A regular **train service** *is run by the State Railway of Thailand; trains depart from
Bangkok Noi Railway Station (* ☎411-3102).

*Full information on fares, frequencies and local attractions available from the
local* **Tourism Authority of Thailand (TAT)** *office (Saeng Chuto Rd.* ☎(034)
511-200 ☒511-200, *open daily 8.30am–4.30pm, closed for lunch 12–1pm).
The* **Tourist Police (** ☎512-795) *share the same offices.*

By car, *take Highway 4 to Km 70 (past Nakhon Pathom), then Highway 323
to Ban Pong and on to Kanchanaburi.*

An excursion to this lovely area usually includes a visit to the famous
bridge over the **River Kwai** and the **Allied War Cemetery**, moving
testaments to the suffering that occurred here during World War II.

Kanchanaburi Province is blessed with some of Thailand's most
spectacular scenery — waterfalls, caves, jungle, and two rivers that meet
just outside the provincial capital, **Kanchanaburi City**.

It is hard to believe that this was the site of the infamous Death Railway
of World War II. About 16,000 Allied prisoners-of-war and 49,000 local

slave-laborers died building a bridge for the Japanese, and more than 16,000 are buried in row upon row of beautifully maintained graves at the two **Allied Cemeteries** nearby.

The bridge, made famous by Pierre Boulle's novel and later by the movie *Bridge Over the River Kwai,* was partly destroyed by bombs in April 1945, but has since been rebuilt and is in use today. Railroad enthusiasts can ride the original line all the way to the terminal at **Nam Tok**, near the Burmese border.

Visitors can also visit the small **JEATH War Museum** *(open daily 8.30am-6pm* 🔊*)* in the riverside precincts of **Wat Chaichumpon**, constructed in the form of an actual POW camp. (The acronym JEATH derives from Japan, England, America, Australia, Thailand and Holland, recalling the national origins of the captors and those captive in this living hell set in a tropical paradise.) Memorabilia include paintings of the original bridge and photographs of some of the prisoners.

In late November–early December, the annual **River Kwai Bridge Festival** is held, a week-long extravaganza organized by TAT, the State Railway and the Ninth Infantry Division of the Royal Thai Army. Festivities include a light-and-sound show, flower floats, beauty contests for "Miss Love and Peace," arts and crafts exhibitions, concerts and even a mini-marathon run.

On a fast *hang yao,* or long-tailed boat, the 1½-hour trip downriver from the River Kwai Village to **Wang Po** is worth doing. The train-ride back to Kanchanaburi goes along the track built by the Allies and shows the difficulties faced in constructing the line.

Going upstream, a nine-hour trip to **Amphoe Sangkhla Buri** is considered by many to be the highlight of a trip to Kanchanaburi Province. From Amphoe Sangkhla Buri there is a three-hour trek to **Phra Chedi Sam Ong**, or Three Pagoda Pass, a point where the railroad line (before being dismantled) crossed the frontier between Thailand and Burma.

GETTING AROUND

Local transport includes trishaws, which can be rented for two or three hours, as can motorcycles or jeeps on Saeng Chuto or Song Kwai Rds. **Boat trips** to **Lawa Cave** and **Sai Yok Yai Waterfall** leave from Pak Saeng pier at Tambon Tha Sao and round trips take about four hours; boats seat 10–12 people. A trip in a long-tail boat to the headquarters of **Nagarind National Park** takes about an hour from Tha Kradan pier; boats seat 10–12 people.

Contact the Tourism Authority of Thailand in Bangkok for help with hotel reservations and rafting trips.

☙ For a better look at this lush, unspoiled tropical countryside, **rafts** with accommodation are available for leisurely trips up- or downriver. There is also the **River Kwai Village**, a 60-room hotel in the upper valley of **Kwai Noi**, near **Nam Tok**, which is a good base for excursions.

You could also stay on one of the stationary hotels (or "floatels") on the way to Amphoe Sangkhla Buri. It is best to make advance reservations through the Tourism Authority of Thailand in Bangkok.

OTHER ATTRACTIONS NEAR BANGKOK

Crocodile Farm

Virtually across the road from ANCIENT CITY (see page 251) in Changwat Samut Prakarn, about 30km (19 miles) sw of Bangkok. **Crocodile wrestling** *and other animal shows staged hourly from 9–11am and 2–4pm daily; extra shows at 5pm on weekends and holidays* ▩ *Open daily 7am–6pm.*

This is home to some 30,000 crocodiles, making it one of the world's largest establishments of its extraordinary kind. Keeping the crocs company are other critters such as elephants, gibbons, lions and snakes.

Rose Garden (Suan Sam Phran)

30km (18 miles) w of Bangkok on Petchkasem Rd., San Phran district, a journey of about 40mins. **Tours** *can be arranged through most tour operators.* **Open** *daily 8am–6pm* ▩ *garden and Thai cultural show* ☎ *253-0295.*

Set on a bank of the Thachin River, in 24ha (60 acres) of beautifully landscaped gardens, the Rose Garden offers an easy escape from the city and a chance to experience different aspects of Thai culture without traveling all over the country. A cultural show takes place every afternoon, and there are folk dance performances, Thai boxing, cock fights, a Buddhist ordination ceremony, a hill-tribe dance and an opportunity to see elephants at work. You can rent boats, and there are Thai-style guesthouses on the banks of the river.

There are also swimming pools, a playground and a golf course. This is a popular weekend retreat for locals and a great place for children.

Samphran Elephant Ground and Zoo

Open daily 9am–6pm ▩ **Crocodile wrestling** *12.45, 2.20, 4.30pm daily and extra 10.30am show Sun;* **Magic show** *1.15, 3pm daily with extra 11am show Sun;* **Elephant show** *1.45, 3.30pm daily with extra show 11.30am Sun* ☎ *284-1873, 284-0273.*

Just 1km ($\frac{1}{2}$-mile) E of **The Rose Garden** (see above), this 9ha (22-acre) site is yet another crocodile-farm-and-zoo combination, featuring what it claims is the world's largest white crocodile.

Longer trips

Traveling farther afield

Thailand is a country of endless variety for the traveler, from the cultural riches of the north to the perfect golden beaches of the south. The island of Phuket, off the south coast, has for some years been a magnet for the long-haul tourist set, and is a destination in its own right. The south has other riches: unsullied coral reefs and paradise islands that remain — precariously — untrampled.

In a different universe, the resort of Pattaya attracts visitors in search of superb hotels, peerless water sports facilities, and life with the accelerator pedal pushed firmly to the floor.

The final trip in this book takes in the ancient northern city of Chiang Mai, with its wealth of historical and architectural interest. The north offers a more rugged side of Thailand, with superb trekking routes into some spectacular countryside.

Phuket and the south

Southern Thailand, famous for its pure-white sandy beaches, beautiful scenery and tiny tropical islands, seems a world away from the ruins and culture of the North. And the farther south you go, the more different things become. Architecture, food, the people and their way of life all differ enormously.

PHUKET ISLAND

*Buses leave the Southern Bus Terminal in Bangkok three times a day for the 14-hour direct journey, and most agents offer **tours**. Monsoon months are May through October* *i* *Tourist Authority of Thailand office, 73–75 Phuket Rd.* ☎*(076) 212-213, 211-036* [Fx]*213-582.*

Phuket Island, in the Andaman Sea 885km (553 miles) sw of Bangkok, is a province with three districts *(Amphoe)* — Amphoe Muang, Amphoe Thalang and Amphoe Kathu — and a world unto itself, although the total population is only about 140,000. The island is and always has been entirely distinctive in its history and economic development from most of the rest of Thailand.

Phuket's ethnic and cultural makeup has been heavily influenced by its proximity to Malaysia (the N provinces of which were under Thai sovereignty until ceded to the British in the 19thC), and by the waves of Chinese laborers who were brought in to work the mines and plantations. Almost a third of the province's population is Muslim — a mosque is as familiar a sight as a Buddhist temple — while the descendants of the original Chinese immigrants have contributed local holidays, such as the **Vegetarian Festival** (see CALENDAR OF EVENTS, page 180), as well as temples and historical monuments (one of which commemorates the putting down of a Chinese miners' rebellion).

But no one comes to Phuket to study Thai culture or Islam. The beaches, the 39 islets nearby and the pristine waters that surround them, are what most attract travelers.

Phuket is now an international tourist destination in its own right, (much like Bali in Indonesia) where about five times the number of tourists arrive each year as there are permanent residents. There are daily domestic flights from Bangkok, Surat Thani and Hat Yai and daily international flights from Penang and Kuala Lumpur in Malaysia, Singapore and Hong Kong.

More than 10,000 hotel or resort rooms have been tucked into this giant island of 570sq.km/220 square miles (50km/31 miles long and 21km/13 miles at its widest), which is Thailand's largest and about the size of Singapore.

Geography

Phuket is connected to Phang Nga on peninsular Thailand by the **Sarasin Bridge**, a 660m (2,160-foot) concrete causeway that crosses Pak Phra Channel (490m wide/1,600 feet) at its N tip. Most of the resorts are strung along the ten magnificent W coast beaches facing across the Bay of Bengal toward India, with which towns along this coastline are believed to have been trading since Biblical times.

Offshore tin dredging and industry are conveniently centered along the sheltered E coast, facing Krabi on Thailand's peninsular mainland.

Phuket Town, the provincial capital, is 20 miles (32km) SE of the international airport, which is near **Naiyang National Park** and its casuarina-lined beach at the extreme NE of the island *(2½ miles/4km W of the airport)*. This is where giant Ridley sea-turtles come ashore to lay their eggs each winter; a **Turtle Release Festival** is held on April 13.

Getting around

Getting around Phuket is easiest by car or *samlor*. There are also hundreds of motorcycles and four-wheel-drive Suzukis for rent. With good roads and short distances — nowhere is much more than an hour away from anywhere else — the island is a driver's delight, despite being 77 percent mountainous. This also makes it a paradise for trekkers, with attractions such as **Khao Phra Thaes Wildlife Park** and its nearby waterfall, in **Ton Sai Forest Park**, or the 13m (40-foot) cascade that spills into a swimming lagoon in **Bang Pae**.

Steep mountain roads are what make the four-wheel-drive vehicles so much fun; curving and undulating beach roads that meander between rocky coves are what drive bikers wild.

Watching **sunsets** from the hills is a popular pastime for drivers. The best spots are: **Rang Hill** N of and overlooking Phuket Town, with a

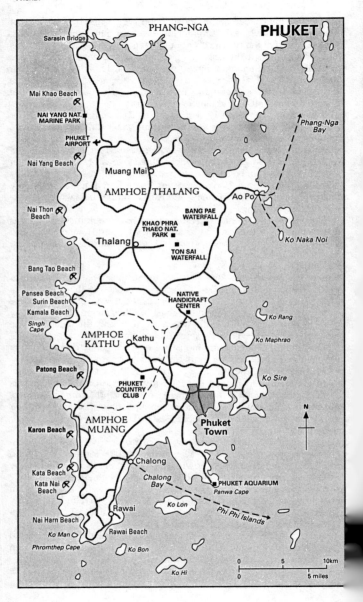

pleasant restaurant, **Tunk-ka Cafe** (☎ *211-500)*, an open pavilion ter-raced into the hillside; **Singh Cape**, 1km (½-mile) from Surin Beach; and **Phromthep Cape**, which marks the extreme s of the island.

PHUKET TOWN

Phuket Town, on the SE coast of the island, is the main city of s Thai-land, and a business and shopping center with a population of 30,000. The town is the island's administrative and market center and frankly does not merit a special trip, unless it is to visit tourist attractions such as **Phuket Aquarium** at Cape Panwa, the **Phuket Butterfly Garden and Aquarium** or the **Native Handicraft Center** on Thepkrasattri Rd.

Some buildings show evidence of Chinese and Portuguese influence and many residents have tried to maintain the original style by conscien-tiously painting and cleaning the intricately patterned carvings and designs on the buildings. However, as of this moment the battle has been all but lost, as more and more residents sell out to property developers.

Worth a look are the **Chartered Bank building** on Phang Nga Rd. and two **Toanit family residences** on Krabi and Yawaraj Rds. The **Provincial Town Hall** was used as the Cambodian French Embassy in the movie, *The Killing Fields*.

✍ The most central accommodation for business travelers is to be found in the **S.T. Hotel** *(5/61 Sakdidej Rd.* ☎ *(076) 223-095* Ⓔ *220-188)*.

PHUKET'S BEACH RESORTS

The beaches on Phuket are its biggest attraction. Virtually all are now dominated by one or more large resort-style hotels, but all but a few also have small, inexpensive bungalows or cabanas, either on the beach or set back in the hills nearby.

Patong

Patong, 15km (9½ miles) from Phuket town, is the safest and most popular beach on the island. Patong's 3km-long (2-mile), curved shore-line protects the bay from the full force of the Andaman Sea swells.

The main area of shops, bungalows, hotels, restaurants and bars runs about four city blocks deep all along its shoreline, between Patong's beachfront Taweewong Rd. and the lanes E off Ratuit Rd., but the predictable pick-up bars concentrate on the sidelanes (especially Bangla Rd.) rather than along the beach road (unlike in Pattaya, where the throng of open-air "go-go" bars gives the main road a seedy quality at night).

✍ At the top end of the market, the plush **Coral Beach Hotel** (☎ *321-106* Ⓔ *321-114)*, part of the Siam Lodge Group, is set on an islet promontory at the s end of the beach.

There are literally scores of service-able alternatives, from the comfortable **Patong Swiss Hotel** (☎ *340-933* Ⓔ *340-522)* and **Holiday Inn**, facing the beach on Taweewong Rd. (☎ *340-608* Ⓔ *340-435)*, to the inexpensive **Nordic Bungalows**, with a small swim-ming pool, around the N corner at Ban-gla Rd. (☎ *321-284* Ⓔ *321-357)*.

The international headquarters of the Hash House Harriers club ("drinkers with a running problem," as they describe themselves; see SPORTS IN BANGKOK, page 243) is the **Expat Rock 'n' Roll Hotel**, a short run from the sea, about five blocks E down Bangla Rd. inland from the beach, on a lane off Ratuit Rd. (☎ *and* Ex *340-300*).

On the small bluff at the N end are some especially pleasant and private converted residences, such as the six units of the **Gene Palmer** (*62/2 Kalim Patong* ☎ *and* Ex *340-346*). Above them is the hillside **Diamond Cliff Resort** (☎ *340-501* Ex *340-507*).

Eating out in Patong is made a joy by the fact that, as in Pattaya, most of its touristic development has been accomplished by foreign tourists who liked the place so much that they settled and became local entrepreneurs. The larger hotels also import fine chefs, particularly those with French owners.

One can sit and look out on the surf breaking over the rocks in **Baan Rim Pa**, a restaurant in the open pavilion style of Thai architecture with a menu developed by Chalie, the famous creator of the Thai Cooking School in Bangkok, run by American Tom McNamara from New York (☎ *and* Ex *340-789*).

A good choice, if your taste is for authentic stateside fare, is **Doolie's Place** (☎ *321-275*), with tasty hamburgers and chicken. Otherwise, you can enjoy excellent Italian food from **Pizzeria Napoli**, prepared by Giulio and Tip Genco (*on Soi Pompong off the beach road* ☎ *340-674*).

There's also **Vecchia Venezia**, run by two scions of restaurant families in Venice, and another Italian restaurant in the Roman style. Amazingly for a place as small as Patong, there are perhaps a dozen Italian restaurants in all, with owners from almost as many locations in Italy, all decked out in the Italian tricolors of red, white and green.

French, German, Scandinavian, Austrian, Japanese, Indian and Chinese cuisines are also to be found in Patong — all prepared by resident foreigners, many of whom have married Thai women and settled here.

In the basement of the **Ocean Supermarket**, on Patong Beach Rd., one can select from 30 kinds of coffee at the **Black Canyon Coffee Legend 2**, a cafe on the Tokyo model.

OTHER BEACHES

Rawai

17km (10½ miles) from Phuket town, with its own **Sea Gypsy Village** on stilts, Rawai is at the extreme S of the island, and its muddy beach is less attractive than many others on the island, so it serves mainly as a setting-off point to many of the small islands out in the bay.

Boat trips are easily organized either at the pier or through one of the many hotels. **Snorkeling** and **scuba equipment** are also available.

North of Patong

Beaches N of Patong, such as contiguous **Mai Khao** and **Nai Yang**, which extend for 9km/5½ miles (*30km/19 miles from Phuket town*), are popular with Thais for picnics.

Other beaches along this coast include: **Nai Thon** and **Bang Tao**, **Pansea** (*24km/15 miles from Phuket town*) and nearby **Surin**, both of which must be reached by descending a cliff, as well as **Kamala**. None of these can really be considered safe for swimming, with strong cross-currents and undertows. You should watch out for, and always heed, the red flags that often go up on all W coast beaches in the rainy season (from May to October).

✍ Choices in Mai Khao and Nai Yang range from inexpensive bungalows on the beach, run by the national park service, to the two "airport resorts," Two good places to stay in are the **Crown Nai Yang Suite Hotel** (☎ 311-516 Fx 311-519) and **Pearl Village**, in 14ha (35 acres) of gardens (☎ 311-376/83 Fx 311-304), popular with in-transit business travelers.

Good hotel choices in Bang Tao include both the **Pacific Islands Club** resort (☎ 324-352), which is akin to a Club Mediterranée resort and founded by former staff, and the brand-new **Sheraton Grande Laguna Beach Resort** (☎ 311-630 Fx 311-637).

Surin can offer the exclusive and extremely expensive **Amanpuri Resort** (☎ 311-394 Fx 311-100).

Between Patong and Rawai

Moving s, there are several great swimming sites, starting with the **Karons** (20km/12$\frac{1}{2}$ miles from Phuket town). **Karon Noi** has now been virtually absorbed into the massive **Le Meridien Hotel** resort complex (☎ 321-480 Fx 321-479). **Karon Yai** has more varied bungalows, small resorts, new condominium complexes and shops. These are separated from the beach by a massive sand dune, behind which carabao bathe in pools formed after rains.

Kata (17km/10$\frac{1}{2}$ miles from Phuket town) is dominated by a massive **Club Mediterranée** (☎ 381-130 Fx 381-462). **Kata Noi** (or "little Kata"), is at the foot of a forested hill. Here, accommodation options include inexpensive bungalows and the **Kata Thani Hotel**, part of the Siam Lodge Group (☎ and Fx 381-124).

Nai Harn (18km/11 miles from Phuket town) is the deep-water home of the stately **Phuket Island Yacht Club and Beach Resort**, where yachties drop anchor behind the protection of Man Island. The beach has a steep drop-off. It's worth making time for sundowners on **The Quarterdeck Terrace** (☎ 381-156 Fx 381-164), with a magnificent view of the bay below.

OTHER SIGHTS

Other interesting sights on Phuket include the rubber plantations, a huge pearl farm on the island of **Ko Naka Noi**, and the **Put Jaw** Chinese temple in the main town, the oldest and largest temple on the island, dedicated to the Goddess of Mercy, Kuan Yin.

The 1907 arrival of the tin-dredger moved mining offshore and stopped the scarring of Phuket, courtesy of Australian Captain Edward Thomas Miles, a feat commemorated in a futuristic monument unveiled at **Saphan Hin** in 1969, 1km ($\frac{1}{2}$ mile) s of Phuket Town. THAISARCO, the country's only tin smelter, is 8km (5 miles) s of town, at Laem Pan Wa.

SPORTS AND ACTIVITIES

Although Phuket is not yet as saturated a tourists' playground as Pattaya, it has an impressive variety of energetic things for visitors to do. There is **horseback riding** at two locations, a **shooting range** that offers the Rambo-set the experience of everything from pistols to M16 assault rifles, a **go-kart track** and **Tarzan's Jungle Bungy Jump** (50m/160 feet dry or wet, into a lagoon below), all of which are short drives from Patong.

There are also three excellent 18-hole golf courses. **Phuket Country Club**, with 160ha (400 acres), is E of Patong Hill on what was a landscape devastated by open-pit tin dredging. It was reborn in late 1988 as the brainchild of a Thai architect, Dr. Suykitti Klangvhisai.

Likewise, **The Blue Canyon**, near the airport in the N of Phuket, turned the lakes created by tin dredgers to advantage as water traps, around which the course is built. It has 49 rooms in its clubhouse and plans a 150-room hotel. The **Banyan Tree Club** is open to guests of three resorts: **Dusit Laguna**, **Pacific Islands Club** and **Sheraton Grande Laguna Beach Resort**. A free golfers' clinic is held on Saturdays at 9am, with free shuttle bus transport from the resorts. The clubhouse also has a squash court and games room with snooker table.

SOUTHERN THAILAND

Krabi, located 180km (112 miles) SE of Phuket, is a typical provincial town of the S. This small and very friendly community is fast developing as another major beach resort, with activity focused on the beautiful beach at **Ao Phra Nang**, just a short ride away. From here, you can rent boats for trips around the islands in the Gulf of Phuket; these can be arranged by one of the many agents along Uttarakit Rd.

One of the most popular of these islands is **Ko Phi Phi**, a two-hour ferry ride W from Krabi *(27 miles/43km)*, with two to four boats departing per day. It is also accessible from Phuket and a two-hour trip from Markham Bay *(29 miles/48km)*, with morning and afternoon departures *(about 8.30am and 2.30pm)*.

Ko Phi Phi actually comprises two islands, **Phi Phi Don** and **Phi Phi Ley**, only the former of which is inhabited. Phi Phi Don, a dumbbell-shaped island of two rocky outcrops linked by a sandbar, is famous for its palm-fringed beaches, translucent water, spectacular coral and powdery white sand. The smaller Phi Phi Ley is renowned for its **Viking Cave**

Nail Island, Phang-Nga Bay

and edible swallows' nests. The Viking Cave contains some interesting but as yet unidentified paintings. The swallows' nests, collected from great heights inside an enormous cavern, form the basis of a thriving industry making bird's-nest soup, a delicacy to the Chinese palate, mainly exported to Hong Kong.

Accommodation is available at about a half-dozen hotels or cabana-style resorts on Phi Phi Don. All development is centered on the two bays at each side of the sandbar.

Back on the mainland, the area around **Phang-Nga Bay**, 94km (58 miles) NE of Phuket, is very scenic. Strange, limestone outcrops loom up out of the water forming all kinds of odd shapes. It is best to go at high tide, when the deep blue waters add to the beauty. Boats can be rented from the Phang-Nga customs pier, which is on the road to Tha Dan, about 4km (2½ miles) outside the town.

The main sights around Phang-Nga Bay are: **Ko Phing Kan**, now touted as **James Bond Island** because scenes from the movie *The Man With The Golden Gun* were filmed here; **Ko Panyi**, for visits to the fishing village on stilts; **Ko Tapu**, because it's just so strange, like a giant spike driven into the Andaman Sea; the archway big enough for boats to pass through at **Tham Lot** with stalactites looming overhead for a distance of about 50m (160 feet); and the beautiful waters of the hidden grotto at **Tham Kaeo**.

There are also some attractive resorts on the other side of the peninsula, on the Gulf of Thailand, particularly **Ko Samui**. For those traveling directly to Ko Samui from the capital, the options are a direct Bangkok Airways turboprop flight *(three times a day)*, or the 12-hour train journey to Surat Thani *(2 trains daily)*, a three-hour boat ride from the island *(30km/18½ miles)* and 651km (406 miles) from Bangkok. There are also connecting flights from Phuket and Hat Yai.

Ko Samui was once touted as the "Phuket of the E coast," and is about half its size *(21km/13 miles at its widest and 25km/15½ miles long)*, but development never really took off, and it has remained a very pleasant, relatively unspoiled island. "Relative" is the operative word: the island can still offer a range of water sports, restaurants from European to Arabian, shopping and nightlife. There are two ferry services, from **Ban Don** *(15mins)* and **Don Sak** *(1hr)* to **Na Thon**, the main town — and landing-place — on the island, from whence a 50km (31-mile) beltway (ring road) circles the coast. You can either go NE through **Maenam**, **Boput** and **Chaweng**, or SE toward **Lamai Beach** and its unique rock formations, most popular with backpackers.

Chaweng is the main beach, where accommodation is plentiful. Motorbikes for rent are the most popular transport. The best white sand beaches are on the E coast, the other coasts have mostly rocky coves. Samui is part of an archipelago whose nearby N islets comprise **Ang Thong Islands National Marine Park**. **Buffalo fighting** is a popular spectator sport at festival times such as Chinese New Year and Songkran (see CALENDAR OF EVENTS, page 178).

On the same coast, but much nearer to Bangkok, is **Hua Hin**, 233km (145 miles) from the capital (a four-hour bus journey). Hua Hin is popular with Thais as a quiet and relaxing weekend retreat from Bangkok. The Thai Royal Family spend part of the summer here at their palace, **Klai Klangwan**, built in the 1920s by King Prajadhipok (Rama VII) and Thailand's first beach resort. It has a golf course and a 3km (2-mile) beach.

Just 27km (17 miles) along the road N toward Phetchburi lies **Cha-am**, even quieter than Hua Hin and with a finer beach.

  At **Phang-Nga**, the **Phang-Nga Bay Resort** *(20 Thadan, Panyee, Phang-Nga ☎ (076) 411-067-70)* is a first-class 90-room hotel by the beach.

On **Ko Samui**, try the **Coral Bay Resort** *(9 Moo 2, Tambol Bophut, Ko Samui, Surat Thani ☎ (077) 272222 ext. 201)*.

A very civilized place to stay in **Hua Hin** is the **Railway Hotel** (*Damnoen Kasem Rd.*), which is set in beautiful gardens. At nearby **Cha-am**, the first-class **Regent Cha-am Resort** *(794/21 Cha-am Beach, Phetchburi* ☎ *(032) 471-480-91)* offers a range of sporting facilities.

FURTHER READING

There are entire guidebooks and tourist maps devoted to just Phuket, or Phuket and the s of Thailand. Besides an extensive booklet in its "Exotic Thailand" series, available from TAT, there are two free tourist guides distributed on the island, *Phuket*, in vestpocket size, published monthly by Shilpa Co. Ltd *(* ☎ *253-5072* Ⓕ*253-0593)* and *Thailand South*, in magazine size, published monthly by Pranee Kaewkool for Asean Journals Co. Ltd *(* ☎ *332-4600* Ⓕ *332-3565)*.

In addition, *Phuket, Phi Phi & Krabi* is a monthly magazine published by Artasia Press Co. Ltd. *(* ☎ *235-3379* Ⓕ*237-3218)*. All of these publishers have offices in both Bangkok and Phuket. Thaiways produces free maps of Phuket, available at most hotels. Compass Publishing in Singapore produces a *Phuket Planner Map* and Prannok Witthaya Publishing House in Bangkok has a bilingual, Thai–English *Tourist Map, Phuket Island*. These last two are sold in souvenir stores.

Pattaya

A resort of a very different character from Hua Hin is Pattaya. Touted as "Thailand's Riviera" and the "Queen of Asia's Resorts," it was first developed as an "R&R" (Rest and Recreation) center for American soldiers on leave from the Vietnam War. It lies on the E side of the Gulf of Thailand, 147km (91 miles) from Bangkok, about a two-hour drive along a relatively fast main road. Air-conditioned buses leave from Don Muang airport, and travel direct to Pattaya *(9am, noon and 8pm)*. Public buses leave at regular intervals from the Eastern Bus Terminal on Sukhumvit Rd.

Pattaya is not everybody's idea of the perfect beach resort. It is crowded, noisy and expensive, and certainly no place for a quiet, away-from-it-all weekend. Its developers have focused on the Recreation and dropped the Rest from its R&R heritage. Pattaya is all about having fun, and if you want to do something more than swim and sunbathe on a deserted beach, this is the resort for you.

Every water sport under the sun can be practiced in Pattaya: waterskiing, windsurfing, snorkeling, scuba diving, parasailing and anything else you can think of, with lessons available although sometimes far from professional. All the necessary equipment can be rented, either from your hotel or at the beach.

For a temporary respite from the hectic pace, there are beautiful islands off Pattaya's shore, where the waters are clearer and the snorkeling more interesting. It is possible to rent a boat for a very modest charge and take a picnic to any or all of these islands.

At night neon lights flash, "The Strip" along the 1.5km (1-mile) Central Pattaya beachfront fills up, and there are nightclubs, bars and discos. The full length of the beach is 4km ($2\frac{1}{2}$ miles), with the N being more sedate and the S especially seedy. Prostitutes of various kinds ply their trade among the thousands of gaping tourists. Many visitors just sit at an outside bar watching the activity and listening to the uncomplicated negotiations.

In among all this activity are some excellent restaurants specializing in seafood but covering every cuisine imaginable. The "shop till you drop" set are catered to with countless tourist outlets. Jeeps with giant wheels and rollbars, vintage sports cars and heavy "CC" motorcycles are available to rent at the curbside. Rock music blasts from every bar and vehicle cruising The Strip. It feels like an adults-only fantasyland based on the movie *American Graffiti*.

There are rooms for every taste and budget, as well as condominium blocks with apartments owned by regulars from Germany, Switzerland, Hong Kong, France and Italy. Within the environs of Pattaya are bowling alleys, billiard halls, shooting galleries, archery, tennis, golf, Go-karts and a Thai cultural show at **Nong Nooch Village**, a short drive up North Pattaya Rd. from the resort town.

Pattaya is a giant theme park whose unashamed subject is *sanuk*, or "have fun" in the Thai language. Despite the naysayers, it remains a beautiful place and has quite enough wholesome attractions to attract family travelers as well as its more legendary clientele of prowling males.

Deep-sea fishing near Pattaya is very popular with Thais and visitors. An expedition can be organized at the **Bang Sare Resort**, just outside Pattaya, or through the **Thailand Game Fishing Association** *(399 Siri Lane, Silom Rd., Bangkok* ☎ *234-7744)*. Species of fish include mackerel, bonito, barracuda, marlin, giant grouper, red snapper, rays and black-tip sharks.

✎ Pattaya has a wide choice of excellent places to stay. Two of the finest hotels are the **Royal Cliff Beach Hotel** *(Pattaya Beach Resort* ☎*(038) 421-421* ⚡*(66-038) 429-926* 🍴 ⚓*)*, which perches on a headland just outside the main town, and the **Royal Garden Resort** *(218 Beach Rd.* ☎*(038) 428-126)*, located right on the beach in the heart of the bustling town.

Chiang Mai and the north

Chiang Mai city sits in a valley 300m (980 feet) above sea level and 710km (443 miles) NW of Bangkok, capital of the 20,000sq.km (7,720 square-mile) province of the same name. Although the second largest city in Thailand, Chiang Mai is still 40 times smaller than the capital. Good air, rail and road links make it very accessible.

- **By bus:** Air-conditioned buses leave Bangkok's Northern Bus Station almost every hour for an eight-hour ride. Private bus companies also offer tours to Chiang Mai and the N.
- **By rail:** Trains, leaving Hualamphong Station, take almost 12 hours, although an overnight trip is more comfortable.

- **By air:** Flights on Thai Airways take about an hour from Bangkok, with usually five flights a day. Daily flights are also available from other northern cities such as Chiang Rai, Phitsanuloke, Phrae and Mae Hong Son. Limited services also operate from Nan and Lampang.

CHIANG MAI

Chiang Mai was founded by King Mengrai in 1296 as capital of his rapidly expanding Lannathai kingdom. After flourishing for 250 years it was captured by the Burmese in 1556, and the Lannathai kingdom became a vassal state of Burma.

The Burmese remained for more than 200 years. After repeated attempts, they were finally expelled first from Ayutthaya and later from Chiang Mai. Chiang Mai remained semi-autonomous and isolated from the new capital city of Bangkok until the late 19thC. It only became easily accessible from Bangkok in the late 1920s.

As a result of its checkered history and long isolation, Chiang Mai has developed along very different lines from Bangkok. This is immediately evident in the art and architecture of the city, much of which survives.

There are more than 300 temples, most of which are in the traditional northern style, with colored tile roofs in two or three levels coming down very low over the side walls, finely carved and gilded wooden pediments and naves flanked by pillars. The four most important temples within the city are **Wat Chiang Man, Wat Chedi Luang, Wat Phra Singh** and **Wat Chet Yot**.

Chiang Mai is also the country's main center for tribal handicrafts. A recent revival of many traditional cottage industries makes it an interesting place to shop. Main shopping areas in the town are **Ta Phae Rd.**, where most things can be found, the **Night Bazaar** on Changkhlan Rd., a great place to find hill-tribe handicrafts, and the regular markets such as **Warorot** on Chang Moi Rd. and the flower market at **Suan Buak Hat** by Suan Prung Gate.

Chiang Mai National Museum *(on the superhighway near Wat Chet Yot, open Wed-Sun 9am-noon, 1-4pm)* has good examples of Buddhas and other artifacts from the Chiang Saen, Haripunchai, Sukhothai, Lopburi and Ayutthaya periods. It also contains other objects peculiar to the N, such as elephant howdahs, hill-tribe costumes and northern-style cookware.

This is a good base for exploring other interesting places in N Thailand. One popular destination is the magnificent **Wat Phrathat**, on the mountain known as **Doi Suthep**, 16km (10 miles) NW of Chiang Mai. Minibuses leave from **White Elephant Gate** several times a day.

The road up to Wat Phrathat offers splendid views of Chiang Mai and the northern countryside. All vehicles must stop at the foot of the final peak; visitors then walk up 290 steps, flanked by a *naga* (sacred snake sculpture atop the balustrades) on either side, in order to reach the temple grounds at some 1,000m (3,280 feet).

Just 4km (2½ miles) from Wat Phrathat lies **Phuping Palace**, the summer residence of the Royal Family. The grounds are open to the

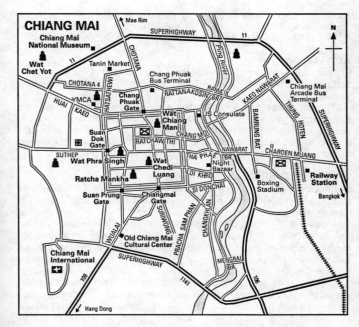

public *(Fri-Sun 8.30am-4.30pm)*, provided the Royal Family is not in residence at the time. The gardens, which are always in bloom but are at their best in January, are quite spectacular.

The nearby village of **Bo Sang** is the place from which Thailand's famous handpainted umbrellas derive. Other popular craft communities are on **Wualai Rd.** for silverware (at least 92.5 percent pure by law), at **San Kamphaeng** for cottons and silks, and **Chiang Mai-Hang Dong Rd.** for lacquerware. The city is also the market center for the hill tribe communities centered in the surrounding mountains and to the N in the **"Golden Triangle"** area, around **Chiang Rai**. There is no better place, apart from the hill tribe villages themselves, in which to buy the marvelous craft works and clothing made by the tribes.

Chiang Mai is also the country's **celadon pottery** center (see SHOPPING, page 232).

The **Rincome Hotel** *(Huey Kaew Rd.* ☎ *(053) 221044* 🏊 '♟' *)* is located 4km (2½ miles) from the center of Chiang Mai, with large grounds accommodating an Olympic-sized swimming pool, The **Chiang Inn** *(100 Chang Klan Rd.* ☎ *(053) 235-655* ♟ *)* is situated in the center of Chiang Mai, with a nightclub, and a shopping arcade next door. A new luxury resort hotel, the **Regent Resort**, part of the Regent group, is due to open in late 1994 on a site in the Mae Rim Valley, around 20 minutes from the city. Its design style is promised to blend Chinese, Indian and other influences.

☰   There are a number of very good restaurants in the city. For a traditional northern-style *khantoke* dinner, complete with a northern classical dance show, try the **Old Chiang Mai Cultural Centre** *(185/3 Wualai Rd. ☎(052) 235-097)*.

ACTIVITIES

Chiang Mai is Thailand's main center for **trekking** (see page 247). **Rafting** on the Kok River from Tha Thon s to Chiang Mai is also popular.

The **Elephant Training Centre** is at the Km 10 marker on Mae Rim–Samoeng Route *(30km/19 miles from town)*. There are daily demonstrations from 9.30–11am (▨) and a 2½-hour jungle tour on elephant-back is offered afterwards *(▨ ☎(053) 236-069)*. **Lanna Golf Course**, at Nong Hoi, 4km (2½ miles) from town, is open to the public.

NORTHERN THAILAND

Sukhothai, the first capital of Thailand, lies 447km (297 miles) N of Bangkok and about 330km (206 miles) s of Chiang Mai. Trains for Chiang Mai, stopping at Phitsanuloke, leave Bangkok three times a day. Buses leave Bangkok twice a day and Thai Airways fly to Phitsanuloke once a day. From there, buses, minibuses and *songthaws* ply the 55km (34-mile) route to Sukhothai. Trains and air-conditioned buses make the trip from Chiang Mai.

The complex at Sukhothai is so vast and interesting that you need to plan your route and time carefully. First visit the **Ramkamhaeng National Museum** *(12km/7½ miles outside new Sukhothai, open Wed-Sun)*, for an idea of what there is to see, and, of course, of the history of the city. Consider staying more than a day: there are hotels in new Sukhothai. Bring good walking shoes and a map.

The main temple site is at **Wat Mahathat**, inside the city walls. Surrounded by walls and a moat, with some 198 *chedis*, and some of the original Buddhas intact, it is thought to date back to the 13thC and the first king of the Sukhothai dynasty. It was completely remodeled in 1345 by King Lo Thai, who added the lotus bud motif peculiar to Sukhothai art and architecture.

Other main sights in the complex are **Wat Sri Sawai**, **Wat Trapang Thong** and **Wat Phra Phai Luang**, whose extensive remains are second only to those of Wat Mahathat.

Clothing sizes chart

LADIES
Suits and dresses

Australia	8	10	12	14	16	18
France	34	36	38	40	42	44
Germany	32	34	36	38	40	42
Italy	38	40	42	44	46	
Japan	7	9	11	13		
UK	6	8	10	12	14	16	18
USA	4	6	8	10	12	14	16

Shoes

USA	6	$6\frac{1}{2}$	7	$7\frac{1}{2}$	8	$8\frac{1}{2}$
UK	$4\frac{1}{2}$	5	$5\frac{1}{2}$	6	$6\frac{1}{2}$	7
Europe	38	38	39	39	40	41

MEN
Shirts

USA, UK Europe, Japan	14	$14\frac{1}{2}$	15	$15\frac{1}{2}$	16	$16\frac{1}{2}$	17
Australia	36	37	38	39.5	41	42	43

Sweaters/T-shirts

Australia, USA, Germany	S		M		L		XL
UK	34		36-38		40		42-44
Italy	44		46-48		50		52
France	1		2-3		4		5
Japan			S-M		L		XL

Suits/Coats

UK, USA	36	38	40	42	44
Australia, Italy, France, Germany	46	48	50	52	54
Japan	S	M	L	XL	

Shoes

UK	7	$7\frac{1}{2}$	$8\frac{1}{2}$	$9\frac{1}{2}$	$10\frac{1}{2}$	11
USA	8	$8\frac{1}{2}$	$9\frac{1}{2}$	$10\frac{1}{2}$	$11\frac{1}{2}$	12
Europe	41	42	43	44	45	46

CHILDREN
Clothing

UK					
Height (ins)	43	48	55	60	62	
Age	4-5	6-7	9-10	11	12	13
USA					
Age	4	6	8	10	12	14
Europe					
Height (cms)	125	135	150	155	160	165
Age	7	9	12	13	14	15

CONVERSION FORMULAE

To convert	Multiply by
Inches to Centimeters	2.540
Centimeters to Inches	0.39370
Feet to Meters	0.3048
Meters to feet	3.2808
Yards to Meters	0.9144
Meters to Yards	1.09361
Miles to Kilometers	1.60934
Kilometers to Miles	0.621371
Sq Meters to Sq Feet	10.7638
Sq Feet to Sq Meters	0.092903
Sq Yards to Sq Meters	0.83612
Sq Meters to Sq Yards	1.19599
Sq Miles to Sq Kilometers	2.5899
Sq Kilometers to Sq Miles	0.386103
Acres to Hectares	0.40468
Hectares to Acres	2.47105
Gallons to Liters	4.545
Liters to Gallons	0.22
Ounces to Grams	28.3495
Grams to Ounces	0.03528
Pounds to Grams	453.592
Grams to Pounds	0.00220
Pounds to Kilograms	0.4536
Kilograms to Pounds	2.2046
Tons (UK) to Kilograms	1016.05
Kilograms to Tons (UK)	0.0009842
Tons (US) to Kilograms	746.483
Kilograms to Tons (US)	0.0013396

Quick conversions

Kilometers to Miles	Divide by 8, multiply by 5
Miles to Kilometers	Divide by 5, multiply by 8
1 meter =	Approximately 3 feet 3 inches
2 centimeters =	Approximately 1 inch
1 pound (weight) =	475 grams (nearly $\frac{1}{2}$ kilogram)
Celsius to Fahrenheit	Divide by 5, multiply by 9, add 32
Fahrenheit to Celsius	Subtract 32, divide by 9, multiply by 5

American Express Travel Guides

spanning the globe....

EUROPE
Amsterdam, Rotterdam
 & The Hague
Athens and the
 Classical Sites
Barcelona, Madrid &
 Seville
Berlin, Potsdam &
 Dresden
Brussels
Dublin
Florence and Tuscany
London
Paris
Prague
Provence and the
 Côte d'Azur
Rome
Venice
Vienna & Budapest

NORTH AMERICA
Boston and New
 England
Los Angeles & San
 Diego
Mexico
New York
San Francisco and
 the Wine Regions
Toronto, Montréal &
 Québec City
Washington, DC

THE PACIFIC
Australia's
 Major Cities
Hong Kong & Taiwan
Singapore &
 Bangkok
Tokyo

Clarity and quality of information, combined with outstanding maps — the ultimate in travelers' guides

Index

- Page numbers in **bold** type indicate main entries.
- *Italic* page numbers indicate illustrations and maps.
- SINGAPORE index: this page. BANGKOK index: page 280.
- See also the LIST OF STREET NAMES on pages 287–8.

Singapore

Bangkok

List of street names

- Listed below are all streets mentioned in the text that fall within the area covered by our color maps of the two cities: Singapore maps **3** and **4** and Bangkok maps **5–7**.
- Map numbers are printed in **bold** type. Some smaller streets are not named on the maps, but the map reference given below will help you locate the correct neighborhood.

Singapore

Alexandra Rd., off **3**D1
Anson Rd., **4**E4–F4
Arab St., **4**B5
Armenian St., **4**C4

Baghdad St., **4**B5
Beach Rd., **4**B6–C5
Bencoolen St., **4**C4–B5
Bideford Rd., **3**B3
Boat Quay, **4**D4
Boon Tat St., **4**E4
Bras Basah Rd., **4**C4–5
Buffalo Rd., **4**C4
Bugis St., **4**B5
Bukit Timah Rd., **3**A3–4B4
Bussorah St., **4**B5

Canning Rise, **4**C4
Cavenagh Rd., **3**A3–B3
Cecil St., **4**E4
Change Alley, **4**D5
Chatsworth Rd., off **3**C1
Cheng Yan Pl., **4**B5
Clemenceau Ave., **3**A3–D3
Coleman St., **4**C4–D4
Collyer Quay, **4**D5
Connaught Drive, **4**D5
Cross St., **3**D3–4E4
Cuppage Rd., **3**B3
Cuppage Tce., **3**B3
Cuscaden Rd., **3**B1–2

Duxton Rd., **3**E3

East Coast Parkway, **4**E5–D6
Emerald Hill, **3**B3
Empress Pl., **4**D4
Erskine Rd., **4**E4
Esplanade,The, **4**D4
Eu Tong Sen St., **3**E3–4D4
Exeter Rd., **3**B3–C3

Fullerton Rd., **4**D5

Grange Rd., **3**B2–C1

Havelock Rd., **3**D3–4D4
Hill St., **4**C4

Jalan Besar, **4**B5–A5
Jalan Kubor, **4**B5
Jalan Rumbia, **3**C3
Jalan Sultan, **4**B5
Java Rd., **4**B6
Jervois Rd., **3**C1

Kaday Awallur St., **4**E4
Kandahar St., **4**B5
Keong Saik Rd., **3**E3
Kerbau Rd., **4**B4
Killiney Rd., **3**C3

Lloyd Rd., **3**C3

Magazine Rd., **3**D3
Maxwell Rd., **4**E4

Miller St., **4**C5
Mosque St., **4**D4
Mount Elizabeth, **3**B3
Murray St., **4**E4
Murray Tce., **4**E4
Muscat St., **4**B5

Nassim Hill, off **3**B1
Nassim Rd., **3**B1
New Bridge Rd., **4**D4
Norris Rd., **4**B5
North Boat Quay, **4**D4
North Bridge Rd., **4**C4–B6

Orange Grove Rd., **3**A1
Orchard Blvd., **3**B1–2
Orchard Rd., **3**B2–4C4
Outram Rd., **3**D2–E3
Oxley Rise, **3**C3

Pagoda St., **4**D4
Peking St., **4**D4
Penang Lane, **4**C4
Penang Rd., **3**C3–4C4
Petain Rd., **4**A5
Phillip St., **4**D4
Prinsep St. **4**B4

Queen St., **4**C4–B5

Race Course Lane, **4**A4–5
Race Course Rd., **4**A4
Raffles Ave., **4**D5
Raffles Blvd., **4**C5

Raffles Quay, **4E4**
River Valley Rd.,
3C2–4D4
Robinson Rd., **4E4**
Rochor Rd., **4B5–C5**

Scotts Rd., **3B2**
Seah St., **4C5**
Selegie Rd., **4B4**
Seng Poh Rd., **3D2**
Serangoon Rd., **4B4–A5**

Shenton Way, **4E4–F4**
Somerset Rd., **3B3**
South Bridge Rd.,
4D4
Stamford Rd., **4C4–5**
Stevens Rd., **3A2**
Sultan Gate, **4B5**

Tanglin Rd., **3B1**
Tanjong Pagar Rd.,
3F3–4E4

Tank Rd., **3C3**
Telok Ayer St., **4E4**
Temple St., **4D4**
Tiong Bahru Rd.,
3D2
Trengganu St.,
3E3–4D4

Victoria St., **4C4–A6**

Waterloo St., **4C4–B5**

Bangkok

Attakarn Prasit Rd., **7F7**

Bamrung Muang Rd.,
5C3–6C4
Boriphat Rd., **5D3**

Captain Bush Lane, **6E4**
Chakraphet Rd., **5D3**
Charoen Krung (New
Rd.), **5D3–6F5**
Chartered Bank Lane,
6F4
Chetuphon Rd., **5D2–3**
Convent Rd., **7E6–F6**

Decho Rd., **6E5–
F5**

Gaysorn Rd., **7D7**

Henri Dunant Rd.,
7D6–E6

Issarapharp, **5D1–E3**

Kasemsan, **7C6–D6**

Lad Ya Rd., **5F3–
6E4**
Lang Suan, **7D7–E7**
Lanluang Rd., **6C4–5**

Mahesak Rd.,**6F5**
Mangkon Rd., **6D4**

Naphrathat Rd., **5C2**
New Rd. (Charoen
Krung), **5D3–6F5**
New Phetburi Rd.,
7C6–7
North (Nua) Sathorn
Rd., **7F6–7**

Oriental Ave., **6F4**

Patpong Rd. 1, 2, 3,
7E6
Phaholyothin Rd.,
7A7–B7
Phetburi Rd., **6C5–7C6**
Phitsanulok Rd., **6B4–C5**
Phra Athit Rd., **5B2–3**
Phyathai Rd., **7C6–E6**
Pipat 1, 2, 3, **7F6**
Ploenchit Rd., **7D7**

Ratchadamnoen Ave.,
6C4
Ratchadamnoen Klang
Rd., **5C3**
Ratchadamnoen Nai
Rd., **5C3**
Ratchadamri Rd.,
7E6–D7
Ratchaprarop Rd.,
7D7–C7
Ratchawithi Rd.,
6A5–7B7
Rajprasong Rd., **7D7–C7**

Rama I Rd., **6C5–7D7**
Rama IV Rd., **6D5–
7F6**
Rama V Rd., **6B4–A5**
Ruamruedi, off **7D7**

Sampeng Lane, **6D4**
Sarasin, **7E7**
Sathorn Rd., **7E6–7**
Siam Sq., **7D6**
Silom Rd., **6F5–7E6**
Siphaya Rd., **6E4–7E6**
Soi Suanphlo Rd., **7F6**
South (Tai) Sathorn Rd.,
7F6–7
Sukhumvit Rd., off **7D7**
Surasak Rd., **6F5**
Surawong Rd., **6F5–7E6**
Si Ayutthaya Rd.,
6A4–7C7
Si Phaya Rd., **6E4–5**
Sua Pa Rd., **6D4**

Tadmai Rd.,
Thaniya Rd., **7E6**
Thanon U Thong Rd.,
6A4
Traimit Rd., **6D4**

Withayu (Wireless) Rd.,
7D7–E7
Worachak Rd., **6B4–D4**

Yaowaraj Rd., **5D3–6D4**

KEY TO MAP PAGES

KEY TO MAP SYMBOLS

City Maps

- Major Place of Interest
- Other Important Building
- Built-up Area
- Park
- † † Cemetery
- ▲ Temple
- ☾ Mosque
- † Church
- ✡ Synagogue
- ⊞ Hospital
- *i* Information Office
- ✉ Post Office
- ✋ Police Station
- ⌖ Parking Lot / Garage
- Ⓗ Hotel
- Ⓜ MRT Station (Singapore only)
- ● Ferry Stop (Bangkok only)
- → One-way Street
- 7 Adjoining Page No.

Singapore Island Map

- ■ Place of Interest
- Built-up Area
- Park
- Natural Vegetation
- ✈ Airport
- ▲ Temple
- ⚐ Golf Course
- =O= Expressway (with access point)
- ▬ Main Road
- ▬ Secondary Road
- ▬ Other Road
- ▭ Railway
- —O— Overground MRT Line
- --O-- Underground MRT Line
- — — Ferry

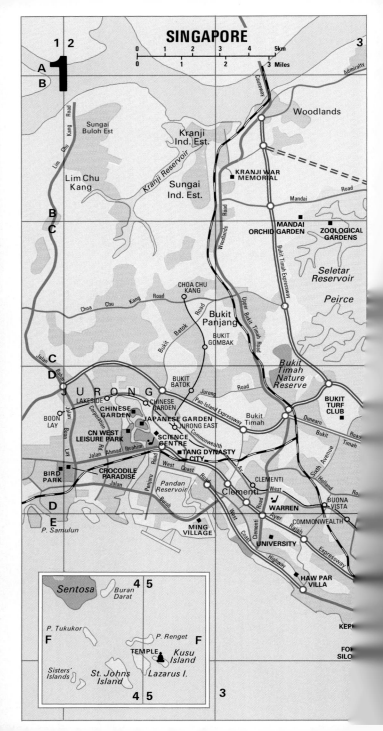

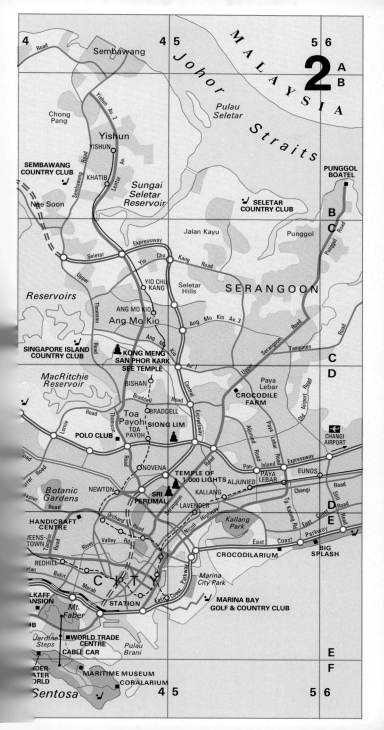

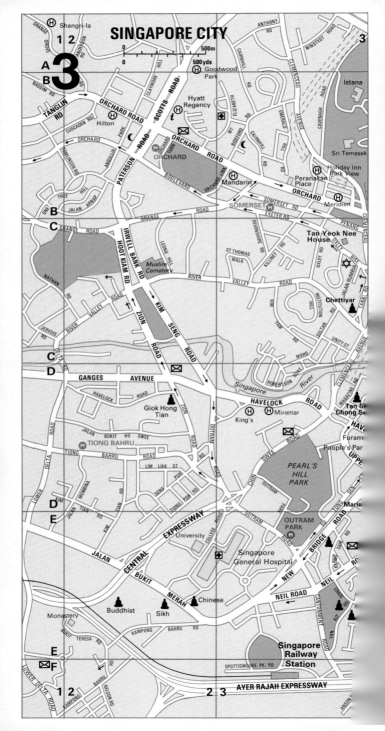

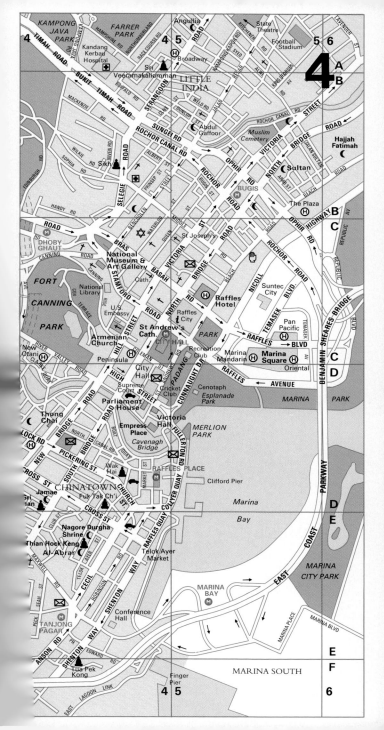

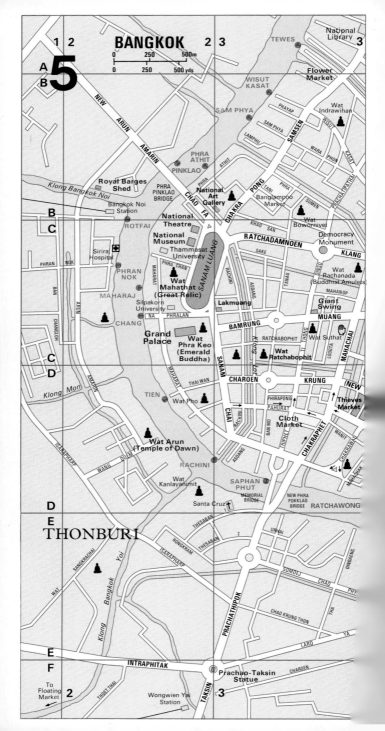

BANGKOK

5

1 2 2 3 3

0 250 500m
0 250 500 yds

A
B

TEWES
National Library

WISUT KASAT
Flower Market

SAM PHYA
PHAYAP
SAM PHYA
LAMPHU
WARA
PHON
Wat Indrawihan

NEW ARUN AMARIN

PHRA ATHIT
PINKLAO
ATHIT
CHAO FA
CHAKRA
PONG
TANI
PHRA
SUMEN
PRACHA TIPATAI

Klong Bangkok Noi
Royal Barges Shed
PHRA PINKLAO BRIDGE
National Art Gallery
Banglampoo Market

Bangkok Noi Station
ROTFAI

B
C
National Theatre
National Museum
Thammasat University
SANAM LUANG
KHAO SAN
Wat Bowornivet

Siriraj Hospital
PHRAN NOK
PHRA CHAN
RACHINI
RATCHADAMNOEN
SAKE
TANAD
DINSO
MAHANOP
Democracy Monument
KLANG
Wat Rachanada (Buddhist Amulets)

PHRAN NOK
MAHARAT
Wat Mahathat (Great Relic)
Lakmuang
Giant Swing
MUANG

BAN
CHANGLOH
ARUN
Silpakorn University
NA
PHRALAN
BAMRUNG
RATCHABOPHIT
THONG
LOOGTA
Wat Suthat
MAHACHAI

CHANG
Grand Palace
Wat Phra Keo (Emerald Buddha)
Klong Lot
SANAM
Wat Ratchabophit

C
D
MAHARAJ
THAI WAN
CHAROEN
KRUNG
(NEW)

Klong Mon
AMARIN
TIEN
Wat Pho
CHAI
ASDANG
RACHINI
PHIRAPONG
PAHURAT
BAN MO
TRIPHET
Cloth Market
CHAKRAPHET
CHAKRAWANG
WANIT
Thieves Market

TSARAPHARP
WANG
ROTFAI
Wat Arun (Temple of Dawn)
Wat Kanlayanimit
Santa Cruz
SAPHAN PHUT
MEMORIAL BRIDGE
MARTHRAK

D
E
NEW PHRA POKKLAO BRIDGE
RATCHAWONG

THONBURI

THESABAN
URHAI
RONGKHAM
THESABAN
2
SOMDEJ
DINDAENG

WAT
SANGKRACHAI
Bangkok Yoi
TSARAPHARP
CHAO PHY
Klong
PRACHATIPHOK
CHAO KRUNG THON
THA
YA

E
F
INTRAPHITAK
Prachao-Taksin Statue

To Floating Market
THOET THAI
Wongwien Yai Station
TAKSIN
LARD
CHAREON

2 3

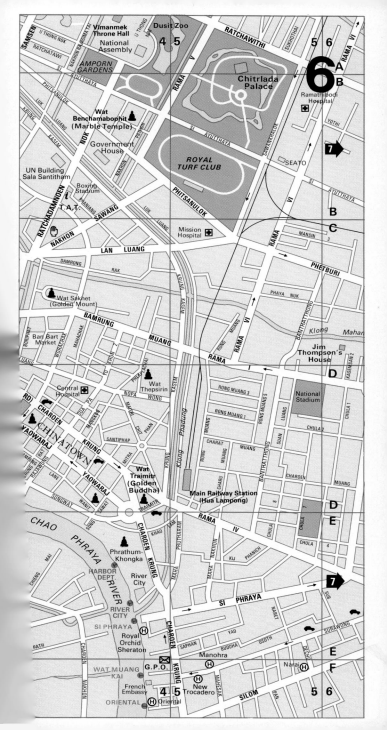

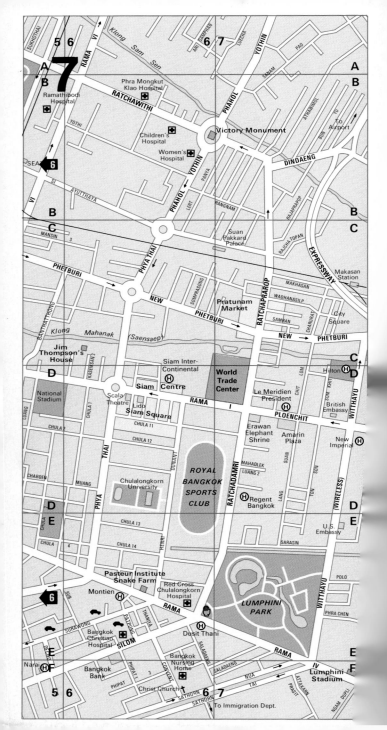